College & Career Success

Fourth Edition

Marsha Fralick

KENDALL/HUNT PUBLISHING COMPANY
4050 Westmark Drive   Dubuque, Iowa 52002

Book Team

Chairman and Chief Executive Officer   Mark C. Falb
President and Chief Operating Officer   Chad M. Chandlee
Vice President, Higher Education   David L. Tart
Director of National Book Program   Paul B. Carty
Editorial Development Manager   Georgia Botsford
Developmental Editor   Lynne Rogers
Vice President, Operations   Timothy J. Beitzel
Assistant Vice President, Production Services   Christine E. O'Brien
Project Coordinator   Charmayne McMurray
Permissions Editor   Elizabeth Roberts
Cover Designer   Sandy Beck
Regional Senior Managing Editor   John Coniglio
Regional Acquisitions Editor   Janice Samuells

Cover images from left to right:
© Yuri Arcurs, 2008. Used under license from Shutterstock, Inc.
© JupiterImages Corporation.
© hfng, 2008. Used under license from Shutterstock, Inc.
© Yuri Arcurs, 2008. Used under license from Shutterstock, Inc.

BRIEF CONTENTS

CONTENTS

5 Improving Memory and Reading 151

6 Taking Notes, Writing, and Speaking 191

10 Communication and Relationships 325

11 Thinking Critically and Creatively 363

12 Maintaining a Healthy Lifestyle 383

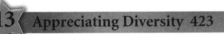

14 Looking Toward the Future 449

13 Appreciating Diversity 423

PREFACE

I have always believed that education provides a means for accomplishing a person's dreams. I guess I learned that idea from my parents and teachers in high school. When I started college at the University of New Mexico, it was the beginning of a great adventure which was to last my lifetime. I can still recall being a college freshman. I had attended a small school in northern New Mexico, Pojoaque High School. I was a good student in high school and was motivated to succeed in college. As a freshman, my career goals were pretty unrealistic and changed from week to week. I thought about becoming the first woman President or a maybe a diplomat. Since Nancy Drew was my heroine, I thought about being a spy or detective like Nancy Drew. Deciding on a major and career was a monumental task.

When I started at the University of New Mexico, I was soon overwhelmed. I did not know how to take notes, remember what I read or manage my time. I remember that I was anxious and stressed out about taking tests. I worked and went to school during the day and tried to study at night. Sometimes I studied all night and then the next day forgot what I had studied. College was not fun, and I wished that someone had written a book on how to survive in college. I decided that I would figure out how to be successful and maybe someday write a book about it so that other people would not have to struggle as much as I did.

I learned how to survive and was very successful in college, completing my bachelor's, master's and doctorate degrees. I enjoyed the college environment so much that I ended up being a college counselor and teacher. That was pretty far from being Nancy Drew, but it has been a career that I have found very satisfying. In 1978 the vice-president of newly opened Cuyamaca College asked if I would design a college success course for the college. I was excited to begin to design a course that would help students to be successful in college. I was motivated because I believed in the value of education and remembered what it was like to be a new college student. Now it is 30 years later and I am still designing and teaching college success courses. Every semester that I teach, I learn more from students and continue to develop ideas for a college success course that makes a positive difference in students' lives. My experiences as a student and faculty member have helped me design a class with proven success. I have also done research on student success and designed this textbook based on my research findings.

What do students need to be successful? First of all they need to know how to study. This includes being able to apply memory techniques, read effectively, listen to lectures, take notes and prepare for exams. Without these skills, students may wrongly decide that they are not capable of doing college work. If students know these techniques and apply them, they can be confident in their abilities and reach their true potential. With confidence, they can begin to relax and meet the challenges of tests and term papers. They might even learn to like education.

Being able to study is not enough. Students need to know what to study, so having a career goal is important. I have observed that students choose their career goals for a variety of reasons. Just like I wanted to be Nancy Drew, some students choose their occupations based on some person that they admire. Some choose their career based on familiarity. They choose occupations that they have observed in their families or communities. Others choose a career by accident; they obtain whatever job is available. We now have a great deal of information on how to choose a satisfying career goal. The first step is personal assessment. What are the students' personality types, interests, aptitudes and values? Once these are determined, what careers match these personal characteristics? What careers will be a good choice for the future? These are all questions that need to be answered in order to continue to study in college.

Managing time and money and setting goals are important. Like many other students, I had always worked while attending college. While getting my master's and doctorate degrees, I worked and had a family. I have felt the pressures of these many roles and learned how to manage them. Students can learn these important life skills to make the journey easier.

Learning how to speak and write well has been a great asset to me in college and in my career. These skills did not come easily. I remember getting papers back with so many red corrections that they looked like decorated Christmas trees. I learned from the mistakes and kept practicing. These are skills that all college students need to master early in their college careers.

One of the goals of a college education is to learn to think critically and creatively. The world is full of com-

plex issues with no easy answers. We find solutions by working with others, questioning the status quo, looking at different alternatives, respecting the opinions of others and constructing our own personal views. Through creative thinking, we can come up with ideas to solve problems in our careers and personal lives.

I had the advantage of growing up with two cultures and speaking two languages. This has given me an appreciation for different groups of people. Appreciating others and working with diverse groups of people are skills needed by everyone today because the world is becoming more diverse. If we have hope for being able to live peacefully in the world, we will need to understand and appreciate this diversity.

Probably the most important skill for success is that of positive thinking. I truly believe that we accomplish what we think we can do. We need to become aware of our thoughts and when they are negative, we need to change them. I often ask students to notice their negative thoughts and then, as if rewinding a tape, change their negative thoughts to positive thoughts. Positive thoughts are powerful influences on attitude and behavior.

What good does it do to attend college if students do not enjoy good health? I have resolved to emphasize achieving wellness and maintaining good health in all my college classes. In the new millennium we are all supposed to live to be 100 years old. I collect stories about seniors who climb mountains, orbit the earth, write bestselling novels and become famous artists. We can learn from them about how to live long, healthy and productive lives.

Through the study of psychology, we have discovered many ways to help people to be successful. I have briefly introduced these theories and the names of the psychologists who have done research in this area. It is not enough to know the theory or idea; it is necessary to know how to apply it. This book contains many exercises designed to assist students apply the material learned.

The sections titled, "Keys to Success," located near the end of each chapter, are my personal philosophies of life developed from being in education for over thirty years. Although I still remember being a college freshman, that was a long time ago; and I have learned a lot since then. If I could survive in college, you can too. I wrote that book that I thought about many years ago. I hope that it makes your journey through college, your career, and your life a little easier.

FEATURES OF THIS BOOK

- Topics from college, career and lifelong success are presented in the text.

- The **Do What You Are (DWYA)** personality assessment and the **Productivity Environmental Preference Survey (PEPS)** learning style inventory are included.

- Personality type and learning style are key themes throughout the text.

- Interactive activities within the text help students to practice the material learned.

- Frequent quizzes and answer keys within the chapters help students with reading comprehension and check understanding of key concepts.

- Journal entries to help students think critically and apply what they have learned to their personal lives.

- Individual and group exercises are included at the end of each chapter.

- The **College Success Website** at http://www.collegesuccess1.com has resources for students and faculty. Student resources include key ideas and Internet links related to each chapter and Word documents for the journal entries. Resources for faculty include the **Instructor Manual** and other resources for teaching college success courses.

ACKNOWLEDGMENTS

I would like to give my sincere thanks to:

- My parents, Betty and Clarence Finley who taught me the value of education

- My seven brothers and sisters who taught me to laugh at life

- My children, Mark and Sara Fralick, who assisted with editing and shared their younger generation perspective

- Paul Delys who provided love and encouragement and shared many of his ideas and materials for this book

- The instructors of Lifelong Success who tried out my material, gave valuable feedback and shared their ideas

- The many students who have taken my course over the years and shared their insights and experiences with me

ABOUT THE AUTHOR

Marsha Fralick has been employed in the field of education for over forty years, including thirty years of teaching college success courses. She has brought together theories from counseling, psychology, career development and health to provide students with strategies for college, career, and lifelong success. Her College and Career Success Program at Cuyamaca College in El Cajon, California, is recognized as an exemplary program by students and statewide organizations. She has a Doctorate from The University of Southern California in higher education with an emphasis in career counseling, Master's Degree in counseling from the University of Redlands and a Bachelor's Degree in Spanish and English from Arizona State University.

LEARNING OBJECTIVES

Read to answer these key questions:

- What do I want from college?

- What is the value of a college education?

- How do I choose my major and career?

- How can I motivate myself to be successful?

- How can I begin habits that lead to success?

- How is persistence a key to success?

© Stephen Coburn, 2008. Under license from Shutterstock, Inc.

Understanding Motivation

Most students attend college with dreams of making their lives better. Some students are there to explore interests and possibilities, and others have more defined career goals. Being successful in college and attaining your dreams begins with motivation. It provides the energy or drive to find your direction and to reach your goals. Without motivation, it is difficult to accomplish anything.

Not everyone is successful in college. As a freshman in college, I attended an orientation in which I was told to look at the student to the left and the student to the right of me. The speaker said that one of us would not make it through the freshman year. I remember telling myself that the speaker must have been talking about one of the other two students and not me. That was the beginning of my motivation to be successful in college. Unfortunately about one-third of college students drop out in the first year. Forty percent of students who start college do not finish their degree. Having a good understanding of your gifts and talents, reasons for attending college, career goals, and how to motivate yourself will help you to reach your dreams.

What Do I Want from College?

Succeeding in college requires time and effort. You will have to give up some of your time spent on leisure activities and working. You will give up some time spent with your friends and families. Making sacrifices and working hard is easier if you know what you want to achieve through your efforts. One of the first steps in motivating yourself to be successful in college is to have a clear and specific understanding of your reasons for attending college. Are you attending college as a way to obtain a satisfying career? Is financial security one of your goals? Will you feel more satisfied if you are living up to your potential? What are your hopes and dreams, and how will college help you to achieve your goals?

When you are having difficulties or doubts about your ability to finish your college education, remember your hopes and dreams and your plans for the future. It is a good idea to write these ideas down, think about them, and revise them from time to time. Complete the exercise "What Do I Want from College?" located at the end of this chapter.

What Is the Value of a College Education?

Many college students say that getting a satisfying job that pays well and achieving financial security are important reasons for attending college. By going to college you can get a job that pays more per hour. You can work fewer hours to earn a living and have more time for leisure activities. You can spend your time at work doing something that you like to do. A report issued by the Census Bureau in 2005 listed the following education and income statistics for all races and both genders throughout the United States.[1] Lifetime income assumes that a person works thirty years before retirement.

Average Earnings Based on Education Level

Education	Yearly Income	Lifetime Income
High school graduate	$29,448	$883,440
Some college, no degree	$31,421	$942,630
Associate degree	$37,990	$1,139,700
Bachelor's degree	$54,689	$1,640,670
Master's degree	$67,898	$2,036,940
Professional degree	$119,009	$3,570,270

Reprinted with special permission of North American Syndicate.

Notice that income rises with the educational level. A person with a bachelor's degree earns almost twice as much as a high school graduate. Of course these are average figures across the nation. Some individuals earn higher or lower salaries. People have assumed that you would certainly be rich if you were a millionaire. College won't make you an instant millionaire, but over a lifetime you earn over a million dollars by having an associate's degree. People fantasize about winning the lottery. The reality is that the probability of winning the lottery is very low. In the long run, you have a better chance of improving your financial status by going to college.

Let's do some further comparisons. A high school graduate earns an average of $883,440 over a lifetime. A college graduate with a bachelor's degree earns $1,640,670 over a lifetime. A college graduate earns $757,230 more than a high school graduate does over a lifetime. So how much is a college degree worth? It is worth $757,230 over a lifetime. Would you go to college if someone offered to pay you $757,230? Here are some more interesting figures we can derive from the table on page 2:

Completing one college course is worth $18,931.
($757,230 divided by 40 courses in a bachelor's degree)

Going to class for one hour is worth $394.
($18,931 divided by 48 hours in a semester class)

Would you take a college class if someone offered to pay you $18,931? Would you go to class today for one hour if someone offered to pay you $394? Of course, if this sounds too good to be true, remember that you will receive these "payments" over a working lifetime of 30 years.

Money is only one of the values of going to college. Can you think of other reasons to attend college? Here are some less tangible reasons.

- College helps you to develop your potential.
- College opens the door to many satisfying careers.

- College prepares you to be an informed citizen and fully participate in the democratic process.
- College increases your understanding and widens your view of the world.
- College allows you to participate in a conversation with the great minds of all times and places. For example, reading the work of Plato is like having a conversation with that famous philosopher. You can continue great conversations with your faculty and fellow students.
- College helps to increase your confidence, self-esteem, and self-respect.

JOURNAL ENTRY #1
What is the value of a college education to you?

Choosing a Major and Career

Having a definite major and career choice is a good motivation for completing your college education. It is difficult to put in the work necessary to be successful if you do not have a clear picture of your future career; however, three out of four college students are undecided about their major. For students who have chosen a major, 30 to 75 percent of a graduating class will change that major two or more times.[2] Unclear or indefinite career goals are some of the most significant factors that identify students at risk of dropping out of college.[3] Students often drop out or extend their stay in college because they are uncertain about their major or want to change their major. Choosing an appropriate college major is one of the most difficult and important decisions that college students can make.

How do people choose a career? There are many complex factors that go into your career choice. This course will help you to become aware of these factors and to think critically about them in order to make a good choice about your career. Some of the factors involved in choosing a career include:

- **Heredity.** You inherit genes from your parents that play a role in shaping who you are.

- **Intelligence.** Every person has a unique mixture of talents and skills. You can work to develop these skills.

- **Experience.** Your experiences can either build your self-confidence or cause you to doubt your abilities.

- **Environment.** What careers have you observed in your environment? Maybe your father was a doctor and you grew up familiar with careers in medicine. Your parents may have encouraged you to choose a particular career. You may want to learn about other possibilities.

- **Social roles.** Maybe you learned that men are engineers and women are teachers because your father is an engineer and your mother is a teacher. It is important to think critically about traditional roles so that your choices are not limited.

- **Learning.** What you have learned will play a part in your career decision. You may need to learn new behaviors and establish new habits.

- **Learning Style.** Knowing how you like to learn can help you be successful in college as well as on the job. Your learning style may provide options for selecting a career as well.

- **Relationships.** We sometimes choose careers to enhance relationships. For example, you may choose a career that gives you time to spend with your family or with people who are important to you.

- **Stress.** Our ability to cope with stress plays a part in career choice. Some enjoy challenges; others value peace of mind.

- **Health.** Good health increases career options and enjoyment of life.

- **Personality.** Your personality is a major factor influencing which career you might enjoy.

- **Values.** What you value determines which career you will find satisfying.

- **Culture.** Your culture has an influence on which careers you value.

- **Traditions.** Traditions often guide career choice.

- **Beliefs.** Your beliefs about yourself and the world determine your behavior and career choice.

- **Interests.** If you choose a career that matches your interests, you can find satisfaction in your career.

Factors in Career Choice[4]

How can you choose the major that is best for you? The best way is to first understand yourself; become aware of your personality traits, learning style, interests, preferred lifestyle, values, gifts, and talents. The next step is to do career research to determine the career that best matches your personal characteristics. Next, plan your education to prepare for your career. Here are some questions to answer to help you understand yourself and what career and major would be best for you.

To learn about yourself, explore these areas:

- **What is my personality type?** Psychologists have studied personality types and career choice. Assessing your personality type will give you some general ideas about careers that will give you satisfaction.
- **What is my learning style?** Being aware of your learning style will help you identify learning strategies that work best for you. Knowing how you learn best can help you identify your gifts and talents and find a career that matches them.
- **What are my interests?** Knowing about your interests is important in choosing a satisfying career.
- **What kind of lifestyle do I prefer?** Think about how you want to balance work, leisure, and family.
- **What are my values?** Knowing what you value (what is most important to you) will help you make good decisions about your life.

To learn about career possibilities, research the following:

- **What career matches my personality, interests, aptitudes and values?** Learn how to do career research to find the best career for you. Find a career that has a good outlook for the future.
- **How can I plan my education to get the career I want?** Once you have identified your area of interest, consult your college catalog or advisor to make an educational plan that matches your career goals.

By following the above steps, you can find the major that is best for you and minimize the time you spend in college.

JOURNAL ENTRY #2

Answer one of the following questions:
1. If you have chosen a major, why is it the best major for you?
2. If you haven't chosen a major yet, what are some steps in choosing the right major and career for you?

How to Be Motivated

There are many ways to be motivated.

- You can **improve your concentration** and motivation for studying by managing your external and internal distractions.
- You can be motivated by internal or external factors called **intrinsic or extrinsic motivation.**
- You can become aware of your **locus of control**, or where you place the responsibility for control over your life. If you are in control, you are more likely to be motivated to succeed.
- You can join a club, organization, or athletic team. **Affiliation motivation** involves taking part in school activities that increase your motivation to stay in college.
- **Achievement** and competition are motivating to some students.
- You can **apply the principles of learning** and use positive reinforcement as a motivation to establish desirable behaviors.

Let's examine each type of motivation in more detail and see if some of these ideas can be useful to you.

Improving Your Concentration

Have you ever watched lion tamers concentrate? If their attention wanders, they are likely to become the lion's dinner. Skilled athletes, musicians, and artists don't have any trouble concentrating. They are motivated to concentrate. Think about a time when you were totally focused on what you were doing. You were motivated to continue. You can improve your concentration and motivation for studying by managing your external and internal distractions.

Manage your external environment. Your environment will either help you to study or distract you from studying. We are all creatures of habit. If you try to study in front of the TV, you will watch TV because that is what you are accustomed to doing in front of the TV. If you study in bed, you will fall asleep because your body associates the bed with sleeping. If you study in the kitchen, you will eat. Find an environment that minimizes distractions. One idea is to study in the library. In the library, there are many cues that tell you to study. There are books and learning resources and other people studying. It will be easier to concentrate in that environment.

You may be able to set up a learning environment in your home. Find a place where you can place a desk or table, your computer, and your materials for learning. When you are in this place, use it for learning and studying only. When you are studying, focus on studying. Make it a habit to study in this place. When you are relaxing, go somewhere else and focus on relaxing.

Because of past experiences and learning, our environment has a powerful influence on our behavior. Choose the right environment for what you are doing. Don't confuse yourself by trying to study in front of the TV! Don't ruin your enjoyment of TV by trying to study while watching it. When you are relaxing, focus on relaxing and don't worry about studying. When you are studying, focus on studying and don't get distracted thinking about relaxing.

Manage your internal distractions. Many of our distractions come from within. Here are some techniques for managing these internal distractions:

1. **Be here now.** Choose where you will place your attention. If you are in a lecture and you begin to think about eating cookies, notice that you are thinking about cookies and bring your attention back to the lecture. You can tell yourself, "Be here now." If you try to force yourself not to think about cookies, you will think about them even more. Just notice when your attention has drifted away and choose to bring it gently back to where you want it. This will take some practice since attention tends to wander often.

2. **The spider technique.** If you hold a tuning fork to a spider web, the web vibrates and the spider senses that it has caught a tasty morsel and goes seeking the food. After awhile, the spider discovers that there is no food and learns to ignore the vibrations caused by the tuning fork. When you are sitting in the library studying and someone walks in talking and laughing, you can choose to pay attention either to the distraction or to studying. Decide to continue to pay attention to studying.

3. **Set up a worry time.** Many times worries interfere with concentration. Some people have been successful in setting up a worry time. Here's how it works:

   • Set a specific time each day for worrying.
   • When worries distract you from your studies, remind yourself that you have set aside time for worrying.
   • Tell yourself, "Be here now."

Managing Internal Distractions

1. Be here now
2. Spider technique
3. Worry time
4. Checkmark technique
5. Increase activity
6. Find an incentive
7. Change topics

- Keep your worry appointment.
- During your worry time, try to find some solutions or take some steps to resolve the things that cause you to worry.

4. **Use the checkmark technique.** When you find yourself distracted from a lecture or from studying, place a checkmark on a piece of paper and refocus your attention on the task at hand. You will find that your checkmarks decrease over time.

5. **Increase your activity.** Take a break. Stretch and move. Read and listen actively by asking questions about the material and answering them as you read or listen.

6. **Find an incentive or reward.** Tell yourself that when you finish, you will do something enjoyable.

7. **Change topics.** Changing study topics may help you to concentrate and avoid fatigue.

JOURNAL ENTRY #3

What concentration techniques can help you be more motivated and study more effectively?

Intrinsic or Extrinsic Motivation

Intrinsic motivation comes from within. It means that you do an activity because you enjoy it or find personal meaning in it. With intrinsic motivation, the nature of the activity itself or the consequences of the activity motivate you. For example, let's say that I am interested in learning to play the piano. I am motivated to practice playing the piano because I like the sound of the piano and feel very satisfied when I can play music that I enjoy. I practice because I like to practice, not because I have to practice. When I get tired or frustrated, I work through it or put it aside and come back to it because I want to learn to play the piano well.

You can be intrinsically motivated to continue in college because you enjoy learning and find the college experience satisfying. Look for ways to enjoy college and to find some personal satisfaction in it. If you enjoy college, it becomes easier to do the work required to be successful. Think about what you say to yourself about college. If you are saying negative things such as, "I don't want to be here," it will be difficult to continue.

Extrinsic motivation comes as a result of an external reward from someone else. Examples of extrinsic rewards are certificates, bonuses, money, praise, and recognition. Taking the piano example again, let's say that I want my child to play the piano. The child does not know if he or she would like to play the piano. I give the child a reward for practicing the piano. I could pay the child for practicing or give praise for doing a good job. There are two possible outcomes of the extrinsic reward. After awhile, the child may gain skills and confidence and come to enjoy playing the piano. The extrinsic reward is no longer necessary because the child is now intrinsically motivated. Or the child may decide that he or she does not like to play the piano. The extrinsic reward is no longer effective in motivating the child to play the piano.

You can use extrinsic rewards to motivate yourself to be successful in college. Remind yourself of the payoff for getting a college degree: earning more money, having a satisfying career, being able to purchase a car and a house. Extrinsic rewards can be a first step in motivating yourself to attend college. With experience and achievement, you may come to like going to college and may become intrinsically motivated to continue your college education.

If you use intrinsic motivation to achieve your goal, you will be happier and more successful. If you do something like playing the piano because you enjoy it, you are more likely to spend the time necessary to practice to achieve your goal. If you view college as something that you enjoy and as valuable to you, it is easier to spend the time to do the required studying. When you get tired or frustrated, tell yourself that you are doing a good job (praise yourself) and think of the positive reasons that you want to get a college education.

JOURNAL ENTRY #4

1. What are your intrinsic motivations for going to college? Remember, intrinsic motivators are those you do because you enjoy them or they are personally meaningful.
2. What are your extrinsic motivators for going to college? Remember, extrinsic motivators are external rewards from someone else.

Locus of Control

Being aware of the concept of locus of control is another way of understanding motivation. The word **locus** means place. Locus of control is where you place the responsibility for control over your life. In other words, who is in charge? If you place the responsibility on yourself and believe that you have control over your life, you have internal locus of control. If you place the responsibility on others and think that luck or fate determines your future, you have external locus of control. Some people use internal or external locus of control in combination or favor one type in certain situations. If you favor an internal locus of control, you believe that to a great extent your actions determine your future. Studies have shown that students who use an internal locus of control are likely to have higher achievement in college.[5] The characteristics of students with internal and external locus of control are listed below.

Students with an internal locus of control:

• Believe that they are in control of their lives.
• Understand that grades are directly related to the amount of study invested.
• Are self-motivated.
• Learn from their mistakes by figuring out what went wrong and how to fix the problem.
• Think positively and try to make the best of each situation.
• Rely on themselves to find something interesting in the class and learn the material.

Students with an external locus of control:

• Believe that their lives are largely a result of luck, fate, or chance.
• Think that teachers give grades rather than students earn grades.
• Rely on external motivation from teachers or others.
• Look for someone to blame when they make a mistake.
• Think negatively and believe they are victims of circumstance.
• Rely on the teacher to make the class interesting and to teach the material.

ACTIVITY
Internal or External Locus of Control

Decide whether the statement represents an internal or external locus of control and put a checkmark in the appropriate column.

Internal	External	
_____	_____	1. Much of what happens to us is due to fate, chance, or luck.
_____	_____	2. Grades depend on how much work you put into it.
_____	_____	3. If I do badly on the test, it is usually because the teacher is unfair.
_____	_____	4. If I do badly on the test, it is because I didn't study or didn't understand the material.
_____	_____	5. I often get blamed for things that are not my fault.
_____	_____	6. I try to make the best of the situation.
_____	_____	7. It is impossible to get a good grade if you have a bad instructor.
_____	_____	8. I can be successful through hard work.
_____	_____	9. If the teacher is not there telling me what to do, I have a hard time doing my work.
_____	_____	10. I can motivate myself to study.
_____	_____	11. If the teacher is boring, I probably won't do well in class.
_____	_____	12. I can find something interesting about each class.
_____	_____	13. When bad things are going to happen, there is not much you can do about it.
_____	_____	14. I create my own destiny.
_____	_____	15. Teachers should motivate the students to study.
_____	_____	16. I have a lot of choice about what happens in my life.

As you probably noticed, the even-numbered statements represent internal locus of control. The odd-numbered statements represent external locus of control. Remember that students with an internal locus of control have a greater chance of success in college. It is important to see yourself as responsible for your own success and achievement and to believe that with effort you can achieve your goals.

JOURNAL ENTRY #5

How can you use the concept of locus of control to improve your chances of success in college?

Affiliation

Human beings are social creatures who generally feel the need to be part of a group. This tendency is called affiliation motivation. People like to be part of a community, family, organization, or culture. You can apply this motivation technique in college by participating in student activities on campus. Join an athletic team, participate in a club, or join the student government. In this way you will feel like you are part of a group and will have a sense of belonging. College is more than going to class; it is participating in social activities, making new friends, and sharing new ideas. Twenty years after you graduate from college, you are more likely to remember the conversations held with college friends than the detailed content of classes. College provides the opportunity to become part of a new group and to start lifelong friendships.

Achievement

Some students are motivated by achievement. Individuals who are achievement motivated have a need for success in school, sports, careers, and other competitive situations. These individuals enjoy getting recognition for their success. They are often known as the best student, the outstanding athlete, or the employee of the year. These persons are attracted to careers that provide rewards for individual achievement, such as sales, law, architecture, engineering, and business. They work hard in order to enjoy the rewards of their efforts. In college, some students work very hard to achieve high grades and then take pride in their accomplishments. One disadvantage of using this type of motivation is that it can lead to excess stress. These students often need to remember to balance their time between work, school, family, and leisure so that they do not become too stressed by the need to achieve.

Applying the Principles of Learning

Psychologists believe that much of our behavior is learned. Understanding these principles of learning can give you some powerful tools for changing your own behavior. We frequently learn through a process called **operant conditioning**. A simple definition of operant conditioning is that behavior is increased or decreased depending on the consequences of the behavior. If you study for the test and receive an A, you will be more likely to study in the future. In operant conditioning, the consequences of a behavior lead to a change in the probability of its occurrence. We are always affected by the consequences of our behavior and are constantly in the process of learning.

If the consequences of your behavior are positive, you are positively reinforced as in our examples above. You are more likely to continue the behavior. If the consequences of your behavior are negative, that behavior is less likely to occur. For example, if you receive a traffic ticket and have to pay a large fine, you are less likely to repeat the offense.

You can use **positive reinforcement** on yourself to manage your own behavior. If you want to increase your studying behavior, follow it by a positive consequence or a reward. Think about what is rewarding to you (watching TV, playing sports, enjoying your favorite music). You could study (your behavior) and then watch a TV program (the positive reinforcement). The timing of your reward is important. To be effective, it must immediately follow the behavior. If you watch TV and then study, you may not get around to studying. If you watch the TV program tomorrow or next week, it is not a strong reinforcement because it is not an immediate reward.

Be careful about the kinds of rewards you use so that you do not get into habits that are detrimental to your health. If you use food as a reward for studying, you may increase your studying behavior, but you may also gain a few pounds. Using alcohol or drugs as a reward can start an addiction. Buying yourself a reward can ruin your budget. Good rewards do not involve too many calories, cost too much money, or involve alcohol or drugs.

You can also use a negative consequence to decrease a behavior. If you touch a hot stove and get burned, you quickly learn not to do it again. You could decide to miss your favorite television program if you do not complete your studying. However, this is not fun and you may feel deprived. You might even rebel and watch your favorite TV show anyway. See if you can find a way to use positive reinforcement (a reward) for increasing a behavior that is beneficial to you rather than using a negative consequence.

When we are young, our attitudes toward education are largely shaped by positive or negative reinforcement. If you were praised for being a good reader as a child, it is likely that you enjoyed reading and developed good reading skills. Maybe a teacher embarrassed you because of your math skills and you learned to be anxious about math. Think about areas of your education in which you excel, and see if you can recall someone praising or otherwise reinforcing that behavior. If you are a good athlete, did someone praise your athletic ability when you were younger? How was it rewarded? If you are not good at math, what were some early messages about your math performance? These early messages have a powerful influence on later behavior. You may need to put in some effort to learn new and more beneficial behaviors.

As a college student, you can use a reward as a powerful motivator. Praise yourself and think positively about your achievements in college even if the achievements come in small steps.

> ## JOURNAL ENTRY #6
> What are some positive rewards that you can give yourself for studying? Remember, good rewards don't have too many calories, don't cost too much, and don't involve drugs or alcohol.

Success Is a Habit

We establish habits by taking small actions each day. Through repetition, these individual actions become habits. I once visited the Golden Gate Bridge in San Francisco and saw a cross section of the cable used to support the bridge. It was made of small metal strands twisted with other strands. Then the cables were twisted together to make a stronger cable. Habits are a lot like cables. We start with one small action and each successive action makes the habit stronger. Have you ever stopped to think that success can be a habit? We all have learned patterns of behavior that either help us to be successful or that interfere with our success. With some effort and some basic understanding of behavior modification, you can choose to establish some new behaviors that lead to success or to get rid of behaviors that interfere with it.

Seven Steps to Change a Habit

You can establish new habits that lead to your success. Once a habit is established, it can become a pattern of behavior that you do not need to think about very much. For example, new students often need to get into the habit of studying. Here is an outline of steps that can be helpful to establish new behaviors.

1. **State the problem.**
   What new habit would you like to start? What are your roadblocks or obstacles? What bad habit would you like to change? Be truthful about it. This is sometimes the most difficult step.

2. **Change one small behavior at a time.**
   If you think about climbing a mountain, the task can seem overwhelming. However, you can take the first step. If you can change one small behavior, you can gain the confidence to change another. For example, a goal to have a better diet is broad and vague. A good way to make it small is to say, "I plan to eat more fruits and vegetables each day." State the behavior you would like to change. Make it small.

3. **State in a positive way the behavior you wish to establish.**
   For example, instead of the negative statement "I will not eat junk food," change it to "I plan to eat fruits and vegetables each day."

4. **Count the behavior.**
   How often do you do this behavior? For example, if you are trying to stop smoking, it is helpful to count the number of cigarettes you smoke each day. If you are trying to improve your diet, write down everything that you eat each day. If you are trying to establish a pattern of studying, write down how much time you spend studying each day. Sometimes just getting an awareness of your habit is enough to begin to make some changes.

5. **Picture in your mind the actions you might take.**
   For example: I see myself in the grocery store buying fruits and vegetables. I see myself packing these fruits and vegetables in my lunch. I see myself putting these foods in a place where I will notice them.

6. **Practice the behavior for ten days.**
   In ten days you can get started on a new pattern of behavior. Once you have started, keep practicing the behavior for about a month to firmly establish your new pattern of behavior. The first three days are the most difficult. If you fail, don't give up. Just realize that you are human and keep trying for ten days. Think positively that you can be successful. Write a journal or note on your calendar about what you have accomplished each day.

7. **Find a reward for your behavior.**
   Remember that we tend to repeat behaviors that are positively reinforced. Find rewards that do not involve too many calories, don't cost too much money, and don't involve alcohol or drugs. Also, rewards are most effective if they directly follow the behavior you wish to reinforce.

Seven Steps to Change a Habit

1. State the problem
2. Change one small behavior at a time
3. Be positive
4. Count the behavior
5. Picture the change
6. Practice the behavior
7. Reward yourself

Ten Habits of Successful College Students

Starting your college education will require you to establish some new habits to be successful.

1. **Attend class.**
   College lectures supplement the material in the text, so it is important to attend class. Many college instructors will drop you if you miss three hours of class. After three absences, most students do not return to class. If your class is online, log in frequently.

2. **Read the textbook.**
   Start early and read a little at a time. If you have a text with 400 pages, read 25 pages a week rather than trying to read it all at once.

3. **Have an educational plan.**
   Counselors or advisors can assist you in making an educational plan so that you take the right classes and accomplish your educational goal as soon as possible.

4. **Use college services.**
   Colleges offer valuable free services that help you to be successful. Take advantage of Tutoring, Counseling, Health Services, Financial Aid, the Learning Resources Center (Library) and many other services.

5. **Get to know the faculty.**
   You can get to know the faculty by asking questions in class or meeting with your instructor during office hours. Your instructor can provide extra assistance and write letters of recommendation for scholarships, future employment or for graduate school.

6. **Don't work too much.**
   Research has shown that full time students should have no more than 20 hours of outside employment a week to be successful in college. If you have to work more than 20 hours a week, reduce your college load. If you are working 40 hours a week or more, take only one or two classes.

7. **Take one step at a time.**
   If you are anxious about going to college, remember that each class you attend takes you another step toward your goal.

8. **Have a goal for the future.**
   Know why you are in college and what you hope to accomplish. What career will you have in the future?

9. **Visualize your success.**
   See yourself walking across the stage and receiving your college diploma. See yourself working at a job you enjoy.

10. **Ask questions if you don't understand.**
    Asking questions not only helps you to find the answers, but it shows you are motivated to be successful. Starting your college education will require you to establish some new habits to be successful.

QUIZ
Motivation

Test what you have learned by selecting the correct answer to the following questions:

1. If the behavior is followed by a reward,

   a. it is likely to be increased.
   b. it is likely to be decreased.
   c. there will probably be no effect.

2. For rewards to be effective, they must occur,

   a. before the behavior.
   b. immediately after the behavior.
   c. either before or after the behavior.

3. Manage your internal distractions by,

   a. forcing yourself to concentrate.
   b. telling yourself not to worry about your problems.
   c. noticing when your attention has wandered and choose where you want to focus your attention.

4. To be successful in college, it is best to use,

   a. intrinsic motivation.
   b. extrinsic motivation.
   c. external locus of control.

5. To change a habit,

   a. set high goals.
   b. focus on negative behavior.
   c. begin with a concrete behavior that can be counted.

How did you do on the quiz? Check your answers: 1. a, 2. b, 3. c, 4. a, 5. c

---

Keys to Success

Persistence

There is an old saying that persistence will get you almost anything eventually. This saying applies to your success in college. The first two to six weeks of college are a critical time in which many students drop out. Realize that college is a new experience and that you will face new challenges and growth experiences. Make plans to persist, especially in the first few weeks. Get to know a college counselor or advisor. These professionals can help you to get started in the right classes and answer any questions you might have. It is important to make a connection with a counselor or faculty member so that you feel comfortable in college and have the resources to obtain needed help. Plan to enroll on time so that you do not have to register late. It is crucial to attend the first class. In the first class, the professor explains the class requirements and expectations and sets the tone for the class. You may even get dropped from the class if you are not there on the first day. Get into the habit of studying right away. Make studying a habit that you start immediately at the beginning of the semester or quarter. If you can make it through the first six weeks, it is likely that you can finish the semester and complete your college education.

It has been said that 90 percent of success is just showing up. Any faculty member will tell you that the number one reason for students dropping out of college is lack of attendance. They know that when students miss three classes in a row, they are not likely to return. Even very capable students who miss class may find that they are lost when they come back. Many students are simply afraid to return. Classes such as math and foreign languages are sequential, and it is very difficult to make up work after an absence. One of the most important ways you can be successful is to make a habit of consistently showing up for class.

You will also need commitment to be successful. Commitment is a promise to yourself to follow through with something. In athletics, it is not necessarily the one with the best physical skills that makes the best athlete. Commitment and practice make a great athlete. Commitment means doing whatever is necessary to succeed. Like the good athlete, make a commitment to accomplishing your goals. Spend the time necessary to be successful in your studies.

When you face difficulties, persistence and commitment are especially important. History is full of famous people who contributed to society through persistence and commitment. Consider these facts about Abraham Lincoln, for example.

- Failed in business at age 21.
- Was defeated in a legislative race at age 22.
- Failed again in business at age 24.
- Overcame the death of his sweetheart at age 26.
- Had a nervous breakdown at age 27.
- Lost a congressional race at age 34.
- Lost a congressional race at age 36.
- Lost a senatorial race at age 45.
- Failed in an effort to become Vice-President at age 47.
- Lost a senatorial race at age 49.
- Was elected President of the United States at age 52.[6]

You will face difficulties along the way in any worthwhile venture. The successful person keeps on trying. There are some precautions about persistence, however. Make sure that the goal you are trying to reach is attainable and valuable to you. As you learn more about yourself, you may want to change your goals. Also, persistence can be misguided if it involves other people. For example, if you decide that you want to marry someone and this someone does not want to marry you, it is better to focus your energy and attention on a different goal.

One of the best ways to be persistent is to accomplish your goals one step at a time. If you look at a mountain, it may seem too high to climb, but you can do it one step at a time. Araceli Segarra became the first Spanish woman to climb Mount Everest. At 29,028 feet, Mount Everest is the highest mountain in the world. It is so high that you need an oxygen tank to breathe at the top. So how did Araceli climb the mountain? She says that it took strength and concentration. She put one foot in front of the other. When she was near the top of the mountain, she was more tired than she had ever been in her life. She told herself that she would take ten more steps. When she took ten steps she said, "I'm OK. I made it." Then she took ten more steps until she reached the top of the mountain.

The goal of getting a college education may seem like a mountain that is difficult to climb. Break it into smaller steps that you can accomplish. See your college counselor or advisor, register for classes, attend the first class, read the first chapter, do the first assignment, and you will be on the road to your success. Then continue to break tasks into small, achievable steps and continue from one step to the next. And remember, persistence will get you almost anything eventually.

JOURNAL ENTRY #7

What steps can you take to make sure that you stay in college to complete your education goals?

Ziggy, © 1996 Ziggy and Friends, Inc. Dist. by Universal Press Syndicate. Reprinted by permission. All rights reserved.

JOURNAL ENTRIES

Understanding Motivation

Go to http://www.collegesuccess1.com/ for Word files of the Journal Entries

Success over the Internet

Visit the *College Success Website* at http://www.collegesuccess1.com/

The *College Success Website* is continually updated with new topics and links to the material presented in this chapter. Topics include:

- How to improve concentration
- Motivation

- Positive attitude
- Balancing work, school, and social life
- Success factors for new college students
- How to change a habit
- Dealing with cravings and urges

Contact your instructor if you have any problems in accessing the College Success website.

Notes

1. U.S. Census Bureau, "The 2008 Statistical/Abstract, Mean Earnings by Highest Degree Earned: 2005," February 2008, retrieved from http://www.census.gov
2. W. Lewallen, "The Impact of Being Undecided on College Persistence," *Journal of College Student Development 34* (1993): 103–12.
3. Marsha Fralick, "College Success: A Study of Positive and Negative Attrition," *Community College Review 20* (1993): 29–36.
4. Ideas from Lina Rocha, Personal Development Instructor, Cuyamaca College, El Cajon, CA.
5. M. J. Findlay and H. M. Cooper, "Locus of Control and Academic Achievement: A Literature Review," *Journal of Personality and Social Psychology 44* (1983): 419–27.
6. Anthony Robbins, *Unlimited Power* (New York: Ballantine Books, 1986), 73.

Name _____   Date _____

Justin

It is the first day of class in the college success course. Justin is feeling excited and a little apprehensive as he walks into the class on the first day. He wonders if this is the right course for him. He managed to be successful in high school without much effort and thinks that college should be the same. His college advisor has recommended the course for all new students. He thinks that this course should be at least an easy A grade and it is not too important to attend every class. Justin has just graduated from high school and is looking forward to more freedom and independence. Justin has just been employed at a local sporting goods store. He is enjoying the job and the extra spending money. He started out working on Saturday only, but has now agreed to work 30 hours a week so that he can buy a new truck. School is not one of his top priorities, but his parents are insisting that he attend college so that he can get a better job in the future. How can Justin motivate himself to be successful in this course?

Anna

Anna walks into the classroom on the first day with a great deal of anxiety. She is returning to school fifteen years after her high school graduation. Her children are getting a little older and she has decided to return to school to finish that degree that she has always wanted. Although having a college degree is a lifelong dream, she is uncertain about which major would be best. She is hoping to choose a major that leads to a good paying job so that she can help her children with college expenses in the near future. She has a busy family life and is not sure how to add all the college activities to her schedule. The college success course seems like a good place to start. She looks around the classroom and notices that she is one of the older students in class and hopes she can keep up with the younger students who have just graduated from high school. What steps can Anna take to be successful in this course?

Behaviors Leading to Success

Name _____   Date _____

Part 1. Think of some behaviors or actions that lead to success for you. Think about success in your personal life, in college, and on the job. What activities help you achieve your goals? For example, you might be successful when you get enough rest, write down assignments, and show up to work on time. Think positively about what works well for you and list ten behaviors here.

I am successful when I

1. _____

2. _____

3. _____

4. _____

5. _____

6. _____

7. _____

8. _____

9. _____

10. _____

Part 2. It is more difficult to think about behaviors that lead to failure. These are actions that interfere with your success. Again consider school, work, and personal life. For example, you might observe that you are not successful when you do not eat right, study at the last minute, and are tired at work. List ten behaviors that interfere with your success.

I am not successful when I

1. _____

2. _____

3. _____

4. _____

5. _____

6. _____

7. _____

8. _____

9. _____

10. _____

Part 3. Look at the two lists above and choose two behaviors you would like to change or establish as a good habit. List them below.

I would like to

1. _____

2. _____

Use the following exercise on how to change a habit to begin working on one of these behaviors.

How to Change a Habit

Name _____   Date _____

The following exercise will help you to practice the process of beginning successful new habits. Choose *one* of these simple 10-day projects:

- Monitor how many minutes you study each day.
- Monitor how many minutes you exercise each day.
- Make a goal of eating breakfast. Write down what you eat for breakfast each day.
- Keep a list of the fruits and vegetables you eat each day.
- Count how many sodas you drink each day.
- Keep a log of time you sleep each night and make a note of how rested you feel the next day.
- Make a goal of making your bed or picking up your clothes. Record your progress each day.
- You can choose another behavior as long as it is realistic and achievable. You must be able to count it or describe the outcome. Consult with your instructor if you choose this option.

1. First, state the problem. Describe the behavior you want to change. What are your roadblocks or obstacles?

    For example:
    I get stressed when I run out of money before my next paycheck. I would like to manage my money better. One obstacle is my attitude that if I have money, I can spend it.

2. Choose one small behavior at a time. If you can change one small behavior, you can gain the confidence to change another.

    For example:
    A goal like improving money management is broad and vague. A good way to begin is to choose a small first step. A good first step is to keep track of expenditures so that you can begin to understand how you spend your money. The projects listed earlier are examples of small behaviors. If you are working on a different project, is it a small behavior that can be counted and one that can realistically be accomplished? List the small behavior that you will use for this project.

State in a positive way the behavior you wish to establish.

For example:
Instead of saying, "I will not spend all of my money before payday," say "I will keep a money monitor for 10 days." Of course the next step would be to work on a budget. If necessary, rewrite your goal in a positive way.

3. Count the behavior. Sometimes just becoming aware of your habit is enough to begin making some changes.

   For example:
   For the next 10 days, I will write down all my expenditures.

4. Picture in your mind the actions you might take to accomplish your goal and write them down in the following space.

   For example:
   I see myself writing down all my expenses on a sheet of paper. I will do this each day so that I can find out where I spend my money and begin to manage my money better. I see myself less stressed because I will have money for the things I need.

5. What reward will you use to reinforce the behavior? Rewards are most effective if they directly follow the behavior you wish to reinforce. Remember that good rewards do not have too many calories, cost too much money, or involve alcohol or drugs. List your rewards.

6. Practice the behavior for *ten days*. The first three days are the most difficult. If you fail, don't give up. Just realize that you are human and keep trying for ten days. Think positively that you can be successful. Use the space below or a separate sheet of paper to count how many times you did the behavior each day and what happened. Remember, you can get started on a new habit in ten days, but you will need to continue for about a month to firmly establish your new pattern of behavior.

Day 1: _____

_____

_____

Day 2: _____

_____

_____

Day 3: _____

_____

_____

Day 4: _____

_____

_____

Day 5: _____

_____

_____

Day 6: _____

_____

Day 7: _____

_____

_____

Day 8: _____

_____

_____

Day 9: _____

_____

_____

Day 10: _____

_____

_____

How did this project work for you?

Name _____   Date _____

You have the potential to earn over a $1,000,000 in your lifetime!

How many years do you think you will work after you earn your degree? _____

Multiply the number of years you will work by the yearly salary of the degrees. Yearly salaries are provided in the textbook.

Degree	Salary		Working Years		Lifetime Earnings
Associate's Degree	_____	×	_____	=	_____
Bachelor's Degree	_____	×	_____	=	_____
Master's Degree	_____	×	_____	=	_____
Professional Degree	_____	×	_____	=	_____

I, _____ have the potential of earning $ _____ in my lifetime.

CHAPTER

2

LEARNING OBJECTIVES

Read to answer these key questions:

- What are the different personality types?

- What is my personality type?

- How is personality type related to choice of a major and career?

- What are the characteristics of my ideal career?

- What careers and majors should I consider based on my personality type?

- What are some other factors in choosing a major?

© Stephen Coburn, 2008. Under license from Shutterstock, Inc.

Exploring Your Personality and Major

To assure your success in college, it is important to choose the major that is best for you. If you choose a major and career that matches your personality, interests, aptitudes and values, you will enjoy your studies and excel in your work. It was Picasso who said that you know you enjoy your work when you do not notice the time passing by. If you can become interested in your work and studies, you are on your way to developing passion and joy in your life. If you can get up each morning and enjoy the work that you do (at least on most days), you will surely have one of the keys to happiness.

Choose a Major That Matches Your Gifts and Talents

The first step in choosing the major that is right for you is to understand your personality type. Psychologists have developed useful theories of personality that can help you understand how personality type relates to the choice of major and career. The personality theory used in this textbook is derived from the work of Swiss psychologist Carl Jung (1875–1961). Jung believed that we are born with a predisposition for certain personality preferences and that healthy development is based on the lifelong nurturing of inborn preferences rather than trying to change a person to become something different. Each personality type has gifts and talents that can be nurtured over a lifetime.

The theories of Carl Jung were further developed by American psychologists Katherine Briggs and her daughter Isabel Myers, who created the Myers-Briggs Type Indicator (MBTI) to measure different personality types. The connection between personality type and career choice was established through statistical analysis. The "Do What You Are" online personality assessment is based on the practical application of the theories of these psychologists.

While assessments are not exact predictors of your future major and career, they provide useful information that will get you started on the path of career exploration and finding the college major that is best suited to you. Knowledge of your personality and an understanding of the personality of others are not only valuable in understanding yourself, but are also valuable in appreciating how others are different. This understanding of self and others will empower you to communicate and work effectively with others. Complete the "Do What You Are" personality assessment that is included with this textbook before you begin this chapter.

Understanding Personality Types

Just as no two fingerprints or snowflakes are exactly alike, each person is a different and unique individual. Even with this uniqueness, however, we can make some general statements about personality. When we make generalizations, we are talking about averages. These averages can provide useful information about ourselves and other people, but it is important to remember that no individual is exactly described by the average. As you read through the following descriptions of personality types, keep in mind that we are talking about generalizations or beginning points for discussion and

5. A person who makes decisions based on logic is a/an:

   a. thinker
   b. perceiver
   c. sensor

6. A person who makes decisions based on their personal values is a/an:

   a. feeling type
   b. thinking type
   c. judging type

7. The perceptive type:

   a. has extrasensory perception
   b. likes to live life in a spontaneous and flexible way
   c. always considers feelings before making a decision

8. The judging type likes to:

   a. judge others
   b. use logic
   c. live in a structured and orderly way

9. Personality assessments are an exact predictor of your best major and career.

   a. true
   b. false

10. Some personality types are better than others.

   a. true
   b. false

How did you do on the quiz? Check your answers: 1. b, 2. a, 3. b, 4. c, 5. a, 6. a, 7. b, 8. c, 9. b, 10. b

Personality and Preferred Work Environment

Knowing your personality type will help you to understand your preferred work environment and provide some insights into selecting the major and career that you would enjoy. Understanding other types will help you to work effectively with co-workers.

Since the **extravert** likes variety, action and talking to others, this type enjoys a work environment that provides the opportunity for social interaction. Extraverts communicate well and meet people easily. They like to talk while working and are interested in other people and what they are doing. They enjoy variety on the job and like to perform their work in different settings. They learn new tasks by talking with others and trying out new ideas. They are career generalists who like to use their skills in a variety of ways.

The **introvert** likes quiet for concentration and likes to focus on a work task until it is completed. They need time to think before taking action. This type often chooses to work alone or with one other person and prefers written communication such as emails to oral communication or presentations. They learn new tasks by reading and reflecting and using mental practice. They are career specialists who develop in depth skills.

The **sensing** type is realistic and practical and likes to develop standard ways of doing the job and following a routine. They are observant and interested in facts and finding the truth. They keep accurate track of details, make lists and are good at doing precise work. This type learns from personal experience and the experience of others. They use their experience to move up the job ladder.

The **intuitive** type likes to follow their inspirations and enjoys working on challenging and complex problems. They like change and finding new ways of doing work. This type focuses on the whole picture rather than the details. The intuitive type is an initiator, promoter and inventor of ideas. They enjoy learning a new skill more than using it. They often change careers to follow their creative inspirations.

The **thinking** type likes to use logical analysis in making decisions. They are objective and rational and treat others fairly. They want logical reasons before accepting any new ideas. They follow policy and are often firm-minded and critical, especially when dealing with illogic in others. They easily learn facts, theories and principles. They are interested in careers with money, prestige or influence.

The **feeling** type likes harmony and the support of co-workers. They are personal, enjoy warm relationships and relate well to most people. Feeling types know their personal values and apply them consistently. They enjoy doing work that provides a service to people and often do work that requires them to understand and analyze their own emotions and those of others. They prefer a friendly work environment and like to learn with others. They enjoy careers in which they can make a contribution to humanity.

The **judging** type likes a work environment that is structured, settled and organized. They prefer work assignments that are clear and definite. The judging type makes lists and plans to get the job done on time. They make quick decisions and like to have the work finished. They are good at doing purposeful and exacting work. They prefer to learn only the essentials that are necessary to do the job. This type carefully plans their career path.

The **perceptive** type likes to be spontaneous and go with the flow. They are comfortable in handling the unplanned or unexpected in the work environment. They prefer to be flexible in their work and feel restricted by structures and schedules. They are good at handling work which requires change and adaptation. They are tolerant and have a "live and let live" attitude toward others. Decisions are often postponed because this type wants to know all there is to know and explore all the options before making a decision. This type is often a career changer who takes advantage of new job openings and opportunities for change.

JOURNAL ENTRY #6
Describe your ideal working environment.

Personality and Decision Making

Your personality type affects how you think and how you make decisions. Knowing how you make decisions will help with self-understanding and working with others in decision making or creative problem solving. Each personality type views the decision making process in a different way. Ideally it would be good to have a variety of types involved in making a decision so that the strengths of each type could be utilized.

The **introvert** thinks up ideas and reflects on the problem before acting. The **extravert** acts as the communicator in the decision making process. Once the decision is made, they take action and implement the decision. The **intuitive** type develops theories and uses intuition to come up with ingenious solutions to the problem. The **sensing type** applies personal experience to the decision making process and focuses on solutions that are practical and realistic.

The thinking and feeling dimensions of personality determine how a decision is made. Of course people use both thinking in feeling in the decision making process, but tend to prefer or trust either thinking or feeling. Those who prefer **thinking** use cause and effect reasoning and solve problems with logic. They use objective and impersonal criteria and include all the consequences of alternative solutions in the decision making process. They are interested in finding out what is true and what is false. They use laws and principles to treat everyone fairly. Once a decision is made, they are firm minded, since the decision was based on logic. This type is often critical of those who do not use logic in the decision making process. The **feeling** type considers human values and motives in the decision making process (whether they are logical or not) and values harmony and maintaining good relationships. They consider carefully how much they care about each of the alternatives and how they will affect other people. They are interested in making a decision that is agreeable to all parties. Feeling types are tactful and skillful in dealing with people.

It is often asked if thinking types have feelings. They do have feelings, but use them as a criterion to be factored into the decision making process. Thinking types are more comfortable when feelings are controlled and often think that feeling types are too emotional. Thinking types may have difficulties when they apply logic in a situation where a feeling response is needed, such as in dealing with a spouse. Thinking types need to know that people are important in making decisions. Feeling types need to know that behavior will have logical consequences and that they may need to keep emotions more controlled to work effectively with thinking types.

Judging and perceptive types have opposite decision making strategies. The judging type is very methodical and cautious in making decisions. Once they have gone through the decision making steps, they like to make decisions quickly so that they can have closure and finish the project. The perceptive type is an adventurer who wants to look at all the possibilities before making a decision. They are open-minded and curious and often resist closure to look at more options.

If a combination of types collaborates on a decision, it is more likely that the decision will be a good one which takes into account creative possibilities, practicality, logical consequences and human values.

JOURNAL ENTRY #7
Describe your decision-making process.

Personality and Time Management

How we manage our time is not just a result of personal habits; it is also a reflection of our personality type. Probably the dimension of personality type most connected to time management is the judging or perceptive trait. **Judging types** like to have their lives planned, orderly, and under control. **Perceptive types** prefer more spontaneity. Understanding the differences between these two types will help you to better understand yourself and others.

Judging types are naturally good at time management. They often use schedules as a tool for time management and organization. Judging types plan their time and work steadily to accomplish goals. They are good at meeting deadlines and often put off relaxation, recreation, and fun. They relax after projects are completed. If they have too many projects, they find it difficult to find time for recreation. Since judging types like to have projects under control, there is a danger that projects will be completed too quickly and that quality will suffer. Judging types may need to slow down and take the time to do quality work. They may also need to make relaxation and recreation a priority.

Perceptive types are more open-ended and prefer to be spontaneous. They take time to relax, have fun, and participate in recreation. In working on a project, perceptive types want to brainstorm all the possibilities and are not too concerned about finishing projects. This type procrastinates when the time comes to make a final decision and finish a project. There is always more information to gather and more possibilities to explore. Perceptive types are easily distracted and may move from project to project. They may have several jobs going at once. These types need to try to focus on a few projects at a time in order to complete them. Perceptive types need to work on becoming more organized so that projects can be completed on time.

Research has shown that students who are judging types are more likely to have a higher grade point average in the first semester.[1] It has also been found that the greater the preference for intuition, introversion, and judgment, the better the grade point average.[2] Why is this true? Many college professors are intuitive types that use intuitive and creative ideas. The college environment requires quiet time for reading and studying, which is one of the preferences of introverts. Academic environments require structure, organization, and completion of assignments. To be successful in an academic environment requires adaptation by some personality types. Extroverts need to spend more quiet time reading and studying. Sensing types need to gain an understanding of intuitive types. Perceptive types need to use organization to complete assignments on time.

JOURNAL ENTRY #8

How does being a judging or a perceptive type explain how you manage your time? In other words, are you usually orderly and organized or do you prefer to be more spontaneous and flexible with how you manage your time? Judging types are generally good with time management, whereas perceptive types need to place greater importance on meeting deadlines. How can you use this information to complete assignments necessary to be successful in college?

Personality and Money

Does your personality type affect how you deal with money? Otto Kroeger and Janet Thuesen make some interesting observations about how different personality types deal with money.

- **Judging types (orderly and organized).**
  These types excel at financial planning and money management. They file their tax forms early and pay their bills on time.

- **Perceptive types (spontaneous).**
  These types adapt to change and are more creative. Perceivers, especially intuitive perceivers, tend to freak out as the April 15 tax deadline approaches and as bills become due.

- **Feeling types (make decisions based on feelings).**
  These types are not very money conscious. They believe that money should be used to serve humanity. They are often attracted to low-paying jobs that serve others.[3]

In studying stockbrokers, these same authors note that ISTJs (introvert, sensing, thinking, and judging types) are the most conservative investors, earning a small but reliable return on investments. The ESTPs (extravert, sensing, thinking, perceptive types) and ENTPs (extravert, intuitive, thinking, perceptive types) take the biggest risks and earn the greatest returns.[4]

JOURNAL ENTRY #9

How does **your** personality affect how you spend money?

Personality and Career Choice

While it is not possible to predict exactly your career and college major by knowing your personality type, it can be helpful in providing opportunities for exploration. Suggestions about career selections are based on the general characteristics of each type, and research that correlates personality type with choice of satisfying career. Here are some general descriptions of personality types and preferred careers. Included are general occupational fields, frequently chosen occupations, and suggested majors. These suggestions about career selections are based on the general characteristics of each type and research that correlates personality type with choice of a satisfying career.[5] Continue your career exploration with the online career database included with the "Do What You Are" personality assessment included with your textbook.

ISTJ

ISTJs are responsible, loyal, stable, practical, down-to-earth, hardworking, and reliable. They can be depended upon to follow through with tasks. They value tradition, family and security. They are natural leaders who prefer to work alone but can adapt to working with teams if needed. They like to be independent and have time to think things through. They are able to remember and use concrete facts and information. They make decisions by applying logic and rational thinking. They appreciate structured and orderly environments and deliver products and services in an efficient and orderly way.

General occupations to consider

business	education	health care
service	technical	military
law and law enforcement		

Specific job titles

business executive	lawyer	electronic technician
administrator	judge	computer occupations
manager	police officer	dentist
real estate agent	detective	pharmacist
accountant	corrections officer	primary care physician
bank employee	teacher (math, trade,	nursing administrator
stockbroker	technical)	respiratory therapist
auditor	educational administrator	physical therapist
hairdresser	coach	optometrist
cosmetologist	engineer	chemist
legal secretary	electrician	military officer or enlistee

College majors

business	engineering	chemistry
education	computers	biology
mathematics	health occupations	vocational training
law		

ISTP

ISTPs are independent, practical, and easygoing. They prefer to work individually and frequently like to work outdoors. These types like working with objects and often are good at working with their hands and mastering tools. They are interested in how and why things work and are able to apply technical knowledge to solving practical problems. Their logical thinking makes them good troubleshooters and problem solvers. They enjoy variety, new experiences, and taking risks. They prefer environments with little structure and have a talent for managing crises. The ISTP is happy with occupations that involve challenge, change, and variety.

General occupations to consider

sales	technical	business and finance
service	health care	vocational training
corrections		

Specific job titles

sales manager	engineer	office manager
insurance agent	electronics technician	small business manager
cook	software developer	banker
fire fighter	computer programmer	economist
pilot	radiologic technician	legal secretary
race car driver	exercise physiologist	paralegal
police officer	coach	computer repair
corrections officer	athlete	airline mechanic
judge	dental assistant/hygienist	carpenter
attorney	physician	construction worker
intelligence agent	optometrist	farmer
detective	physical therapist	military officer or enlistee

College majors

business	computers	health occupations
vocational training	biology	physical education
law		

ISFJ

ISFJs are quiet, friendly, responsible, hardworking, productive, devoted, accurate, thorough, and careful. They value security, stability, and harmony. They like to focus on one person or project at a time. ISFJs prefer to work with individuals and are very skillful in understanding people and their needs. They often provide service to others in a very structured way. They are careful observers, remember facts, and work on projects requiring accuracy and attention to detail. They have a sense of space and function that leads to artistic endeavors such as interior decorating or landscaping. ISFJs are most comfortable working in environments that are orderly, structured, and traditional. While they often work quietly behind the scenes, they like their contributions to be recognized and appreciated.

General occupations to consider

health care	education	artistic
social service	business	religious occupations
corrections	technical	vocational training

Specific job titles

nurse	social worker	counselor
physician	social services	secretary
medical technologist	administrator	cashier
dental hygienist	child care worker	accountant
health education	speech pathologist	personnel administrator
practitioner	librarian	credit counselor
dietitian	curator	business manager
physical therapist	genealogist	paralegal
nursing educator	corrections worker	computer occupations
health administrator	probation officer	engineer
medical secretary	teacher (preschool, grades	interior decorator
dentist	1–12)	home economist
medical assistant	guidance counselor	religious educator
optometrist	educational administrator	clergy
occupational therapist		

College majors

health occupations	education	graphics
biology	business	religious studies
psychology	engineering	vocational training
sociology	art	

ISFP

ISFPs are quiet, reserved, trusting, loyal, committed, sensitive, kind, creative, and artistic. They have an appreciation for life and value serenity and aesthetic beauty. These types are individualistic and generally have no desire to lead or follow; they prefer to work independently. They have a keen awareness of their environment and often have a special bond with children and animals. ISFPs are service-oriented and like to help others. They like to be original and unconventional. They dislike rules and structure and need space and freedom to do things in their own way.

General occupations to consider

artists	technical	business
health care	service	vocational training

Specific job titles

artist	recreation services	forester
designer	physical therapist	botanist
fashion designer	radiologic technician	geologist
jeweler	medical assistant	mechanic
gardener	dental assistant/hygienist	marine biologist
potter	veterinary assistant	teacher (science, art)
painter	veterinarian	police officer
dancer	animal groomer/trainer	beautician
landscape designer	dietician	merchandise planner
carpenter	optician/optometrist	stock clerk
electrician	exercise physiologist	store keeper
engineer	occupational therapist	counselor
chef	art therapist	social worker
nurse	pharmacy technician	legal secretary
counselor	respiratory therapist	paralegal

College majors

art	forestry	psychology
health occupations	geology	counseling
engineering	education	social work
physical education	business	vocational training
biology		

INFJ

INFJs are idealistic, complex, compassionate, authentic, creative, and visionary. They have strong value systems and search for meaning and purpose to life. Because of their strong value systems, INFJs are natural leaders or at least follow those with similar ideas. They intuitively understand people and ideas and come up with new ideas to provide service to others. These types like to organize their time and be in control of their work.

General occupations to consider

counseling	religious occupations	health care
education	creative occupations	social services
		business

Specific job titles

career counselor	director of religious	dental hygienist
psychologist	education	speech pathologist
teacher (high school or	fine artist	nursing educator
college English, art,	playwright	medical secretary
music, social sciences,	novelist	pharmacist
drama, foreign	poet	occupational therapist
languages,	designer	human resources manager
health)	architect	marketer
librarian	art director	employee assistance
home economist	health care administrator	program
social worker	physician	merchandise planner
clergy	biologist	environmental lawyer

College majors

psychology	drama	architecture
counseling	foreign languages	biology
education	English	business
art	health occupations	law
music	social work	

INFP ⭐

INFPs are loyal, devoted, sensitive, creative, inspirational, flexible, easygoing, complex, and authentic. They are original and individualistic and prefer to work alone or with other caring and supportive individuals. These types are service-oriented and interested in personal growth. They develop deep relationships because they understand people and are genuinely interested in them. They dislike dealing with details and routine work. They prefer a flexible working environment with a minimum of rules and regulations.

General occupations to consider

creative arts	counseling	health care
education	religious occupations	organizational
		development

Specific job titles

artist	photographer	dietician
designer	carpenter	psychiatrist
writer	teacher (art, drama,	physical therapist
journalist	music, English, foreign	occupational therapist
entertainer	languages)	speech pathologist
architect	psychologist	laboratory technologist
actor	counselor	public health nurse
editor	social worker	dental hygienist
reporter	librarian	physician
journalist	clergy	human resources
musician	religious educator	specialist
graphic designer	missionary	social scientist
art director	church worker	consultant

College majors

art	foreign languages	medicine
music	architecture	health occupations
graphic design	education	social work
journalism	religious studies	counseling
English	psychology	business

INTJ

INTJs are reserved, detached, analytical, logical, rational, original, independent, creative, ingenious, innovative, and resourceful. They prefer to work alone and work best alone. They can work with others if their ideas and competence are respected. They value knowledge and efficiency. They enjoy creative and intellectual challenges and understand complex theories. They create order and structure. They prefer to work with autonomy and control over their work. They dislike factual and routine kinds of work.

General occupations to consider

business and finance	education	law
technical occupations	health care and medicine	creative occupations

Specific job titles

management consultant	astronomer	dentist
human resources planner	computer programmer	biomedical engineer
economist	biomedical researcher	attorney
international banker	software developer	manager
financial planner	network integration	judge
investment banker	specialist	electrical engineer
scientist	teacher (university)	writer
scientific researcher	school principal	journalist
chemist	mathematician	artist
biologist	psychiatrist	inventor
computer systems analyst	psychologist	architect
electronic technician	neurologist	actor
design engineer	physician	musician

College majors

business	physics	journalism
finance	education	art
chemistry	mathematics	architecture
biology	medicine	drama
computers	psychology	music
engineering	law	vocational training
astronomy	English	

INTP

INTPs are logical, analytical, independent, original, creative, and insightful. They are often brilliant and ingenious. They work best alone and need quiet time to concentrate. They focus their attention on ideas and are frequently detached from other people. They love theory and abstract ideas and value knowledge and competency. INTPs are creative thinkers who are not too interested in practical application. They dislike detail and routine and need freedom to develop, analyze, and critique new ideas. These types maintain high standards in their work.

General occupations to consider

planning and development	technical	academic
health care	professional	creative occupations

Specific job titles

computer software designer	pharmacist	historian
computer programmer	engineer	philosopher
research and development	electrician	college teacher
systems analyst	dentist	researcher
financial planner	veterinarian	logician
investment banker	lawyer	photographer
physicist	economist	creative writer
plastic surgeon	psychologist	artist
psychiatrist	architect	actor
chemist	psychiatrist	entertainer
biologist	mathematician	musician
pharmaceutical researcher	archaeologist	inventor

College majors

computers	philosophy	mathematics
business	music	archeology
physics	art	history
chemistry	drama	English
biology	engineering	drama
astronomy	psychology	music
medicine	architecture	vocational training

ESTP

ESTP's have great people skills, are action-oriented, fun, flexible, adaptable, and resourceful. They enjoy new experiences and dealing with people. They remember facts easily and have excellent powers of observation that they use to analyze other people. They are good problem solvers and can react quickly in an emergency. They like adventure and risk and are alert to new opportunities. They start new projects but do not necessarily follow through to completion. They prefer environments without too many rules and restrictions.

General occupations to consider

sales	entertainment	technical
service	sports	trade
active careers	health care	business
finance		

Specific job titles

marketing professional	insurance agent	dentist
fire fighter	sportscaster	carpenter
police officer	news reporter	farmer
corrections officer	journalist	construction worker
paramedic	tour agent	electrician
detective	dancer	teacher (trade, industrial,
pilot	bartender	technical)
investigator	auctioneer	chef
real estate agent	professional athlete or	engineer
exercise physiologist	coach	surveyor
flight attendant	fitness instructor	radiologic technician
sports merchandise sales	recreation leader	entrepreneur
stockbroker	optometrist	land developer
financial planner	pharmacist	retail sales
investor	critical care nurse	car sales

College majors

business	vocational training	English
physical education	education	journalism
health occupations		

ESTJ

ESTJs are loyal, hardworking, dependable, thorough, practical, realistic, and energetic. They value security and tradition. Because they enjoy working with people and are orderly and organized, these types like to take charge and be the leader. This personality type is often found in administrative and management positions. ESTJs work systematically and efficiently to get the job done. These types are fair, logical, and consistent. They prefer a stable and predictable environment filled with action and a variety of people.

General occupations to consider

managerial	service	professional
sales	technical	military leaders

Specific job titles

retail store manager
fire department manager
small business manager
restaurant manager
financial or bank officer
school principal
sales manager
top-level manager in city/
    county/state
    government
management consultant
corporate executive

military officer or enlistee
office manager
purchasing agent
police officer
factory supervisor
corrections
insurance agent
detective
judge
accountant
nursing administrator
mechanical engineer

physician
chemical engineer
auditor
coach
public relations worker
cook
personnel or labor
    relations worker
teacher (trade, industrial,
    technical)
mortgage banker

College majors

business
business management
accounting
finance

small business
    management
engineering

law
education
vocational training

ESFP

ESFPs are practical, realistic, independent, fun, social, spontaneous, and flexible. They have great people skills and enjoy working in environments that are friendly, relaxed, and varied. They know how to have a good time and make an environment fun for others. ESFPs have a strong sense of aesthetics and are sometimes artistic and creative. They often have a special bond with people or animals. They dislike structure and routine. These types can handle many activities or projects at once.

General occupations to consider

education
social service

health care
entertainment

business and sales
service

Specific job titles

child care worker
teacher (preschool,
    elementary school,
    foreign languages,
    mathematics)
athletic coach
counselor
library assistant
police officer
public health nurse
respiratory therapist
physical therapist
physician
emergency medical
    technician
dental hygienist

medical assistant
critical care nurse
dentist
dental assistant
exercise physiologist
dog obedience trainer
veterinary assistant
travel or tour agent
recreation leader or
    amusement site worker
photographer
designer
film producer
musician
performer
actor

promoter
special events coordinator
editor or reporter
retail merchandiser
fund raiser
receptionist
real estate agent
insurance agent
sporting equipment sales
retail sales
retail management
waiter or waitress
cashier
cosmetologist
hairdresser
religious worker

College majors

education
psychology
foreign languages
mathematics
physical education

health occupations
art
design
photography
English

journalism
drama
music
business
vocational training

ESFJ

ESFJs are friendly, organized, hardworking, productive, conscientious, loyal, dependable, and practical. These types value harmony, stability, and security. They enjoy interacting with people and receive satisfaction from giving to others. ESFJs enjoy working in a cooperative environment in which people get along well with each other. They create order, structure, and schedules and can be depended on to complete the task at hand. They prefer to organize and control their work.

General occupations to consider

health care
education

social service
counseling

business

Specific job titles

medical or dental assistant
nurse
radiologic technician
dental hygienist
speech pathologist
occupational therapist
dentist
optometrist
dietician
pharmacist
physician
physical therapist
health education
    practitioner
medical secretary
teacher (grades 1–12,
    foreign languages,
    reading)

coach
administrator of
    elementary
    or secondary school
administrator of student
    personnel
child care provider
home economist
social worker
administrator of social
    services
police officer
counselor
community welfare
    worker
religious educator
clergy

sales representative
hairdresser
cosmetologist
restaurant worker
recreation or amusement
    site worker
receptionist
office manager
cashier
bank employee
bookkeeper
accountant
sales
insurance agent
credit counselor
merchandise planner

College majors

health occupations
biology
foreign languages
English

education
psychology
counseling
sociology

religious studies
business
vocational training

ENFP ⭐

ENFPs are friendly, creative, energetic, enthusiastic, innovative, adventurous, and fun. They have great people skills and enjoy providing service to others. They are intuitive and perceptive about people. ENFPs are good at anything that interests them and can enter a variety of fields. These types dislike routine and detailed tasks and may have difficulty following through and completing tasks. They enjoy occupations in which they can be creative and interact with people. They like a friendly and relaxed environment in which they are free to follow their inspiration and participate in adventures.

General occupations to consider

creative occupations
marketing
education

counseling
health care

social service
entrepreneurial business

Specific job titles

journalist	public relations	physical therapist
musician	counselor	consultant
actor	clergy	inventor
entertainer	psychologist	sales
fine artist	teacher (health, special	human resources manager
playwright	education, English, art,	conference planner
newscaster	drama, music)	employment development
reporter	social worker	specialist
interior decorator	dental hygienist	restauranteur
cartoonist	nurse	merchandise planner
graphic designer	dietician	environmental attorney
marketing	holistic health practitioner	lawyer
advertising		

College majors

journalism	business (advertising,	religious studies
English	marketing, public	health occupations
drama	relations)	law
art	counseling	vocational training
graphic design	psychology	

ENFJ

ENFJs are friendly, sociable, empathetic, loyal, creative, imaginative, and responsible. They have great people skills and are interested in working with people and providing service to them. They are good at building harmony and cooperation and respect other people's opinions. These types can find creative solutions to problems. They are natural leaders who can make good decisions. They prefer an environment that is organized and structured and enjoy working as part of a team with other creative and caring people.

General occupations to consider

religious occupations	counseling	health care
creative occupations	education	business
communications	human services	

Specific job titles

director of religious
   education
minister
clergy
public relations
marketing
writer
librarian
journalist
fine artist
designer
actor
musician or composer
fund-raiser
recreational director
TV producer

newscaster
politician
editor
crisis counselor
school counselor
vocational or career
   counselor
psychologist
alcohol and drug
   counselor
teacher (health, art,
   drama, English, foreign
   languages)
child-care worker
college humanities
   professor

social worker
home economist
nutritionist
speech pathologist
occupational therapist
physical therapist
optometrist
dental hygienist
family practice physician
psychiatrist
nursing educator
pharmacist
human resources trainer
travel agent
small business executive
sales manager

College majors

religious studies
business (public relations,
   marketing)
art
graphic design
drama

music
journalism
English
foreign languages
humanities
psychology

counseling
sociology
health occupations
business
vocational training

ENTP

ENTPs are creative, ingenious, flexible, diverse, energetic, fun, motivating, logical, and outspoken. They have excellent people skills and are natural leaders, although they dislike controlling other people. They value knowledge and competence. They are lively and energetic and make good debaters and motivational speakers. They are logical and rational thinkers who can grasp complex ideas and theories. They dislike environments that are structured and rigid. These types prefer environments that allow them to engage in creative problem solving and the creation of new ideas.

General occupations to consider

creative occupations
politics

law
business

health care

Specific job titles

photographer	politician	computer professional
marketing professional	political manager	corrections officer
journalist	political analyst	sales manager
actor	social scientist	speech pathologist
writer	psychiatrist	health education
musician or composer	psychologist	practitioner
editor	engineer	respiratory therapist
reporter	construction laborer	dental assistant
advertising director	research worker	medical assistant
radio/TV talk show host	electrician	critical care nurse
producer	lawyer	counselor
art director	judge	human resources planner
new business developer	corporate executive	

College majors

art	music	political science
photography	business (advertising,	psychology
journalism	marketing,	health occupations
drama	management,	computers
English	human resources)	vocational training

ENTJ

ENTJs are independent, original, visionary, logical, organized, ambitious, competitive, hardworking, and direct. They are natural leaders and organizers who identify problems and create solutions for organizations. ENTJs are often in management positions. They are good planners and accomplish goals in a timely manner. These types are logical thinkers who enjoy a structured work environment where they have opportunity for advancement. They enjoy a challenging, competitive, and exciting environment in which accomplishments are recognized.

General occupations to consider

business
finance
law

Specific job titles

executive	manager in city/county/	accountant
manager	state government	auditor
supervisor	management trainer	financial manager
personnel manager	school principal	real estate agent
sales manager	bank officer	lawyer, judge
marketing manager	computer systems analyst	consultant
human resources planner	computer professional	engineer
corporate executive	credit investigator	corrections, probation
college administrator	mortgage broker	officer
health administrator	stockbroker	psychologist
small business owner	investment banker	physician
retail store manager	economist	

College majors

business management   computers   engineering
finance   law   psychology
economics   medicine   vocational training

Dilbert reprinted by permission of United Feature Syndicate, Inc.

Other Factors in Choosing a Major

Choosing your college major is one of the most difficult and important decisions you will make during your college years. After assessing their personality types, students often come up with many different options for a major and career. Future chapters will help you to think about your interests, values, and preferred lifestyle. This information will help you to narrow down your choices.

Once you have completed a thorough self-assessment, you may still have several majors to consider. At this point, it is important to do some research on the outlook for a selected career in the future and the pay you would receive. Sometimes students are disappointed after graduation when they find there are few job opportunities in their chosen career field. Sometimes students graduate and cannot find jobs with the salary they had hoped to earn. It is important to think about the opportunities you will have in the future. If you have several options for a career you would enjoy, you may want to consider seriously the career that has the best outlook and pay.

Majors and Earnings[6]

Major	Earnings
Chemical Engineering	$56,269
Electrical Engineering	$53,500
Mechanical Engineering	$51,732
Computer Science	$50,744
Information Sciences and Systems	$47,182
Civil Engineering	$46,084
Accounting	$44,928
Economics/Finance	$44,588
Business Administration Management	$41,155
Political Science and Government	$33,094
History	$33,071
English	$31,385
Sociology	$31,096
Psychology	$30,369

Every career counselor can tell stories about students who ask, "What is the career that makes the most money? That's the career I want!" However, if you choose a career based on money alone, you might find it difficult and uninteresting for a lifetime of work. You might even find yourself retraining later in life for a job that you really enjoy. Remember that the first step is to figure out who you are and what you like. Then look at career outlook and opportunity. If you find your passion in a career that is in demand and pays well, you will probably be very happy with your career choice. If you find your passion in a career that offers few jobs and does not pay well, you will have to use your ingenuity to find a job and make a living. Many students happily make this informed choice and find a way to make it work.

JOURNAL ENTRY #10

Answer one of the following questions:

1. If you have chosen a major, is it one that is suggested by your personality type? If your major is not suggested for your personality type, how can you apply your personality strengths to being successful in your chosen career?

2. If you have not chosen a major, are there some suggested careers that you are interested in considering? How would your personality strengths be an asset in these careers?

Find Your Passion

Mark Twain said, "The secret of success is making your vocation your vacation." Find what you like to do. Better yet, find your passion. If you can find your passion, it is easy to invest the time and effort necessary to be successful. Aviator Charles Lindbergh said, "It is the greatest shot of adrenaline to be doing what you've wanted to do so badly. You almost feel like you could fly without the plane."[7] We may not be as excited about our careers as Charles Lindbergh, but we can find a career that matches our personalities and talents and provides meaning to our lives.

How do you know when you have found your passion? You have found your passion when you are doing an activity and you do not notice that the time is passing. The great painter Picasso often talked about how quickly time passed while he was painting. He said, "When I work, I relax; doing nothing or entertaining visitors makes me tired." Whether you are an artist, an athlete, a scientist, or a business entrepreneur, passion provides the energy needed to be successful. It helps you to grow and create. When you are using your talents to grow and create, you can find meaning and happiness in your life.

Psychologist Martin Seligman has written a book entitled *Authentic Happiness,* in which he writes about three types of work orientation: a job, a career, and a calling.[8] A job is what you do for the paycheck at the end of the week. Many college students have jobs to earn money for college. A career has deeper personal meaning. It involves achievement, prestige, and power. A calling is defined as "a passionate commitment to work for its own sake."[9] When you have found your calling, the job itself is the reward. He notes that people who have found their calling are consistently happier than those who have a job or even a career. One of the ways that you know you have found your calling is when

you are in the state of "flow." The state of "flow" is defined as "complete absorption in an activity whose challenges mesh perfectly with your abilities."[10] People who experience "flow" are happier and more productive. They do not spend their days looking forward to Friday. Understanding your personal strengths is the beginning step to finding your calling.

Seligman adds that any job can become a calling by using your personal strengths to do the best possible job. He cited a study of hospital cleaners. Although some viewed their job as drudgery, others viewed the job as a calling. They believed that they helped patients get better by working efficiently and anticipating the needs of doctors and nurses. They rearranged furniture and decorated walls to help patients feel better. They found their calling by applying their personal talents to their jobs. As a result, their jobs became a calling.

Sometimes we wait around for passion to find us. That probably won't happen. The first step in finding your passion is to know yourself. Then find an occupation in which you can use your talents. You may be able to find your passion by looking at your present job and finding a creative way to do it based on your special talents. It has been said that there are no dead-end jobs, just people who cannot see the possibilities. Begin your search for passion by looking for possibilities. If the job that you have now is not your passion, see what you can learn from it and then use your skills to find a career where you are more likely to find your passion.

Success is not the key to happiness; happiness is the key to success. If you love what you are doing, you will be successful.

—Anonymous

JOURNAL ENTRIES

Personality

Go to http://www.collegesuccess1.com/ for Word files of the Journal Entries

Success over the Internet

Visit the *College Success Website* at http://www.collegesuccess1.com/

The *College Success Website* is continually updated with new topics and links to the material presented in this chapter. Topics include:

• Personality profiles
• Online personality assessments
• Personality types of famous people in history

• Personality types and relationships
• Personality types and marriage
• Personality and careers
• Personality and communication
• Choosing your major
• Topics just for fun

Contact your instructor if you have any problems in accessing the *College Success Website*.

Notes

1. Judith Provost and Scott Anchors, eds., *Applications of the Myers-Briggs Type Indicator in Higher Education* (Palo Alto, CA: Consulting Psychologists Press, 1991), 51.
2. Ibid., 49.
3. Otto Kroeger and Janet Thuesen, *Type Talk: The 16 Personality Types That Determine How We Live, Love and Work* (New York: Dell, 1989), 204.
4. Ibid.
5. Allen L. Hammer and Gerald P. Macdaid, *MBTI Career Report Manual* (CA: Consulting Psychologist Press, 1998), 57–89.
6. Rob Kelly, "Most Lucrative Degrees for College Grads," CNN Money.com, October 27, 2006.
7. Quoted in Rob Gilbert, ed., *Bits and Pieces,* December 2, 1999.
8. Martin Seligman, *Authentic Happiness* (Free Press, 2002).
9. Martin Seligman, as reported by Geoffrey Cowley, "The Science of Happiness," *Newsweek,* September 16, 2002, 49.
10. Ibid.

Personality Preferences

Name _____   Date _____

Use the textbook and personality assessment to think about your personality type. Place an X on the scale to show your degree of preference for each dimension of personality.

Introvert _____|_____ Extravert

Sensing _____|_____ INtuitive

Thinking _____|_____ Feeling

Judging _____|_____ Perceptive

Write a key word or phrase to describe each preference.

Introvert

Extravert

Sensing

INtuitive

Thinking

Feeling

Judging

Perceptive

What careers are suggested by your personality assessment?

Was the personality assessment accurate and useful to you?

Name _____   Date _____

Look at the charts at the beginning of the chapter that describe the ideal work environment and the section on Personality and Preferred Work Environment. Based on this information and the items you have highlighted, describe your ideal work environment.

Are there other characteristics of your ideal job? For example, do you want a job that provides financial security, helps you stay in the same geographical area, provides opportunity for travel, and lets you have time to be with your family? Write two additional characteristics of your ideal job.

What are the five most important characteristics of your ideal job?

1. _____

2. _____

3. _____

4. _____

5. _____

Look at the careers that match your personality type. List the careers that seem interesting to you. Include any careers that you have been considering, whether they are on the list or not.

Describe Your Personality

Name _____   Date _____

Review the following material to prepare for writing a description of your personality type.

- The material on personality in this chapter

- The results of your "Do What You Are" personality assessment.

- Additional materials provided by your professor or located on the Internet at www.personalitypage.com.

Using the outline below, write a description of your personality type on a separate sheet of paper.

1. In the introduction, give the four-letter abbreviation for your type (such as ISFJ) and explain in your own words what each letter means.

2. Using the material you have reviewed, write a general description of your personality type.

3. Describe the first letter of your code (E or I). Include preferences in the workplace. Give an example of how this preference affects your social life, school, and work.

4. Describe the second letter of your code (S or N). Include preferences in the workplace. Give an example of how this preference affects your social life, school, and work.

5. Describe the third letter of your code (T or F). Include preferences in the workplace. Give an example of how this preference affects your social life, school, and work.

6. Describe the fourth letter of your code (J or P). Include preferences in the workplace. Give an example of how this preference affects your social life, school, and work.

7. Tell how your personality is suited to specific careers and majors.

8. In the last paragraph, tell what you thought of the personality assessment. Was it useful to you? Did it give you ideas for your major or career?

Name _____   Date _____

Directions: Please read the chapter on personality before commenting on these scenarios. Keep in mind the theory that we are all born with certain personality types and there are no good or bad types. Each type has gifts and talents that can be used to be a successful and happy person. Relate your comments to the concepts in this chapter. Your instructor may have you do this exercise as a group activity in class.

Scenario 1 (Sensing vs. Intuitive): Julie is a pre-school teacher. She assigns her class to draw a picture of a bicycle. Students share their pictures with the class. One of the students has drawn a bicycle with wings. Another student laughs at the drawing and says, "Bicycles don't have wings!" How should the teacher handle this situation?

Scenario 2 (Thinking vs. Feeling): John has the almost perfect girlfriend. She is beautiful, intelligent and fun to be with. She only has one flaw. John thinks that she is too emotional and wishes she could be a little more rational. When his girlfriend tries to talk to him about emotional issues, he analyzes her problems and proposes a logical solution. His girlfriend doesn't like the solutions that John proposes. Should John find a new girlfriend?

Scenario 3 (Introvert vs. Extravert): Mary is the mother of 2 children ages 5 (daughter) and 8 (son). The 5-year old is very social and especially enjoys birthday parties. At the last party she invited 24 girls and they all showed up at the party. Everyone had a great time. The 8-year old is very quiet and spends his time reading, doing art work, building models and hanging out with his one best friend. Mary is concerned that her son does not have very many friends. She decides to have a birthday party for her son also. The only problem is that he cannot come up with a list of children to invite to the party. What should Mary do?

Scenario 4 (Judging vs. Perceptive): Jerry and Jennifer have just been married and they love each other very much. Jennifer likes to keep the house neat and orderly and likes to plan out activities so that there are no surprises. Jerry likes creative disorder. He leaves his things all over the house. He often comes up with creative ideas for having fun. How can Jerry and Jennifer keep their good relationship going?

CHAPTER **3**

LEARNING OBJECTIVES

Read to answer these key questions:

- What is my learning style?

- What is the best learning environment for me?

- What are some specific learning strategies that match my learning style?

- How is learning style connected to personality type?

- What are some specific learning strategies based on personality type?

- How can I understand and adapt to my professor's personality type (or "psych out" the professor)?

- What kinds of intelligence do I have?

- How can I create my success?

© Répási Lajos Atilla, 2008. Under license from Shutterstock, Inc.

Learning Style and Intelligence

Knowing about your learning style can help you to choose effective strategies for learning in school and on the job. Knowing about your preferred learning environment can help you increase productivity. Discovering your multiple intelligences will help you to gain an appreciation of your gifts and talents that can be used to develop your self-confidence and choose the career that is right for you.

What Is Learning Style?

Just as each individual has a unique personality, each individual has a unique learning style. It is important to remember that there are no good or bad learning styles. Learning style is simply your preferred way of learning. It is how you like to learn and how you learn best. By understanding your learning style, you can maximize your potential by choosing the learning techniques that work best for you. Many factors determine how you learn best. Each individual also has a preferred learning environment. Knowing about your preferred learning environment and learning style helps you be more productive, increase achievement, be more creative, improve problem solving, make good decisions, and learn effectively. Personality type also influences how we learn. Another way to think about learning style is through an awareness of the many kinds of intelligences that we possess. Knowing about how you learn best helps to reduce frustration and increase your confidence in learning.

Gary Price has developed the Productivity Environmental Preference Survey (PEPS) which is included with your textbook. It identifies 20 different elements of learning style and environment including the immediate environment, emotional factors, sociological needs, and physical needs. As you read the description of each of these elements, think about your preferences.

1. Sound.
Some students need a quiet environment for study, whereas others find it distracting if it is too quiet.
•   If you prefer quiet, use the library or find another quiet place. If you cannot find a quiet place, sound-blocking earphones or earplugs may be helpful. Remember that not all people need a quiet environment for study.
•   If you study better with sound, play soft music or study in open areas. Use headphones for your music if you are studying with those who prefer quiet.

2. Light.
Some students prefer bright light to see what they are studying, whereas others find bright light uncomfortable or irritating.
•   If you prefer bright light, study near a window with light shining over your shoulder or invest in a good study lamp.
•   If you prefer dim lights, sit away from direct sunlight or use a shaded light.

3. Temperature.
Some students perform better in cool temperatures and others prefer warmer temperatures.
•   If you prefer a warm environment, remember to bring your sweater or jacket. Sit near a window or other source of heat.
•   If you prefer a cooler environment, study in a well-ventilated environment or even outside in the shade.

4. Design.
Some students study best in a more formal environment or less formal environment.
•   If you prefer a formal environment, sit in a straight chair and use a desk.

- If you prefer an informal environment, sit on the sofa or a soft chair or on some pillows on the floor.

5. Motivation.
Some students are self-motivated to learn, and others lack motivation.
- If you are self-motivated, you usually like school and enjoy learning on your own.
- If you lack motivation, think about your reasons for attending college and review the material in the motivation chapter of this book.

6. Persistence.
Some students finish what they start, whereas others have many things going on at once and may not finish what they have started.
- If you are persistent, you generally finish what you start.
- If you lack persistence, you may get bored or distracted easily. You may find it easier to break tasks into small steps and work steadily toward completing assignments on time.

7. Responsibility (Conforming).
This element has a unique meaning in the area of learning style.
- Some students like to please others by doing what is asked of them.
- Other students are less likely to conform. They prefer to complete assignments because they want to rather than because someone else wants the assignment done. These students may need to look for something interesting and personally meaningful in school assignments.

8. Structure.
Students prefer more or less structure.
- Students who prefer structure want the teacher to give details about how to complete the assignment. They need clear directions before completing an assignment.
- Students who prefer less structure want the teacher to give assignments in which the students can choose the topic and organize the material on their own.

9. Alone/Peer.
Some students prefer to study alone, and others prefer to study with others.
- You may find other people distracting and prefer to study alone. You need to study in a private area.
- You may enjoy working in a group because talking with others helps you to learn.

10. Authority Figures Present.
Some students are more or less independent learners.
- Some students prefer to have the professor available to guide learning. In the college environment, students may prefer traditional face-to-face classes.
- Others prefer to work on their own and report later. In the college environment, students may prefer online classes or independent study.

11. Several Ways.
Some students learn in several ways, and others have definite preferences.
- Some students like variety and can learn either on their own or with others.
- Some students definitely prefer learning on their own or prefer learning with others.

12. Auditory.
Some students prefer to learn through listening and talking.
- Those who prefer auditory learning find it easier to learn through lectures, audio materials, discussion, and oral directions.

- Those who do not prefer auditory learning may find their mind wandering during lectures and become confused with oral directions. They do not learn through others talking about the topic. These students should read and take notes before the lecture.

13. Visual.
Some students learn through reading or seeing things.
- Those who prefer visual learning benefit from pictures and reading.
- Those who are not visual learners may dislike reading. If auditory learning is preferred, attend the lecture first to hear the lecturer talk about the subject and then do the reading.

14. Tactile.
Some students prefer to touch the material as they learn.
- Students who prefer tactile learning prefer manipulative and three-dimensional materials. They learn from working with models and writing.
- Students who are not tactile learners should use visual or auditory preferences.

15. Kinesthetic.
Kinesthetic learning is related to tactile learning. Students learn best by acting out material to be learned or moving around while learning.
- Students who prefer kinesthetic learning enjoy field trips, drama, and becoming physically involved with learning. For example, they can learn fractions by slicing an apple into parts or manipulating blocks. It is important to be actively involved in learning.
- Students who are not kinesthetic learners will use another preferred method of learning such as auditory or visual.

16. Intake.
Some students need to chew or drink something while learning.
- If you prefer intake while learning, drink water and have nutritious snacks such as fruits and vegetables.
- Some students do not need intake to study and find food items distracting.

17. Evening/Morning.
Some students are more awake in the morning and prefer to go to bed early at night. If this is your preference, schedule your most challenging studying in the morning and do your routine tasks later.

18. Late Morning.
Some students are more awake from 10:00 A.M. until noon. If this is your preference, use this time for studying. Use other times for more routine tasks.

19. Afternoon.
Some students are most productive in the afternoon. If this is your preference, schedule your study time in the afternoon. Do your routine tasks at other times.

20. Mobility.
Some students like to move around while studying.
- If you prefer mobility, you may find it difficult to sit still for a long time. Take a break every 15 or 20 minutes to move around. When choosing an occupation, consider one that requires you to move around.
- If you don't need to move around while studying, a stationary desk and chair is sufficient to help you concentrate on learning.

Learning Techniques

It is important to connect specific learning strategies to your preferred learning style. Even if you have definite preferences, you can experiment with other styles to improve your learning. If you become frustrated with a learning task, first try a familiar technique that you have used successfully in the past. If that does not work, experiment with different ways of learning. If one technique does not work, try another. It is powerful to combine techniques. For example, it is a good idea to make pictures of what you want to remember (visual), recite the ideas you want to remember (auditory), and take notes (tactile).

The following are specific techniques for each type of learner. Underline or highlight techniques that are useful to you.

Visual Learning Techniques

- Make a mental photograph or mental video of what you want to remember. Put action and color in the picture.
- Use flash cards and look at them frequently.
- Use different colors to highlight or underline your reading and lecture notes.
- Draw pictures to remember what you are learning.
- Use symbols or pictures in the margin to emphasize important points.
- Draw a map or outline of important points.

Auditory Learning Techniques

- Discuss what you have learned with others.
- Participate in study groups.
- Teach others what you want to learn.
- Use music to study if it does not distract you or break your concentration.
- Use music as a study break.
- Add rhythm or music to the items you are trying to remember.
- Recite aloud or silently in your mind while you are reading.
- Use flash cards and say the items on the cards.
- Use a tape recorder to recite and review important points from the reading or lecture.

Kinesthetic and Tactile Learning Techniques

- Read while walking or pacing.
- Study outside when practical.
- Take notes on lectures.
- Highlight or underline your reading material and lecture notes.
- Write summaries of the material to be learned.
- Outline chapters.
- Think of practical applications for abstract material.
- Act out the material as in a play.

- Use puzzles, games, and computers.
- Make a game out of flash cards. Count the number of answers you get correct. Set a time limit and see if you can get through the cards in the time allowed.
- Take something apart and put it together again.

JOURNAL ENTRY #2

Based on your visual, auditory, kinesthetic, and tactile learning preferences, list some useful learning techniques.

Personality and Learning Preferences

Learning preferences are also connected to personality type. As a review, according to the work of Carl Jung, and Katherine Briggs and Isabel Myers, personality has four dimensions:

1. Extraversion or Introversion
2. Sensing or Intuitive
3. Thinking or Feeling
4. Judging or Perceptive

What is your personality type? To review, here are brief descriptions of each type:

Extraverts focus their energy on the world outside themselves. They enjoy interaction with others and get to know a lot of different people. They enjoy and are usually good at communication. They are energized by social interaction and prefer being active. These types are often described as talkative and social.

Introverts focus their energy on the world inside of themselves. They enjoy spending time alone and think about the world in order to understand it. Introverts like more limited social contacts, preferring smaller groups or one-on-one relationships. These types are often described as quiet or reserved.

Sensing persons prefer to use the senses to take in information (what they see, hear, taste, touch, smell). They focus on "what is" and trust information that is concrete and observable. They learn through experience.

INtuitive persons rely on instincts and focus on "what could be." While we all use our five senses to perceive the world, the intuitive person is interested in relationships, possibilities, meanings, and implications. They value inspiration and trust their "sixth sense" or hunches. We all use our senses and intuition in our daily lives, but we usually have a preference for one mode or another.

Thinking individuals make decisions based on logic. They are objective and analytical. They look at all the evidence and reach an impersonal conclusion. They are concerned with what they think is right.

Feeling individuals make decisions based on what is important to them and matches their personal values. They are concerned about what they feel is right.

Judging types like to live in a structured, orderly, and planned way. They are happy when their lives are structured and matters are settled. They like to have control over their lives. Judging does not mean to judge others. Think of this type as orderly and organized.

Perceptive types like to live in a spontaneous and flexible way. They are happy when their lives are open to possibilities. They try to understand life rather than control it. Think of this type as spontaneous and flexible.

ACTIVITY

Circle your personality type (as determined in chapter 2).

Extravert or Introvert

Sensing or Intuitive

Thinking or Feeling

Judging or Perceptive

Each personality type has a natural preference for how to learn. When learning something new, it may be easiest and most efficient to use the style that matches your personality type. It is also a good idea to experiment with using new techniques commonly used by other types. There is no learning style that works best in all situations. You may need to adapt your learning style based on the learning activity. Underline or highlight your learning preferences below.

Learning Preferences Associated with Personality Types[2]

Extraversion
Learn best when in action
Value physical activity
Like to study with others
Say they're above average in verbal and interpersonal skills
Say they need training in reading and writing papers
Background sounds help them study
Want faculty who encourage discussion

Introversion
Learn best by pausing to think
Value reading
Prefer to study individually
Say they're below average in verbal expression
Say they need training in public speaking
Need quiet for concentration
Want faculty who give clear lectures

Sensing
Seek specific information
Memorize facts
Value what is practical
Follow instructions
Like hands-on experience
Trust material as presented
Want faculty who give clear assignments

INtuition
Seek quick insights
Use imagination to go beyond facts
Value what is original
Create their own directions
Like theories to give perspective
Read between the lines
Want faculty who encourage independent thinking

Thinking
Want objective material to study
Logic guides learning
Like to critique new ideas
Can easily find flaws in an argument
Learn by challenge and debate
Want faculty who make logical presentations

Feeling
Want to be able to relate to the material personally
Personal values are important
Like to please instructors
Can easily find something to appreciate
Learn by being supported and appreciated
Want faculty who establish personal rapport with students

Judging
Like formal instructions for solving problems
Value dependability
Plan work well in advance
Work steadily toward goals
Like to be in charge of events
Drive toward closure (finish)
Want faculty to be organized

Perceiving
Like to solve problems informally
Value change
Work spontaneously
Work impulsively with bursts of energy
Like to adapt to events
Stay open to new information
Want faculty to be entertaining and inspiring

JOURNAL ENTRY #3

What is your personality type? How does your personality type affect your learning preferences?

Learning Strategies for Different Personality Types

Based on the above descriptions of learning preferences, the following learning strategies are suggested along with some cautions for each type. Highlight those suggestions and cautions that apply to you.

Extravert

1. Since extraverts learn best when talking, discuss what you have learned with others. Form a study group.
2. Extraverts like variety and action. Take frequent breaks and do something active during your break such as walking around.
3. *Caution!* You may become so distracted by activity and socialization so your studying does not get done.

Introvert

1. Since introverts like quiet for concentration, find a quiet place to study by yourself.
2. Plan to study for longer periods of time and in a way that minimizes interruptions. Unplug the phone or study in the library.
3. *Caution!* You may miss out on sharing ideas and the fun social life of college.

Sensing

1. Sensing types are good at mastering facts and details.
2. Think about practical applications in order to motivate yourself to learn. Ask, "How can I use this information?"
3. *Caution!* You may miss the big picture or general outline by focusing too much on the facts and details. Make a general outline to see the relationship and meaning of the facts.

Intuitive

1. Intuitive types are good at learning concepts and theories.
2. As you are reading, ask yourself, "What is the main point?"
3. *Caution!* Because this type focuses on general concepts and theories, they are likely to miss details and facts. To learn details, organize them into broad categories that have meaning for you.

Thinking

1. Thinking types are good at logic.
2. As you are reading, ask yourself, "What do I think of these ideas?" Discuss or debate your ideas with others.
3. Allow time to think and reflect on your studies.
4. If possible, pick instructors whom you respect and who are intellectually challenging.
5. *Caution!* Others may be offended by your ideas. Learn to respect the ideas of others.

Feeling

1. Feeling types need a comfortable environment in order to concentrate.
2. For motivation, search for personal meaning in your studies. Ask how the material affects you or others. Look for a supportive environment or study group.
3. Help others to learn.
4. When possible, choose classes that relate to your personal interests.
5. If possible, select instructors who get to know the students and establish a positive learning environment.
6. *Caution!* You may neglect studying because of time spent helping others or may find it difficult to pay attention to material that is not personally meaningful.

Judging

1. Judging types are orderly and organized. Find ways to organize the material to learn it easier.
2. If possible, select instructors who present material in an organized way.
3. Set goals and use a schedule to motivate yourself. This type is naturally good at time management.
4. Use a daily planner, calendar, or to-do list.

5. *Caution!* Being too structured and controlled may limit your creativity and cause conflict with others. Judging types are sometimes overachievers who get stressed easily.

Perceptive

1. Perceptive students are good at looking at all the possibilities and keeping options open.
2. Allow enough time to be thorough and complete your work.
3. Keep learning fun and interesting.
4. Study in groups that have some perceptive types and some judging types. In this way, you can explore possibilities, have fun, and be organized.
5. *Caution!* Work on managing your time to meet deadlines. Be careful not to overextend yourself by working on too many projects at once.

Understanding Your Professor's Personality

Different personality types have different expectations of teachers.

*   Extraverts want faculty who encourage class discussion.
*   Introverts want faculty who give clear lectures.
*   Sensing types want faculty who give clear assignments.
*   Intuitive types want faculty who encourage independent thinking.
*   Thinking types want faculty who make logical presentations.
*   Feeling types want faculty who establish personal rapport with students.
*   Judging types want faculty to be organized.
*   Perceptive types want faculty to be entertaining and inspiring.

What can you do if your personality and the professor's personality are different? This is often the case. In a study reported by *Consulting Psychologist Press,* college faculty are twice as likely than students to be introverted intuitive types interested in abstractions and learning for its own sake.[3] College students are twice as likely than faculty to be extraverted sensing types who are interested in practical learning. There are three times more sensing and perceptive students than faculty. Faculty tend to be intuitive and judging types. Students expect faculty to be practical, fun, and flexible. Faculty tend to be theoretical and organized. In summary:

College faculty tend to be:	College students tend to be:
Introverted	Extraverted
Intuitive	Sensing
Judging	Perceptive

Of course, the above is not always true, but there is a good probability that you will have college professors who are very different from you. First, try to understand the professor's personality. This has been called "psyching out the professor." You can usually tell the professor's personality type on the first day of class by examining class materials and observing his or her manner of presentation. If you understand the professor's personality type, you will know what to expect. Next, try to appreciate what the professor has to offer. You may need to adapt your style to fit. If you are a perceptive type, be careful to meet the due dates of your assignments. Experiment with different study techniques so that you can learn the material presented.

QUIZ
Multiple Intelligences

Test what you have learned by selecting the correct answer to the following questions.

1. Multiple intelligences are defined as
   a. the many parts of intelligence as measured by an IQ test
   b. the ability to design something valued in at least one culture
   c. the ability to read, write and do mathematical computations

2. The concept of multiple intelligences is significant because
   a. it measures the intelligence of students in schools
   b. it does not use culture in measuring intelligence
   c. it broadens the scope of human potential and includes all cultures

3. Intelligences are measured by
   a. IQ tests
   b. performance in activities related to the intelligence
   c. performance in the classroom

4. Each individual's life history contains crystallizers that
   a. promote the development of the intelligences
   b. inhibit the development of the intelligences
   c. cause the individual to be set in their ways

5. Multiple intelligences include
   a. getting good grades in college
   b. bodily kinesthetic skills
   c. good test taking skills

How did you do on the quiz? Check your answers: 1. b, 2. c, 3. b, 4. a, 5. b

Keys to Success

Create Your Success

We are responsible for what happens in our lives. We make decisions and choices that create the future. Our behavior leads to success or failure. Too often we believe that we are victims of circumstance. When looking at our lives, we often look for others to blame for how our life is going:

- My grandparents did it to me. I inherited these genes.
- My parents did it to me. My childhood experiences shaped who I am.
- My teacher did it to me. He gave me a poor grade.
- My boss did it to me. She gave me a poor evaluation.
- The government did it to me. All my money goes to taxes.
- Society did it to me. I have no opportunity.

These factors are powerful influences in our lives, but we are still left with choices. Concentration camp survivor Viktor Frankl wrote a book, *Man's Search for Meaning,* in which he describes his experiences and how he survived his ordeal. His parents, brother, and wife died in the camps. He suffered starvation and torture. Through all of his sufferings and imprisonment, he still maintained that he was a free man because he could make choices.

> *We who lived in concentration camps can remember the men who walked through the huts comforting others, giving away their last piece of bread. They may have been few in number, but they offer sufficient proof that everything can be taken from a man but one thing: the last of the human freedoms—to choose one's attitude in any given set of circumstances, to choose one's own way. . . . Fundamentally, therefore, any man can, even under such circumstances, decide what shall become of him— mentally and spiritually. He may retain his human dignity even in a concentration camp.[6]*

Viktor Frankl could not choose his circumstances at that time, but he did choose his attitude. He decided how he would respond to the situation. He realized that he still had the freedom to make choices. He used his memory and imagination to exercise his freedom. When times were the most difficult, he would imagine that he was in the classroom lecturing to his students about psychology. He eventually did get out of the concentration camp and became a famous psychiatrist.

Christopher Reeve is another example of a person who maintained his freedom to make choices in difficult circumstances. Christopher Reeve, who once played the character Superman, was paralyzed from the neck down as the result of an accident he suffered when he was thrown from his horse. When he first awoke after the accident, he saw little reason for living. With the help of his family, he made the decision to keep fighting and do as much as he could to promote research on spinal cord injuries. He succeeded in raising awareness and money for this cause. As a result, there have been many advancements in the study and treatment of spinal cord injuries. Reeve believed that he and others in similar circumstances would walk again some day. Sadly, Reeve passed away in 2004. However, his advocacy for the cause of finding a cure for spinal injuries has led to research that will help others in the future.

Hopefully none of you will ever have to experience the circumstances faced by Viktor Frankl or Christopher Reeve, but we all face challenging situations. It is empowering to think that our behavior is more a function of our decisions rather than our circumstances. It is not productive to look around and find someone to blame for your problems. Psychologist Abraham Maslow says that instead of blaming we should see how we can make the best of the situation.

> *One can spend a lifetime assigning blame, finding a cause, "out there" for all the troubles that exist. Contrast this with the responsible attitude of confronting the situation, bad or good, and instead of asking, "What caused the trouble? Who was to blame?" asking, "How can I handle the present situation to make the best of it?"[7]*

Author Steven Covey suggests that we look at the word responsibility as "response-ability."[8] It is the ability to choose responses and make decisions about the future. When you are dealing with a problem, it is useful to ask yourself what decisions you made that led to the problem. How did you create the situation? If you created the problem, you can create a solution.

At times, you may ask, "How did I create this?" and find that the answer is that you did not create the situation. We certainly do not create earthquakes or hurricanes for example. But we do create or at least contribute to many of the things that happen to us. Even if you did not create your circumstances, you can create your reaction to the situation. In the case of an earthquake, you can decide to panic or find the best course of action at the moment.

Steven Covey believes that we can use our resourcefulness and initiative in dealing with most problems. When his children were growing up and they asked him how to solve a certain problem, he would say, "Use your R and I!" He meant resourcefulness and initiative. He notes that adults can use this R and I to get a good job.

But the people who end up with the good jobs are the proactive ones who are solutions to problems, not problems themselves, who seize the initiative to do whatever is necessary, consistent with correct principles, to get the job done.[9]

Use your resourcefulness and initiative to create the future that you want.

JOURNAL ENTRIES

Learning Style and Intelligence

Go to http://www.collegesuccess1.com/ for Word files of the Journal Entries

Success over the Internet

Visit the *College Success Website* at http://www.collegesuccess1.com/

The *College Success Website* is continually updated with new topics and links to the material presented in this chapter. Topics include:

- Learning style assessments
- Learning style and memory
- Learning style and personality type

Contact your instructor if you have any problems accessing the *College Success Website*.

Notes

1. Gary E. Price, "Productivity Environmental Preference Survey," Price Systems, Inc., Box 1818, Lawrence, KS 66044-8818.
2. Modified and reproduced by special permission of the Publisher, Consulting Psychologist Press, Inc., Palo Alto, CA 94303, from *Introduction to Type in College* by K. Ditiberio, Allen L. Hammer. Copyright 1993 by Consulting Psychologist Press, Inc. All rights reserved. Further reproduction is prohibited without the Publisher's written consent.
3. John K. Ditiberio and Allen L. Hammer, *Introduction to Type in College* (Palo Alto, CA: Consulting Psychologist Press, 1993), 7.

4. Howard Gardner, *Intelligence Reframed: Multiple Intelligences for the Twenty-First Century* (Boulder, CO: Basic Books, 1999).

5. Thomas Armstrong, *Multiple Intelligences in the Classroom* (Alexandria, VA: Association for Curriculum Development, 1994).

6. Viktor Frankl, *Man's Search for Meaning* (New York: Pocket Books, 1963), 104–5.

7. Quoted in Rob Gilbert, ed., *Bits and Pieces*, November 4, 1999.

8. Stephen Covey, *The Seven Habits of Highly Effective People* (New York: Simon and Schuster, 1989), 71.

9. Ibid., 75.

Learning Style Applications

Name _____   Date _____

How would you use the knowledge of your learning style to deal with the following college situations? Your instructor may use this exercise for a group activity and class discussion.

1. You have just been assigned a 10 page term paper.

2. You have to study for a challenging math test.

3. You have to write up a lab report for a biology class. It included drawings of a frog you have dissected.

4. You are taking a required course for your major and it is taught by only one professor. You dislike this professor.

5. You are taking a business class and have been assigned a group project to design a small business. It is worth 50 percent of your grade.

6. You have signed up for an economics course and find it difficult to stay awake during the lecture.

7. You signed up for a philosophy course to meet a humanities requirement. The vocabulary in this course is unfamiliar.

8. As part of the final exam, you have to prepare a five minute presentation for your art history class.

Crystallizers and Paralyzers

Name _____   Date _____

Complete the "Describing Your Multiple Intelligences" activity in this chapter before doing this exercise.

Each individual's life history contains **crystallizers** that promote the development of intelligences. Look at your highest scores on the multiple intelligences activity. List your highest scores below. Write down at least two crystallizers you experienced that may have helped you to develop these intelligences. For example, you may have been praised for your athletic skills and developed your bodily kinesthetic intelligence.

My highest scores:

Crystallizers:

Each individual's life history also contains **paralyzers** that inhibit the development of intelligences. Look at your lowest scores on the multiple intelligences activity. Write down two paralyzers that may have discouraged you from developing this intelligence. For example, you may have been corrected many times on your piano lessons and gave up learning the piano. Paralyzers often involve shame, guilt, fear or anger.

My lowest scores:

Paralyzers:

Are there some scores that you need to improve to accomplish your career and educational goals?

Based on the above analysis, write a discovery statement about what you have learned. I discovered that I . . . .

Create Your Success

Name _____   Date _____

1. Have you been displeased about anything that has happened to you recently? Think about the last several weeks and briefly describe some problem you have faced. If you cannot think of a problem, describe something that was a success in your life.

2. This question is more difficult. It requires courage and honesty as well as looking at things a little differently. Whether you described a problem situation or a success above, ask yourself, "How did I create this situation?" If you did not create it, how did you choose to react to it?

LEARNING OBJECTIVES

Read to answer these key questions:

- What are my lifetime goals?

- How can I manage my time to accomplish my goals?

- How much time do I need for study and work?

- How can I make an effective schedule?

- What are some time management tricks?

- How can I deal with procrastination?

- How can I manage my money to accomplish my financial goals?

- What are some ways to save money?

- How can I pay for my education?

- How can I use priorities to manage my time?

© EUL, 2008. Under license from Shutterstock, Inc.

Managing Time and Money

Success in college requires that you manage both time and money. You will need time to study and money to pay for your education. The first step in managing time and money is to think about the goals that you wish to accomplish in your life. Having goals that are important to you provides a reason and motivation for managing time and money. This chapter provides some useful techniques for managing time and money so that you can accomplish the goals you have set for yourself.

What Are My Lifetime Goals?

Setting goals helps you to establish what is important and provides direction for your life. Goals help you to focus your energy on what you want to accomplish. Goals are a promise to yourself to improve your life. Setting goals can help you turn your dreams into reality. Steven Scott in his book *A Millionaire's Notebook,* lays out five steps in this process:

1. Dream or visualize.
2. Convert the dream into goals.
3. Convert your goals into tasks.
4. Convert your task into steps.
5. Take your first step, and then the next.[1]

As you begin to think about your personal goals in life, make your goals specific and concrete. Rather than saying, "I want to be rich," make your goal something that you can break into specific steps. You might want to start learning about money management or begin a savings plan. Rather than setting a goal for happiness, think about what brings you happiness. If you want to live a long and healthy life, think about the health habits that will help you to accomplish your goal. You will need to break your goals down into specific tasks to be able to accomplish them.

Here are some criteria for successful goal setting:

1.   Is it achievable?
Do I have the skills, abilities and resources to accomplish this goal? If not, am I willing to spend the time to develop the skills, abilities and resources needed to achieve this goal?

2.   Is it realistic?
Do I believe I can achieve it? Am I positive and optimistic about this goal?

3.   Is it specific and measurable?
Can it be counted or observed? The most common goal mentioned by students is happiness in life. What is happiness and how will you know when you have achieved it? Is happiness a career you enjoy, owning your own home or a travel destination?

4.   Do you want to do it?
Is this a goal you are choosing because it gives you personal satisfaction rather than meeting a requirement or an expectation of someone else?

5.   Are you motivated to achieve it?
What are your rewards for achieving it?

6.   Does the goal match your values?
Is it important to you?

7. **What steps do you need to take to begin?**
Am I willing to take action to start working on it?

8. **When will you finish this goal?**
Set a date to accomplish your goal.

JOURNAL ENTRY #1

What are your lifetime goals? Begin your thinking about lifetime goals by answering the following questions:

1. What is your career goal? If you do not know what your career goal is, describe the work environment. Would your ideal career require a college degree? Would you work in an office or outside? Would you have the freedom to design your own projects or would you enjoy working in a more structured and stable environment? Would your career involve power and money? Would your career goal involve helping other people?

2. What are your family goals? Are you interested in marriage and family? What would be your important family values?

3. Describe your desired social life.

4. Where would you like to live, and what kind of house would you have?

5. What kind of recreational activities would you have?

6. When you are older and look back on your life, what are the three most important life goals that you would want to make sure to accomplish?

A Goal or a Fantasy?

One of the best questions ever asked in my class was, "What is the difference between a goal and a fantasy?" As you look at your list of lifetime goals, are some of these items goals or fantasies? Think about this question as you read the following scenario:

When Linda was a college student, she was walking through the parking lot and noticed a beautiful red sports car and decided that it would become a lifetime goal to own a similar car one day. However, with college expenses and her part-time job, it was not possible to buy the car. She would have to be content with the used car that her dad had given her so that she could drive to college. Years passed by, and Linda now has a good job, a home, and a family. She is reading a magazine and sees a picture of a similar red sports car. She cuts out this picture and tapes it to the refrigerator. After it has been on the refrigerator for several months, her children ask her why the picture is on the refrigerator. Linda replies, "I just like to dream about owning this car." One day as Linda is driving past a car dealership, she sees the red sports car on display and stops in for a test drive. To her surprise, she decides that she does not like driving the car. It doesn't fit her lifestyle either. She enjoys outdoor activities that would require a larger car. Buying a second car would be costly and reduce the amount of money that the family could spend on vacations. She decides that vacations are more important than owning the sports car. Linda goes home and removes the picture of the red sports car from the refrigerator.

"In life, as in football, you won't go far unless you know where the goalposts are."

Arnold Glasgow

There are many differences between a goal and a fantasy. A fantasy is a dream that may or may not become a reality. A goal is something that we actually plan to achieve. Sometimes we begin with a fantasy and later it becomes a goal. A fantasy can become a goal if steps are taken to achieve it. In the preceding example, the sports car is a fantasy until Linda actually takes the car for a test drive. After driving the car, she decides that she really does not want it. The fantasy is sometimes better than the reality. Goals and fantasies change over a lifetime. We set goals, try them out, and change them as we grow and mature and find out what is most important in life. Knowing what we think is important, and what we value most, helps us make good decisions about lifetime goals.

What is the difference between a goal and a fantasy? A goal is something that requires action. Ask yourself if you are willing to take action on the goals you have set for yourself. Begin to take action by thinking about the steps needed to accomplish the goal. Then take the first step and continue. Change your goals if they are no longer important to you.

JOURNAL ENTRY #2

Using one of the most important goals you have identified for yourself in the previous exercise, list some steps needed to accomplish it. What is the first step? Are you willing to begin taking these steps?

The ABCs of Time Management

The **ABCs of time management** is a system of thinking about priorities. Priorities are what you think is important. An **A priority** is a task that relates to your lifetime goal. For example, if my goal is to earn a college degree, studying becomes an A priority. This activity would become one of the most important tasks that I could accomplish today. If my goal were to be healthy, an A priority would be to exercise and plan a healthy diet. If my goal is to have a good family life, an A priority would be to spend time with family members. Knowing about your lifetime goals and spending time on those items that are most important to you will help you to accomplish the goals that you have set for yourself. If you do not spend time on your goals, you may want to look at them again and decide which ones are fantasies that you do not really value or want to accomplish.

A **B priority** is an activity that you have to do but is not directly related to your lifetime goal. Examples of B priorities might be getting out of bed, taking a shower, buying groceries, paying bills, or getting gas for the car. These activities are less important but still are necessary for survival. If I do not put gas in the car, I cannot even get to school or work. If I do not pay the bills, I will soon have financial difficulties. While we often cannot postpone these activities in order to accomplish lifetime goals, we can learn efficient time management techniques to accomplish these tasks quickly.

A **C priority** is something that I can postpone until tomorrow with no harmful effect. For example, I could wait until tomorrow or another day to wash my car, do the laundry, buy groceries, or organize my desk. As these items are postponed, however, they can move up the list to a B priority. If I cannot see out of my car window or have no clean clothes to wear, it is time to move these tasks up on my list of priorities.

Have you ever been a victim of "**C fever**"? This is an illness in which we do the C activities first and do not get around to doing the A activities that are connected to lifetime goals. Tasks required to accomplish lifetime goals are often ones that are more difficult, challenge our abilities and take some time to accomplish. These tasks are often more difficult than the B or C activities. The C activities can fill our time and exhaust the energy we need to accomplish the A activities. An example of C fever is the student who cleans the desk or organizes the CD collection instead of studying. C fever is doing the endless tasks that keep us from accomplishing goals that are really important to us. Why do we fall victim to C fever? C activities are often easy to do and give us a sense of accomplishment. We can see immediate progress without too much effort. I can wash my car and get a sense of accomplishment and satisfaction in my shiny clean car. The task is easy and does not challenge my intellectual capabilities.

ACTIVITY
Setting Priorities

To see how the ABCs of time management work, read the profile of Justin, a typical college student, below.

Justin is a 19-year-old college student who plans to major in physical therapy. He is athletic and values his good health. He cares about people and likes helping others. He has a part-time job working as an assistant in the gym, where he monitors proper use of the weight-lifting machines. Justin is also a member of the soccer team and practices with the team every afternoon.

Here is a list of activities that Justin would like to do today. Label each task as follows:

        A if it relates to the Justin's lifetime goals
        B if it is something necessary to do
        C if it is something which could be done tomorrow or later

_____ Get up, shower, get dressed.
_____ Eat breakfast.
_____ Go to work.
_____ Go to class.
_____ Visit with friends between classes.
_____ Buy a new battery for his watch.
_____ Go shopping for new gym shoes.
_____ Attend soccer practice.
_____ Do weight-lifting exercises.

_____ Study for biology test that is tomorrow.
_____ Meet friends for pizza at lunch.
_____ Call girlfriend.
_____ Eat dinner.
_____ Unpack gear from weekend camping trip.
_____ Watch football game on TV.
_____ Play video games.
_____ Do math homework.

While Justin is the only one who can decide how to spend his time, he can take some steps toward accomplishing his lifetime goal of being healthy by eating properly, exercising, and going to soccer practice. He can become a physical therapist by studying for the biology test and doing his math homework. He can gain valuable experience related to physical therapy by working in the gym. He cares about people and likes to maintain good relationships with others. Any tasks related to these goals are high-priority A activities.

What other activities are necessary B activities? He certainly needs to get up, shower, and get dressed. What are the C activities that could be postponed until tomorrow or later? Again Justin needs to decide. Maybe he could postpone shopping for a new watch battery and gym shoes until the weekend. He would have to decide how much time to spend visiting with friends, watching TV, or playing video games. Since he likes these activities, he could use them as rewards for studying for the biology test and doing his math homework.

How to Estimate Study and Work Time

Students are often surprised at the amount of time necessary for study to be successful in college. A general rule is that you need to study two hours for every hour spent in a college class. A typical weekly schedule of a full-time student would look like this:

Typical College Schedule

15 hours of attending class

+30 hours of reading, studying, and preparation

45 hours total

A full-time job involves working 40 hours a week. A full-time college student spends 45 hours or more attending classes and studying. Some students will need more than 45 hours a week if they are taking lab classes, need help with study and learning skills, or are taking a heavy course load.

Some students try to work full-time and go to school full-time. While some are successful, this schedule is extremely difficult.

The Nearly Impossible Schedule

15 hours attending class

30 hours studying

+40 hours working

85 hours total

This schedule is the equivalent of having two full-time jobs! Working full-time makes it very difficult to find the time necessary to study for classes. Lack of study causes students to do poorly on exams and to doubt their abilities. Such a schedule causes stress and fatigue that make studying difficult. Increased stress can also lead to problems with personal relationships and emotional problems. These are all things that lead to dropping out of college.

Many students today work and go to college. Working during college can provide some valuable experience that will help you to find a job when you finish college. Working can teach you to manage your time efficiently and give you a feeling of independence and control over your own future. Many people need to work to pay for their education. A general guideline is to work no more than 20 hours a week if you plan to attend college full-time. Here is a workable schedule.

Part-Time Work Schedule

12 hours attending class

24 hours studying

+20 hours working

56 hours total

A commitment of 56 hours a week is like having a full-time job and a part-time job. While this schedule takes extra energy and commitment, many students are successful with it. Notice that the course load is reduced to 12 hours. This schedule involves taking one less class per semester. The class missed can be made up in summer school, or the time needed to graduate can be extended. Many students take five years to earn the bachelor's degree because they work part-time. It is better to take longer to graduate than to drop out of college or to give up because of frustration. If you must work full-time, consider reducing your course load to one or two courses. You will gradually reach your goal of a college degree.

Part-Time Student Schedule

  6 hours attending class
12 hours studying
+40 hours working
_____
58 hours total

Add up the number of hours you are attending classes, double this figure for study time and add to it your work time as in the above examples. How many hours of commitment do you have? Can you be successful with your current level of commitment to school, work, and study?

To begin managing your schedule, use the weekly calendar located at the end of this chapter to write in your scheduled activities such as work, class times, and athletics.

Schedule Your Success

If you have not used a schedule in the past, consider trying a schedule for a couple of weeks to see if it is helpful in completing tasks and working toward your lifetime goals. There are several advantages to using a schedule:

- It gets you started on your work.
- It helps you avoid procrastination.
- It relieves pressure because you have things under control.
- It frees the mind of details.
- It helps you find time to study.
- It eliminates the panic caused by doing things at the last minute.
- It helps you find time for recreation and exercise.

Once you have made a master schedule that includes classes, work, and other activities, you will see that you have some blanks that provide opportunities for using your time productively. Here are some ideas for making the most of your schedule:

1. Fill in your study times. Use the time immediately before class for previewing and the time immediately after class for reviewing. Remember that you need to study two hours or more for each hour spent in a college class.

Frank & Ernest reprinted by permission of Newspaper Enterprise Association, Inc.

2. Break large projects such as a term paper or test into small tasks and begin early. Double your time estimates for completion of the project. Larger projects often take longer than you think. If you finish early, use the extra time for something fun.

3. Use the daylight hours when you are most alert for studying. It may take you longer to study if you wait until late in the day when you're tired.

4. Think about your day and see if you can determine when you are most alert and awake. Prime time differs with individuals, but it is generally earlier in the day. Use the prime time when you are most alert to accomplish your most challenging tasks. For example, do your math homework during prime time. Wash your clothes during nonprime time, when you are likely to be less alert.

5. Set priorities. Make sure you include activities related to your lifetime goals.

6. Allow time for sleep and meals. It is easier to study if you are well rested and have good eating habits.

7. Schedule your time in manageable blocks of an hour or two. Having every moment scheduled leads to frustration when plans change.

8. Leave some time unscheduled to use as a shock absorber. You will need unscheduled time to relax and to deal with unexpected events.

9. Leave time for recreation, exercise, and fun.

Return to the schedule at the end of this chapter. After you have written in classes, work times, and other scheduled activities, use the scheduling ideas listed earlier to write in your study times and other activities related to your lifetime goals. Leave some unscheduled time to provide flexibility in the schedule.

If You Dislike Schedules

Some personality types like more freedom and do not like the structure that a schedule provides. There are alternatives for those who do not like to use a schedule. Here are some additional ideas.

1. A simple and fast way to organize your time is to use a to-do list. Take an index card or small piece of paper and simply write a list of what you need to do during the day. You can prioritize the list by putting an A or star by the most important items. Cross items off the list as you accomplish them. A list helps you focus on what is important and serves as a reminder not to forget certain tasks.

2. Another idea is to use monthly or yearly calendars to write down important events, tasks, and deadlines. Use these calendars to note the first day of school, when important assignments are due, vacations, and final exams. Place the calendars in a place where they are easily seen.

3. Alan Lakein, who wrote a book titled *How to Get Control of Your Time and Your Life,* suggests a simple question to keep you on track.[2] Lakein's question is, "What is the best use of my time right now?" This question works well if you keep in mind your goals and priorities.

4. Use reminders and sticky notes to keep on track and to remind yourself of what needs to be done each day. Place the notes in a place where you will see them, such as your computer, the bathroom mirror, or the dashboard of your car.

5. Some families use their refrigerator as a time management device. Use the refrigerator to post your calendars, reminders, goals, tasks and to-do lists. You will see these reminders every time you open the refrigerator.

6. Invent your own unique ideas for managing time. Anything will work if it helps to accomplish your goals.

QUIZ
Time Management, Part I

Test what you have learned by selecting the correct answer to the following questions.

1. The most important difference between a goal and a fantasy is

   a. imagination.
   b. procrastination.
   c. action.

2. An A priority is

   a. related to your lifetime goals.
   b. something important.
   c. something you have to do.

3. A general rule for college success is that you must spend _____ hours studying for every hour spent in a college class.

   a. one hour
   b. four hours
   c. two hours

4. For a workable study schedule,

   a. fill in all the blank time slots.
   b. leave some unscheduled time to deal with the unexpected.
   c. plan to study late at night.

5. To complete a large project such as a term paper,

   a. break the project into small tasks and begin early.
   b. schedule large blocks of time the day before the paper is due.
   c. leave time for exercise, recreation, and fun before beginning on the project.

How did you do on the quiz? Check your answers: 1. c, 2. a, 3. c, 4. b, 5. a

---

JOURNAL ENTRY #3

List ten items that you have to do today. Place an A next to the items that are related to your lifetime goals.

Time Management Tricks

Life is full of demands for work, study, family, friends, and recreation. Time management tricks can help you get started on the important tasks and make the most of your time. Try the following techniques when you are feeling frustrated and overwhelmed.

Divide and Conquer

When large tasks seem overwhelming, think of the small tasks needed to complete the project and start on the first step. For example, suppose you have to write a term paper. You have to take out a paper and pencil, log onto your computer, brainstorm some ideas, go to the library to find information, think about your main ideas, and

Time Management Tricks

- Divide and conquer
- Do the first small step
- 80/20 rule
- Aim for excellence, not perfection
- Make learning fun
- Take a break
- Study in the library
- Learn to say no

write the first sentence. Each of these steps is manageable. It's looking at the entire project that can be intimidating.

I once set out hiking on a mountain trail. When I got to the top of the mountain and looked down, I enjoyed a spectacular view and was amazed at how high I had climbed. If I had thought about how high the mountain was, I might not have attempted the hike. I climbed the mountain by taking it one step at a time. That's the secret to completing any large project. Break it into small, manageable parts; then take the first step and keep going.

Learning a small part at a time is also easy and helps with motivation for learning. While in college, carry around some material that you need to study. Take advantage of five or ten minutes of time to study a small part of your material. In this way you make good use of your time and enhance memory by using distributed practice. Don't wait until you have large blocks of uninterrupted study time to begin your studies. You may not have the luxury of large blocks of time, or you may want to spend that time in other ways.

Do the First Small Step

The most difficult step in completing any project is the first step. If you have a challenging project to do, think of a small first step and complete that small step. Make the first step something that you can accomplish easily and in a short amount of time. Give yourself permission to stop after the first step. However, you may find that you are motivated to continue with the project. If you have a term paper to write, think about some small step you can take to get started. Log onto your computer and look at the blank screen. Start writing some ideas. Type the topic into a computer search engine and see what information is available. Go to the library and see what is available on your topic. If you can find some interesting ideas, you can motivate yourself to begin the project. Once you have started the project, it is easier to continue.

The 80/20 Rule

Alan Lakein is noted for many useful time management techniques. One that I have used over the years is the 80/20 rule. Lakein says, "If all items are arranged in order of value, 80 percent of the value would come from only 20 percent of the items, while the remaining 20 percent of the value would come from 80 percent of the items."[3] For example, if you have a list of ten items to do, two of the items on the list are more important than the others. If you were to do only the two most important items, you would have accomplished 80 percent of the value. If you are short on time, see if you can choose the 20 percent of the tasks that are the most valuable. Lakein noted that the 80/20 rule applies to many situations in life:

- 80 percent of file usage is in 20 percent of the files.
- 80 percent of dinners repeat 20 percent of the recipes.
- 80 percent of the washing is done on the 20 percent of the clothes worn most frequently.
- 80 percent of the dirt is on 20 percent of the floor used most often.

Think about how the 80/20 rule applies in your life. It is another way of thinking about priorities and figuring out which of the tasks are C priorities. This prioritizing is especially important if you are short on time. The 80/20 rule helps you to focus on what is most important.

Aim for Excellence, Not Perfection

Are you satisfied with your work only if it is done perfectly? Do you put off a project because you cannot do it perfectly? Aiming for perfection in all tasks causes anxiety and procrastination. There are times when perfection is necessary. Dave Ellis calls this time management technique "It Ain't No Piano."[4] If a construction worker bends a nail in the framing of a house, it does not matter. The construction worker simply puts in another nail. After all, "it ain't no piano." It is another matter if you are building a fine cabinet or finishing a piano. Perfection is more important in these circumstances. We need to ask: Is the task important enough to invest the time needed for perfection? A final term paper needs to be as perfect as we can make it. A rough draft is like the frame of a house that does not need to be perfect.

In aiming for excellence rather than perfection, challenge yourself to use perspective to see the big picture. How important is the project and how perfect does it need to be? Could your time be better invested accomplishing other tasks? This technique requires flexibility and the ability to change with different situations. Do not give up if you cannot complete a project perfectly. Do the best that you can in the time available. In some situations, if life is too hectic, you may need to settle for completing the project and getting it in on time rather than doing it perfectly. With this idea in mind, you may be able to relax and still achieve excellence.

Make Learning Fun by Finding a Reward

Time management is not about restriction, self-control, and deprivation. Used correctly, time can be used to get more out of life and to have fun while doing it. Remember that behavior is likely to increase if followed by a reward. Think about activities that you find rewarding. In our time management example with Justin who wants to be a physical therapist, he could use many tasks as rewards for completing his studies. He could meet friends for pizza, call his girlfriend, play video games, or watch TV. The key idea is to do the studying first and then reward the behavior. Maybe Justin will not be able to do all of the activities we have mentioned as possible rewards, but he could choose what he enjoys most.

Studying first and then rewarding yourself leads to peace of mind and the ability to focus on tasks at hand. While Justin is out having pizza with his friends, he does not have to worry about work that he has not done. While Justin is studying, he does not have to feel that he is being deprived of having pizza with friends. In this way, he can focus on studying while he is studying and focus on having a good time while relaxing with his friends. It is not a good idea to think about having pizza with friends while studying or to think about studying while having pizza with friends. When you work, focus on your work and get it done. When you play, enjoy playing without having to think about work.

> "Don't say you don't have enough time. You have exactly the same number of hours per day that were given to Helen Keller, Pasteur, Michelangelo, Mother Theresa, Leonardo da Vinci, Thomas Jefferson, and Albert Einstein."
>
> H. Jackson Brown

Take a Break

If you are overwhelmed with the task at hand, sometimes it is best to just take a break. If you're stuck on a computer program or a math problem, take a break and do something else. As a general rule, take a break of ten minutes for each hour of study. During the break, do something totally different. It is a good idea to get up and move around. Get up and pet your cat or dog, observe your goldfish, or shoot a few baskets. If time is really a premium, use your break time to accomplish other important tasks. Put your clothes in the dryer, empty the dishwasher, or pay a bill.

Study in the Library

If you are having difficulty with studying, try studying at school in the library. Libraries are designed for studying, and other people are studying there as well. It is hard to do something else in the library without annoying the librarian or other students. If you can complete your studying at school, you can go home and relax. This may be especially important if family, friends, or roommates at home easily distract you.

Learn to Say No Sometimes

Learn to say no to tasks that you do not have time to do. Follow your statement with the reasons for saying no: you are going to college and need time to study. Most people will understand this answer and respect it. You may need to say no to yourself as well. Maybe you cannot go out on Wednesday night if you have a class early on Thursday morning. Maybe the best use of your time right now is to turn off the TV or get off the Internet and study for tomorrow's test. You are investing your time in your future.

> **JOURNAL ENTRY #4**
>
> What time management techniques can you use to accomplish your goal of getting a college degree?

Dealing with Time Bandits

Time bandits are the many things that keep us from spending time on the things we think are important. Another word for a time bandit is a time waster. In college, it is tempting to do many things other than studying. We are all victims of different kinds of bandits.

ACTIVITY

Put a checkmark next to the items that waste your time. Add your own personal time wasters at the end of the list.

_____ TV	_____ Other electronic devices	_____ Daydreaming
_____ Stereo	_____ Saying yes when you mean no	_____ Friends
_____ Internet	_____ Social time	_____ Family
_____ Phone	_____ Household chores	_____ Roommates
_____ Video games	_____ Partying	_____ Children
_____ iPod	_____ Waiting time	_____ Girlfriend, boyfriend, spouse
_____ Sleeping in	_____ Shopping	_____ Being easily distracted
_____ Studying at a bad time	_____ Reading magazines	_____ Studying in a distracting
_____ Movies	_____ Commuting time (travel)	place

List some of your personal time bandits here.

_____

_____

Here are some ideas for keeping time bandits under control:

Schedule time for other people. Friends and family are important, so we do not want to get rid of them! Discuss your goal of a college education with your friends and family. People who care about you will respect your goals. You may need to use a Do Not Disturb sign at times. If you are a parent, remember that you are a role model for your children. If they see you studying, they are more likely to value their own education. Plan to spend quality time with your children and the people who are important to you. Make sure they understand that you care about them.

Remember the rewards. Many of the time bandits listed above make good rewards for completing your work. Put the time bandits to work for you by studying first and then enjoying a reward. Enjoy the TV, Internet, iPod, video games, or phone conversations after you have finished your studies. Aim for a balance of work, study, and leisure time.

Use your prime time wisely. Prime time is when you are most awake and alert. Use this time for studying. Use non-prime time for the time bandits. When you are tired, do household chores and shopping. If you have little time for household chores, you might find faster ways to do them. If you don't have time for shopping, you will notice that you spend less and have a better chance of following your budget.

Remind yourself about your priorities. When time bandits attack, remind yourself of why you are in college. Think about your personal goals for the future. Remember that college is not forever. By doing well in college, you will finish in the shortest time possible.

Use a schedule. Using a schedule or a to-do list is helpful in keeping you on track. Make sure you have some slack time in your schedule to handle unexpected phone calls and deal with the unplanned events that happen in life. If you cannot stick to your schedule, just get back on track as soon as you can.

Dealing with Procrastination

Procrastination means putting off things until later. We all use delaying tactics at times. Procrastination that is habitual, however, can be self-destructive. Understanding some possible reasons for procrastination can help you use time more effectively and be more successful in accomplishing goals.

Why Do We Procrastinate?

There are many psychological reasons for procrastinating. Just becoming aware of these may help you deal with procrastination. If you have serious difficulty managing your time for psychological reasons, visit the counseling center at your college or university. Do you recognize any of these reasons for procrastination in yourself or others?

- **Fear of failure.** Sometimes we procrastinate because we are afraid of failing. We see our performance as related to how much ability we have and how worthwhile we are as human beings. We may procrastinate in our college studies because of doubts about our ability to do the work. Success, however, comes from trying and learning from mistakes. There is a popular saying: falling down is not failure, but failing to get up or not even trying is failure.
- **Fear of success.** Most students are surprised to find out that one of the reasons for procrastination is fear of success. Success in college means moving on with your life, getting a job, leaving a familiar situation, accepting increased responsibility, and sometimes leaving friends behind. None of these tasks is easy. An example of fear of success is not taking the last step required to be successful. Students sometimes do not take the last class needed to graduate. Some good students do not show up for the final exam or do not turn in a major project. If you ever find yourself procrastinating on an important last step, ask yourself if you are afraid of success and what lies ahead in your future.
- **Perfectionism.** Some people who procrastinate do not realize that they are perfectionists. Perfectionists expect more from themselves than is realistic and more than others expect of themselves. There is often no other choice than to procrastinate because perfectionism is usually unattainable. Perfectionism generates anxiety that further hinders performance. Perfectionists need to understand that perfection is seldom possible. They need to set a time limit on projects and do their best within those time limits.
- **Need for excitement.** Some students can only be motivated by waiting until the last minute to begin a project. These students are excited and motivated by playing a game of "Beat the Clock." They like living on the edge and the adrenaline rush of responding to a crisis. Playing this game provides motivation, but it does not leave enough time to achieve the best results. Inevitably, things happen at the last minute to make the game even more exciting and dangerous: the printer breaks, the computer crashes, the student gets ill, the car breaks down, or the dog eats the homework. These students need to start projects earlier to improve their chances of success. It is best to seek excitement elsewhere, in sports or other competitive activities.

- **Excellence without effort.** In this scenario, students believe that they are truly outstanding and can achieve success without effort. These students think that they can go to college without attending classes or reading the text. They believe that they can pass the test without studying. They often do not succeed in college the first semester, which puts them at risk of dropping out of school. They often return to college later and improve their performance by putting in the effort required.
- **Loss of control.** Some students fear loss of control over their lives and procrastinate to gain control. An example is students who attend college because others (such as parents) want them to attend. Procrastination becomes a way of gaining control over the situation by saying, "You can't make me do this." They attend college but accomplish nothing. Parents can support and encourage education, but students need to choose their own goals in life and attend college because it is important to them.

Tips for Dealing with Procrastination

When you find yourself procrastinating on a certain task, think about the consequences. Will the procrastination lead to failing an exam or getting a low grade? Think about the rewards of doing the task. If you do well, you can take pride in yourself and celebrate your success. How will you feel when the task is completed? Will you be able to enjoy your leisure time without guilt about not doing your work? How does the task help you to achieve your lifetime goals?

Maybe the procrastination is a warning sign that you need to reconsider lifetime goals and change them to better suit your needs.

Procrastination Scenario

George is a college student who is on academic probation for having low grades. He is required to make a plan for improving grades in order to remain in college. George tells the counselor that he is making poor grades because of his procrastination. He is an accounting major and puts off doing homework because he dislikes it and does not find it interesting. The counselor asks George why he had chosen accounting as a major. He replies that accounting is a major that is in demand and has a good salary. The counselor suggests that George consider a major that he would enjoy more. After some consideration, George changes his major to psychology. He becomes more interested in college studies and is able to raise his grades to stay in college.

Most of the time, you will reap benefits by avoiding procrastination and completing the task at hand. Jane Burka and Lenora Yuen suggest the following steps to deal with procrastination:

1. Select a goal.
2. Visualize your progress.
3. Be careful not to sabotage yourself.
4. Stick to a time limit.
5. Don't wait until you feel like it.
6. Follow through. Watch out for excuses and focus on one step at a time.
7. Reward yourself after you have made some progress.
8. Be flexible about your goal.
9. Remember that it does not have to be perfect.[5]

QUIZ
Time Management Part II

Test what you have learned by selecting the correct answer to the following questions.

1. To get started on a challenging project,

    a. think of a small first step and complete it.
    b. wait until you have plenty of time to begin.
    c. wait until you are well-rested and relaxed.

2. In completing a To Do List of 10 items, the 80/20 rule states that

    a. 80% of the value comes from completing most of the items on the list.
    b. 80% of the value comes from completing two of the most important items.
    c. 80% of the value comes from completing half of the items on the list.

3. It is suggested that students aim for

    a. perfection.
    b. excellence.
    c. passing.

4. Sometimes students procrastinate because of

    a. fear of failure.
    b. fear of success.
    c. all of the above.

5. Playing the game "Beat the Clock" when doing a term paper results in

    a. increased motivation and success.
    b. greater excitement and quality work.
    c. increased motivation and risk.

How did you do on the quiz? Check your answers: 1. a, 2. b, 3. b, 4. c, 5. c

---

JOURNAL ENTRY #5

What techniques can you use to avoid procrastination in accomplishing the goals that are important to you?

Managing Your Money

To be successful in college and in life, you will need to manage not only time but money. One of the top reasons that students drop out of college is that they cannot pay for their education or that they have to work so much that they do not have time for school. Take a look at your lifetime goals. Most students have a goal related to money, such as becoming financially secure or becoming wealthy. If financial security or wealth is one of your goals, you will need to begin to take some action to accomplish that goal. If you don't take action on a goal, it is merely a fantasy.

How to Become a Millionaire

Save regularly. Frances Leonard, author of *Time Is Money,* cites some statistics on how much money you need to save to become a millionaire.[6] You can retire with a million dollars by age 68 by saving the following amounts of money at various ages. These figures assume a 10 percent return on your investment.

> At age 22, save $87 per month
> At age 26, save $130 per month
> At age 30, save $194 per month
> At age 35, save $324 a month

Notice that the younger you start saving, the less money is required to reach the million-dollar goal. (And keep in mind that even a million dollars may not be enough money to save for retirement.) How can you start saving money when you are a student struggling to pay for college? The answer is to practice money management techniques and to begin a savings habit, even if the money you save is a small amount to buy your books for next semester. When you get that first good job, save 10 percent of the money. If you are serious about becoming financially secure, learn about investments such as real estate, stocks and bonds, and mutual funds. Learning how to save and invest your money can pay big dividends in the future.

Think thrifty. Money management begins with looking at your attitude toward money. Pay attention to how you spend your money so that you can accomplish your financial goals such as getting a college education, buying a house or car, or saving for the future. The following example shows how one woman accomplished her financial goals through being thrifty. Amy Dacyczyn, author of *The Tightwad Gazette* says, "A lot of people get a thrill out of buying things. Frugal people get a rush from the very act of saving. Saving can actually be fun—we think of it almost as a sport."[7] She noticed that people are working harder and harder for less and less. Amy Dacyczyn had the goals of marriage, children, and a New England farmhouse to live in. She wanted to stay home and take care of her six children instead of working. In seven years she was able to accomplish her goals with her husband's income of $30,000 a year. During this time she saved $49,000 for the down payment on a rural farmhouse costing $125,000. She also paid cash for $38,000 worth of car, appliance, and furniture purchases while staying at home with her children. How did she do this? She says that she just started paying attention to how she was spending her money.

To save money, Amy Dacyczyn made breakfast from scratch. She made oatmeal, pancakes, and muffins instead of purchasing breakfast cereals. She saved $440 a year in this way. She purchased the family clothing at yard sales. She thought of so many ideas to save money that she began publishing *The Tightwad Gazette* to share her money saving ideas with others. At $12 per subscription, she grosses a million dollars a year!

Challenge yourself to pay attention to how you spend your money and make a goal of being thrifty in order to accomplish your financial goals. With good money management, you can work less and have more time for college and recreational activities.

Managing Your Money

- Monitor your spending
- Prepare a budget
- Beware of credit and interest
- Watch spending leaks

Budgeting: The Key to Money Management

It is important to control your money, rather than letting your money control you. One of the most important things that you can do to manage your money and begin saving is to use a budget. A budget helps you become aware of how you spend your money and will help you make a plan for how you would like to spend your money.

> "Money is, in some respects like fire; it is a very excellent servant, but a terrible master."
>
> P. T. Barnum

Monitor how you spend your money. The first step in establishing a workable budget is to monitor how you are actually spending your money at the present time. For one month, keep a list of the date, purchase, and amount of money spent. You can do this on a sheet of paper, on your calendar, or on index cards. If you write checks for items, include the checks written as part of your money monitor. At the end of the month, group your purchases in categories such as food, gas, entertainment, and credit card payments and add them up. Doing this will yield some surprising results. For example, you may not be aware of just how much it costs to eat at a fast-food restaurant or to buy lunch or coffee every day.

Prepare a budget. One of the best tools for managing your money is a budget. At the end of this chapter you will find a simple budget sheet that you can use as a college student. After you finish college, update your budget and continue to use it. Follow these three steps to make a budget:

1. Write down your income for the month.
2. List your expenses. Include tuition, books, supplies, rent, telephone, utilities (gas, electric, water, cable TV), car payments, car insurance, car maintenance (oil, repairs), parking fees, food, personal grooming, clothes, entertainment, savings, credit card payments, loan payments, and other bills. Use your money monitor to discover how you are spending your money and include categories that are unique to you.
3. Subtract your total expenses from your total income. You cannot spend more than you have. Make adjustments as needed.

Beware of credit and interest. College students are often tempted to use credit cards to pay for college expenses. This type of borrowing is costly and difficult to repay. It is easy to pull out a plastic credit card and buy items that you need and want. Credit card companies earn a great deal of money from credit cards. Jane Bryant Quinn gives an example of the cost of credit cards.[8] She says that if you owe $3,000 at 18 percent interest and pay the minimum payment of $60 per month, it will take you thirty years and ten months to get out of debt! Borrowing the $3,000 would cost about $22,320 over this time! If you use a credit card, make sure you can pay it off in one to three months. It is good to have a credit card in order to establish credit and to use in an emergency.

Watch those spending leaks. We all have spending problem areas. Often we spend small amounts of money each day that add up to large spending leaks over time. For example, if you spend $2 on coffee each weekday for a year, this adds up to $520 a year! If you eat lunch out each weekday and spend $6 for lunch, this adds up to $1,560 a year! Here are some common areas for spending leaks:

- Fast food and restaurants
- Entertainment and vacations
- Clothing
- Miscellaneous cash
- Gifts

To identify your spending problem areas, write down all of your expenditures for one month. Place a three-by-five card in your wallet to monitor your cash expenditures. At the end of the month, organize your expenditures into categories and total them up. Then ask yourself if this is how you want to spend your money.

Need More Money?

You may be tempted to work more hours to balance your budget. Remember that to be a full-time college student, it is recommended that you work no more than 20 hours per week. If you work more than 20 hours per week, you will probably need to decrease your course load. Before increasing your work hours, see if there is a way you can decrease your monthly expenses. Can you make your lunch instead of eating out? Can you get by without a car? Is the item you are purchasing a necessity, or do you just want to have it? These choices are yours.

1. **Check out financial aid.** All students can qualify for some type of financial aid. Visit the Financial Aid Office at your college for assistance. Depending on your income level, you may qualify for one or more of the following forms of aid.

   - **Loans.** A loan must be paid back. The interest rate and terms vary according to your financial need. With some loans, the federal government pays the interest while you are in school.
   - **Grants.** A grant does not need to be repaid. There are both state and federal grants based on need.
   - **Work/Study.** You may qualify for a federally subsidized job depending on your financial need.

   The first step in applying for financial aid is to fill out the Free Application for Federal Student Aid (FAFSA). This form determines your eligibility for financial aid. You can obtain this form from your college's financial aid office or over the Internet at www.fafsa.ed.gov/

   Here are some other financial aid resources that you can obtain from your financial aid office or over the Internet.

   - **Student Guide.** The Student Guide, published by the U.S. Department of Education, describes in detail the kinds of financial aid available and eligibility requirements. It is available over the Internet at studentaid.ed.gov/students/publications/student_guide/index.html
   - **How to Apply for Financial Aid.** Learn how to apply for federal financial aid and scholarships at this website www.finaid.org/
   - Visit the ed.gov site for parents and students for current information and publications on federal financial aid at http://www.ed.gov/about/offices/list/index.htm/?scr = mr

2. **Apply for a scholarship.** Applying for a scholarship is like having a part-time job, only the pay is often better, the hours are flexible, and you can be your own boss. For this part-time job, you will need to research scholarship opportunities and fill out applications. There are multitudes of scholarships available, and sometimes no one even applies for them. Some students do not apply for scholarships because they think that high grades and financial need are required. While many scholarships are based on grades and financial need, many are not. Any person or organization can offer a scholarship for any reason they want. For example, scholarships can be based on hobbies, parent's occupation, religious background, military service, and personal interests, to name a few.

   There are several ways to research a scholarship. As a first step, visit the financial aid office on your college campus. This office is staffed with persons knowledgeable about researching and applying for scholarships. Organizations or persons wishing to fund scholarships often contact this office to advertise opportunities.

   You can also research scholarships through your public or college library. Ask the reference librarian for assistance. You can use the Internet to research scholarships as well. Use a search engine such as yahoo.com and simply type in the keyword *scholarships*. The following websites index thousands of scholarships:

   fastweb.com
   princetonreview.com/college/finance
   college-scholarships.com/
   guaranteed-scholarships.com/
   collegenet.com/mach25/
   srnexpress.com/index.cfm
   collegeboard.com/paying
   collegeanswer.com/index.jsp

To apply for scholarships, start a file of useful material usually included in scholarship applications. You can use this same information to apply for many scholarships.

- Three current letters of recommendation
- A statement of your personal goals
- A statement of your financial need
- Copies of your transcripts
- Copies of any scholarship applications you have filled out

Be aware of scholarship scams. You do not need to pay money to apply for a scholarship. No one can guarantee that you will receive a scholarship. Use your college scholarship office and your own resources to research and apply for scholarships.

The Best Ideas for Becoming Financially Secure

Financial planners provide the following ideas as the best way to build wealth and independence.[9] If you have financial security as your goal, plan to do the following.

1. Use a simple budget to track income and expenses.
Do not spend more than you earn.

2. Have a financial plan.
Include goals such as saving for retirement, purchasing a home, paying for college or taking vacations.

3. Save 10 percent of your income.
As a college student, you may not be able to save this much, but plan to do it as soon as you get your first good-paying job. If you cannot save 10 percent, save something to get in the habit of saving. Save to pay for your tuition and books.

4. Don't take on too much debt.
Be especially careful about credit cards and consumer debt. Credit card companies often visit college campuses and offer high-interest credit cards to students. It is important to have a credit card, but pay off the balance each month. Consider student loans instead of paying college fees by credit card.

5. Don't procrastinate.
The earlier you take these steps toward financial security, the better.

Tips for Managing Your Money

Keeping these guidelines in mind can help you to manage your money.

- Don't let friends pressure you into spending too much money. If you can't afford something, learn to say no.
- Keep your checking account balanced or use online banking so you will know how much money you have.
- Don't lend money to friends. If your friends cannot manage their money, your loan will not help them.
- Use comparison shopping to find the best prices on the products that you buy.
- Get a part-time job while in college. You will earn money and gain valuable job experience.
- Don't use shopping as a recreational activity. When you visit the mall, you will find things you never knew you needed and will wind up spending more money than intended.
- Make a budget and follow it. This is the best way to achieve your financial goals.

Do What Is Important First

The most important thing you can do to manage time and money is to spend it on what is most important. Manage time and money to help you live the life you want. How can you do this? Author Steven Covey wrote a book titled *The Seven Habits of Highly Effective People*. One of the habits is "Put first things first." Covey suggests that in time management, the "challenge is not to manage our time but to manage ourselves."[10]

How can you manage yourself? Our first thoughts in answering this question often involve suggestions about willpower, restriction, and self-control. Schedules and budgets are seen as instruments for self-control. It seems that the human spirit resists attempts at control, even when we aim to control ourselves. Often the response to control is rebellion. With time and money management, we may not follow a schedule or budget. A better approach to begin managing yourself is to know your values. What is important in your life? Do you have a clear mental picture of what is important? Can you describe your values and make a list of what is important to you? With your values and goals in mind, you can begin to manage both your time and your money.

When you have given some thought to your values, you can begin to set goals. When you have established goals for your life, you can begin to think in terms of what is most important and establish your priorities. Knowing your values is essential in making decisions about how to invest your time and money. Schedules and budgets are merely tools for helping you accomplish what you have decided is important. Time and money management is not about restriction and control but about making decisions regarding what is important in your life. If you know what is important, you can find the strength to say no to activities and expenditures that are less important.

As a counselor, I have the pleasure of working with many students who have recently explored and discovered their values and are highly motivated to succeed. They are willing to do what is important first. I recently worked with a young couple who came to enroll in college. They brought with them their young baby. The new father was interested in environmental engineering. He told me that in high school he never saw a reason for school and did just the minimum needed to get by. He was working as a construction laborer and making a living but did not see a future in the occupation. He had observed an environmental engineer who worked for the company and decided that was what he wanted for his future. As he looked at his new son, he told me that he needed to have a better future for himself and his family.

He and his wife decided to do what was important first. They were willing to make the sacrifice to attend school and invest the time needed to be successful. The father planned to work during the day and go to school at night. Later, he would go to school full-time and get a part-time job in the evening. His wife was willing to get a part-time job also, and they would share in taking care of the baby. They were willing to manage their money carefully to accomplish their goals. As they left, they added that their son would be going to college as well.

How do you get the energy to work all day, go to school at night, and raise a family? You can't do it by practicing self-control. You find the energy by having a clear idea of what you want in your life and focusing your time and resources on the goal. Finding what you want to do with your life is not easy either. Many times people find what they want to do when some significant event happens in their lives.

Begin to think about what you want out of life. Make a list of your important values and write down your lifetime goals. Don't forget about the people who are important to you and include them in your priorities. Then you will be able to do what is important first.

JOURNAL ENTRY #6
What is your plan for managing your money?

JOURNAL ENTRIES

Managing Time and Money

Go to http://www.collegesuccess1.com/ for Word files of the Journal Entries

Success over the Internet

**Visit the *College Success Website* at
http://www.collegesuccess1.com/**

The *College Success Website* is continually
updated with new topics and links to the material
presented in this chapter. Topics include:

- Suggestions for time management
- How to overcome procrastination
- How to deal with perfectionism

- Goal setting
- Goal setting in sports
- Goal setting and visualization
- Scholarship websites
- Recognizing scholarship scams
- Financial aid websites

Ask your instructor if you need any assistance
in accessing the *College Success Website.*

Notes

1. Quoted in Rob Gilbert, ed., *Bits and Pieces,* 4 November 1999, 15.
2. Alan Lakein, *How to Get Control of Your Time and Your Life* (New York: Peter H. Wyden, 1973).
3. Ibid., 70–71.
4. Dave Ellis, *Becoming a Master Student* (Boston: Houghton Mifflin, 1998).
5. Jane Burka and Lenora Yuen, *Procrastination* (Reading, MA: Addison-Wesley, 1983).
6. Frances Leonard, *Time Is Money,* (Addison-Wesley) cited in the *San Diego Union Tribune,* 14 October 1995.
7. Amy Dacyczyn, *The Tightwad Gazette II* (Villard Books), cited in the *San Diego Union Tribune,* 20 February 1995.
8. Jane Bryant Quinn, "Money Watch," *Good Housekeeping,* November 1996, 80.
9. Robert Hanley, "Breaking Bad Habits," *San Diego Union Tribune,* 7 September 1992.
10. Steven R. Covey, *The Seven Habits of Highly Effective People* (New York: Simon and Shuster, 1990), 150.

My Lifetime Goals: Brainstorming Activity

Name _____   Date _____

1. Think about the goals that you would like to accomplish in your life. At the end of your life, you do not want to say, "I wish I would have _____." Set a timer for five minutes and write whatever comes to mind about what you would like to do and accomplish over your lifetime. Include goals in these areas: career, personal relationships, travel, and financial security or any area that is important to you. Write down all your ideas. The goal is to generate as many ideas as possible in five minutes. You can reflect on which ones are most important later. You may want to do this as part of a group activity in your class.

Look over the ideas you wrote above and highlight or underline the goals that are most important to you.

2. Ask yourself what you would like to accomplish in the next five years. Think about where you want to be in college, what you want to do in your career, and what you want to do in your personal life. Set a timer and write whatever comes to mind in five minutes. The goal is to write down as many ideas as possible.

Again, look over the ideas you wrote and highlight or underline the ideas that are most important to you.

3. What goals would you like to accomplish in the next year? What are some steps that you can begin now to accomplish your lifetime goals? Consider work, study, leisure and social goals. Set your timer for five minutes and write down your goals for the next year.

Review what you wrote and highlight or underline the ideas that are most important to you. When writing your goals, include fun activities as well as taking care of others.

Looking at the items that you have highlighted or underlined, make a list of your Lifetime Goals using the form that follows. Make sure your goals are specific enough so that you can break them into steps you can achieve.

Name _____   Date _____

Using the ideas that you brainstormed in the previous exercise, make a list of your lifetime goals. Make sure your goals are specific and concrete. Begin with goals that you would like to accomplish over a lifetime. In the second section, think about the goals you can accomplish over the next one to three years.

Long-Term Goals (lifetime goals)

Short-Term Goals (one to three years)

What are some steps you can take now to accomplish intermediate and long-term goals?

Successful Goal Setting

Name _____ Date _____

Look at your list of lifetime goals. Which one is most important? Write the goal here:

Answer these questions about the goal you have listed above.

1. What skills, abilities and resources do you have to achieve this goal? What skills, abilities and resources will you need to develop to achieve this goal?

2. Do you believe you can achieve it? Write a brief positive statement about achieving this goal.

3. State your goal in specific terms that can be observed or counted. Rewrite your goal if necessary.

4. Write a brief statement about how this goal will give you personal satisfaction.

5. How will you motivate yourself to achieve this goal?

6. What are your personal values that match this goal?

7. List some steps that you will take to accomplish this goal.

8. When will you finish this goal?

9. What roadblocks will make this goal difficult to achieve?

10. How will you deal with these roadblocks?

Weekly College Schedule

Name _____ Date _____

Copy the following schedule to use in future weeks or design your own schedule. Fill in this schedule and try to follow it for at least one week. First fill in scheduled commitments (classes, work, activities). Next fill in the time you need for studying. Put in some tasks related to your lifetime goals. Leave some blank time as a shock absorber to handle unexpected activities.

Time	Monday	Tuesday	Wednesday	Thursday	Friday	Saturday	Sunday
7 A.M.							
8							
9							
10							
11							
Noon							
1 P.M.							
2							
3							
4							
5							
6							
7							
8							
9							
10							
11							

Study Schedule Analysis

Name _____   Date _____

Before completing this analysis, use the schedule form to create a master schedule. A master schedule blocks out class and work times as well as any regularly scheduled activities. Looking at the remaining time, write in your planned study times. It is recommended that you have 2 hours of study time for each hour in class. For example, a 3-unit class would require 6 hours of study time. A student with 12 units would require 24 hours of study time. You may need more or fewer hours, depending on your study skills, reading skills, and difficulty of courses.

1.   How many units are you enrolled in?

2.   How many hours of planned study time do you have?

3.   How many hours do you work each week?

4.   How many hours do you spend in relaxation/social activities?

5.   Do you have time planned for exercise?

6.   Do you get enough sleep?

7.   What are some of your time bandits (things that take up your time and make it difficult to accomplish your goals)?

Write a few discovery statements about how you use your time.

1. Are you spending enough time to earn the grades you want to achieve? Do you need to spend more time studying to become successful?

2. Does your work schedule allow you enough time to study?

3. How can you deal with your time bandits?

4. How can you use your time more effectively to achieve your goals?

Weekly "To Do" Chart

Name _____   Date _____

Using a "To Do" list is an easy way to remind yourself of important priorities each day. This chart is divided into three areas that represent tasks that college students need to balance: academic, personal, and social.

Weekly "To Do" List

	Monday	Tuesday	Wednesday	Thursday	Friday
Academic					
Personal					
Social					

Name _____   Date _____

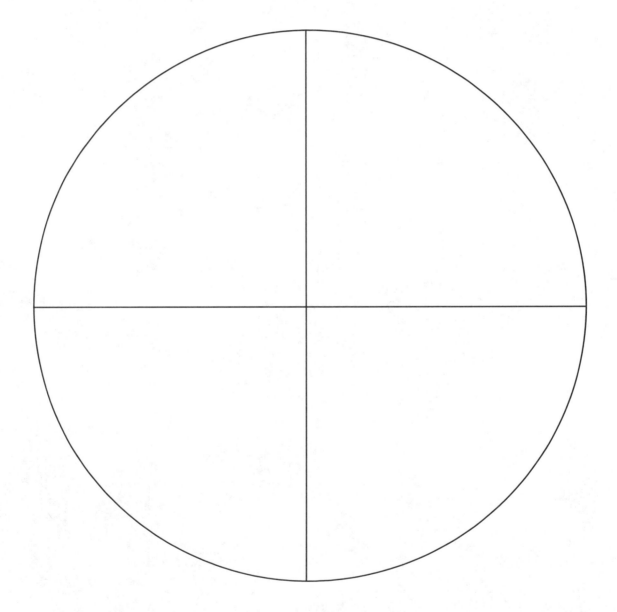

This circle represents 24 hours. Each piece is 6 hours. Draw a slice of pie to represent how much time you spend on these activities on a typical day: sleeping, attending classes, studying, work, family, friends, and other activities.

Thinking about your values is the first step in setting goals. How you spend your time determines whether you will accomplish these goals. Are you using your time to accomplish your goals? Make some intention statements for the future on how you want to spend your time.

I intend to:

The College Student's Tightwad Gazette

Name _____   Date _____

List five ideas for saving money that could be included in a publication called "The College Student's Tightwad Gazette."

1. _____

2. _____

3. _____

4. _____

5. _____

Get together with other students in the class and come up with five additional ideas that college students can use to save money or increase income.

1. _____

2. _____

3. _____

4. _____

5. _____

List five ways that college students can have fun without spending much money.

1. _____

2. _____

3. _____

4. _____

5. _____

Budgeting for College

Name _____   Date _____

Before you complete this budget, monitor your expenses for one month. Write down all expenditures and then divide them into categories that have meaning for you. Then complete the following budget and try to follow it for at least two months. Do this exercise on your own, since it is likely to contain private information.

College Student Monthly Budget

Monthly Income for _____ (month)	
Income from job _____	
Money from home _____	**Total Income:**
Financial aid _____	
Other _____	
Budgeted Monthly Expenses:	**Actual Monthly Expenses:**
Total Budgeted:	**Total Actual:**

Total Income _____ **Minus Total Budgeted** _____ **Equals** _____

CHAPTER 5

LEARNING OBJECTIVES

Read to answer these key questions:

- How does the memory work?

- Why do we forget?

- How can I remember what I study?

- What are some memory tricks?

- How can I apply memory techniques to reading?

- What is a reading system for college texts?

- What are some ways to improve reading speed and comprehension?

- Why is positive thinking a key to remembering and reading?

© Diego Cervo, 2008. Under license from Shutterstock, Inc.

Improving Memory and Reading

Learning how to improve your memory and remember what you read will be great assets in college, on the job, and in life in general. This chapter describes how memory works and provides some practical techniques for improving your memory. Once you understand how memory works, you can apply these techniques to remembering what you read. Positive thinking will help you be successful in remembering and reading effectively.

Improving Your Memory

How Does the Memory Work?

Understanding how the memory works provides the framework for effective study techniques. There are three stages of memory: **sensory register, short-term memory** and **long-term memory.** Understanding these stages of memory will help you to learn how to store information in your long-term memory which lasts a lifetime.

- **Sensory register.** The first stage of memory is called sensory register. It is the initial moment of perception. This stage of memory lasts less than a second and is used to record sensory experience (what you see, hear, taste, touch, or do). It is like a quickly fading snapshot of what your senses perceive. The purpose of the sensory register is to allow the brain to process information and to focus on relevant information. To remember information for more than a second, it must be transferred to short-term memory.
- **Short-term memory (STM).** Paying attention to the information you have perceived in the sensory register transfers the information to STM. STM is temporary and limited, lasting only about half a minute. The information must be rehearsed or renewed for longer storage. STM records what we see, hear, feel, taste, or touch. Information is best stored in STM through recitation or mentally talking to ourselves. If the information is not repeated, it is very quickly lost. For example, when you look up a number in the telephone book, you say it to yourself and quickly dial the number before it is forgotten. The purpose of STM is to ponder the significance of the stimuli we have received, detect patterns, and decide if the information is important enough to remember.

    Grouping together or chunking bits of information can increase the limited capacity of STM. George Miller of Harvard University found that the optimum number of chunks or bits of information that we can hold in STM is five to nine chunks.[1] For example, we remember telephone numbers of seven digits by using a hyphen to separate the numbers into two more easily remembered chunks. We divide our social security numbers into three chunks for easier recall.

    According to George Miller's research, we often use the "Magical Number Seven" technique to remember material. It is much easier to remember material that is grouped in chunks of seven or less. You can find many examples of groups of seven used to enhance memory. There are seven days of the week and seven numbers in your driver's license and license plate. There are also seven dwarfs, seven deadly sins, and seven wonders of the world!
- **Long-term memory (LTM).** Long-term memory has a large capacity and is used to store information more permanently. You will want to use your LTM to store important information that you want to be able to recall at a later date. Most psychologists agree that once information is in LTM, it is there forever. Although the information is available, the problem becomes how to access it. Think of LTM as a library in which many available books are stored. If the books in the library are randomly stored, retrieval of information becomes extremely difficult. If the books are properly stored and indexed, we can find them more easily.

How are long-term memories formed? Short-term memories become long-term through repetition or meaningful association. Creating long-term memories takes some purposeful action. We are motivated to take some purposeful action to remember if the information has some survival value. When we touch a hot stove, this memory moves from sensory register to short-term memory and then is stored in long-term memory to avoid injury in the future. In an academic setting, we must convince ourselves of the survival value of what we are learning. Is the information needed to pass a test, be successful in a career or for personal reasons? If so, it is easier to take the action required to store information in long term memory. Emotions such as fear, anger or joy are also involved in the storing of memories. In the hot stove example, fear elevates the importance of the memory and helps us to store it in long-term memory. In the educational setting, an interest or joy in learning helps to store information in long-term memory.

It is interesting to note that computers are designed much like STM and LTM. The Random Access Memory (RAM) is the working and calculating part of the computer and can be compared to the STM. When the computer is turned off, the contents of RAM disappear just as information quickly disappears in STM. The Read Only Memory (ROM) is the permanent storage component, similar to LTM.

In summary, when you are trying to store information in your memory, the first step is receiving information through the five senses to store in the sensory register, similar to entering data in a computer through the use of a keyboard. This takes less than a second. The next step involves paying attention to the sensory stimulus in order to transfer it to STM for the purpose of seeing patterns and judging significance or importance. Information only stays in STM for thirty seconds or less unless rehearsed or repeated. If you decide that the information is likely to be on a test and you need to remember it, you must organize the material in a meaningful way or repeat it to store the information in LTM. Information must be stored in LTM in order for you to remember it permanently. Effective techniques for storing information in LTM will be presented later in this chapter.

Why Do We Forget?

Is it true that we never forget? Material that is stored in the sensory register is forgotten in less than one second. Material stored in STM is forgotten in thirty seconds unless rehearsed or repeated. We do not forget material stored in LTM, but we can lose access to the information, similar to when a book is filed incorrectly in the library. The book is in the library, but we cannot find it.

Examining the following lists of items frequently forgotten or remembered can give us insight into why forgetting or losing access occurs.

We frequently forget these things:

* Unpleasant experiences
* Names of people, places, or things
* Numbers and dates
* What is barely learned
* Material we do not fully understand
* What we try to remember when embarrassed, frustrated, tired, or ill
* Material we have learned by cramming
* Ideas or theories that conflict with our beliefs

We tend to remember these things:

* Pleasant experiences
* Material that is important to us
* What we have put an effort into learning

- What we have reviewed or thought about often
- Material that is interesting to us
- What is used frequently
- Muscular skills such as riding a bike
- What we had an important reason to remember
- Items we discuss with others
- Material that we understand
- Frequently used information

Theories of Forgetting

An understanding of theories of forgetting is also helpful in developing techniques for effective study and learning. There are many theories about why we forget or lose access to information stored in LTM.

1.   I Forgot.
If you forget a name, number, or fact, you might just say, "I forgot." The information was stored in STM and never made it to LTM. Have you ever been introduced to a person and really didn't listen to the name? You didn't forget it. You never learned it.

2.   The Mental Blur.
If you are studying and don't understand the material, you will not remember it.

3.   The Decay Theory.
If you do not use information, you lose access to it, just as weeds grow over a path that is seldom used.

4.   Interference Theory.
New memories interfere with old memories, and old memories interfere with new memories. Interference is especially likely when the memories are similar. For example, when I meet my students in the hallway, it is difficult to remember which class they are in because I have several similar classes.

5.   Reactive Interference.
We tend not to remember ideas or subjects that we dislike.

6.   Reconstruction Theory.
What we remember becomes distorted over time. Our personal biases affect what we remember.

7.   Motivated Forgetting.
We choose to remember pleasant experiences and to forget unpleasant experiences.

Minimizing Forgetting

Herman Ebbinghaus (1850–1909), a German psychologist and pioneer in research on forgetting, described a curve of forgetting.[2] He invented nonsense syllables such as WUX, CAZ, BIJ, and ZOL. He chose these nonsense syllables so that there would be no meaning, associations, or organizations that could affect the memory of the words. He would learn these lists of words and measure forgetting over time. The following is a chart of time and forgetting of nonsense syllables.

Time	Percent Forgotten
After 20 minutes	47
After 1 day	62
After 2 days	69
After 15 days	75
After 31 days	78

We can draw three interesting conclusions from examining these figures. First, most of the forgetting occurs within the first twenty minutes. Immediate review or at least review during the first twenty minutes would prevent most of the forgetting. Second, forgetting slows down over time. The third conclusion is that forgetting is significant after 31 days. Fortunately we do not need to memorize nonsense syllables. We can use meaning, associations, organization, and proper review to minimize forgetting.

Review is important in transferring information from short-term to long-term memory. You can also minimize forgetting over time through the proper use of review.[3] Let's assume that you spend 45 minutes studying and learning something new. The optimum schedule for review would look like this:

After 10 minutes	Review for 5 minutes
After 1 day	Review for 5 minutes
After 1 week	Review for 3 minutes
After 1 month	Review for 3 minutes
After 6 months	Review for 3 minutes

By spending about 20 minutes in review time, you can remember 90 to 100 percent of the material. The short periods of review are much easier to accomplish than spending larger periods of review. Make good use of your time by having material for review immediately available. When you have three to five minutes available, review some material that you have learned previously. You will be improving access to material stored in long-term memory, and you will be able to easily recall the information for an exam or for future use in your career.

Memorization Tips

- Meaningful organization
- Visualization
- Recitation
- Develop an interest
- See the big picture first
- Intend to remember
- Learn small amounts frequently
- Basic background
- Relax

QUIZ
Improving Your Memory

Test what you have learned by circling the letter of the correct answer to the following questions.

1. Information is stored permanently in the

   a. sensory register.
   b. short-term memory (STM).
   c. long-term memory (LTM).

2. You never forget. True or false?

   a. False.
   b. True.
   c. This is true only if the information is stored properly in long-term memory.

3. According to Ebbinghaus, the greatest rate of forgetting occurs

   a. within the first 20 minutes.
   b. within the first day.
   c. within the first 15 days.

4. If you do not review information stored in long-term memory, you will

   a. still remember it because it is in long-term memory.
   b. probably lose access to the information.
   c. lose the information forever.

5. The best way to review is

   a. in a 45-minute study session.
   b. in a 20-minute study session.
   c. in 3- to 5-minute study sessions spaced out over time.

How did you do on the quiz? Check your answers: 1. c, 2. c, 3. a, 4. b, 5. c

How Can I Remember What I Study?

Based on the above theories of memory and forgetting, here are some practical suggestions for storing information in LTM. Information stored in LTM can be retrieved for tests in college and for success in your career and personal life.

Meaningful Organization

There is no better method of memory improvement than imposing your own form of personal organization on the material you are trying to remember. Psychologists have even suggested that your intelligence quotient (IQ) may be related to how well you have organized material you learned in the past. When learning new material, cluster facts and ideas into categories that are meaningful to you.

ACTIVITY

Remember George Miller's Magical Number Seven theory? It is more efficient to limit the number of categories to seven or less, although you can have subcategories. Examine the following list of words.

goat	horse	cow
carrot	cat	lettuce
banana	tomato	pig
celery	orange	peas
cherry	apple	strawberry

Look at the list for one minute. Then look away from the list and write down all the words you can recall. Record the number of words you remembered: _____

Note that the following lists are divided into categories: animals, crops, and tropical fruits.

animals	**crops**	**tropical fruits**
lion	wheat	banana
giraffe	beans	kiwi
kangaroo	corn	mango
coyote	hay	guava
bear	oats	orange

Look at the above list for one minute. Then look away from the list and write down the words you recall. Record the number of words you remembered: _____

You probably remembered more from the second list because the list is organized into categories. Notice that there are only five words in each category. Remember that it is easier to remember lists with seven items or less. If these words have some meaning for you, it is easier to remember them. A farmer from the Midwest would probably have an easier time remembering the crops. A person from Hawaii would probably remember the list of tropical fruits. We also tend to remember unusual items and the first and last items on the list. If you need to memorize a list, pay more attention to the mundane items and the items in the middle of the list.

Visualization

Another very powerful memorization technique is visualization. The right side of the brain specializes in visual pictures and the left side in verbal functions. If you focus on the words only, you are using only half of your brain. If you can focus on the words and accompany them with pictures, you are using your brain in the most efficient way. Advertisers use pictures as powerful influences to motivate you to purchase their products. You can use the same power of visualization to enhance your studying. While you are studying history, picture what life would be like in that time period. In engineering, make pictures in your mind or on paper to illustrate scientific principles. Challenge yourself to see the pictures along with the words. Add movement to your pictures, as in a video. During a test, relax and recall the pictures.

Recitation

Although scientists are still researching and learning how the memory works and how information is stored, we do know that recitation, rehearsal, and reviewing the ideas are powerful techniques for learning. Memories exist in the brain in the form of a chemical neural trace. Some researchers think that it takes about four or five seconds for this neural trace to be established in LTM. It is through recitation that we keep the ideas in our mind long enough to store them in LTM. Often students say they cannot remember the material that they have just read. The reason for this problem is not a lack of intelligence but rather a simple lack of rehearsal. If information obtained through reading is stored in STM, it is very quickly forgotten. Say aloud or to yourself the material you want to remember. This process takes about five seconds.

Applying the recitation technique can help you remember names. When you are introduced to someone, first pay attention to make sure that you have heard the name correctly. Ask the person to repeat their name if necessary. Repeat the name out loud or in your mind. Say something like, "Glad to meet you, *Lydia*." Say the name silently to yourself five times to establish the neural trace. If possible, make a visual connection with the name. If the person's name is Frank, you might picture a hot dog, for example. Thinking about the name or reviewing it will help to access the name in the future.

Remember that most of the forgetting occurs in the first twenty minutes after learning something. Reviewing the material within 20 minutes is the fastest and most effective way to remember it. You will also need to review the information you have stored in LTM periodically so it is more accessible. This periodic review can be done effectively in three to five minutes.

Develop an Interest

We tend to remember what interests us. People often have phenomenal memories when it comes to sports, automobiles, music, stamp collecting, or anything they consider fun or pursue as a hobby. Find something interesting in your college studies. If you are not interested in what you are studying, look for something interesting or even pretend that you are interested. Reward yourself for studying by doing something enjoyable.

Attitude has a significant impact on memory. Approaching your studies with a positive attitude will help you to find something interesting and make it easier to remember. In addition, the more you learn about a topic, the more interesting it becomes. Often we judge a subject as boring because we know nothing about it.

Another way to make something interesting is to look for personal meaning. How can I use this information in my future career? Does the information relate to my personal experience in some way? How can I use this information? What is the importance of this information? And finally, is this information likely to be on the test?

See the Big Picture First

Imagine looking at a painting one inch at a time. It would be difficult to understand or appreciate a painting in this way. College students often approach reading a textbook in the same way. They focus on the small details without first getting an idea of the main points. By focusing on the details without looking at the main points, it is easy to get lost.

The first step in reading is to skim the chapter headings to form a mental outline of what you will be learning. Then read for detail. Think of the mind as a file cabinet or a computer. Major topics are like folders in which we file detailed information. When we need to find or access the information, we think of the major topic and look in the folder to find the details. If we put all of our papers into the file drawer without organization, it is difficult to find the information we need. Highlight or underline key ideas to focus on the main points and organize what you are learning.

Be selective and focus on key ideas to increase learning efficiency. Herman Ebbinghaus studied the length of time needed to remember a series of six nonsense syllables and twelve nonsense syllables.[4] We might assume that it would take twice as long to remember twelve syllables as it would six syllables. Ebbinghaus found that it took fifteen times longer to memorize twelve syllables. The Magic Number Seven theory seems to apply to the number of items that can be memorized efficiently.

Does this mean that we should try to remember only seven or less ideas in studying a textbook chapter? No, it is most efficient to identify seven or fewer key ideas and then cluster less important ideas under major headings. In this way, you can remember the key ideas in the chapter you are studying. The critical thinking required by this process also helps in remembering ideas and information.

Intend to Remember

Tell yourself that you are going to remember. If you think you won't remember, you won't remember. This step also relates to positive thinking and self-confidence and will take some practice to apply. Once you have told yourself to remember, apply some of the above techniques such as organizing, visualizing, and reciting. If you intend to remember, you will pay attention, make an effort to understand, and use memory techniques to strengthen your memory.

One practical technique that involves intent to remember is the memory jogger. This involves doing something unusual to jog, or trigger your memory. If you want to be sure to remember your books, place your car keys on the books. Since you cannot go anywhere without your keys, you will find them and remember the books too. Another application is putting your watch on your right hand to remember to do something. When you look at your left hand and notice that the watch is not there, the surprise will jog your memory for the item you wish to recall. You can be creative with this technique and come up with your own memory joggers.

Distribute the Practice

Learning small amounts of material and reviewing frequently is more effective than a marathon study session. One research study showed that a task that took thirty minutes to learn in one day could be learned in twenty-two minutes if spread over two days. This is almost a 30 percent increase in efficiency.[5]

If you have a list of vocabulary words or formulas to learn, break the material into small parts and frequently review each part for a short period of time. Consider putting these facts or figures on index cards to carry with you in your purse or pocket. Use small amounts of time to quickly review the cards. This technique works well because it prevents fatigue and helps to keep motivation high. One exception to the distributed practice rule is creative work such as writing a paper or doing an art project, where a longer time period is needed for creative inspiration and immediate follow-through.

A learning technique for distributed practice is summed up in the acronym **SAFMEDS**, which stands for Say All Fast for one Minute Each Day and Shuffle.[6] With this technique you can easily and quickly learn 100 or more facts. To use this technique, prepare flash cards that contain the material to be learned (vocabulary, foreign language words, numbers, dates, places, names, formulas). For example, if you are learning Spanish, place the Spanish word on one side of the card and the English word on the other side. Just writing out the flash cards is an aid to learning and is often sufficient for learning the material. Once the cards are prepared, *say* the Spanish word and see if you can remember what it means in English. Look at the back of the card to see if your answer is correct. Do this with *all* of the cards as *fast* as you can for *one minute each day*. Then *shuffle* the cards and repeat the process the next day.

It is important that you do this activity quickly. Don't worry if you do not know the answer. Just flip the card over, quickly look at the answer and put the card that you missed into a separate pile. At the end of the minute, count the number of cards you answered correctly. You can learn even faster if you take the stack of cards you missed and practice them quickly one more time. Shuffling the cards helps you to remember the actual meanings of the words, instead of just the order in which they appear. In the case of the Spanish cards, turn the cards over and say each English word to see if you can remember the equivalent word in Spanish. Each day, the number of correct answers will increase, and you will have a concrete measure of your learning. Consider this activity as a fun and fast-moving game to challenge yourself.

Create a Basic Background

You remember information by connecting it to things you already know. The more you know, the easier it is to make connections that make remembering easier. You will even find that it is easier to remember material toward the end of a college class because you have established a basic background at the beginning of the semester. With this in mind, freshman-level courses will be the most difficult in college because they form the basic background for your college education. College does become easier as you establish this basic background and practice effective study techniques.

You can enhance your basic background by reading a variety of books. Making reading a habit also enhances vocabulary, writing, and spelling. College provides many opportunities for expanding your reading horizons and areas of basic knowledge.

Relax While Studying

The brain works much better when it is relaxed. As you become more confident of your study techniques, you can become more relaxed. Here are some suggestions to help you relax during study time.

- Use distributed practice to take away some of the pressure of learning; take breaks between periods of learning. Give yourself time to absorb the material.
- Plan ahead so that you do not have to cram. Waiting until the last minute to study produces anxiety that is counterproductive.
- If you are anxious, try a physical activity or relaxation exercise before study sessions. For example, imagine a warm, relaxing light beginning at the feet and moving slowly up the body to the top of the head. Feel each part of the body relax as the light makes contact with it. You will find other relaxation techniques in Chapter 12.
- If you are feeling frustrated, it is often a good idea to stop and come back to your studies later. You may gain insight into your studies while you are more relaxed and doing something else. You can often benefit from a fresh perspective.

Memorization Tricks

- Acrostics
- Acronyms
- Peg systems
- Loci systems
- Visual clues
- Say it aloud
- Have a routine
- Write it down

Using Mnemonics and Other Memory Tricks

Memory tricks can be used to enhance your memory. These memory tricks include acrostics, acronyms, peg, and loci systems. These systems are called mnemonics from the Greek word *mneme* which means "to remember."

Mnemonic devices are very effective. A research study by Gerald R. Miller found that students who used mnemonic devices improved their test scores by up to 77 percent.[7] Mnemonics are effective because they help to organize material. They have been used throughout history, in part as a way to entertain people with amazing memory feats.

Mnemonics are best used for memorizing facts. They are not helpful for understanding or thinking critically about the information. Be sure to memorize your mnemonics carefully and review them right before exam time. Forgetting the mnemonic or a part of it can cause major problems.

Acrostics

Acrostics are creative rhymes, songs, poems, or sentences that help us to remember. Maybe you previously learned some of these in school.

- Days in each month: Thirty days hath September, April, June, and November. All the rest have 31, except February which has 28 until leap year gives it 29.
- Spelling rules: *i* before *e* except after *c*, or when sounding like *a* as in neighbor and weigh.
- Numbers: Can I remember the reciprocal? To remember the reciprocal of pi, count the letters in each word of the question above. The reciprocal of pi = .3 1 8 3 10
- Notes on the treble clef in music: Every Good Boy Does Fine (E, G, B, D, F)
- Classification in biology: Kings Play Cards on Fairly Good Soft Velvet (Kingdom, Phylum, Class, Order, Family, Genus, Species, Variety)

An effective way to invent your own acrostics is to first identify key ideas you need to remember. Underline these key words or write them down as a list. Think of a word that starts with the letter of the idea you want to remember. Rearrange the words if necessary to form a sentence. The more unusual the sentence, the easier it is to remember.

Mnemonics become more powerful when used with visualization. For example, if you are trying to remember the planets, use a mnemonic and then visualize Saturn as a hulahoop dancer to remember that it has rings. Jupiter could be a king with a number of maids to represent its moons.

Acronyms

Acronyms are commonly used as a shortcut in our language. The military is especially fond of using acronyms. For example, NASA is the acronym for the National Aeronautics and Space Administration. You can invent your own acronyms as a memory trick. Here are some common ones that students have used:

- The colors of the spectrum: Roy G. Biv (red, orange, yellow, green, blue, indigo, violet)
- The Great Lakes: HOMES (Huron, Ontario, Michigan, Erie, Superior)
- The stages of cell division in biology: IPMAT (interphase, prophase, metaphase, and telephase)

To make your own acronym, list the items you wish to remember. Use the first letter of each word to make a new word. The word you make can be an actual word or an invented word.

Peg Systems

Peg systems start with numbers, typically 1 to 100. Each number is associated with an object. The object chosen to represent each number can be based on rhyme or on a logical association. The objects are memorized and used with a mental picture to recall a list. There are entertainers who can have the audience call out a list of 100 objects and then repeat all of the objects through use of a peg system. Here is an example of a commonly used peg system based on rhyme:

One	Bun	Six	Sticks
Two	Shoe	Seven	Heaven
Three	Tree	Eight	Gate
Four	Door	Nine	Wine
Five	Hive	Ten	Hen

For example, if I want to remember a grocery list consisting of milk, eggs, carrots, and butter, I would make associations between the peg and the item I want to remember. The more unusual the association is, the better. I would start by making a visual connection between *bun*, my peg word, and *milk*, the first item on the list. I could picture dipping a bun into a glass of milk for a snack. Next I would make a connection between *shoe* and *eggs*. I could picture eggs being broken into my shoe as a joke. Next I would picture a *tree* with orange *carrots* hanging from it and then a *door* with *butter* dripping from the doorknob. The technique works because of the organization provided by the pegs and the power of visualization.

There are many variations of the peg system. One variation is using the letters of the alphabet instead of numbers. Another variation is to visualize objects and put them in a stack, one on top of the other, until you have a great tottering tower, like a totem pole telling a story. Still another variation is to use your body or your car as a peg system. Using our example of the grocery list above, visualize balancing the milk on your head, carrying eggs in your hands, having carrots tied around your waist and smearing butter on your feet. Remember that the more unusual the pictures, the easier they are to remember.

Loci Systems

Loci or location systems use a series of familiar places to aid the memory. The Roman orators often used this system to remember the outline of a speech. For example, the speaker might connect the entry of a house with the introduction, the living room with the first main point, and each part of the speech with a different room. Again, this technique works through organization and visualization.

Another example of using a loci system to remember a speech or dramatic production is to imagine a long hallway. Mentally draw a picture of each topic or section you need to remember, and then hang each picture on the wall. As you are giving your speech or acting out your part in the play, visualize walking down the hallway and looking at the pictures on the wall to remind yourself of the next topic. For multiple topics, you can place signs over several hallway entrances labeling the contents of each hallway.

Visual Clues

Visual clues are helpful memory devices. To remember your books, place them in front of the door so you will see them on your way to school. To remember to take your finished homework to school, put it in your car when you are done. To remember to fill a prescription, put the empty bottle on the front seat of your car. Tie a bright ribbon on your backpack to remind you to attend a meeting with your study group. When parking your car in the mall, look around and notice landmarks such as nearby stores or row numbers. When you enter a large department store, notice the items that are near the door you entered. Are you worried that you left the iron on? Tie a ribbon around the handle of the iron each time you turn it off or unplug it. To find out if you have all the items you need to go skiing, visualize yourself on the ski slope wearing all those items.

Say It Aloud

Some people are auditory learners and can remember items by repeating them out loud. For example, if you want to remember where you hid your diamond ring, say it out loud a few times. Then reinforce the memory by making a visual picture of where you have hidden the ring. You can also use your auditory memory by making a rhyme or song to remember something. Commercials use this technique all the time to try to get you to remember a product and purchase it.

Have a Routine

Do you have a difficult time trying to remember where you left your keys, wallet, or purse? Having a routine can greatly simplify your life and help you to remember. As you enter your house, hang your keys on a hook each time. Decide where you will place your wallet or purse and put it in the same place each time. When I leave for work, I have a mental checklist with four items: keys, purse, glasses, and cell phone.

Write It Down

One of the easiest and most effective memory techniques is to simply write something down. Make a grocery list or to-do list, send yourself an e-mail, or tape a note to your bathroom mirror or the dashboard of your car.

Remembering Names

Many people have difficulty remembering names of other people in social or business situations. The reason we have difficulty in remembering names is that we do not take the time to store the name properly in our memories. When we first meet someone, we are often distracted or thinking about ourselves. We are trying to remember our own names or wondering what impression we are making on the other person.

   To remember a name, first make sure you have heard the name correctly. If you have not heard the name, there is no way you can remember it. Ask the person to repeat his or her name or check to see if you have heard it correctly. Immediately use the name. For example, say "It is nice to meet you, *Nancy*." If you can mentally repeat the name about five times, you have a good chance of remembering it. You can improve the chances of remembering the name if you can make an association. For example, you might think, "She looks like my daughter's friend Nancy." Some people remember names by making a rhyme such as "fancy Nancy."

JOURNAL ENTRY #2

Look at the list of memory tricks above. List and briefly explain at least three memory tricks you are willing to try.

Optimize Your Brain Power

The mind can be strengthened and remain healthy throughout life. Scientists have studied a group of nuns from Mankato, Minnesota, who have lived long lives and suffer less from dementia and brain diseases than the general population. These nuns have lived a long time because they do not drink to excess or smoke. Their minds have remained healthy into old age by staying mentally active. They keep active by discussing current events, playing cards, practicing math problems, and doing crossword puzzles. Arnold Scheibel, head of the UCLA Brain Institute gives the following suggestions for strengthening your mind.

- Do jigsaw and crossword puzzles.
- Play a musical instrument.
- Fix something. The mental challenge stimulates the brain.
- Participate in the arts. Draw or paint something.
- Dance. Exercise and rhythm is good for the brain.
- Do aerobic exercise. This promotes blood flow to the brain.
- Meet and interact with interesting people.
- Read challenging books.
- Take a college class.[8]

Doing these kinds of activities can actually stimulate the development of neurons and nerve connections in the brain so that the brain functions more efficiently. The good news is that you can do this at any age.

Besides doing exercises to strengthen your brain, you can take other actions to keep your brain healthy. Here are some ideas:

1. Do aerobic exercise.
Exercise improves the flow of oxygen to the brain. The brain needs oxygen to function. Researchers have just announced that the human brain can grow new nerve cells by putting subjects on a three month aerobic workout regimen. It was interesting to note these new nerve cells could be generated at any age and are important in reversing the aging process and delaying the onset of Alzheimer's disease or other cognitive disorders.[9] For optimum health and learning, it is important to exercise the body as well as the mind.

2. Get enough rest.
Nobel Laureate Francis Crick, who studies the brain at the Salk Institute, proposes that the purpose of sleep is to allow the brain to "take out the trash." Sleep provides time for the brain to review the events of the day and to store what is needed and discard what is not worth remembering. During sleep, the brain sorts memories and stores

significant ones in long-term memory. Studies have shown that when humans and lab animals are taught a new task and deprived of sleep, they do not perform the task the next day as well as non-sleep-deprived subjects.[10] Chronic lack of sleep can even lead to death.

3. **Eat a balanced, low-fat diet.**
The brain needs nutrients, vitamins, and minerals to be healthy. Low-fat diets have been shown to improve mental performance.[11]

4. **Eat proteins and carbohydrates.**
Proteins are the building blocks of neurotransmitters that increase mental activity. Carbohydrates provide energy and are the building blocks of neurotransmitters that have a calming effect.[12]

5. **Drink caffeine in moderation.**
Caffeine can make you feel stressed, making it difficult to think.

6. **Don't abuse drugs or alcohol.**
These substances kill brain cells and change brain chemistry.

7. **Use safety gear.**
Wear a seat belt when driving and a helmet when biking or skating to reduce head injuries.

> ## JOURNAL ENTRY #3
> What can you do to keep your brain healthy?

Improving Your Reading
Myths about Reading

Effective reading techniques are crucial to college success. The level and quantity of reading may be greatly increased over what you have experienced in the past. The following are some myths about reading that cause problems for many college students.

1. **"If I read a chapter, I should remember what I read."**
Many students say that they read the chapter, but "it goes in one ear and out the other." After such a frustrating experience, students often conclude that they cannot read well or are not intelligent enough to succeed in college. If you just read the chapter, you have stored it in short-term memory, which lasts about 30 seconds. Reading a chapter takes a lot of effort. You want to make sure the effort you have invested pays off by storing the material in long-term memory. You can then retrieve the information in the future, as well as pass exams. Material is stored in long-term memory through rehearsal or review. Without review, you will not remember.

2. **"I do not need to read if I go to class."**
The role of the college professor is to supplement material in the text and increase student understanding of the material. Some professors do not even cover topics contained in the text and consider it the student's responsibility to learn textbook material. If you do not read the text, you may miss out on important material that is not presented during class. Reading the text also helps you understand the material that the professor presents.

3.   **"Practice makes perfect."**
Students think that if they keep reading the way they are reading, their reading will get better. The truth is "Perfect practice makes perfect." If you are reading in a way that enhances memory, you will get better and better. Success in college reading may mean learning some new reading habits. You will learn about effective reading habits in this chapter.

4.   **"Learn the facts that will be on the test."**
Focusing on details without looking at the big picture can slow down learning and lead to frustration. Start with the big picture or outline and then it is easier to learn the details.

JOURNAL ENTRY #4

College success depends on reading and remembering a large amount of material. How will you fit this reading into your schedule?

Getting Started with a New Text: Skimming

Skimming a textbook before you begin a course is a good way to prepare for learning. Skimming will give you an organized preview of what's ahead. Here are the steps to skimming a new text:

1.   **Quickly read the preface or introduction.**
Read as if you were having a conversation with the author of the text. In the preface or introduction, you will find out how the author has organized the material, the key ideas, and his or her purpose in writing the text.

2.   **Look at the major topics in the table of contents.**
You can use the table of contents as a window into the book. It gives a quick outline of every topic in the text. As you read the table of contents, look for topics of special interest to you.

3.   **Spend five to fifteen minutes quickly looking over the book.**
Turn the pages quickly, noticing boldfaced topics, pictures, and anything else that catches your attention. Again, look for important or interesting topics. Do not spend too much time on this step.

4.   **Notice the items located at the back of the book.**
Is there an index, glossary of terms, answers to quiz questions, or solutions to math problems? These sections will be of use to you as you read.

Skimming a text before you begin to read has several important benefits. The first benefit is that it gets you started in the learning process. It is an easy and quick step that can help you avoid procrastination. It increases motivation by helping you notice items that have appeal to you. Previewing the content will help you to relax as you study and remember the information. Early in the course, this step will help you verify that you have chosen the correct course and that you have the prerequisites to be successful in the class.

Study System

1. Survey and question
2. Read and recite
3. Review and reflect

A Study System for Reading a College Text: SQ4R

There are many systems for reading a college textbook. All successful systems involve ways to store information in long-term memory: recognizing major points, organizing material to be learned, reviewing, intending to remember, and critical thinking about reading. The crucial step in transferring information to long-term memory is rehearsal, reviewing, or reciting. You need to keep information in your mind for five to fifteen seconds in order for it to be stored in long-term memory. **The SQ4R system (Survey, Question, Read, Recite, Review, Reflect)** is a simple and effective way to store information in long-term memory. This system was derived from an information-processing theory developed by Francis P. Robinson in 1941 and was originally developed for use by military personnel attending college during World War II. Since that time the system has been used by many colleges to teach students effective study skills. The system can be broken down into three steps.

Step 1: Survey and Question.   The first step is to survey and question the chapter before you begin reading. Read the title and first paragraph or introduction to the chapter and then look quickly through the chapter, letting your eyes glide across bold headings, diagrams, illustrations, and photos. Read the last paragraph or summary of the chapter. This process should take five minutes or less for a typical chapter in a college textbook.

While you are surveying the chapter, ask yourself questions. Take each major heading in the chapter and turn it into a question. For example, in this section of the book you might ask: What is a system for reading a college text? Why do I need a system? What is SQ4R? What is the first step of SQ4R? You can also ask some general questions as you survey the chapter: What is the main point? What will I learn? Do I know something about this? Can I find something that interests me? How can I use this? Does this relate to something said in class? What does this mean? Is this a possible test question? Asking questions will help you to become an active reader and to find some personal meaning in the content that will help you remember it. If you at least survey and question the relevant textbook material before you go to class, you will have the advantage of being familiar with some of the key ideas to be discussed.

There are several benefits to taking this first step:

- This is the first step in rehearsal for storage of information into long-term memory.
- The quick survey is a warmup for the brain, similar to an athlete's warmup before exercise.
- A survey step is also good practice for improving your reading speed.
- Reading to answer questions increases comprehension, sparks interest, and has the added bonus of keeping you awake while reading.

If you want to be able to read faster, improve your reading comprehension, and increase retention of your reading material, practice the survey and question step before you begin your detailed reading.

Step 2: Read and Recite.   The second step in reading a text is to read and recite. Read each paragraph and look for the most important point or topic sentence. If the point is important, highlight or underline it. You might use different colors to organize the ideas. You can also make a notation or outline in the margin of the text if the point is especially significant, meaningful, useful, or likely to appear on an exam. A picture, diagram, or chart drawn in the margin is a great way to use visualization to improve retention of the material.

Next, look away and see if you can say the main point to yourself either silently or out loud. Reciting is even more powerful if you combine it with visualization. Make a video in your head to illustrate what you are learning. Include color, movement, and sound if possible. Reciting is crucial to long-term memory storage. It will also keep you awake. Beginning college students will find this step a challenge, but practice makes it a habit that becomes easier and easier.

If you read a paragraph or section and do not understand the main point, try these techniques:

1. **Notice any vocabulary or technical terms that are unfamiliar.**
Look up these words in a dictionary or in the glossary at the back of the book. Use index cards to write the words on one side and the definition on the other side. Use the SAFMEDS technique (Say All Fast in one Minute Each Day Shuffle) as discussed earlier in this chapter. You are likely to see these vocabulary words on quizzes and exams.

2. **Read the paragraph again.**
Until you get into the habit of searching for the main point, you may need to reread a paragraph until you understand. If this does not work, reread the paragraph before and after the one you do not understand.

3. **Write a question in the margin and ask your instructor or tutor to explain.**
College instructors have office hours set aside to assist students with questions, and faculty are generally favorably impressed with students who care enough to ask questions. Most colleges offer tutoring free of charge.

4. **If you are really frustrated, put your reading away and come back to it later.**
You may be able to relax and gain some insight about the material.

5. **Make sure you have the proper background for the course.**
Take the introductory course first.

6. **Assess your reading skills.**
Colleges offer reading assessments, and counselors can help you understand your skill level and suggest appropriate courses. Most colleges offer reading courses that can help you to be successful in college.

7. **If you have always had a problem with reading, you may have a learning disability.**
A person with a learning disability is of average or higher-than-average intelligence but has a problem that interferes with learning. Most colleges offer assessment that can help you understand your learning disability and tutoring that is designed to help you to compensate for the disability.

Step 3: Review and Reflect. The last step in reading is to review and reflect. After each section, quickly review what you have highlighted or underlined. Again, ask questions. How can I use this information? How does it relate to what I already know? What is most important? What is likely to be on the exam? Is it true? Learn to think critically about the material you have learned.

When you finish the chapter, quickly (in a couple of minutes) look over the highlights again. This last step, review and reflect, is another opportunity for rehearsal. At this point, you have stored the information in long-term memory and want to make sure that you can access the information again in the future. Think of this last step as a creative step in which you put the pieces together, gain an understanding, and begin to think of how you can apply your new knowledge to your personal life. This is the true reward of studying.

Review is faster, easier, and more effective if done immediately. As discussed previously in this chapter, most forgetting occurs in the first 20 minutes after exposure to new information. If you wait 24 hours to review, you will probably have forgotten 80 percent of the material and will have to spend a longer time in review. Review periodically to make sure that you can access the material easily in the future, and review again right before the test.

As you read about the above steps, you may think that this process takes a lot of time. Remember that it is not how much you read but how you read that is important. In reality, the SQ4R technique is a time-saver in that you do not have to reread all the material before the test. You just need to quickly review information that is stored in long-term memory. Rereading can be purely mechanical and consume your time with little payoff. Rather than rereading, spend your time reciting the important points. With proper review, you can remember 80 to 90 percent of the material.

In his book *Accelerated Learning*, Colin Rose states that you can retain 88 percent of the material you study using the following review schedule.[13] He also notes that the rate of retention using this schedule is four times better than the expected curve of forgetting.

1. Review immediately within 30 seconds.
2. Review after a few minutes.
3. Review after one hour.
4. Review a day later after an overnight rest.
5. Review after a week.
6. Review after one month.

Suggestions for review schedules vary, but the key point is that review is most effective when it is done in short sessions spaced out over time.

In summary, here are the three steps of SQ4R:

1.   Survey and Question.
Quickly skim or survey the chapter. Turn the section headings into questions.

2.   Read and Recite.
Read each paragraph, asking yourself, "What is the main point?" Look away and see if you can say this idea to yourself either mentally or out loud. Use visualization along with reciting. Highlight or mark the idea if it is important.

3.   Review and Reflect.
Quickly review the main ideas as you finish each section. Review the chapter when finished. Review periodically. As you review, think critically about the material.

The following chart summarizes the speed and purpose of each step.

	Survey and Question	Read and Recite	Review and Reflect
Speed	Fast	Read slowly Recite quickly	Fast
Purpose	Speed-reading Comprehension	Memory Comprehension	Memory Understanding

Guidelines for Marking Your Textbook

Marking your textbook can help you pick out what is important, save time, and review the material. It is a great way to reinforce your memory and help you access the material you have learned. In high school, you were given the command, "Thou shalt not mark in thy book!" College is different. You have paid for the book and need to use it as a tool. Even if you plan to sell your book, you can still mark it up. Here are some guidelines for marking your book:

- Underline or mark the key ideas in your text. You don't have to underline complete sentences; just underline enough to make sense when you review your markings. This technique works especially well for kinesthics or tactile learners.
- Aim for marking or highlighting about 20 percent of the most important material. If you mark too much of your reading, it will be difficult to review the main points.
- Read each paragraph first. Ask yourself, "What is the main point?" Highlight or mark the main point if it is important. Not every paragraph has a main point that needs to be marked.
- Use other marks to help you organize what you have read. Write in numbers or letters and use different colors to help you organize ideas.
- Most college texts have wide margins. Use these margins to write down questions, outlines, or key points to remember.
- Learn to be brief, fast, and neat in your marking or highlighting.
- If you are tempted to mark too much, use the double system of first underlining with a pencil as much as you want and then using a highlighter to pick out the most important 20 percent of the material in the chapter.
- Use different kinds of marks and symbols, such as the following:
  - Single or double underlines
  - Brackets around an important paragraph
  - Numbers or letters to organize points
  - Circles or squares to make important words stand out
  - An asterisk or star in the margin for a very important idea
  - A question mark next to something you do not understand
  - "DEF" in the margin to point out a definition
  - Use your imagination to come up with your own symbols

- Learn to recognize organizing patterns in your reading. These patterns will help you to pick out and mark the important ideas.
  - **The listing pattern.** Identify and mark the items in the list. Use numbers and letters to identify the parts of a list.
  - **The sequence pattern.** This pattern presents a list in a certain order. Note the items in the list and the order by using numbers or letters.
  - **The definition pattern.** Circle the word being defined. Underline the definition.
  - **The comparison/contrast pattern.** This pattern explains similarities or differences. Underline or mark these.
  - **The cause/effect pattern.** This pattern describes the reasons things happen. Underline or mark the cause and the effect.

- Quickly review the important points after you have marked each section. Quickly review again when you have finished the chapter. If you review within 20 minutes, the review will be faster and easier.

QUIZ
Improving Reading

Test what you have learned by circling the letter of the correct answer to the following questions.

1. If you have read the chapter and can't remember what you have read,

   a. read the chapter again.
   b. remember to select important points and review them.
   c. the material is stored in long-term memory.

2. When you start reading a new textbook,

   a. begin with chapter one.
   b. focus on the details you will need to remember.
   c. skim over the text to get a general idea of what you will be reading.

3. The first step in reading a chapter in a college textbook is to

   a. survey and question.
   b. read and recite.
   c. review and reflect.

4. As you are reading each paragraph in a college textbook, it is most important to

   a. read quickly.
   b. identify the main point and recite it.
   c. question what you are reading.

5. When marking a college textbook, it is recommended to mark about

   a. 50%.
   b. 30%.
   c. 20%.

How did you do on the quiz? Check your answers: 1. b, 2. c, 3. a, 4. b, 5. c

Reading Strategies for Different Subjects

While the SQ4R technique is a good general strategy for reading textbook material, there are steps that you will need to add depending on the subject area you are studying.

Math

1. Make sure you have the proper prerequisites or background courses before you begin your math class.
2. When skimming a math book, keep in mind that many of the topics will be unfamiliar to you. You should be able to understand the first few pages and build your knowledge from there. If all the concepts are familiar to you, you may be taking a class that you do not need.
3. It is not enough to read and understand mathematical concepts. Make sure that you add practice to your study system when studying math. Practice gives you the self-confidence to relax when working with math.
4. It is helpful to read over your math book before you go to class so that you will know what areas need special attention.
5. Focus on understanding the math problems and concepts rather than on memorizing problems.
6. Do not get behind in your math studies. You need to understand the first step before you can go on to the next.
7. Ask for help as soon as you have difficulties.

Science

1. In science classes the scientific method is used to describe the world. The scientific method relies on questioning, observing, hypothesizing, researching, and analyzing. You will learn about theories and scientific principles. Highlight or mark theories, names of scientists, definitions, concepts, and procedures.
2. Understand the scientific principles and use flash cards to remember details and formulas.
3. Study the charts, diagrams, tables, and graphs. Draw your own pictures and graphs to get a visual picture of the material.
4. Use lab time as an opportunity to practice the theories and principles that you have learned.

Social and Behavioral Sciences

1. Social and behavioral scientists focus on principles of behavior, theories, and research. Notice that there are different theories that explain the same phenomena. Highlight, underline, and summarize these theories in your own words.
2. When looking at the research, ask yourself what the point of the research was, who conducted the research, when the research was completed, what data was collected, and what conclusions were drawn.
3. Think of practical applications of theories.
4. Use flash cards to remember details.

Literature Courses

When taking a course in literature, you will be asked to understand, appreciate, interpret, evaluate, and write about the literature.

1. Underline the names of characters and write plot summaries.
2. Write notes about your evaluation of literary works.
3. Make flash cards to remember literary terms.
4. Write down important quotes or note page numbers on a separate piece of paper so that you don't have to go back and find them later when you are writing about a work.

Foreign Language Courses

Foreign language courses require memorization and practice.

1. Distribute the practice. Practice a small amount each day. It is not possible to learn everything at once.
2. Complete the exercises as a way to practice and remember.
3. Study out loud.
4. Practice speaking the language with others.
5. Use flash cards to remember vocabulary.
6. Make charts to practice verb conjugations.
7. Ask for help if you do not understand.
8. Learn to think in the foreign language. Translating from English causes confusion because the structures of languages are different.

Reading for Speed and Comprehension

In *How to Read for Speed and Comprehension*, Gordon Wainwright suggests using different gears, or speeds, when reading for different purposes.[14] Understanding these four gears can be helpful for college students.

1. **Studying.**

In this gear, the maximum reading speed is about 200 words per minute. It is used for material that is difficult or unfamiliar, such as a college textbook. For this material high quality of retention is required. It involves the steps described in SQ4R.

2. **Slow reading.**

In this gear, reading speed ranges from 150 to 300 wpm. It is used for material that is fairly difficult when a good quality of retention is desired.

3. **Rapid reading.**

In rapid reading, speeds range from 300 to 800 wpm. It is used for average or easy material. Use this gear for review of familiar material.

4. **Skimming.**

Skimming is a type of very fast reading done at 800 to 1000 wpm. With practice, it is possible to skim at 2000 to 3000 wpm. Using this technique, the eyes glide quickly down the page looking for specific information. Not every group of words or line is read. The eyes focus quickly on key ideas, bold headings, and titles. The purpose is to get a quick overview of the important ideas in the material.

Different reading speeds are used for different purposes. In college reading, it is more important to have good comprehension and retention than speed. However, we all live busy lives, and many college students today try to combine study, work, family, and social life. Learning to read faster is important to survival.

Efficient readers are those who can read quickly with good comprehension.[14] The following chart offers practical suggestions for attaining the skills and characteristics of an efficient reader.

Becoming an Efficient Reader

Reading Skill	What is it?	How to Practice
Wide eye span	You can read faster if you can see groups of words instead of one word at a time.	Skimming your textbook helps to increase eye span.
Minimal subvocalization	Saying words silently to yourself as you read slows reading speed. The average speaking speed is 200 words per minute. Thinking speed is much faster.	Skim your text quickly in the survey and review steps. Subvocalization decreases as reading speed increases.
Understanding complex reading material	College level texts require more in depth and active reading.	For complex material, slow down reading speed and use any of these techniques that work for you: subvocalization, reading aloud, visualization, highlighting, note taking.
Good vocabulary	Knowing the meaning of the words is essential to reading speed and comprehension.	Look up unfamiliar words and learn the definitions. You are likely to see these vocabulary words on the tests in your college courses.
Reading purpose	Reading a college textbook and reading for pleasure require different reading techniques.	To read a college textbook, use a study system such as SQ4R that helps to store information in long-term memory. When reading for pleasure, a study system is not necessary.
Broad base of knowledge	It is easier to learn when you can connect new material to what you know already. The more you know, the easier it is to learn new material.	Take a variety of general education courses. Although these courses can be difficult, they will expand your base of knowledge and make future learning easier.

Improving Reading Concentration

Hank Aaron said that what separates the superstar from the average ballplayer is that the superstar concentrates just a little longer. Athletes are very aware of the power of concentration in improving athletic performance. Coaches remind athletes to focus on the ball and to develop good powers of concentration and visualization. Being able to concentrate on your reading helps you to study more efficiently.

It is important to have a regular place for studying that has all the needed materials. You will need a table or desk with space for a computer, space for writing, and a comfortable chair. Keep a good supply of writing materials, computer supplies, and reference materials. To minimize fatigue and eye strain, good lighting is essential. It is best to have an overhead light and a lamp. Place the lamp to your left if you are right-handed. In this way, you will not be writing in a shadow. Do the reverse if you are lefthanded. If you have space, use two lamps with one placed on each side. Eliminate glare by using a lampshade. Study lamps often come with a deflector on the bottom of the lampshade that further eliminates glare. Lighter colors on your desk and wall also help to eliminate glare and fatigue.

In setting up your regular place for studying, keep in mind your environmental preferences as identified by your PEPS learning style inventory. Consider these factors:

Improving Reading Concentration

1. Become an active reader.
2. Remember your purpose.
3. Use daydreaming to relax.
4. Solve personal problems.
5. Plan to deal with worry.
6. Break tasks into small parts.
7. Record when your attention wanders.
8. Focus your attention.

- Do you need a quiet environment to focus on your studies?
- Do you prefer bright or dim light?
- Do you prefer a warm or cool environment?
- Do you prefer learning by yourself or with others?
- Do you study best in the morning or the afternoon?

Having and using a well-equipped and comfortable study place reduces external distractions. Internal distractions are many and varied and may be more difficult to manage. Internal distractions include being hungry, tired, or ill. It is a good idea to eat and be well rested before reading any course material. If you are ill, rest and get well. Study when you feel better. Many internal distractions are mental, such as personal problems, worrying about grades, lack of interest or motivation, frustration, or just daydreaming.

Here are some ideas for dealing with internal mental distractions while reading.

1.   Become an active reader.
Read to answer questions. Search for the main idea. Recite or re-say the main idea in your mind. Reflect and think critically about the material you are reading. Mark or highlight the text. Visualize what you are reading.

2.   Remind yourself of your purpose for reading.
Think of your future college and career goals.

3.   Give yourself permission to daydream.
If you like to daydream, give yourself permission to daydream as a break from your studies. Come back to your studies with a more relaxed attitude.

4.   Take steps to solve personal problems.
If you are bothered by personal problems, take steps to solve them. See your college counselor for assistance. Another strategy is to make a plan to deal with the problem later so that you can study now.

5.   Plan to deal with worry.
Worry is not a very good motivator and it interferes with memory. Take some positive action to deal with problems that cause you to worry. If you are worried about your grades, what can you do right now to improve your chances of making better grades?

LUANN reprinted by permission of United Feature Syndicate, Inc.

6.   Break the task into small parts.

If the task seems overwhelming, break it into small parts and do the first part. If you have 400 pages to read in ten days, read 40 pages each day. Make a schedule that allows time to read each day until you have accomplished your goal. Use distributed practice in your studies. Study for a short time each day rather than holding a marathon study session before the test.

7.   Record times when your attention wanders.

Keep an index card by your book and make a mark on the card each time your attention wanders. With practice, you will have fewer marks on your card.

8.   Focus your attention.

Willpower is not enough! If you focus on concentrating, the mind seems to disobey. You will be concentrating on concentrating and not on your studies. In addition you will end up with lots of wrinkles in your forehead. Dave Ellis, author of *Becoming a Master Student*, reminds us to "be here now," which means to keep your mind and body in the same place.[15] As I'm sure you have experienced, your body can be at the desk reading, but your mind can be in lots of different and exciting places. When your mind wanders, notice that you have drifted off and gently return your attention to your reading.

Reading Speed, Comprehension, and Concentration

Test what you have learned by circling the letter of the correct answer to the following questions.

1. When reading a math book, you will need to add _____ to your study system.

   a. speed reading.
   b. practice.
   c. memorization.

2. Learn to increase your reading speed by

   a. applying all steps of SQ4R.
   b. starting with skimming.
   c. learning to concentrate.

3. Improve reading comprehension by

   a. applying the steps of SQ4R.
   b. reading as quickly as possible.
   c. reading slowly and carefully.

4. Improve reading concentration by

   a. reading in bed.
   b. reading in the kitchen.
   c. having a regular place for studying with needed materials.

5. To deal with mental distractions that interfere with reading,

   a. practice "Be Here Now."
   b. ignore personal problems.
   c. do your reading in large blocks of time.

How did you do on the quiz? Check your answers: 1. b, 2. b, 3. a, 4. c, 5. a

Keys to Success

Positive Thinking

You can improve your memory and your reading (as well as your life) by using positive thinking. Positive thinking involves two aspects: thinking about yourself and thinking about the world around you. When you think positively about yourself, you develop confidence in your abilities and become more capable of whatever you are attempting to do. When you think positively about the world around you, you look for possibilities and find interest in what you are doing.

Golfer Arnold Palmer has won many trophies but places high value on a plaque on his wall that says:

> If you think you are beaten, you are.
> If you think you dare not, you don't.
> If you like to win but think you can't,
> It's almost certain that you won't.
>
> Life's battles don't always go
> To the stronger woman or man,
> But sooner or later, those who win
> Are those who think they can.[16]

Success in athletics, school or any other endeavor begins with positive thinking. To remember anything, you first have to believe that you can remember. You need to trust in your abilities. Then apply memory techniques to help you to remember. If you think that you cannot remember, you will not even try. To be a good reader, you need to think that you can become a good reader and then work toward learning, applying, and practicing good reading techniques.

The second part of positive thinking involves thinking about the world around you. If you can convince yourself that the world and your college studies are full of interesting possibilities, you can start on a journey of adventure to discover new ideas. It is easier to remember and to read if you can find the subject interesting. If the topic is interesting, you will learn more about it. The more you learn about a topic, the more interesting it becomes and you are well on your way in your journey of discovery. If you tell yourself that the task is boring, you will struggle and find the task difficult. You will also find it difficult to continue.

You can improve your reading through positive thinking. Read with the intent to remember and use reading techniques that work for you. We remember what interests us, and having a positive attitude helps to find something interesting. To find something interesting, look for personal meaning. How can I use this information? Does it relate to something I know? Will this information be useful in my future career? Why is this information important? Write down your personal goals and remind yourself of your purpose for attending college. You are not just completing an assignment; you are on a path to discovery.

To be successful in college and to remember what you read, start with the belief that you can be successful. Anticipate that the journey will be interesting and full of possibilities. Enjoy the journey!

JOURNAL ENTRY #5

How can you use positive thinking to improve memory, reading, and success in college?

JOURNAL ENTRIES

Improving Memory and Reading

Go to http://www.collegesuccess1.com/ for Word files of the Journal Entries

Success over the Internet

Visit the *College Success Website* at http://www.collegesuccess1.com/

The *College Success Website* is continually updated with new topics and links to the material presented in this chapter. Topics include

- Memory techniques
- Reading strategies
- How to concentrate

- How to highlight a textbook
- Speed reading
- How to study science
- Study groups
- Examples of mnemonics

Contact your instructor if you have any problems in accessing the *College Success Website*.

Notes

1. G. A. Miller, "The Magical Number Seven, Plus or Minus Two: Some Limits on Our Capacity for Processing Information," *Psychological Review* 63 (March 1956): 81–97.
2. Colin Rose, *Accelerated Learning* (New York: Dell Publishing, 1985), 33–36.
3. Colin Rose, *Accelerated Learning* (New York: Dell Publishing, 1985), 50–51.
4. Walter Pauk, *How to Study in College* (Boston: Houghton Mifflin, 1989), 96–97.
5. Rose, *Accelerated Learning*, 34.
6. Adapted from Paul Chance, *Learning and Behavior* (Pacific Grove, CA: Brooks/Cole, 1979), 301.
7. Pauk, *How to Study in College*, 108.
8. Daniel Golden, "Building a Better Brain," *Life Magazine* July 1994, 63–70.
9. Mary Carmichael, "Stronger, Faster, Smarter," *Newsweek* March 26, 2007, 38–46.
10. Scott LaFee, "A Chronic Lack of Sleep Can Lead to the Big Sleep," *San Diego Union Tribune*, 8 October 1997.
11. Randy Blaun, "How to Eat Smart," *Psychology Today*, May/June 1996, 35.
12. Ibid.
13. Rose, *Accelerated Learning*, 51.
14. Gordon R. Wainwright, *How to Read for Speed and Comprehension* (NJ: Prentice-Hall, 1977), 100–101.
15. Dave Ellis, *Becoming a Master Student* (Boston: Houghton Mifflin, 1998), 74–75.
16. Rob Gilbert, ed., *Bits and Pieces* (Fairfield, NJ: The Economics Press), Vol. R, No. 40, p. 12, copyright 1998.

Name _____   Date _____

Review the main ideas on improving memory and reading. Based on these ideas, how would you be successful in the following situations? You may want to do this as a group activity in your class.

1. You just read the assigned chapter in economics and cannot remember what you read. It went in one ear and out the other.

2. In your anatomy and physiology class, you are required to remember the scientific name for 100 different muscles in the body.

3. You signed up for a philosophy class because it meets general education requirements. You are not interested in the class at all.

4. You have a mid-term in your literature class and have to read 400 pages in one month.

5. You must take American history to graduate from college. You think that history is boring.

6. You have been introduced to an important business contact and would like to remember his/her name.

7. You are enrolled in an algebra class. You continually remind yourself that you have never been good at math. You don't think that you will pass this class.

8. You have noticed that your grandmother is becoming very forgetful. You want to do whatever is possible to keep your mind healthy as you age.

Memory Test

Name _____   Date _____

Part 1. Your professor will read a list of 15 items. Do not write them down. After listening to this list, see how many you can remember and write them here.

1.   6.   11.

2.   7.   12.

3.   8.   13.

4.   9.   14.

5.   10.   15.

After your professor has given you the answers, write the number of words you remembered: _____

Part 2. Your professor will discuss memory techniques that you can use to improve your test scores and then will read another list. Again, do not write the words down, but try to apply the recommended techniques. Write as many words as you can remember.

1.   6.   11.

2.   7.   12.

3.   8.   13.

4.   9.   14.

5.   10.   15.

How many words did you remember this time? _____

Practice with Mnemonics

Name _____   Date _____

Join with a group of students in your class to invent some acrostics and acronyms.

Acrostics

Acrostics are creative rhymes, songs, poems, or sentences that help us to remember. To write an acrostic, think of a word that starts with the letter of the idea you want to remember. Sometimes you can rearrange the words if necessary to form a sentence. At other times, it is necessary to keep the words in order. The more unusual the sentence, the easier it is to remember.

Example:
Classification in biology: Kings Play Cards on Fairly Good Soft Velvet (Kingdom, Phylum, Class, Order, Family, Genus, Species, Variety)

Create an acrostic for the planets in the solar system. Keep the words in the same order as the planets from closest to the sun to farthest from the sun.

Mercury, Venus, Earth, Mars, Jupiter, Saturn, Uranus, Neptune, Pluto

_____

_____

_____

Acronyms

To make your own acronym, list the items you wish to remember. Use the first letter of each word to make a new word. The new word you invented can be an actual word or an invented word.

Example:
The Great Lakes: HOMES (Huron, Ontario, Michigan, Erie and Superior)

The following are the excretory organs of the body. Make an acronym to remember them. Rearrange the words if necessary.

     intestines, liver, lungs, kidneys, skin

_____

_____

_____

Write down any acrostics or acronyms that you know. Share them with your group.

Check Your Textbook Reading Skills

Name _____   Date _____

As you read each of the following statements, mark your response using this key:

1   I seldom or never do this.
2   I occasionally do this, depending on the class.
3   I almost always or always do this.

_____ 1.   Before I read the chapter, I quickly skim through it to get main ideas.

_____ 2.   As I skim through the chapter, I form questions based on the bold printed section headings.

_____ 3.   I read the introductory and summary paragraphs in the chapter before I begin reading.

_____ 4.   As I read each paragraph, I look for the main idea.

_____ 5.   I recite the main idea so I can remember it.

_____ 6.   I underline or highlight the main ideas.

_____ 7.   I write notes or outlines in the margin of the text.

_____ 8.   After reading each section, I do a quick review.

_____ 9.   I quickly review the chapter immediately after reading it.

_____ 10. During or after reading, I reflect on how the material is useful or meaningful to me.

_____ 11. I read or at least skim the assigned chapter before I come to class.

_____ 12. I have planned reading time in my weekly schedule.

_____ **Total points**

Check your score

30–36   You have good college reading skills.

24–29   You have good skills, but can improve.

18–23   Some changes are needed.

12–17   Major changes are needed.

Name _____   Date _____

1. Based on your responses to the reading skills checklist on the previous page, list some of your good reading habits.

2. Based on this same checklist, what are some areas you need to improve?

3. Review the material on SQ4R and reading for speed and comprehension. Make a list of reading techniques you are willing to try in order to become a more efficient reader.

4. Review the material on how to concentrate while reading. List some ideas that you can use.

Textbook Skimming

Name _____   Date _____

Use this text or any new text to answer the following questions. Challenge yourself to do this exercise quickly. Remember that a textbook survey should take no longer than five to fifteen minutes. Try to complete this exercise in fifteen minutes to allow time for writing. Notice the time when you start and finish.

1. Write two key ideas found in the introduction or preface to the book.

2. Looking at the table of contents, list the first five main ideas covered in the text.

3. Write down five interesting topics that you found in the book.

4. What did you find at the back of the book (e.g., index, glossary, appendixes)?

5. How long did it take you to do this exercise? _____

6. Briefly, what did you think of this textbook skimming exercise?

Name _____   Date _____

Using the *next chapter* assigned in this class or any other class, answer these questions. Again, challenge yourself to do this activity quickly. Can you finish the exercise in five to seven minutes? Notice your beginning and end times.

1. What is the title of the chapter? Write the title in the form of a question. For example, the title of this chapter is, "Improving Memory and Reading." A good question would be, "How can I improve my memory and reading?"

2. Briefly list one key idea mentioned in the introduction or first paragraph.

3. Write five questions you asked yourself while surveying this chapter. Read the bold section headings in the chapter and turn them into questions. For example, one heading in this chapter is, "Myths about Reading." This heading might prompt you to ask: What are some myths about reading? Do I believe in some of these myths?

4. List three topics that interest you.

5. Briefly write one key idea from the last paragraph or chapter summary.

6. How long did it take you to do this exercise? Write your time here. _____

7. What did you think of this exercise on surveying and questioning a chapter? _____

LEARNING OBJECTIVES

Read to answer these key questions:

- Why is it important to take notes?

- What are some good listening techniques?

- What are some tips for taking good lecture notes?

- What are some note taking systems?

- What is the best way to review my notes for the test?

- What is power writing?

- How can I make a good speech?

© PhotoCreate, 2008. Under license from Shutterstock, Inc.

Taking Notes, Writing, and Speaking

Knowing how to listen and take good notes can make your college life easier and may help you in your future career as well. Professionals in many occupations take notes as a way of recording key ideas for later use. Whether you become a journalist, attorney, architect, engineer, or other professional, listening and taking good notes can help you to get ahead in your career.

Good writing and speaking skills are important to your success in college and in your career. In college you will be asked to write term papers and complete other writing assignments. The writing skills you learn in college will be used later in jobs involving high responsibility and good pay. On the job, you will write reports, memos, and proposals. You will probably take a speech class and give oral reports in other classes. On the job, you will present your ideas orally to your colleagues and business associates.

> ## JOURNAL ENTRY #1
> What is your evaluation of your note taking skills?

Why Take Notes?

The most important reason for taking notes is to remember important material for the test or for future use in your career. If you just attend class without taking notes, you will forget most of the material by the next day.

How does taking notes enhance memory?

- In college, the lecture is a way of supplementing the written material in the text-book. Without good notes, an important part of the course is missing. Note taking provides material to rehearse or recite, so that it can be stored in long-term memory.
- By taking notes and imposing your own organization on them, the notes become more personally meaningful. If they are meaningful, they are easier to remember.
- Taking notes helps you to make new connections. New material is remembered by connecting it to what you already know.
- For kinesthetic and tactile learners, the physical act of writing the material is help-ful in learning and remembering it.
- For visual learners, notes provide a visual map of the material to be learned.
- For auditory learners, taking notes is a way to listen carefully and record informa-tion to be stored in the memory.
- Note taking helps students to concentrate, maintain focus, and stay awake.
- Attending the lectures and taking notes helps you to understand what the profes-sor thinks is important and to know what to study for the exam.

The College Lecture

You will experience many different types of lectures while in college. At larger univer-sities many of the beginning-level courses are taught in large lecture halls with 300 people or more. More advanced courses tend to have fewer students. In large lecture situations, it is not always possible or appropriate to ask questions. Under these cir-cumstances, the large lecture is often supplemented by smaller discussion sessions where you can ask questions and review the lecture material. Although attendance may not be checked, it is important to attend both the lectures and the discussion session.

A formal college lecture is divided into four parts. Understanding these parts will help you to be a good listener and take good notes.

1. Introduction.

The professor uses the introduction to set the stage and to introduce the topic of the lecture. Often an overview or outline of the lecture is presented. Use the introduction as a way to begin thinking about the organization of your notes and the key ideas you will need to write down.

2. Thesis.

The thesis is the key idea in the lecture. In a one-hour lecture, there is usually one thesis statement. Listen carefully for the thesis statement and write it down in your notes. Review the thesis statement and related ideas for the exam.

3. Body.

The body of the lecture usually consists of five or six main ideas with discussion and clarification of each idea. As a note taker, your job is to identify the main ideas, write them in your notes and put in enough of the explanation or examples to understand the key ideas.

4. Conclusion.

In the conclusion, the professor summarizes the key points of the lecture and sometimes asks for questions. Use the conclusion as an opportunity to check your understanding of the lecture and to ask questions to clarify the key points.

How to Be a Good Listener

Effective note taking begins with good listening. What is good listening? Sometimes students confuse listening with hearing. Hearing is done with the ears. Listening is a more active process done with the ears and the brain engaged. Good listening requires attention and concentration. Practice these ideas for good listening:

- **Be physically ready.** It is difficult to listen to a lecture if you are tired, hungry, or ill. Get enough sleep so that you can stay awake. Eat a balanced diet without too much caffeine or sugar. Take care of your health and participate in an exercise program so that you feel your best.

- **Prepare a mental framework.** Look at the course syllabus to become familiar with the topic of the lecture. Use your textbook to read, or at least survey, the material to be covered in the lecture. If you are familiar with the key concepts from the textbook, you will be able to understand the lecture and know what to write down in your notes. If the material is in your book, there is no need to write it down in your notes.

  The more complex the topic, the more important it is for you to read the text first. If you go to the lecture and have no idea what is being discussed, you may be overwhelmed and find it difficult to take notes on material that is totally new to you. Remember that it is easier to remember material if you can connect it to material you already know.

- **Find a good place to sit.** Arrive early to get a good seat. The best seats in the classroom are in the front and center of the room. If you were buying concert tickets, these would be the best and most expensive seats. Find a seat that will help you to hear and focus on the speaker. You may need to find a seat away from your friends to avoid distractions.

- **Have a positive mental attitude.** Convince yourself that the speaker has something important to say and be open to new ideas. This may require you to focus on your goals and to look past some distractions. Maybe the lecturer doesn't have the best speaking voice or you don't like his or her appearance. Focus on what you can learn from the professor rather than outward appearances.

- **Listen actively to identify the main points.** As you are listening to the lecture, ask yourself, "What is the main idea?" In your own words, write the main points down in your notes. Do not try to write down everything the professor says. This will be impossible and unnecessary. Imagine that your mind is a filter and you are actively sorting through the material to find the key ideas and write them down in your notes. Try to identify the key points that will be on the test and write them in your notes.

- **Stay awake and engaged in learning.** The best way to stay awake and focused is to listen actively and take notes. Have a mental debate with the professor. Listen for the main points and the logical connection between ideas. The physical act of writing the notes will help to keep you awake.

Tips for Good Note Taking

Here are some suggestions for taking good notes:

1. Attend all of the lectures. Because many professors do not take attendance, students are often tempted to miss class. If you do not attend the lectures, however, you will not know what the professor thinks is important and what to study for the test. There will be important points covered in the lectures that are not in the book.
2. Have the proper materials. A three-ring notebook and notebook paper are recommended. Organize notes chronologically and include any handouts given in class. You can have a small notebook for each class or a single large notebook with dividers for each class. Just take the notebook paper to class and later file it in your notebook at home.
3. Begin your notes by writing the date of the lecture, so you can keep your notes in order.
4. Write notes on the front side only of each piece of paper. This will allow you to spread the pages out and see the big picture or pattern in the lectures when you are reviewing.
5. Write notes neatly and legibly so you can read and review them easily.
6. Do not waste time recopying or typing your notes. Your time would be better spent reviewing your notes.
7. As a general rule, do not rely on a tape recorder for taking notes. With a tape recorder, you will have to listen to the lecture again on tape. For a semester course this would be about forty-five hours of tape! It is much faster to review carefully written notes.
8. Copy down everything written on the board and the main points from transparencies or visual presentations. If it is important enough for the professor to write on the board, it is important enough to be on the test.
9. Use key words and phrases in your notes. Leave out unimportant words and don't worry about grammar.

10. Use abbreviations as long as you can read them. Entire sentences or paragraphs are not necessary and you may not have time to write them.
11. Don't loan your whole notebook to someone else because you may not get it back. If you want to share your notes, make copies.
12. If the professor talks too fast, listen carefully for the key ideas and write them down. Leave spaces in your notes to fill in later. You may be able to find the information in the text or get the information from another student.

QUIZ
Listening and Note Taking

Test what you have learned by selecting the correct answer to the following questions.

1. When taking notes on a college lecture, it is most important to

   a. write down everything you hear.
   b. write down the main ideas and enough explanation to understand them.
   c. write down names, dates, places, and numbers.

2. To be a good listener,

   a. read or skim over the material before you attend the lecture.
   b. attend the lecture first and then read the text.
   c. remember that listening is more important than note taking.

3. To stay awake during the lecture,

   a. drink lots of coffee.
   b. sit near your friends so you can make some comments on the lecture.
   c. listen actively by taking notes.

4. Since attendance is not always checked in college classes,

   a. it is not necessary to attend class if you read the textbook.
   b. it is acceptable to miss lectures as long as you show up for the exams.
   c. it is up to you to attend every class.

5. When taking notes, be sure to

   a. use complete sentences and good grammar.
   b. write down whatever is written on the board or the visual presentations.
   c. write the notes quickly without worrying about neatness.

How did you do on the quiz? Check your answers: 1. b, 2. a, 3. c, 4. c, 5. b

Note-Taking Systems

- Cornell format
- Outline method
- Mind map

Note-Taking Systems

There are several systems for taking notes. How you take notes will depend on your learning style and the lecturer's speaking style. Experiment with these systems and use what works best for you.

The Cornell Format

The Cornell format is an efficient method of taking notes and reviewing them. It appeals to students who are logical, orderly and organized and lectures that fit into this pattern. The Cornell format is especially helpful for thinking about key points as you review your notes.

The Cornell Format

Date	Title of Lecture
Recall column	Key idea Minor point or explanation More details
Key words	Key idea Details Details Details
	Key idea Details Details Details

Step 1: Prepare. To use the Cornell format, you will need a three-ring notebook with loose-leaf paper. Draw or fold a vertical line 2 ½ inches from the left side of the paper. This is the recall column that can be used to write key ideas when reviewing. Use the remaining section of the paper for your notes. Write the date and title of the lecture at the top of the page.

Step 2: Take notes. Use the large area to the right of the recall column to take notes. Listen for key ideas and write them just to the right of the recall column line as in the diagram above. Indent your notes for minor points and illustrative details. Then skip a space and write the next key idea. Don't worry about using numbers or letters as in an outline format. Just use the indentations and spacing to highlight and separate key ideas. Use short phrases, key words, and abbreviations. Complete sentences are not necessary, but write legibly so you can read your notes later.

Step 3: Use the recall column for review. Read over your notes and write down key words or ideas from the lecture in the recall column. Ask yourself, "What is this about?" Cover up the notes on the right-hand side and recite the key ideas of the lecture. Another variation is to write questions in the margin. Find the key ideas and then write possible exam questions in the recall column. Cover your notes and see if you can answer the questions.

The Outline Method

If the lecture is well organized, some students just take notes in outline format. Sometimes lecturers will show their outline as they speak.

- Use Roman numerals to label main topics. Then use capital letters for main ideas and Arabic numerals for related details or examples.
- You can use a free-form outline using just indentation to separate main ideas and supporting details.
- Leave spaces to fill in material later.
- Use a highlighter to review your notes as soon as possible after the lecture.

The Mind Map

A mind map shows the relationship between ideas in a visual way. It is much easier to remember items that are organized and linked together in a personally meaningful way. As a result, recall and review is quicker and more effective. Mind maps have appeal to visual learners and those who do not want to be limited by a set structure as in the outline formats. They can also be used for lectures that are not highly structured. Here are some suggestions for using the mind-mapping technique:

- Turn your paper sideways to give you more space. Use standard-size notebook paper or consider larger sheets if possible.
- Write the main idea in the center of the page and circle it.
- Arrange ideas so that more important ideas are closer to the center and less important ideas are farther out.
- Show the relationship of the minor points to the main ideas using lines, circles, boxes, charts, and other visual devices. Here is where you can use your creativity and imagination to make a visual picture of the key ideas in the lecture.
- Use symbols and drawings.
- Use different colors to separate main ideas.
- When the lecturer moves to another main idea, start a new mind map.
- When you are done with the lecture, quickly review your mind maps. Add any written material that will be helpful in understanding the map later.
- A mind map can also be used as
  - a review tool for remembering and relating the key ideas in the textbook.
  - a preparation tool for essay exams in which remembering main ideas and relationships are important.
  - the first step in organizing ideas for a term paper.

The Outline Method

Date	Title of Lecture

I. Main Idea
    A. Important Idea
        1. Detail or example
        2. Detail
        3. Detail
    B. Important Idea
        1. Detail
        2. Detail
(Leave space here.)

II. Main Idea
    A. Important Idea
        1. Detail or example
        2. Detail
        3. Detail

Mind Map

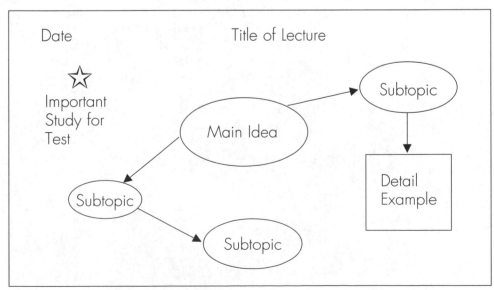

Improving Note-Taking Efficiency

Improve note-taking efficiency by listening for key words that signal the main ideas and supporting details. Learn to write faster by using telegraphic sentences, abbreviations, and symbols.

Signal Words

Signal words are clues to understanding the structure and content of a lecture. Recognizing signal words can help you identify key ideas and organize them in your notes. The table on the following page lists some common signal words and their meaning.

Telegraphic Sentences

Telegraphic sentences are short, abbreviated sentences used in note taking. They are very similar to the text messages sent on a cell phone. There are four rules for telegraphic sentences:

1. Write key words only.
2. Omit unnecessary words (*a, an, the*).
3. Ignore rules of grammar.
4. Use abbreviations and symbols.

Here is an example of a small part of a lecture followed by a student's telegraphic notes:

Heavy drinking of alcoholic beverages causes students to miss class and to fall behind in schoolwork. College students who are considered binge drinkers are at risk for many alcohol-related problems. Binge drinking is simply drinking too much alcohol at one time. Binge drinking is defined by researchers as men who drink five or more drinks in a row or women who drink four or more drinks in a row. Researchers estimate that two out of five college students (40 percent) are binge drinkers.

> Binge drinking—too much alcohol at one time
> Men = 5 in row
> Women = 4
>
> 2 out of 5 (40%) college students binge

Signal Words

Type	Examples	Meaning
Main idea words	And most important A major development The basic concept is Remember that The main idea is We will focus on The key is	Introduce the key points that need to be written in your notes.
Example words	To illustrate For example For instance	Clarify and illustrate the main ideas in the lecture. Write these examples in your notes after the main idea. If multiple examples are given, write down the ones you have time for or the ones that you understand the best.
Addition words	In addition Also Furthermore	Add more important information. Write these points down in your notes.
Enumeration words	The five steps First, second, third Next	Signal a list. Write down the list in your notes and number the items.
Time words	Before, after Formerly Subsequently Prior Meanwhile	Signal the order of events. Write down the events in the correct order in your notes.
Cause and effect words	Therefore As a result If . . ., then	Signal important concepts that might be on the exam. When you hear these words, label them "cause" and "effect" in your notes and review these ideas for the exam.
Definition words	In other words It simply means That is In essence	Provide the meanings of words or simplify complex ideas. Write these definitions or clarifications in your notes.
Swivel words	However Nevertheless Yes, but Still	Provide exceptions, qualifications, or further clarification. Write down qualifying comments in your notes.
Compare and contrast words	Similarly Likewise In contrast	Present similarities or differences. Write these similarities and differences in your notes and label them.
Summary words	In conclusion To sum up In a nutshell	Restate the important ideas of the lecture. Write the summaries in your notes.
Test words	This is important. Remember this. You'll see this again. You might want to study this for the test.	Provide a clue that the material will be on the test. Write these down in your notes and mark them in a way that stands out. Put a star or asterisk next to these items or highlight them. Each professor has his or her own test clue words.

Abbreviations

If you have time, write out words in their entirety for ease of reading. If you are short on time, use any abbreviation as long as you can read it. Here are some ideas:

1. Use the first syllable of the word.

democracy	dem
education	ed
politics	pol
different	diff
moderate	mod
characteristic	char
develop	dev

2. Use just enough of the word so that you can recognize it.

republican	repub
prescription	prescrip
introduction	intro
intelligence	intell
association	assoc

3. Abbreviate or write out the word the first time, then use an acronym. For example, for the United States Department of Agriculture, abbreviate it as "US Dept of Ag" and then write it as USDA in subsequent references. Other examples:

short-term memory	STM
as soon as possible	ASAP

4. Omit vowels.

background	bkgrnd
problem	prblm
government	gvt

5. Use g in place of ing.

checking	ckg
decreasing	decrg

Symbols

Use common symbols or invent your own to speed up the note-taking process.

Common Symbols Used in Note Taking

Symbol	Meaning	Symbol	Meaning
&	and	B4	before
w	with	BC	because
wo	without	esp	especially
wi	within	diff	difference
<	less than	min	minimum
>	more than	gov	government
@	at	ex	example
/	per	↑	increasing

2	to, two, too	↓	decreasing
∴	therefore	=	equal
vs	versus, against	≠	not equal

JOURNAL ENTRY #3

How can you improve your note-taking efficiency?

How to Review Your Notes

Immediate review. Review your notes as soon as possible after the lecture. The most effective review is done immediately or at least within twenty minutes. If you wait until the next day to review, you may already have forgotten much of the information. During the immediate review, fill in any missing or incomplete information. Say the important points to yourself. This begins the process of rehearsal for storing the information in long-term memory.

There are various methods for review depending on your note-taking system:

- For the Cornell format, use the recall column to write in key words or questions. Cover your notes and see if you can recall the main ideas. Place a checkmark by the items you have mastered. Don't worry about mastering all the key points from the beginning. With each review, it will be easier to remember the information.
- For the outline format, use a highlighter to mark the key ideas as you repeat them silently to yourself.
- For mind maps, look over the information and think about the key ideas and their relationships. Fill in additional information or clarification. Highlight important points or relationships with color.

Intermediate review. Set up some time each week for short reviews of your notes and the key points in your textbook from previous weeks. Quickly look over the notes and recite the key points in your mind. These intermediate reviews will help you to master the material and avoid test anxiety.

Test review. Complete a major review as part of your test preparation strategy. As you look through your notes, turn the key ideas into possible test questions and answer them.

Final review. The final review occurs after you have received the results of your test. Ask yourself these questions:

- What percentage of the test questions came from the lecture notes?
- Were you prepared for the exam? Is so, congratulate yourself on a job well done. If not, how can you improve next time?
- Were your notes adequate? If not, what needs to be added or changed?

QUIZ
Note-Taking Efficiency

Test what you have learned by selecting the correct answer to the following questions.

1. Recognizing signal words will help you to
   a. know when the lecture is about to end.
   b. identify the key ideas and organize them in your notes.
   c. know when to pay attention.

2. When taking notes, be sure to
   a. write your notes in complete sentences.
   b. use correct grammar.
   c. use telegraphic sentences.

3. The best time to review your notes is
   a. as soon as possible after the lecture.
   b. within 24 hours.
   c. within one week.

4. Using abbreviations in note taking is
   a. not a good idea.
   b. a good idea as long as you can read them.
   c. makes review difficult.

5. To avoid test anxiety,
   a. review your notes just before the test.
   b. review your notes the week before the test.
   c. review your notes periodically throughout the semester.

How did you do on the quiz? Check your answers: 1. b, 2. c, 3. a, 4. b, 5. c

---

JOURNAL ENTRY #4

What is your plan for reviewing your notes?

Power Writing

- Prepare
- Organize
- Write
- Edit
- Revise

Power Writing

Effective writing will help you in school, on the job, and in your personal life. Good writing will help you to create quality term papers. The writing skills that you learn in college will be used later in jobs involving high responsibility and good pay. You can become an excellent writer by learning about the steps in POWER writing: prepare, organize, write, edit and revise.

Prepare

Plan your time. The first step in writing is to plan your time so that the project can be completed by the due date. Picture this scene: It is the day that the term paper is due. A few students proudly hand in their term papers and are ready to celebrate their accomplishments. Many of the students in the class are absent, and some will never return to the class. Some of the students look as though they haven't slept the night

© Lynn Johnston Productions, Inc./Distributed by United Feature Syndicate, Inc.

before. They look stressed and weary. At the front of the class is a line of students wanting to talk with the instructor. The instructor has heard it all before:

- I had my paper all completed and my printer jammed.
- My hard drive crashed and I lost my paper.
- I was driving to school and my paper flew off my motorcycle.
- I had the flu.
- My children were sick.
- I had to take my dog to the vet.
- My dog ate my paper.
- My car broke down and I could not get to the library.
- My grandmother died and I had to go to the funeral.
- My roommate accidentally took my backpack to school.
- I spilled salad dressing on my paper, so I put it in the microwave to dry it out and the writing disappeared!

To avoid being in this uncomfortable and stressful situation, plan ahead. Plan to complete your project at least one week ahead of time so that you can deal with life's emergencies. Life does not always go as planned. You or your children may get sick, or your dog may do strange things to your homework. Your computer may malfunction, leading you to believe it senses stress and malfunctions just to frustrate you even more.

To avoid stress and do your best work, start with the date that the project is due and then think about the steps needed to finish. Write these dates on your calendar or on your list of things to do. Consider all these components:

Project due date: _____

To do	By when?
1. Brainstorm ideas.	_____
2. Choose a topic.	_____
3. Gather information.	_____
4. Write a thesis statement.	_____
5. Write an outline.	_____
6. Write the introduction.	_____
7. Write the first draft.	_____

Prepare

- Plan your time
- Find space and time
- Choose general topic
- Gather information
- Write thesis statement

8. Prepare the bibliography.   _____
9. Edit.   _____
10. Revise.   _____
11. Print and assemble.   _____

Find a space and time. Find a space where you can work. Gather the materials that you will need to write. Generally writing is best done in longer blocks of time. Determine when you will work on your paper and write the time on your schedule. Start right away to avoid panic later.

Choose a general topic. This task will be easy if your topic is already clearly defined by your instructor or your boss at work. Make sure that you have a clear idea of what is required, such as length, format, purpose, and method of citing references and topic. Many times the choice of a topic is left to you. Begin by doing some brainstorming. Think about topics that interest you. Write them down. You may want to focus your attention on brainstorming ideas for five or ten minutes, and then put the project aside and come back to it later. Once you have started the process of thinking about the ideas, your mind will continue to work and you may have some creative inspiration. If inspiration does not come, repeat the brainstorming process.

Gather information. Go to your college library and use the Internet to gather your information. As you begin, you can see what is available, what is interesting to you, and what the current thinking is on your topic. Note the major topics of interest that might be useful to you. Once you have found some interesting material, you will feel motivated to continue your project. As you find information relevant to your topic, make sure to write down the source of your information to use in the bibliography. The bibliography contains information about where you found your material. Write down the author, title of the publication, publisher, place and date of publication. For Internet resources, list the address of the website and the date accessed.

Write the thesis statement. The thesis statement is the key idea in your paper. It provides a direction for you to follow. It is the first step in organizing your work. To write a thesis statement, review the material you have gathered and then ask these questions:

- What is the most important idea?
- What question would I like to ask about it?
- What is my answer?

For example, if I decide to write a paper for my health class on the harmful effects of smoking, I would look at current references on the topic. I might become interested in how the tobacco companies misled the public on the dangers of smoking. I would think about my thesis statement and answer the questions stated above.

- **What is the most important idea?** Smoking is harmful to your health.

- **What question would I like to ask about it?** Did the tobacco companies mislead the public about the health hazards of smoking?

- **What is my answer?** The tobacco companies misled the public about the hazards of smoking in order to protect their business interests.

- **My thesis statement:** Tobacco companies knew that smoking was hazardous to health, but to protect their business interests they deliberately misled the public.

The thesis statement helps to narrow the topic and provide direction for the paper. I can now focus on reference material related to my topic: research on health effects of smoking, congressional testimony relating to regulation of the tobacco industry, and how advertising influences people to smoke.

Organize

At this point you have many ideas about what to include in your paper, and you have a central focus, your thesis statement. Start to organize your paper by listing the topics that are related to your thesis statement. Here is a list of topics related to my thesis statement about smoking:

Organize
- List related topics
- Arrange in logical order
- Have an organizational structure

- Tobacco companies' awareness that nicotine is addictive
- Minimizing health hazards in tobacco advertisements
- How advertisements encourage people to smoke
- Money earned by the tobacco industry
- Health problems caused by smoking
- Statistics on numbers of people who have health problems or die from smoking
- Regulation of the tobacco industry
- Advertisements aimed at children

Think about the topics and arrange them in logical order. Use an outline, a mind map, a flowchart, or a drawing to think about how you will organize the important topics. Keep in mind that you will need an introduction, a body, and a conclusion. Having an organizational structure will make it easier for you to write because you will not need to wonder what comes next.

Write

Write the First Sentence
Begin with the main idea.

Write the Introduction
This is the road map for the rest of the paper. The introduction includes your thesis statement and establishes the foundation of the paper. It introduces topics that will be discussed in the body of the paper. The introduction should include some interesting points that provide a "hook" to motivate the audience to read your paper. For example, for a paper on the hazards of smoking, you might begin with statistics on how many people suffer from smoking-related illnesses and premature death. Note the large profits earned by the tobacco industry. Then introduce other topics: deception, advertisements, and regulation. The introduction provides a guide or outline of what will follow in the paper.

Write
- First sentence
- Introduction
- Body
- Conclusion
- References

Write the Body of the Paper
The body of the paper is divided into paragraphs that discuss the topics that you have introduced. As you write each paragraph, include the main idea and then explain it and give examples. Here are some good tips for writing:

1. Good writing reflects clear thinking. Think about what you want to say and write about it so the reader can understand your point of view.
2. Use clear and concise language. Avoid using too many words or scholarly sounding words that might get in the way of understanding.

3. Don't assume that the audience knows what you are writing about. Provide complete information.
4. Provide examples, stories, and quotes to support your main points. Include your own ideas and experiences.
5. Beware of plagiarism. Plagiarism is copying the work of others without giving them credit. It is illegal and can cause you to receive a failing grade on your project or even get you into legal trouble. You can avoid plagiarism by using quotation marks around an author's words and providing a reference indicating where you found the material. You can also avoid plagiarism by writing about others' ideas in your own words.

Write the Conclusion

The conclusion summarizes the topics in the paper and presents your point of view. It makes reference to the introduction and answers the question posed in your thesis statement. It often makes the reader think about the significance of your point and the implications for the future. Make your conclusion interesting and powerful.

Include References

No college paper is complete without references. References may be given in footnotes, endnotes, a list of works cited, or a bibliography. You can use your computer to insert these references. There are various styles for citing references depending on your subject area. There are computer programs that put your information into the correct style. Ask your instructor which style to use for your particular class or project. Three frequently used styles for citing references are APA, Chicago, and MLA.

1. The American Psychological Association (APA) style is used in psychology and other behavioral sciences. Consult the *Publication Manual of the American Psychological Association*, 5th ed. (Washington, DC: American Psychological Association, 2001). You can find this source online at www.apastyle.org
2. Chicago style is used by many professional writers in a variety of fields. Consult the *Chicago Manual of Style*, 15th ed. (Chicago: University of Chicago Press, 2003). You can find this source online at http://www.chicagomanualofstyle.org/home.html
3. The Modern Language Association (MLA) style is used in English, classical languages, and the humanities. Consult the *MLA Handbook for Writers of Research Papers*, 6th ed. (New York: Modern Language Association, 2003). This source is available online at www.mla.org/style

Each of these styles uses a different format for listing sources but all include the same information. Make sure you write down this information as you collect your reference material. If you forget this step, it is very time-consuming and difficult to find later.

- Author's name
- Title of the book or article
- Publisher
- City where book was published
- Publication date
- Page number (and volume and number if available)

Here are some examples of citations in the APA style:

- Book
  Include author, title, city of publication, publisher, date of publication.
  Fralick, M. *College and Career Success*, 4th ed., Dubuque, IA; Kendall/Hunt 2008

- Journal article
  Include author, title, name of journal, date, volume and number, pages.
  Fralick, M. "College Success: A Study of Positive and Negative Attrition." *Community College Review,* Spring 1993, *20* (5), 29–36.

- Website
  Include author, date listed or updated, document title or name of website, the URL or website address and the date it was accessed. Include as many of the above items as possible. Methods of citing information in the Internet are still evolving.
  Fralick, M. (2009, January). "Note Taking." Retrieved April, 2009 from College Success 1 at http://collegesuccess1.com

Save Your Work

As soon as you have written the first paragraph, save it on your computer. Save your work in two places. Save it on your hard drive and on a flash drive or external hard drive. At the end of each section, save your work again to both of these places. When you are finished, print your work and save a paper copy. In this way, if your hard drive crashes, you will still have your work at another location. If your file becomes corrupted, you will still have the paper copy. Following these procedures can save you a lot of headaches. Any writer can tell you stories of lost work because of computer problems, lightning storms, power outages, and other unpredictable events.

Put It Away for a While

The last step in writing the first draft is easy. Put it away for a while and come back to it later. In this way, you can relax and gain some perspective on your work. You will be able to take a more objective look at your work to begin the process of editing and revising.

Writer's Block

Many people who are anxious about writing experience "writer's block." You have writer's block if you find yourself staring at that blank piece of paper or computer screen not knowing how to begin or what to write. Here are some tips for avoiding writer's block.

Tips to Overcome Writer's Block

1. Write freely
2. Use brainstorming
3. Realize it's a first draft
4. Read reference materials
5. Break up assignment
6. Find a good place to write
7. Beware of procrastination

- **Write freely.** Just write anything about your topic that comes to mind. Don't worry about organization or perfection at this point. Don't censure your ideas. You can always go back to organize and edit later. Free-writing helps you to overcome one of the main causes of writer's block: you think it has to be perfect from the beginning. This expectation of perfection causes anxiety. You freeze up and become unable to write. Perhaps you have past memories of writing where the teacher made many corrections on your paper. Maybe you lack confidence in your writing skills. The only way you will become a better writer is to keep writing and perfecting your writing skills, so to start the writing process, just write what comes to mind. Don't worry how great it is. You can fix it later. Just begin.

- **Use brainstorming if you get stuck.** For five minutes, focus your attention on the topic and write whatever comes to mind. You don't even need to write full sentences; just jot down ideas. If you are really stuck, try working on a different topic or take a break and come back to it later.

- **Realize that it is only the first draft.** It is not the finished product and it does not have to be perfect.

- **Read through your reference materials.** The ideas you find can get your mind working. Also, reading can make you a better writer.

- **Break the assignment up into small parts.** If you find writing difficult, write for five minutes at a time. Do this consistently and you can get used to writing and can complete your paper.

- **Find a good place for writing.** If you are an introvert, look for a quiet place for concentration. If you are an extrovert, go to a restaurant or coffee shop and start your writing.

- **Beware of procrastination.** The more you put off writing, the more anxious you will become and the more difficult the task will be. Make a schedule and stick to it.

Edit and Revise

The editing and revising stage allows you to take a critical look at what you have written. It takes some courage to do this step. Once people see their ideas in writing, they become attached to them. With careful editing and revising, you can turn in your best work and be proud of your accomplishments. Here are some tips for editing and revising:

1.   Read your paper as if you were the audience.
Pretend that you are the instructor or another person reading your paper. Does every sentence make sense? Did you say what you meant to say? Read what you have written, and the result will be a more effective paper.

2. Read paragraph by paragraph.

Does each paragraph have a main idea and supporting details? Do the paragraphs fit logically together? Use the cut-and-paste feature on your computer to move sentences and paragraphs around if needed.

3. Check your grammar and spelling.

Use the spell check and grammar check on your computer. These tools are helpful, but they are not thorough enough. The spell check will pick up only misspelled words. It will skip words that are spelled correctly but not the intended word, for example, if you use "of" instead of "on" or "their" instead of "there." To find such errors, you need to read your paper after doing a spell check.

4. Check for language that is biased in terms of gender, disability, or ethnic group.

Use words that are gender neutral. If a book or paper uses only the pronoun "he" or "she," half of the population is left out. You can often avoid sexist language by using the plural form of nouns:

(singular)   The successful student knows *his* values and sets goals for the future.

(plural)   Successful students know *their* values and set goals for the future.

After all, we are trying to make the world a better place, with opportunity for all. Here are some examples of biased language and better alternatives.

Biased Language	Better Alternatives
policeman	police officer
chairman	chair
fireman	fire fighter
draftsman	drafter
mankind	humanity
manmade	handcrafted
housewife	homemaker
crippled and disabled persons	persons with disabilities

5. Have someone else read your paper.

Ask your reader to check for clarity and meaning. After you have read your paper many times, you do not really see it anymore. If you need assistance in writing, colleges offer tutoring or writing labs where you can get help with editing and revising.

6. Review your introduction and conclusion.

They should be clear, interesting and concise. The introduction and conclusion are the most powerful parts of your paper.

7. Prepare the final copy.

Check your instructor's instructions on the format required. If there are no instructions, use the following format:

- Use double-spacing.
- Use ten- or twelve-point font.
- Use one-inch margins on all sides.
- Use a three-inch top margin on the first page.
- Single-space footnotes and endnotes.
- Number your pages.

Tips for Editing and Revising

1. Read your paper objectively
2. Read paragraph by paragraph
3. Check grammar and spelling
4. Check for biased language
5. Have someone else read your paper
6. Review the introduction and conclusion
7. Prepare final copy
8. Prepare title page

8.   Prepare the title page.
Center the title of your paper and place it one third of the page from the top. On the bottom third of the page, center your name, the professor's name, the name of the class, and the date.

Final Steps

Make sure you follow instructions about using a folder or cover for your paper. Generally professors dislike bulky folders or notebooks because they are difficult to carry. Imagine your professor trying to carry fifty notebooks to his or her office! Unless asked to do so, do not use plastic page protectors. Professors like to write comments on papers, and it is extremely difficult to write on papers with page protectors.

Turning your paper in on time is very important. Some professors do not accept late papers. Others subtract points if your paper is late. Put your paper in the car or someplace where you will have to see it before you go to class. **Then reward yourself for a job well done!**

> **JOURNAL ENTRY #5**
> What is your evaluation of your writing skills?

Effective Public Speaking

You may need to take a speech class in order to graduate from college, and many of your classes will require oral presentations. Being a good speaker can contribute to your success on the job as well. A study done at Stanford University showed that one of the top predictors of success in professional positions was the ability to be a good public speaker.[1] You will need to present information to your boss, your colleagues, and your customers or clients.

Learn to Relax

Whenever I tell students that they will need to take a speech class or make an oral presentation, I see a look of panic on many faces. Good preparation can help you to feel confident about your oral presentation. Professional speaker Lilly Walters believes that you can deal with 75 percent of your anxiety by being well prepared.[2] You can deal with the remaining 25 percent by using some relaxation techniques.

- If you are anxious, admit to yourself that you are anxious. If it is appropriate, as in a beginning speech class, you can even admit to the audience that you are anxious. Once you have admitted that you are anxious, visualize yourself confidently making the speech.
- You do not have to be perfect; it is okay to make mistakes. Making mistakes just shows you are human like the rest of us.
- If you are anxious before your speech, take three to five deep breaths. Breathe in slowly and hold your breath for five seconds, and then breathe out slowly. Focus your mind on your breathing rather than your speech.
- Use positive self-talk to help you to relax. Instead of saying to yourself, "I will look like a fool up there giving the speech," tell yourself, "I can do this" or "It will be okay."

- Once you start speaking, anxiety will generally decline.
- With experience, you will gain confidence in your speaking ability and will be able to relax more easily.

Preparing and Delivering Your Speech

Write the Beginning of the Speech

The beginning includes a statement of your objective and what your speech will be about. It should prepare the audience for what comes next. You can begin your speech with a personal experience, a quote, a news article, or a joke. Jokes can be effective, but they are risky. Try out your joke with your friends to make sure that it is funny. Do not tell jokes that put down other people or groups.

Write the Main Body of the Speech

The main body of the speech consists of four or five main points. Just as in your term paper, state your main points and then provide details, examples, or stories that illustrate them. As you present the main points of your speech, consider your audience. Your speech will be different depending on whether it is made to a group of high school students, your college classmates, or a group of professionals. You can add interest to your speech by using props, pictures, charts, overhead transparencies, music, or video clips. College students today are increasingly using PowerPoint software to make classroom presentations. If you are planning to enter a professional career, learning how to make PowerPoint presentations will be an asset.

Write the Conclusion

In your conclusion, summarize and review the key points of your speech. The conclusion is like the icing on a cake. It should be strong, persuasive, and interesting. Invest some time in your ending statement. It can be a call to action, a recommendation for the future, a quote, or a story.

Practice your Speech

Practice your speech until you feel comfortable with it. Prepare a memory system or notes to help you deliver your speech. You will want to make eye contact with your audience, which is difficult if you are trying to read your speech. A memory system useful for delivering speeches is the loci system. Visualize a house, for example: the entryway is the introduction, and each room represents a main point in the speech. Visualize walking into each room and what you will say in each room. Each room can have items that remind you of what you are going to say. At the conclusion, you say good-bye at the door. Another technique is to prepare brief notes or outlines on index cards or sheets of paper. When you are practicing your speech, time it to see how long it is. Keep your speech within the time allowed. Most people tend to speak longer than necessary.

Review the Setup

If you are using props, make sure that you have them ready. If you are using equipment, make sure it is available and in working condition. Make arrangements in advance for the equipment you need and, if possible, check to see that it is running properly right before your presentation.

Deliver the Speech

Wear clothes that make you feel comfortable, but not out of place. Remember to smile and make eye contact with members of the audience. Take a few deep breaths if you are nervous. You will probably be less nervous once you begin. If you make a mistake, keep your sense of humor. I recall the famous chef Julia Childs doing a live television production on how to cook a turkey. As she took the turkey out of the oven, it slipped and landed on the floor right in front of the television cameras. She calmly picked it up and said, "And remember that you are the only one that really knows what goes on in the kitchen." It is one of the shows that made her famous.

JOURNAL ENTRY #6

What is your evaluation of your public speaking skills?

QUIZ
Writing and Speaking

Test what you have learned by selecting the correct answer to the following questions.

1. To make sure to get your paper done on time,

    a. have someone remind you of the deadline.
    b. write the due date on your calendar and the date for completion of each step.
    c. write your paper just before the due date to increase motivation.

2. The thesis statement is the

    a. most important sentence in each paragraph.
    b. the key idea in the paper.
    c. the summary of the paper.

3. If you have writer's block, it is helpful to

    a. delay writing your paper until you feel relaxed.
    b. make sure that your writing is perfect from the beginning.
    c. begin with brainstorming or free writing.

4. No college paper is complete without

    a. the references.
    b. a professional looking cover.
    c. printing on quality paper.

5. You can deal with most of your anxiety about public speaking by

    a. striving for perfection.
    b. visualizing your anxiety.
    c. being well prepared.

How did you do on the quiz? Check your answers: 1. b, 2. b, 3. c, 4. a, 5. c

Keys to Success

Be Selective

Psychologist and philosopher William James said, "The essence of genius is knowing what to overlook."[3] This saying has a variety of meanings. In reading, note taking, marking a college textbook, and writing, it is important to be able to pick out the main points first and then identify the supporting details. Imagine you are trying to put together a jigsaw puzzle. You bought the puzzle at a garage sale and all the pieces are there, but the lid to the box with the picture of the puzzle is missing. It will be very difficult, if not impossible to put this puzzle together. Reading, note taking, marking, and writing are very much like putting a puzzle together. First you will need an understanding of the main ideas and then you can focus on the details.

How can you get the overall picture? When reading, you can get the overall picture by skimming the text. As you skim the text, you get a general outline of what the chapter contains and what you will learn. In note taking, actively listen for the main ideas and write them down in your notes. In marking your text, try to pick out about 20 percent of the most important material and underline or highlight it. In writing, think about what is most important, write your thesis statement, and then provide the supporting details. To select what is most important, be courageous, think, and analyze.

Does this mean that you should forget about the details? No, you will need to know some details too. The supporting details help you to understand and assess the value of the main idea. They help you

to understand the relationship between ideas. Being selective means getting the general idea first, and then the details will make sense to you and you will be able to remember them. The main ideas are like scaffolding or a net that holds the details in some kind of framework so you can remember them. If you focus on the details first, you will have no framework or point of reference for remembering them.

Experiment with the idea of being selective in your personal life. If your schedule is impossibly busy, be selective and choose to do the most important or most valuable activities. This takes some thinking and courage too. If your desk drawer is stuffed with odds and ends and you can never find what you are looking for, take everything out and only put back what you need. Recycle, give away, or throw away surplus items around the house. You can take steps toward being a genius by being selective and taking steps to simplify and organize your life and your work.

> ### JOURNAL ENTRY #7
> How can being selective help you achieve success in college?

JOURNAL ENTRIES

Taking Notes, Writing, and Speaking

Go to http://www.collegesuccess1.com/ for Word files of the Journal Entries

Success over the Internet

Visit the *College Success Website* at http://www.collegesuccess1.com/

The *College Success Website* is continually updated with new topics and links to the material presented in this chapter. Topics include:

- Note taking
- Mind maps
- Memory and note taking
- Telegraphic sentences
- Signal words

- Listening to lectures
- Grammar and style
- Quotes to use in speeches and papers
- The virtual public speaking assistant
- Researching, organizing, and delivering a speech
- Best speeches in history

Contact your instructor if you have any problems accessing the *College Success Website*.

Notes

1. T. Allesandra and P. Hunsaker, *Communicating at Work* (New York: Fireside, 1993), 169.
2. Lilly Walters, *Secrets of Successful Speakers: How You Can Motivate, Captivate, and Persuade* (New York: McGraw-Hill), 203.
3. Quoted in Rob Gilbert, ed., *Bits and Pieces,* August 12, 1999, 15.

Place a checkmark next to the note-taking skills you have now.

Note-Taking Checklist

Name _____ Date _____

_____ I attend every (or almost every) lecture in all my classes.

_____ I check the syllabus to find out what is being covered before I go to class.

_____ I read or at least skim through the reading assignment before attending the lecture.

_____ I attend lectures with a positive attitude about learning as much as possible.

_____ I am well rested so that I can focus on the lecture.

_____ I eat a light, nutritious meal before going to class.

_____ I sit in a location where I can see and hear easily.

_____ I have a three-ring binder, loose-leaf paper, and a pen for taking notes.

_____ I avoid external distractions (friends, sitting by the door).

_____ I am alert and able to concentrate on the lecture.

_____ I have a system for taking notes that works for me.

_____ I am able to determine the key ideas of the lecture and write them down in my notes.

_____ I can identify signal words that help to understand key points and organize my notes.

_____ I can write quickly using telegraphic sentences, abbreviations, and symbols.

_____ If I don't understand something in the lecture, I ask a question and get help.

_____ I write down everything written on the board or on visual materials used in the class.

_____ I review my notes immediately after class.

_____ I have intermediate review sessions to review previous notes.

_____ I use my notes to predict questions for the exam.

_____ I have clear and complete notes that help me to prepare adequately for exams.

Evaluate Your Note-Taking Skills

Name _____   Date _____

Use the note-taking checklist on the previous page to answer these questions.

1. Look at the items that you checkmarked. What are your strengths in note taking?

2. What are some areas that you need to improve?

3. Write at least three intention statements about improving your listening and note-taking skills.

216

A Case Study

Name _____   Date _____

John is a new college student who needs help with college success skills. Using what you have learned in this chapter, give John some advice on how to take notes in class. This exercise can be done individually or as a group exercise in class.

> John is a new college student who has just graduated from high school. He is not sure what he wants to do with his life, but his parents want him to go to college. He misses the first class in Psychology 101 because he thinks nothing important happens on the first day. On the second day of class, John walks into class and finds some friends from high school. He takes a seat near them and starts a lively conversation. He has no books, paper, or pencil.
>
> The lecture is on the biological foundations of behavior. The topic is new for John and he is unfamiliar with the terms and concepts used in the lecture. He notices that the professor is wearing a tie that he must have purchased in 1970 and has an irritating habit of scratching his head. In addition, he is boring and speaks in a dull and monotonous way. John finds it difficult to concentrate. He becomes sleepy and starts to doze off during the lecture. At the end of the lecture, John realizes that he is going to have problems with psychology. For the next class, John brings a tape recorder and records the class. Again he finds it difficult to stay awake during the lecture. He works late at night and has scheduled this class for 8:00 in the morning.

What are the five most important suggestions you could make to help John take notes and be successful in this class?

1.

2.

3.

4.

5.

Assess Your College Writing Skills

Name _____ Date _____

Directions: Read the following statements and rate how true they are for you at the present time. Use the following scale:

5   Definitely true
4   Mostly true
3   Somewhat true
2   Seldom true
1   Never true

_____ I am generally confident of my writing skills.

_____ I have a system for reminding myself of due dates for writing projects.

_____ I start writing projects early so that I am not stressed by finishing them at the last minute.

_____ I have the proper materials and a space to write comfortably.

_____ I know how to use the library and the Internet to gather information for a term paper.

_____ I can write a thesis statement for a term paper.

_____ I know how to organize a term paper.

_____ I know how to write the introduction, body, and conclusion of a paper.

_____ I can cite references in the appropriate style for my subject.

_____ I own reference books that have rules for APA, MLA, or Chicago style.

_____ I know what plagiarism is and know how to avoid it.

_____ I can deal with "writer's block" and get started on my writing project.

_____ I know how to edit and revise a paper.

_____ I know where I can get help with my writing.

_____ **Total**

60–70   You have excellent writing skills, but can always learn new ideas.

50–59   You have good writing skills, but there is room for improvement.

Below 50   You need to improve writing skills. The skills presented in this chapter will help. Consider taking a writing class early in your college studies.

Name _____   Date _____

List 10 suggestions from this chapter that could help you improve your writing skills.

1.

2.

3.

4.

5.

6.

7.

8.

9.

10.

CHAPTER

7

Test Taking

An important skill for survival in college is the ability to take tests. Passing tests is also important in careers that require licenses, certificates, or continuing education. Knowing how to prepare for and take tests with confidence will help you to accomplish your educational and career goals while maintaining your good mental health. Once you have learned some basic test-taking and relaxation techniques, you can turn your test anxiety into motivation and good test results.

Preparing for Tests

Attend Every Class

The most significant factor in poor performance in college is lack of attendance. Students who attend the lectures and complete their assignments have the best chance for success in college. Attending the lectures help you to be involved in learning and to know what to expect on the test. College professors know that students who miss three classes in a row are not likely to return, and some professors drop students after three absences. After three absences, students can fall behind in their schoolwork and become overwhelmed with makeup work.

Distribute the Practice

The key to successful test preparation is to begin early and do a little at a time. Test preparation begins the first day of class. During the first class, the professor gives an overview of the course content, requirements, tests, and grading. These items are usually described in writing in the class calendar and syllabus. It is very important to attend the first class to obtain this essential information. If you have to miss the first class, make sure to ask the professor for the syllabus and calendar and read it carefully.

Early test preparation helps you to take advantage of the powerful memory technique called distributed practice. In distributed practice, the material learned is broken up into small parts and reviewed frequently. Using this method can enable you to learn a large quantity of material without becoming overwhelmed. Here are some examples of using distributed practice:

- If you have a test on 50 Spanish vocabulary words in two weeks, don't wait until the day before the test to try to learn all 50 words. Waiting until the day before the test will result in difficulty remembering the words, test anxiety, and a dislike of studying Spanish. If you have 50 Spanish vocabulary words to learn in two weeks, learn five words each day and quickly review the words you learned previously. For example, on Monday you would learn five words and on Tuesday, you would learn five new words and review the ones learned on Monday. Give yourself the weekends off as a reward for planning ahead.
- If you have to read a history book with 400 pages, divide that number by the number of days in the semester or quarter. If there are 80 days in the semester, you will only have to read five pages per day or ten pages every other day. This is a much easier and more efficient way to master a long assignment.
- Don't wait until the last minute to study for a midterm or final exam. Keep up with the class each week. As you read each chapter, quickly review a previous chapter. In this way you can comfortably master the material. Just before a major test, you can review the material that you already know and feel confident about your ability to get a good grade on the test.

Schedule a Time and a Place for Studying

To take advantage of distributed practice, you will need to develop a study schedule. Write down your work time and school time and other scheduled activities. Identify times that can be used for studying each day. Get in the habit of using these available times for studying each week. As a general rule you need two hours of study time for each hour spent in a college classroom. If you cannot find enough time for studying, consider either reducing your course load or reducing work hours.

Use your study schedule or calendar to note the due dates of major projects and all test dates. Schedule enough time to complete projects and to finish major reviews for exams. Look at each due date and write in reminders to begin work or review well in advance of the due date. Give yourself plenty of time to meet the deadlines. It seems that around exam time, students are often ill or have problems that prevent them from being successful. Having some extra time scheduled will help you to cope with the many unexpected events that happen in everyday life.

Try to schedule your study sessions during your prime time, when you are awake and refreshed. For many people, one hour of study during the daylight hours is worth one and a half hours at night. Trying to study late at night may not be the best idea because it is difficult to motivate yourself to study when you are tired. Save the time at the end of the day for relaxing or doing routine chores.

Find a place to study. This can be an area of your home where you have a desk, computer, and all the necessary supplies for studying. As a general rule, do not study at the kitchen table, in front of the television, or in your bed. These places provide powerful cues for eating, watching television, or sleeping instead of studying. If you cannot find an appropriate place at home, use the college library as a place to study. The library is usually quiet and others are studying, so there are not too many distractions.

Test Review Tools

There are a variety of tools you can use to review for tests. Choose the tools according to your learning style and what works for you. Learning styles include visual, auditory, kinesthetic, and tactile modes of learning. **Visual learners** find it easy to make mental pictures of the material to be learned. **Auditory learners** prefer listening and reciting material out loud. **Kinesthetic learners** benefit from moving around or acting out material to be learned. **Tactile learners** benefit from physical activities such as writing down items to be remembered.

Review Tools

- Flash cards
- Summary sheets
- Mind maps
- Study groups

- **Flash cards.** Flash cards are an effective way to learn facts and details for objective tests such as true-false, multiple-choice, matching, and fill-in-the-blank. For example, if you have 100 vocabulary words to learn in biology, put the word on one side and the definition on the other side. First, look at each definition and see if you can recall the word. If you are a visual learner, look at the word and see if you can recall the definition. If you are an auditory learner, say the words and definitions. If you are a tactile or kinesthetic learner, carry the cards with you and briefly look at them as you are going about your daily activities. Make a game of studying by sorting the cards into stacks of information you know and information you still have to practice. Work with flash cards frequently and review them quickly. Don't worry about learning all items at once. Each day that you practice, you will recall the items more easily.

- **Summary sheets.** Summary sheets are used to record the key ideas from your lecture notes or textbook. It is important to be selective; write only the most important ideas on the summary sheets. At the end of the semester, you might have approximately ten pages of summary sheets from the text and ten pages from your notes. If you are a kinesthetic learner, writing down the items you wish to remember will help you learn them. If you are a visual learner, the summary sheet becomes a picture of the ideas you need to remember. If you are an auditory learner, recite aloud the important ideas on the summary sheets.

- **Mind maps.** A mind map is a visual picture of the items you wish to remember. Start in the center of the page with a key idea and then surround it with related topics. You can use drawings, lines, circles, or colors to link and group the ideas. A mind map will help you to learn material in an organized way that will be useful when writing essay exams.

- **Study groups.** A study group is helpful in motivating yourself to learn through discussions of the material with other people. For the study group, select three to seven people who are motivated to be successful in class and can coordinate schedules. Study groups are often used in math and science classes. Groups of students work problems together and help each other understand the material. The study group is also useful in studying for exams. Give each member a part of the material to be studied. Have each person predict test questions and quiz the study group. Teaching the material to the study group can be the best way to learn it.

Reviewing Effectively

Begin your review early and break it into small parts. Remember that repetition is one of the effective ways to store information in long-term memory. Here are some types of review that help you to store information in long-term memory:

- **Immediate review.** This type of review is fast and powerful and helps to minimize forgetting. It is the first step in storing information in long-term memory. Begin the process by turning each bold-faced heading in the text into a question. Read each section to answer the question you have asked. Read your college texts with a highlighter in hand so that you can mark the key ideas for review. Some students use a variety of colors to distinguish main ideas, supporting points, and key examples, for instance. When you are finished using the highlighter, quickly review the items you have marked. As you complete each section, quickly review the main points. When you finish the chapter, immediately review the key points in the entire chapter again. As soon as you finish taking your lecture notes, take a few minutes to review them. To be most effective, immediate review needs to occur as soon as possible or at least within the first twenty minutes of learning something.

- **Intermediate review.** After you have finished reading and reviewing a new chapter in your textbook, spend a few minutes reviewing an earlier one. This step will help you to master the material and to recall it easily for the midterm or final exam. Another way to do intermediate review is to set up time periodically in your study schedule for reviewing previous chapters and classroom notes. Doing intermediate reviews helps to access the materials you have stored in long-term memory.

- **Final review.** Before a major exam, organize your notes, materials, and assignments. Estimate how long it will take you to review the material. Break the material into manageable chunks. For an essay exam, use mind maps or summary sheets to write down the main points that you need to remember and recite these ideas frequently. For objective tests, use flash cards or lists to remember details and concepts that you expect to be on the test. Here is a sample seven-day plan for reviewing ten chapters for a final exam:

Day 1   Gather materials and study chapters 1 and 2 by writing key points on summary sheets or mind maps. Make flash cards of details you need to remember. Review and highlight lecture notes and handouts on these chapters.

Day 2   Review chapters 1 and 2. Study chapters 3 and 4 and the corresponding lecture notes.

Day 3   Review chapters 1 to 4. Study chapters 5 and 6 and the corresponding lecture notes.

Day 4   Review chapters 1 to 6. Study chapters 7 and 8 along with the corresponding lecture notes.

Day 5   Review chapters 1 to 8. Study chapters 9 and 10 along with corresponding lecture notes.

Day 6   Review notes, summary sheets, mind maps and flash cards for chapters 1 to 10. Relax and get a good night's sleep. You are well prepared.

Day 7   Do one last quick review of chapters 1 to 10 and walk into the test with the confidence that you will be successful on the exam.

Predicting Test Questions

There are many ways to predict the questions that will be on the test. Here are some ideas that might be helpful:

- Look for clues from the professor about what will be on the test. Many times the professors put information about the tests on the course syllabus. During lectures, they often give hints about what will be important to know. If a professor repeats something more than once, make note of it as a possible test question. Anything written on the board is likely to be on the test. Sometimes the professor will even say, "This will be on the test." Write these important points in your notes and review them.
- College textbooks are usually written in short sections with bold headings. Turn each bold-faced heading into a question and read to answer the question. Understand and review the main idea in each section. The test questions will generally address the main ideas in the text.
- Don't forget to study and review the handouts that the professor distributes to the class. If the professor has taken the time and effort to provide extra material, it is probably important and may be on the test.
- Form a study group and divide up the material to be reviewed. Have each member of the group write some test questions based on the important points in each main section of the text. When the study group meets, take turns asking likely test questions and providing the answers.
- When the professor announces the test, make sure to ask what material is to be covered on the test and what kind of test it is. If necessary, ask the professor which concepts are most important. Know what kind of test questions will be asked (essay, true-false, multiple-choice, matching, or short-answer). Some professors may provide sample exams or math problems.
- Use the first test to understand what is expected and how to study for future tests.

Preparing for an Open-Book Test

In college you may have some open-book tests. Open-book tests are often used in very technical subjects where specific material from the book is needed to answer questions. For example, in an engineering course, tables and formulas in the book may be needed to solve engineering problems on an exam. To study for an open-book test, focus on understanding the material and being able to locate key information for the exam. Consider making index tabs for your book so that you can locate needed information quickly. Be sure to bring your book, calculator, and other needed material to the exam.

Emergency Procedures

If it is a day or two before the test and you have not followed the above procedures, it is time for the college practice known as "cramming." There are two main problems that result from this practice. First you cannot take advantage of distributed practice, so it will be difficult to remember large amounts of material. Second it is not fun, and if done often will result in anxiety and a dislike of education. Because of these problems, some students who rely on cramming wrongly conclude that they are not capable of finishing their education.

If you must cram for a test, here are some emergency procedures that may be helpful in getting the best grade possible under difficult circumstances:

- When cramming *it is most important to be selective*. Try to identify the main points and recite and review them.
- Focus on reviewing and reciting the lecture notes. In this way, you will cover the main ideas the professor thinks are important.
- If you have not read the text, skim and search each chapter looking for the main points. Highlight and review these main points. Read the chapter summaries. In a math textbook, practice sample problems.
- Make summary sheets containing the main ideas from the notes and the text. Recite and review the summary sheets.
- For objective tests, focus on learning new terms and vocabulary related to the subject. These terms are likely to be on the test. Flash cards are helpful.
- For essay tests, develop an outline of major topics and review the outline so you can write an essay.
- Get enough rest. Staying up all night to review for the test can result in confusion, reduced mental ability, and test anxiety.
- Hope for the best.
- Plan ahead next time so that you can get a better grade.

If you have very little time to review for a test, you will probably experience information overload. One strategy for dealing with this problem is based on the work of George Miller of Harvard University. He found that the optimum chunks of information that we can remember is seven plus or minus two (or five to nine chunks of information).[1] This is also known as the Magical Number Seven Theory. For this last-minute review technique, start with five sheets of paper. Next, identify five key concepts that are likely to be on the test. Write one concept on the top of each sheet of paper. Then check your notes and text to write an explanation, definition, or answer for each of these topics. If you have more time, find two to four more concepts and research them, writing the information on additional sheets. You should have no more than nine sheets of paper. Arrange the sheets in order of importance. Review and recite the key ideas on these sheets. Get a regular night's sleep before the test and do some relaxation exercises right before the test.

Ideas That Don't Work

Some students do poorly on tests for the following reasons.

- Attending a party or social event the evening before a major test rather than doing the final review will adversely affect your test score. Study in advance and reward yourself with the party after the test.
- Skipping the major review before the test may cause you to forget some important material.
- Taking drugs or drinking alcohol before a test may give you the impression that you are relaxed and doing well on the test, but the results are disastrous to your success on the exam and your good health.
- Not knowing the date of the test can cause you to get a low grade because you are not prepared.
- Not checking or knowing about the final exam schedule can cause you to miss the final.
- Missing the final exam can result in a lower grade or failing the class.
- Arriving late for the exam puts you at a disadvantage if you don't have time to finish or have to rush through the test.
- Deciding not to buy or read the textbook will cause low performance or failure.
- Having a fight, disagreement, or argument with parents, friends, or significant others before the test will make it difficult to focus on the exam.
- Sacrificing sleep, exercise, or food to prepare for the exam makes it difficult to do your best.
- Cheating on an exam can cause embarrassment, a lower grade, or failure. It can even lead to expulsion from college.
- Missing the exam because you are not prepared and asking the professor to let you make up the exam later is a tactic that many students try. Most professors will not permit you to take an exam late.
- Inventing a creative excuse for missing an exam is so common that some professors have a collection of these stories that they share with colleagues. Creative excuses don't work with most professors.
- Arriving at the exam without the proper materials such as a pencil, scantron, paper, calculator, or book (for open-book exams) can cause you to miss the exam or start the exam late.

> **JOURNAL ENTRY #1**
>
> What is your own evaluation of your strengths and weaknesses in preparing for tests? List and briefly explain at least three test preparation ideas that you find useful.

Dealing with Test Anxiety

Some anxiety is a good thing. It can provide motivation to study and prepare for exams. However, it is common for college students to suffer from test anxiety. Too much anxiety can lower your performance on tests. Some symptoms of test anxiety include:

- Fear of failing a test even though you are well prepared

- Physical symptoms such as perspiring, increased heart rate, shortness of breath, upset stomach, tense muscles, or headache
- Negative thoughts about the test and your grade
- Mental blocking of material you know and remembering it once you leave the exam

You can minimize your test anxiety by being well prepared and by applying the memory strategies described in earlier chapters. Prepare for your exams by attending every class, keeping up with your reading assignments, and reviewing during the semester. These steps will help increase your self-confidence and reduce anxiety. Apply the principles of memory improvement to your studying. As you are reading, find the important points and highlight them. Review these points so that they are stored in your long-term memory. Use distributed practice and spread out learning over time rather than trying to learn it all at once. Visualize and organize what you need to remember. Trust in your abilities and intend to remember what you have studied.

If you find that you are anxious, here are some ideas you can try to cope with the anxiety. Experiment with these techniques to see which ones work best for you.

- **Do some physical exercise.** Physical exercise helps to use up stress hormones. Make physical activity a part of your daily routine. Arrive for your test a little early and walk briskly around campus for about twenty minutes. This exercise will help you to feel relaxed and energized.

- **Get a good night's sleep before the test.** Lack of sleep can interfere with memory and cause irritability, anxiety, and confusion.

- **Take deep breaths.** Immediately before the test, take a few deep breaths; hold them for three to five seconds and let them out slowly. These deep breaths will help you to relax and keep a sufficient supply of oxygen in your blood. Oxygen is needed for proper brain function.

Tips to Minimize Anxiety

- Exercise
- Sleep
- Take deep breaths
- Visualize success
- Acknowledge anxiety
- Easy questions first
- Yell "Stop!"
- Daydream
- Practice perspective
- Give yourself time
- Get help

- **Visualize and rehearse your success.** Begin by getting as comfortable and relaxed as possible in your favorite chair or lying down in bed. Visualize yourself walking into the exam room. Try to imagine the room in as much detail as possible. If possible, visit the exam room before the test so that you can get a good picture of it. See yourself taking the exam calmly and confidently. You know most of the answers. If you find a question you do not know, see yourself circling it and coming back to it later. Imagine that you find a clue on the test that triggers your recall of the answers to the difficult questions. Picture yourself handing in the exam with a good feeling about doing well on the test. Then imagine you are getting the test back and you get a good grade on the test. You congratulate yourself for a job well done. If you suffer from text anxiety, you may need to rehearse this scene several times. When you enter the exam room, the visual picture that you have rehearsed will help you to relax.

- **Acknowledge your anxiety.** The first step in dealing with anxiety is to admit that you are anxious rather than trying to fight it or deny it. Say to yourself, "I am feeling anxious." Take a few deep breaths and then focus your attention on the test.

- **Do the easy questions first** and mark the ones that may be difficult. This will help you to relax. Once you are relaxed, the difficult questions become more manageable.

- **Yell "Stop."** Negative and frightening thoughts can cause anxiety. Here are some examples of negative thoughts:

  I'm going to fail this test.
  I don't know the answer to number ten!
  I never do well on tests.
  Essays! I have a hard time with those.
  I'll never make it through college.
  I was never any good in math!

  These types of thoughts don't help you do better on the test, so stop saying them. They cause you to become anxious and to freeze up during the test. If you find yourself with similar thoughts, yell "stop" to yourself. This will cause you to interrupt your train of thought so that you can think about the task at hand rather than becoming more anxious. Replace negative thoughts with more positive ones such as these:

  I'm doing the best I can.
  I am well prepared and know most of the answers.
  I don't know the answer to number ten, so I'll just circle it and come back to it later.
  I'll make an outline in the margin for the essay question.
  College is difficult, but I'll make it!
  Math is a challenge, but I can do it!

- **Daydream.** Think about being in your favorite place. Take time to think about the details. Allow yourself to be there for a while until you feel more relaxed.

- **Practice perspective.** Remember, one poor grade is not the end of the world. It does not define who you are. If you do not do well, think about how you can improve your preparation and performance the next time.

- **Give yourself time.** Test anxiety develops over a period of time. It will take some time to get over it. Learn the best ways to prepare for the exam and practice saying positive thoughts to yourself.

- **Get help.** If these techniques do not work for you, seek help from your college health or counseling center.

Studying Math and Dealing with Math Anxiety

When I mention to students that they need to take math, I often see a look of fear on their faces. Everyone needs to take math. Most colleges require math classes and demonstrated math competency in order to graduate. Math is essential for many high-paying technical and professional occupations. Being afraid of math and avoiding it will limit your career possibilities.

Begin your study of math with some positive thinking. You may have had difficulty with math in the past, but with a positive attitude and the proper study techniques, you can meet the challenge. The first step to success in math is to put in the effort required. Attend class, do your homework, and get help if needed. If you put in the effort and hard work, you will gain experience in math. If you gain experience with math, you will become more confident in your ability to do math. If you have confidence, you will gain satisfaction in doing math. You may even learn to like it! If you like the subject, you can gain competence. The process looks like this:

Hard work $\rightarrow$ Experience $\rightarrow$ Confidence $\rightarrow$ Satisfaction $\rightarrow$ Competence

Although you may have had difficulty with math in the past, you can become successful by following these steps. Your reward is self-satisfaction and increased opportunity in technical and professional careers.

- **Don't delay taking math.** You may need a sequence of math courses in order to graduate. If you delay taking math, you may delay your graduation from college.

- **Think positively about your ability to succeed in math.** You may have had difficulties in math classes before. Think about your educational history. Can you recall having difficulties in the past? These past difficulties cause a fear of math. You may have a picture of failure in your mind. You need to replace it with a picture of success. Acknowledge that you are afraid because of past experiences with math. Acknowledge that the future can be different, and spend the time and effort needed to be successful.

- **Start at the beginning.** Assess where your math skills are at the present time. If you have not taken math classes for some time, you may need to review. Take the college math assessment test, read the college catalog, and speak to a counselor about where you should start.

- **Ask questions in class.** Students are often afraid to ask questions in math classes because they are afraid other students will think they are not smart. It is more likely that other students are wishing that someone would ask a question because they don't understand either. Ask your questions early, as soon as you find something you don't understand.

- **Get help early.** If you are having difficulties, get tutoring right away. If you are confused, you will not understand the next step either.

- **Don't miss your math classes.** It is difficult to catch up if you miss class.

- **Do your math homework regularly.** Math skills depend on practice. Make sure you understand the examples given in the textbook. Practice as many questions as you can until you feel comfortable solving the problems. Assign yourself extra problems if necessary. It is difficult to cram for a math test.

- **Use a study group.** Work with groups of students to study math. Get the phone number of other students in the study group. If you do not understand, other students may be able to help.

- **Study for the math test.** Start early so that you will have time to go over each topic in the book and practice doing problems from each section. Check your work against the solutions given in the text.

- **Do the easiest problems first on a math test.** In this way, you can gain confidence and relax. Then focus on the problems that are worth the most points. Don't be distracted by problems that you do not know and that use up test time.

- **Solve problems systematically.** First make sure you understand the problem. Write out the given facts and equations you may need to use before working out the problem. Then make a plan for solving it. What have you learned in class that will help you to solve the problem? Carry out the plan. Then check your answer. Does the answer make sense? Check your calculator work over again at the end of the test.

- **Check for careless errors.** Go over your math test to see if you have made any careless errors. Forgetting a plus or minus sign or adding or subtracting incorrectly can have a big impact on your grade. Save at least five minutes to read over your test.

- **Get enough sleep before the math test.** If you are mentally sharp, the test will be easier.

JOURNAL ENTRY #2

What are some techniques that you can use to deal with text anxiety or math anxiety?

QUIZ

Test Preparation

Test what you have learned by selecting the correct answer to the following questions.

1. In test preparation, it is important to use this memory technique.

   a. Distribute the practice.
   b. Read every chapter just before the test.
   c. Do most of the review right before the test to minimize forgetting.

2. Schedule your study sessions

   a. late at night.
   b. during your prime time, which is generally earlier in the day.
   c. after all other activities are done.

3. Effective tools to learn facts and details are

   a. mind maps.
   b. summary sheets.
   c. flash cards.

4. The best way to review is

   a. to start early and break it into small parts.
   b. immediately before the test.
   c. in large blocks of time.

5. The best way to deal with text anxiety is to

   a. visualize your failure on the exam.
   b. start with the difficult questions first.
   c. be well prepared and visualize your success on the exam.

How did you do on the quiz? Check your answers: 1. a, 2. b, 3. c, 4. a, 5. c

Ten Rules for Success

Here are ten rules for success on any test. Are there any new ideas you can put into practice?

1. **Make sure to set your alarm,** and consider having a backup in case your alarm doesn't go off. Set a second alarm or have someone call to make sure you are awake on time.

2. **Arrive a little early for your exam.** If you are taking a standardized test like the Scholastic Aptitude Test (SAT) or Graduate Record Exam (GRE), familiarize yourself with the location of the exam. If you arrive early, you can take a quick walk around the building to relax or spend a few minutes doing a review so that your brain will be tuned up and ready.

3. **Eat a light breakfast including some carbohydrates and protein.** Be careful about eating sugar and caffeine before a test because this can contribute to greater anxiety and low blood sugar by the time you take the test. The worst breakfast would be something like a doughnut and coffee or a soda and candy bar. Examples of good breakfasts are eggs, toast, and juice or cereal with milk and fruit.

4. **Think positively about the exam.** Tell yourself that you are well prepared and the exam is an opportunity to show what you know.

5. **Make sure you have the proper materials:** scantrons, paper, pencil or pen, calculator, books and notes (for open-book exams).

6. **Manage your time.** Know how long you have for the test and then scan the test to make a time management plan. For example, if you have one hour and there are 50 objective questions, you have about a minute for each question. Half way through the time, you should have completed 25 questions. If there are three essay questions in an hour, you have less than 20 minutes for each question. Save some time to look over the test and make corrections.

7. **Neatness is important.** If your paper looks neat, the professor is more likely to have a positive attitude about the paper before it is even read. If the paper is hard to read, the professor will start reading your paper with a negative attitude, possibly resulting in a lower grade.

8. **Read the test directions carefully.** On essay exams, it is common for the professor to give you a choice of questions to answer. If you do not read the directions, you may try to answer all of the questions and then run out of time or give incomplete answers to them.

9. **If you get stuck on a difficult question, don't worry about it.** Just mark it and find an easier question. You may find clues on the rest of the test that will aid your recall or you may be more relaxed later on and think of the answer.

10. **Be careful not to give any impression that you might be cheating.** Keep your eyes on your own paper. If you have memory aids or outlines memorized, write them directly on the test paper rather than a separate sheet so that you are not suspected of using cheat notes.

Taking Tests
True-False Tests

Many professors use objective tests such as true-false and multiple-choice because of their ease in grading. The best way to prepare for these types of tests is to study the key points in the textbook, lecture notes, and class handouts. In the textbook, take each bold-faced topic and turn it into a question. If you can answer the question, you will be successful on objective tests.

In addition to studying for the test, it is helpful to understand some basic test-taking techniques that will help you to determine the correct answer. Many of the techniques used to determine whether a statement is true or false can also be used to eliminate wrong answers on multiple-choice tests.

To develop strategies for success on true-false exams, it is important to understand how a teacher writes the questions. For a true-false question, the teacher identifies a key point in the book or lecture notes. Then he or she has two choices. For a true statement, the key idea is often written exactly as it appears in the text or notes. For a false statement, the key idea is changed in some way to make it false.

One way to make a statement false is to add a **qualifier** to the statement. Qualifiers that are **absolute** or extreme are generally, but not always, found in false statements. **General** qualifiers are often found in true statements.

Absolute Qualifiers (false)		General Qualifiers (true)	
all	none	usually	frequently
always	never	often	sometimes
only	nobody	some	seldom
invariably	no one	many	much
best	worst	most	generally
everybody	everyone	few	ordinarily
absolutely	absolutely not	probably	a majority
certainly	certainly not	might	a few
no	every	may	apt to

Seven Tips for Success on True-False Tests

1. **Identify the key ideas in the text and class notes and review them.**

2. **Accept the question at face value.** Don't overanalyze or create wild exceptions in your mind.

3. **If you don't know the answer, assume it is true.** There are generally more true statements because we all like the truth (especially teachers) and true questions are easier to write. However, some teachers like to test students by writing all false statements.

4. **If any part of a true-false statement is false, the whole statement is false.** Carefully read each statement to determine if any part of it is false. Students sometimes assume a statement is true if most of it is true. This is not correct.

    Example: Good relaxation techniques include deep breathing, exercise, and visualizing your failure on the exam.

    This statement is false because visualizing failure can lead to test anxiety and failure.

5. **Notice any absolute or general qualifiers.** Remember that absolute qualifiers often make a statement false. General qualifiers often make a statement true.

    Example: The student who crams **always** does poorly on the exam.

    This statement is false because **some** students are successful at cramming for an exam.

Be careful with this rule. Sometimes the answer can be absolute.

Example: The grade point average is always calculated by dividing the number of units attempted by the grade points. (true)

6.   **Notice words such as *because, therefore, consequently,* and *as a result.*** They may connect two things that are true but result in a false statement.

Example: Martha does not have test anxiety. (true)

Martha makes good grades on tests. (true)

Martha does not have test anxiety and therefore makes good grades on tests.

This statement is false because she also has to prepare for the exam. Not having test anxiety could even cause her to lack motivation to study and do poorly on a test.

7.   **Watch for double negatives.** Two no's equal a yes. If you see two negatives in a sentence, read them as a positive. Be careful with negative prefixes such as: un-, im-, mis-, dis-, il-, and ir-. For example, the phrase "not uncommon" actually means "common." Notice that the word "not" and the prefix "un-" when used together form a double negative that equals a positive.

Example: **Not** being **un**prepared for the test is the best way to earn good grades.

The above sentence is confusing. To make it clearer, change both of the negatives into a positive:

Being prepared for the test is the best way to earn good grades.

ACTIVITY
Practice True-False Test

Answer the following questions by applying the tips for success in the previous section. Place a T or an F in the blanks.

_____ 1.   If a statement has an absolute qualifier, it is always false.

_____ 2.   Statements with general qualifiers are frequently true.

_____ 3.   If you don't know the answer, you should guess true.

_____ 4.   Studying the key points for true-false tests is not unimportant.

_____ 5.   Good test-taking strategies include eating a light breakfast that includes carbohydrates and protein and drinking plenty of coffee to stay alert.

_____ 6.   Ryan attended every class this semester and therefore earned an A in the class.

How did you do on the test?

Answers: 1. F, 2. T, 3. T, 4. T, 5. F, 6. F

Multiple-Choice Tests

College exams often include multiple-choice questions rather than true-false questions because it is more difficult to guess the correct answer. On a true-false exam, the student has a 50 percent chance of guessing the correct answer while on a multiple-choice question the odds of guessing correctly are only 25 percent. You can think of a multiple-choice question as four true-false questions in a row. First, read the question and try to answer it without looking at the options. This will help you to focus on the question and determine the correct answer. Look at each option and determine if it is true or false. Then choose the **best** answer.

To choose the best option, it is helpful to understand how a teacher writes a multiple-choice question. Here are the steps a teacher uses to write a multiple-choice exam:

1. Find an important point in the lecture notes, text, or handouts.
2. Write a **stem**. This is an incomplete statement or a question.
3. Write the correct answer as one of the options.
4. Write three or four plausible but incorrect options that might be chosen by students who are not prepared. These incorrect options are called **decoys**. Here is an example:

Stem: If you are anxious about taking math tests, it is helpful to

A.   Stay up the night before the test to review thoroughly. (**decoy**)
B.   Visualize yourself doing poorly on the test so you will be motivated to study. (**decoy**)
C.   Practice math problems regularly during the semester. (**correct answer**)
D.   Do the most difficult problem first. (**decoy**)

Being well prepared for the test is the most reliable way of recognizing the correct answer and the decoys. In addition, becoming familiar with the following rules for recognizing decoys can help you determine the correct answer or improve your chances of guessing the correct answer on an exam. If you can at least eliminate some of the wrong answers, you will improve your odds of selecting the correct answer.

Rules for recognizing a decoy or wrong answer:

1. **The decoys are all true or all false statements.**
    Read each option and determine which options are false and which statements are true. This will help you to find the correct answer.

    Example: To manage your time on a test, it is important to

    A.   Skip the directions and work as quickly as possible. (false)
    B.   Skim through the test to see how much time you have for each section. (true)
    C.   Do the most difficult sections first. (false)
    D.   Just start writing as quickly as possible. (false)

    Read the stem carefully because sometimes you will be asked to identify one false statement in a group of true statements.

2. **The decoy may contain an absolute qualifier.**
    The option with the absolute qualifier (e.g., always, only, every) is likely to be false because few things in life are absolute. There are generally exceptions to any rule.

3. **The decoy can be partly true.**
    However, if one part of the statement is false, the whole statement is false and an incorrect answer.

Rules for Recognizing a Decoy

1. Decoys are all true or all false
2. Decoys contain absolute qualifiers
3. Decoys can be partly true
4. Decoys have conjunctions that make them false
5. Decoys have double negatives
6. Decoys can be foolish
7. Decoys are high or low numbers
8. Decoys can look correct
9. Decoys are often the shorter answer
10. Decoys may be grammatically incorrect
11. Decoys may be an opposite
12. Decoys may be the same as another answer

4. **The decoy may have a conjunction or other linking words that makes it false.**
Watch for words and phrases such as *because, consequently, therefore,* and *as a result.*

5. **The decoy may have a double negative.**
Having two negatives in a sentence makes it difficult to understand. Read the two negatives as a positive.

6. **The decoy may be a foolish option.**
Writing multiple decoys is difficult, so test writers sometimes throw in foolish or humorous options.

   Example: In a multiple-choice test, a decoy is

   A. a type of duck.
   B. an incorrect answer.
   C. a type of missile used in air defense.
   D. a type of fish.

The correct answer is B. Sometimes students are tempted by the foolish answers.

7. **The decoy is often a low or high number.**
If you have a multiple-choice question with numbers, and you are not sure of the correct answer, choose the number in the middle range. It is often more likely to be correct.

   Example: George Miller of Harvard University theorized that the optimum number of chunks of material that we can remember is:

   A. 1–2 (This low number is a decoy)
   B. 5–9 (correct answer)
   C. 10–12 (close to the correct answer)
   D. 20–25 (This high number is a decoy)

There is an exception to this rule when the number is much higher or lower than the average person thinks is possible.

8. **The decoy may look like the correct answer.**
When two options look alike, one is incorrect and the other may be the correct answer. Test writers often use words that look alike as decoys.

   Example: In false statements, the qualifier is often

   A. absolute.
   B. resolute.
   C. general.
   D. exaggerated.

The correct answer is A. Answer B is an incorrect look-alike option.

9. **Decoys are often shorter than the correct answer.**
Longer answers are more likely to be correct because they are more complete. Avoid choosing the first answer that seems to be correct. There may be a better and more complete answer.

   Example: Good test preparation involves

   A. doing the proper review for the test.
   B. good time management.
   C. a positive attitude.
   D. having good attendance, studying and reviewing regularly, being able to deal with test anxiety, and having a positive mental attitude.

Option D is correct because it is the most complete and thus the best answer.

10. **Decoys may be grammatically incorrect.**
The correct answer will fit the grammar of the stem. A stem ending with "a" will match an answer beginning with a consonant; stems ending with "an" will match a word beginning with a vowel. The answer will agree in gender, number, and person with the stem.

Example: In test taking, a decoy is an

    A. incorrect answer.
    B. correct answer.
    C. false answer.
    D. true answer.

The correct answer is A. It is also the only answer that grammatically fits with the stem. Also note that decoys can be all true or all false. In standardized tests, the grammar is usually correct. On teacher-made tests, the grammar can be a clue to the correct answer.

11. **A decoy is sometimes an opposite.**
When two options are opposites, one is incorrect and the other is sometimes, but not always, correct.

Example: A decoy is

    A. a right answer.
    B. a wrong answer.
    C. a general qualifier.
    D. a true statement.

The two opposites are answers A and B. The correct answer is B.

12. **A decoy may be the same as another answer.**
If two answers say the same thing in different ways, they are both decoys and incorrect.

Example: A true statement is likely to have this type of qualifier:

    A. extreme
    B. absolute
    C. general
    D. factual

Notice that answers A and B are the same and are incorrect. The correct answer is C.

Example: How much does a gallon of water weigh?

    A. 8.34 pounds
    B. 5.5 pounds
    C. 5 pounds 8 ounces
    D. 20 pounds

B and C are the same and are therefore incorrect answers. Answer D is a high number. The correct answer is A.

If you are unable to identify any decoys, these suggestions may be helpful:

- Mark the question and come back to it later. You may find the answer elsewhere on the test or some words that help you remember the answer. After answering some easier questions, you may be able to relax and remember the answer.
- Trust your intuition and choose something that sounds familiar.
- Do not change your first answer unless you have misread the question or are sure that the answer is incorrect. Sometimes students overanalyze a question and then choose the wrong answer.

- The option "All of the above" is often correct because it is easier to write true statements rather than false ones. Options like A and B, B and D, or other combinations are also likely to be correct for the same reason.
- If you have no idea about the correct answer, guess option B or C. Most correct answers are in the middle.

ACTIVITY
Practice Multiple-Choice Test

Circle the letter of the correct answer. Then check your answers using the key at the end of this section.

1. The correct answer in a multiple-choice question is likely to be
   a. the shortest answer.
   b. the longest and most complete answer.
   c. the answer with an absolute qualifier.
   d. the answer that has some truth in it.

2. When guessing on a question involving numbers, it is generally best to
   a. choose the highest number.
   b. choose the lowest number.
   c. choose the mid-range number.
   d. always choose the first option.

3. If you have test anxiety, what questions should you answer first on the test?
   a. The most difficult questions
   b. The easiest questions
   c. The questions at the beginning
   d. The questions worth the least points

4. When taking a multiple-choice test, you should
   a. pick the first choice that is true.
   b. read all the choices and select the best one.
   c. pick the first choice that is false.
   d. choose the extreme answer.

5. A good method for guessing is to
   a. identify which choices are true and false.
   b. use the process of elimination.
   c. notice absolute qualifiers and conjunctions.
   d. all of the above.

6. The key to success when taking a multiple-choice test is
   a. cheating.
   b. good preparation.
   c. knowing how to guess.
   d. being able to recognize a qualifier.

7. The following rule about decoys is correct:
   a. A decoy is always absolute.
   b. A decoy can be partly true.
   c. Every decoy has a qualifier.
   d. Decoys are invariably false statements.

8. An example of an absolute qualifier is
   a. generally.
   b. never.
   c. sometimes.
   d. frequently.

9. Statements with absolute qualifiers are generally
   a. true.
   b. false.
   c. irrelevant.
   d. confusing.

10. If two multiple-choice options are the same or very similar, they are most likely
    a. a decoy and a correct answer.
    b. a correct answer.
    c. a true answer.
    d. a mistake on the test.

11. It is generally not a good idea to change your answer unless
    a. you are very anxious about the test.
    b. you do not have good intuition.
    c. you notice that your intelligent friend has a different answer.
    d. you have misread the question and you are sure that the answer is incorrect.

Answers:

1. b, 2. c, 3. b, 4. b, 5. d, 6. b, 7. b (notice the absolute qualifiers in the decoys), 8. b, 9. b (notice the opposites), 10. a (notice the grammar), 11. d

Matching Tests

A matching test involves two lists of facts or definitions that must be matched together. Here are some tips to help you successfully complete a matching exam:

1. Read through both lists to discover the pattern or relationship between the lists. The lists might give words and definitions, people and accomplishments, or other paired facts.
2. Count the items on the list of answers to see if there is only one match for each item or if there are some extra answer choices.
3. Start with one list and match the items that you know. In this way, you have a better chance of guessing on the items that you do not know.
4. If you have difficulty with some of the items, leave them blank and return later. You may find the answers or clues on the rest of the test.

ACTIVITY
Practice Matching Test

Match the items in the first column with the items in the second column. Write the letter of the matching item in the blank at the left.

_____ 1. Meaningful organization   A. Learn small amounts and review frequently.
_____ 2. Visualization   B. The more you know, the easier it is
                                          to remember.
_____ 3. Recitation   C. Tell yourself you will remember.

_____ 4. Develop an interest   D. Pretend you like it.

_____ 5. See the big picture   E. Make a mental picture.

_____ 6. Intend to remember   F. Rehearse and review.

_____ 7. Distribute the practice   G. Focus on the main points first.

_____ 8. Create a basic background   H. Personal organization.

Answers: 1. H, 2. E, 3. F, 4. D, 5. G, 6. C, 7. A, 8. B

Sentence-Completion or Fill-in-the-Blank Tests

Fill-in-the-blank and sentence-completion tests are more difficult than true-false or multiple-choice tests because they require the **recall** of specific information rather than the **recognition** of the correct answer. To prepare for this type of test, focus on facts such as definitions, names, dates, and places. Using flash cards to prepare can be helpful. For example, to memorize names, place the name on one side of the card and some identifying words on the other side. Practice looking at the names on one side of the card and then recalling the identifying words on the other side of the card. Then turn the cards over and look at the identifying words to recall the names.

Sometimes the test has clues that will help you to fill in the blank. Clues can include the length of the blanks and the number of blanks. Find an answer that makes sense in the sentence and matches the grammar of the sentence. If you cannot think of an answer, write a general description and you may get partial credit. Look for clues on the rest of the test that may trigger your recall.

ACTIVITY
Practice Fill-in-the-Blank Test

Complete each sentence with the appropriate word or words.

1. Fill-in-the-blank tests are more difficult because they depend on the _____ of specific information.

2. On a true-false test, a statement is likely to be false if it contains an _____ qualifier.

3. Test review tools include _____, _____, and _____.

4. When studying for tests, visualize your _____.

Answers: 1. recall, 2. absolute, 3. flash cards, summary sheets, and mind maps (also study groups and highlighters), 4. success

Essay Tests

Many professors choose essay questions because they are the best way to show what you have learned in the class. Essay questions can be challenging because you not only have to know the material but must be able to organize it and use good writing techniques in your answer.

Essay questions contain key words that will guide you in writing your answer. One of the keys to success in writing answers to essay questions is to note these key words and then structure your essay accordingly. As you read through an essay question, look for these words:

Analyze	Break into separate parts and discuss, examine, or interpret each part.
Argue	State an opinion and give reasons for the opinion.
Comment	Give your opinion.
Compare	Identify two or more ideas and identify similarities and differences.
Contrast	Show how the components are the same or different.
Criticize	Give your opinion and make judgments.
Defend	State reasons.
Define	Give the meaning of the word or concept as used within the course of study.
Describe	Give a detailed account or provide information.
Demonstrate	Provide evidence.
Diagram	Make a drawing, chart, graph, sketch, or plan.

Differentiate	Tell how the ideas are the same and how they are different.
Describe	Make a picture with words. List the characteristics, qualities and parts.
Discuss	Describe the pros and cons of the issues. Compare and contrast.
Enumerate	Make a list of ideas, events, qualities, reasons, and so on.
Explain	Make an idea clear. Show how and why.
Evaluate	Describe it and give your opinion about something.
Illustrate	Give concrete examples and explain them. Draw a diagram.
Interpret	Say what something means. Describe and then evaluate.
Justify	Prove a point. Give the reasons why.
Outline	Describe the main ideas.
Prove	Support with facts. Give evidence or reasons.
Relate	Show the connections between ideas or events.
State	Explain precisely. Provide the main points.
Summarize	Give a brief, condensed account. Draw a conclusion.
Trace	Show the order of events.

Here are some tips on writing essays:

1. To prepare for an essay test, use a mind map or summary sheet to summarize the main ideas. Organize the material in the form of an outline or mental pictures that you can use in writing.
2. The first step in writing an essay is to quickly survey the test and read the directions carefully. Many times you are offered a choice of which and how many questions to answer.
3. Manage your time. Note how many questions need to be answered and how many points each question is worth.

   For example, if you have three questions to answer in one hour, you will have less than 20 minutes for each question. Save some time to check over your work.

   If the questions are worth different points, divide up your time proportionately. In the above example with three questions, if one question is worth 50 points and the other two are worth 25 points, spend half the time on the 50-point question (less than 30 minutes) and divide the remaining time between the 25-point questions (less than 15 minutes each).
4. If you are anxious about the test, start with an easy question in order to relax and build your confidence. If you are confident of your test-taking abilities, start with the question that is worth the most points.
5. Get organized. Write a brief outline in the margin of your test paper. Do not write your outline on a separate sheet of paper because you may be accused of using cheat notes.
6. In the first sentence of your essay, rephrase the question and provide a direct answer. Rephrasing the question keeps you on track and a direct answer becomes the thesis statement or main idea of the essay.

   Example: (Question:) Describe a system for reading a college textbook.

   (Answer:) A system for reading a college textbook is Survey, Question, Read, Review, Recite, and Reflect (SQ4R). (Then you would go on to expand on each part of the topic.)

7. Use the principles of good composition. Start with a thesis statement or main idea. Provide supporting ideas and examples to support your thesis. Provide a brief summary at the end.

8. Write your answer clearly and neatly so it is easy to grade. Grading an essay involves an element of subjectivity. If your paper looks neat and is easy to read, the professor is likely to read your essay with a positive attitude. If your paper is difficult to read, the professor will probably read your paper with a negative attitude.

9. Determine the length of your essay by the number of points it is worth. For example, a five-point essay might be a paragraph with five key points. A 25-point essay would probably be a five-paragraph essay with at least 25 key points.

10. Save some time at the end to read over your essays. Make corrections, make sure your answers make sense, and add any key information you may have forgotten to include.

JOURNAL ENTRY #3

List and explain at least three ideas that you can use to improve your essay exams.

Math Tests

Taking a math test involves some different strategies:

1. Some instructors will let you write down formulas on an index card or a small crib sheet. Prepare these notes carefully, writing down the key formulas you will need for the exam.

2. If you have to memorize formulas, review them right before the test and write them on the test immediately.

3. As a first step, quickly look over the test. Find a problem you can solve easily and do this problem first.

4. Manage your time. Find out how many problems you have to solve and how much time is available for each problem. Do the problems worth the most points first. Stay on track.

5. Try this four-step process:
   a. Understand the problem.
   b. Devise a plan to solve the problem. Write down the information that is given. Think about the skills and techniques you have learned in class that can help you to solve the problem.
   c. Carry out the plan.
   d. Look back to see if your answer is reasonable.

6. If you cannot work a problem, go on to the next question. Come back later when you are more relaxed. If you spend too much time on a problem you cannot work, you will not have time for the problems that you can work.

7. Even if you think an answer is wrong, turn it in. You may get partial credit.

8. Show all the steps in your work and label your answer. On long and complex problems, it is helpful to use short sentences to explain your steps in solving the problem.

9. Estimate your answer and see if it makes sense or is logical.

10. Write your numbers as neatly as possible to avoid mistakes and to make them legible for the professor.

Tips for Avoiding Common Math Errors[2]

- Any quantity multiplied by zero is zero.
- Any quantity raised to the zero power is one.
- Any fraction multiplied by its reciprocal is one.
- Only like algebraic terms may be combined.
- Break down to the simplest form in algebra.
- In algebra, multiply and divide before adding and subtracting.
- If an algebraic expression has more than one set of parentheses, get rid of the inner parenthesis first and work outward.
- Any operation performed on one side of the equation must be performed on the other side.

11. Leave space between your answers in case you need to add to them later.
12. If you have time left over at the end, recheck your answers.

What to Do When Your Test Is Returned

When your test is returned, use it as feedback for future test preparation in the course. Look at your errors and try to determine how to prevent these errors in the future.

- Did you study correctly?
- Did you study the proper materials?
- Did you use the proper test-taking techniques?
- Was the test more difficult than you expected?
- Did you run out of time to take the test?
- Was the test focused on details and facts or on general ideas and principles?
- Did you have problems with test anxiety?

Analyzing your test performance can help you to do better in the future.

Peanuts reprinted by permission of United Feature Syndicate, Inc.

 **Keys to Success**

Be Prepared

The key idea in this chapter is to be prepared. Good preparation is essential for success in test taking as well as in many other areas of life. Being successful begins with having a vision of the future and then taking steps to achieve your dream.

> The secret of getting ahead is getting started. The secret of getting started is breaking your complex, overwhelming tasks into small manageable tasks, and then starting on the first one.
> —Mark Twain

Sometimes people think of success in terms of good luck. Thomas Jefferson said, "I'm a great believer in luck, and I find the harder I work, the more I have of it." Don't depend on good luck. Work to create your success.

You can reach your dream of attaining a college education through preparation and hard work. Use the ideas in this chapter to ensure your success. Remember that preparation begins on the first day of class; it does not begin when the professor announces a test. On the first day of class, the professor provides an overview, or outline, of what you will learn. Attend every class. The main points covered in the class will be on the test. Read your assignments a little at a time starting from the first day. If you distribute your practice, you will find it easier to learn and to remember.

When it comes time to review for the test, you will already know what to expect on the test; and you will have learned the material by attending the lectures and reading your text. Reviewing for the test is just review; it is not original learning. It is a chance to strengthen what you have learned so that you can relax and do your best on the test. Review is one of the final steps in learning. With review you will gain a sense of confidence and satisfaction in your studies.

If you are not prepared, you will need to cram for the test and you may not be as successful on the test as you could be. If you are not successful, you may get the mistaken idea that you cannot be successful in college. Cramming for the test produces stress since you will need to learn a great deal of information in a short time. Stress can interfere with memory and cause you to freeze up on exams. It is also difficult to remember if you have to cram. The memory works best if you do a small amount of learning regularly over a period of time. Cramming is hard work and no fun. The worst problem with cramming is that it causes you to dislike education. It is difficult to continue to do something that you have learned to dislike.

Good preparation is the key to success in many areas of life. Whether you are taking a college course, playing a basketball game, going on vacation, planning a wedding, or building a house, good preparation will help to guarantee your success. Begin with your vision of the future and boldly take the first steps. The best preparation for the future is the good use of your time today.

> The future starts today, not tomorrow.
> —Pope John Paul II

JOURNAL ENTRY #4

What is the ideal strategy for preparation for a major exam such as a midterm or final?

JOURNAL ENTRIES

Test Taking

Go to http://www.collegesuccess1.com/ for Word files of the Journal Entries

Success over the Internet

Visit the *College Success Website* at http://www.collegesuccess1.com/

The *College Success Website* is continually updated with new topics and links to the material presented in this chapter. Topics include

- Tips for taking tests
- Dealing with math anxiety

- How to study for math tests
- How to take math tests
- How to guess on a test
- Test anxiety
- Multiple-choice exams
- Dealing with difficult questions

Contact your instructor if you have any problems in accessing the *College Success Website*.

Notes

1. G. A. Miller, "The Magical Number Seven, Plus or Minus Two: Some Limits on Our Capacity for Processing Information," *Psychological Review* 63 (March 1956): 81–97.
2. From Aguilar et al., *The Community College: A New Beginning*, 2nd ed. Copyright 1998 by Kendall/Hunt Publishing Company.

Test-Taking Checklist

Name _____ Date _____

Place a checkmark next to the test-taking skills you have now.

_____ Attend every class (or almost every class)

_____ Have a copy of the course syllabus with test dates

_____ Start test preparation early and study a little at a time

_____ Do not generally cram for exams

_____ Have a place to study (not the kitchen, TV room, or bedroom)

_____ Participate in a study group

_____ Review immediately after learning something

_____ Review previous notes and reading assignments on a regular basis

_____ Schedule a major review before the exam

_____ Know how to predict the test questions

_____ Get enough rest before a test

_____ Visualize my success on the exam

_____ Complete my math homework on a regular basis

_____ Eat a light but nutritious meal before the exam

_____ Maintain a regular exercise program

_____ Read all my textbook assignments before the exam

_____ Review my classroom notes before the exam

_____ Skim through the test and read all directions carefully before starting the test

_____ Answer the easy questions first and return later to answer the difficult questions

_____ Check over my test before handing it in

_____ Write an outline before beginning my essay answer

_____ Manage my study time to adequately prepare for the test

_____ Review my returned tests to improve future test preparation

_____ Write the test neatly and make sure my writing is legible

_____ Avoid test anxiety by being well prepared and practicing relaxation techniques

_____ Prepare adequately for tests

Analyze Your Test-Taking Skills

Name _____ Date _____

Use the test-taking checklist on the previous page to answer the following questions.

1. My strengths in test taking skills are

2. Some areas I need to improve are

3. Write three intention statements about improving your test-taking skills.

Name _____   Date _____

Your professor may ask you to do this as a classroom exercise. Review the section in the text on how to write a short essay. Answer the following short essay worth five points.

1. Explain how you can improve your chances of success when preparing for exams. Include the physical, mental, and emotional preparation necessary for success.

2. Rate your essay. Did you do the following?

    _____ I read the directions and the essay question thoroughly before I began.

    _____ I organized my thoughts or made a brief outline before starting.

    _____ The first sentence was a direct answer and rephrased the question.

    _____ My thesis statement or main idea was clear.

    _____ The remaining sentences in the essay supported my main idea.

    _____ Since this is a five point essay, I made at least five key points in the essay.

    _____ My answer was written clearly and neatly. My handwriting was legible.

    _____ I spelled the words correctly and used good grammar.

    _____ I read over my essay to make sure it made sense.

3. For essay exams, I need to work on

Name _____   Date _____

1. Read all of the directions before you do anything.

2. Put your name at the top of this page.

3. In the bottom right-hand corner, write the name of this class.

4. In the bottom left-hand corner, write the name of your instructor.

5. Put a box around the class name.

6. Put a circle around your instructor's name.

7. Write the name of your college at the bottom of this page.

8. You have now completed the exercise, so let the class know you are finished by calling out "Done."

9. Return to the beginning and only do number one.

CHAPTER

8

LEARNING
OBJECTIVES

Read to answer these key
questions:

• What are my interests?

• What lifestyle do I prefer?

• How do my interests relate
to possible careers?

• What are my values?

• How do I put my values into
action?

© Laurence Gough, 2008. Under license from Shutterstock, Inc.

Exploring Interests and Values

Holland's Basic Categories of Career Interests

- Realistic
- Investigative
- Artistic
- Social
- Enterprising
- Conventional

Becoming aware of your interests and values will increase self-understanding and help you to make good decisions about your college major and future career. Interests and values are also important considerations in thinking about your preferred lifestyle.

Using Interests to Choose a Career

Interests are simply what a person likes to do. Interests are a result of many factors, including personality, family life, values, and the environment. Knowing about your interests is helpful in planning a satisfying career. By studying people who are satisfied with their careers, psychologists have been able to help people choose careers based on their interests. John L. Holland proposed one of the most widely used theories of career development. He described six basic categories of occupational interests that are widely used today in career counseling: realistic, investigative, artistic, social, enterprising, and conventional.[1] As you read the descriptions below, think about which occupational areas you prefer.

Realistic Persons

- Enjoy working with tools, machines, and equipment
- Work outdoors with animals, machines, or nature
- Prefer active and adventurous activities
- Like jobs that produce concrete results, such as fixing, building, and repairing
- Have good mechanical abilities
- Are employed in manufacturing, construction, transportation, and engineering

Investigative Persons

- Have a strong interest in science
- Work with abstract theories, analyze data, and solve problems
- Work independently doing research and analysis
- Are analytical, curious, original, and creative
- Have good skills in mathematics and science
- Are employed in science or laboratory work

Artistic Persons

- Enjoy visual arts, music, drama, or writing
- Are creative and value self-expression
- Appreciate beauty and aesthetic qualities
- Work in unstructured and flexible environments
- Have artistic talent
- Work in museums, theaters, concert halls, advertising, and other artistic careers

Social Persons

- Like to work with people
- Enjoy helping, nurturing, and caring for others
- Have social, communication, and teaching skills
- Work with people through leading, directing, or persuading
- Are often humanistic, idealistic, kind, and understanding
- Work in schools, social services, religious occupations, health care, and mental health facilities

QUIZ
Interests

Test what you have learned by selecting the correct answer to the following questions.

1. Realistic people are likely to choose a career in

    a.   construction or engineering
    b.   accounting or real estate
    c.   financial investments or banking

2. Investigative people are likely to choose a career in

    a.   art or music
    b.   teaching or social work
    c.   science or laboratory work

3. Enterprising people are likely to choose a career in

    a.   computer programming or accounting
    b.   business management or government
    c.   health care or social services

4. Conventional people are likely to choose a career in

    a.   health care or social services
    b.   financial investments or banking
    c.   manufacturing or transportation

5. Social types generally

    a.   enjoy working with tools and machines
    b.   are humanistic and idealistic
    c.   have skills in selling and communication

How did you do on the quiz? Check your answers: 1. a, 2. c, 3. b, 4. b, 5. b

Using Values to Make Important Life Decisions

Values are what we think is important and what we feel is right and good. Values come from many sources, including our parents, friends, the media, our religious background, our culture, our society, and the historical time in which we live. Our values make us different and unique individuals. Knowing our values helps us to make good decisions about work and life. For example, consider a situation in which a person is offered a high-paying job that involves a high degree of responsibility and a lot of stress. If the person values challenge and excitement and views stress as a motivator, the chances are that it would be a good decision to take the job. If the person values peace of mind and has a difficult time coping with stress, it might be better to forgo the higher income and maintain quality of life. Making decisions consistent with our values is one of the keys to happiness and success.

Values and needs are closely related. Humanistic psychologist Abraham Maslow[4] theorized that we adopt certain values to fulfill psychological or physical needs. He described needs and values in terms of a pyramid in which needs are organized in a hierarchy arranged from the most basic to the most complex and personal. We cannot move to the next higher level until lower-level needs are met. These needs, listed in order from most basic to most complex can be defined as follows:

Biological needs. Basic needs for survival including food, water, air, and clothing

Safety needs. Basic needs for shelter and a safe and predictable environment

Love and belongingness. Includes love, respect, and caring from our family and friends

Self-esteem. Feeling good about yourself and having confidence in your abilities

Intellectual. Having the knowledge and understanding needed for survival

Aesthetic. Having an appreciation of beauty

Self-actualization. Developing and reaching your fullest potential, enabling you to contribute to society

An example of a practical application of this theory is finding a solution for homeless people in society. It is easy to say that they should just go get a job. Applying Maslow's hierarchy of needs, we would say that the first step in helping the homeless is to meet their biological needs. Before they can worry about employment, they need food, water, and clothing. Next they need shelter so they have a safe and predictable environment. They need to know that people care about them so they can develop self-esteem. Once people have self-esteem and confidence, they can begin to be trained and educated. Once they have skills, they can become employed and enjoy the good life, appreciate beauty, and reach their potential. A person who is employed pays taxes and may do volunteer work to contribute to society.

Self-actualization is another word for success. It means knowing about and using your talents to fulfill your potential. It means being healthy and creative. It is being the best that you can be. Abraham Maslow said, "We may still often (if not always) expect that a new discontent and restlessness will soon develop, unless the individual is doing what he's fitted for. A musician must make music, an artist must paint, a poet must write, if he's to be ultimately at peace. What a person can be, he must be. This need we call self-actualization."[5]

We are all ultimately aiming for self-actualization. Here are some characteristics of the self-actualized person:

Calvin and Hobbs, © 1993 Watterson. Dist. by Universal Press Syndicate. Reprinted with permission. All rights reserved.

- Feels secure, loved, respected, and makes a connection with others
- Values self and others
- Is independent

- Can make decisions and accept responsibility
- Appreciates other people and cares for the world
- Is open to new ideas
- Resists conformity
- Has little need for status symbols
- Is emotionally balanced
- Is not burdened with anxiety, guilt, or shame
- Treats others with respect
- Feels at one with humankind
- Has deep and caring relationships
- Can look at life with a sense of humor
- Is creative, passionate, and enjoys life
- Takes time for self-renewal and relaxation
- Has strong values and a philosophy of life

This sounds great, but may be difficult. Remember that we are always on the road to self-actualization. Life is about growing and changing. If we do not grow and change, life becomes boring. It all begins with basic needs for survival. Once we have the basic needs for survival, we can focus on wants or desires (the possibilities). We can't have everything, so we determine what is important or what we value the most. Knowing what we value helps us to make good decisions about life goals. In setting our goals, we put values into practice. Meeting the challenges of our lives and accomplishing our goals leads to satisfaction and happiness. The process looks like this:

Needs $\longrightarrow$ Wants $\longrightarrow$ Values $\longrightarrow$
Meet basic survival needs. What is possible? What is important?

Decisions $\longrightarrow$ Goals $\longrightarrow$ Accomplish goals
Make choices based on values. Decide on life goals. Become self-actualized.

JOURNAL ENTRY #3
Picture yourself as a self-actualized person. Describe what life would be like.

ACTIVITY
Values Checklist

Assessing Your Personal Values

Use the following checklist to begin to think about what values are important to you.
Place a checkmark next to any value that is important to you. There are no right or wrong answers. If you think
of other values that are important to you, add them to the bottom of the list.

_____ Having financial security

_____ Making a contribution to humankind

_____ Being a good parent

_____ Being honest

_____ Acquiring wealth

_____ Being a wise person

_____ Becoming an educated person

_____ Believing in a higher power (God)

_____ Preserving civil rights

_____ Never being bored

_____ Enjoying life and having fun

_____ Making something out of my life

_____ Being an ethical person

_____ Feeling safe and secure

_____ Having a good marriage

_____ Having good friends

_____ Having social status

_____ Being patriotic

_____ Having power

_____ Having good morals

_____ Being creative

_____ Having control over my life

_____ Growing and developing

_____ Feeling competent

_____ Feeling relaxed

_____ Having prestige

_____ Improving society

_____ Having good mental health

_____ Being a good athlete

_____ Enjoying the present moment

_____ Maintaining peace of mind

_____ Having good family relationships

_____ Preserving the environment

_____ Having the respect of others

_____ Becoming famous

_____ Happiness

_____ Freedom and independence

_____ Common sense

_____ Having pride in my culture

_____ Doing community service

_____ Achieving my goals in life

_____ Having adventures

_____ Having leisure time

_____ Having good health

_____ Being loyal

_____ Having a sense of accomplishment

_____ Participating in church activities

_____ Being physically fit

_____ Helping others

_____ Being a good person

_____ Having time to myself

_____ Loving and being loved

_____ Being physically attractive

_____ Achieving something important

_____ Accepting who I am

_____ Appreciating natural beauty

_____ Using my artistic talents

_____ Feeling good about myself

_____ Making a difference

_____ Other: _____

_____ Other: _____

_____ Other: _____

JOURNAL ENTRY #4
What is your most important value? Why is it important to you?

Keys to Success

Act on Your Values

Values are what are most important to you; they are your highest principles. They provide the road map to your success and happiness. You will face important turning points along life's journey. Should I go to college? What will be my major? What career will I have? Who should I marry? What job should I take? Where shall I live? You can find good answers to these questions by being aware of your values and using them to make decisions and guide your actions. If your decisions follow your values, you can get what you want out of life.

The first step is knowing your values. You may need some time to think about your values and change them if they are not right for you. What values were you taught as a child? What values do you want to keep as an adult? Look around at people that you admire. What are their values? What values have you learned from your religion? Are these values important to you? Ask your friends about their values and share yours. Revise and rethink your values periodically. Make sure your values are your own and not necessarily values that someone has told you were important. When you begin to think about values, you can come up with many things that are important. The key is to find out which values are most important. In this way, when you are faced with a choice, you will not be confused. You will know what is most important to you.

Knowing about values is not enough. It is important to act consistently with your values and to follow them. For example, if people value health but continue to smoke, they are saying one thing but doing another. If they value family but spend all of their time at work, they are not acting consistently with their values. As a result, they might find that their family is gone and they have lost something that is really valuable.

Use your actions to question or reaffirm your values. Do you really value your health and family?

If so, take action to preserve your good health and spend time with your family. It is necessary to periodically look at your patterns of behavior. Do you act out of habit or do you act according to what is important to you? Habits might need to be changed to get what you value most out of life.

In times of doubt and difficulty, your values can keep you going. If you truly value getting a college education, you can put in the effort to accomplish your goal. When you have doubts about whether you can be successful, examine your values again and remind yourself of why you are doing what you are doing. For example, if you value being an independent business entrepreneur, you will put in the effort to be successful. If you value being a good parent, you will find the patience and develop the skill to succeed. Reminding yourself of your values can help you to continue your commitment to accomplishing your goals.

By knowing your values and following them, you have a powerful tool for making decisions, taking action, and motivating yourself to be successful.

JOURNAL ENTRY #5

Write down your most important value. Write an intention statement about how you plan to act on this value. For example, my most important value is to maintain my good health. I intend to act on this value by eating right and exercising.

QUIZ
Values

Test what you have learned by selecting the correct answer to the following questions.

1. Values are

   a. What we find interesting
   b. What we find important
   c. What we find entertaining

2. Abraham Maslow described values as a

   a. Circle
   b. Pyramid
   c. Square

3. According to Maslow, our most basic needs are

   a. Social
   b. Biological
   c. Intellectual

4. According to Maslow, we are all aiming for

   a. Independence
   b. Wealth
   c. Self-actualization

5. Knowing what we value helps us to make good

   a. Wages
   b. Decisions
   c. Expenditures

How did you do on the quiz? Check your answers: 1. b, 2. b, 3. b, 4. c, 5. b

JOURNAL ENTRIES

Exploring Interests and Values

Go to http://www.collegesuccess1.com/ for Word files of the Journal Entries

Success over the Internet

Visit the *College Success website* at http://www.collegesuccess1.com/

The *College Success Website* is continually updated with new topics and links to the material presented in this chapter. Topics include

- Occupations for realistic, investigative, artistic, social, enterprising, and conventional interests

- Holland's self-directed search
- Various self-assessments
- Being a self-actualized person

Contact your instructor if you have any problems in accessing the *College Success Website.*

Notes

1. John L. Holland, *Making Vocational Choices: A Theory of Careers* (Englewood Cliffs, NJ: Prentice-Hall, 1973).
2. Lenore W. Harmon, Jo-Ida C. Hansen, Fred H. Borgen, and Allen L. Hammer, *Strong Interest Inventory Applications and Technical Guide* (Stanford, CA: Stanford University Press, 1994).
3. The Lifestyle Triangle adapted with permission from NTL Institute, "Urban Middle-Class Lifestyles in Transition," by Paula Jean Miller and Gideon Sjoberg, p. 149, *Journal of Applied Behavioral Science*, Vol. 9, Nos. 2/3, copyright 1973.
4. Abraham Maslow, *Motivation and Personality* (New York: Harper and Row, 1970).
5. Maslow, *Motivation and Personality*, 91.

Values in Action

Name _____   Date _____

Knowing your values is important to making good decisions. Read the following scenarios and think about the values of the person described. Make a recommendation to answer the question posed in each case. You may want to do this exercise in a group with other students.

Scenario 1: What should be my major?

Shawn is 20 years old and has completed two years of college. He has been trying to decide whether to major in engineering or music. He has completed all of his general education requirements as well as several courses in music, math, and physics. As a child, Shawn was interested in science and dreamed of making new inventions. He always took things apart to see how they worked. Math was always easy for Shawn, and he received awards for achievement in science.

He also took part in band throughout his school years and learned to play several instruments. As a teenager, he had a garage band and became so interested in playing the piano that he spent two hours a day practicing. Shawn's dilemma was that he was becoming stressed out trying to do both majors and no longer had time to do well in both music and engineering. He also wanted to have time to get a part-time job in order to become more independent. Shawn's top five values are being independent and living on his own, having a secure future, doing interesting work, achieving something important, and being able to relax.

What are Shawn's values?

What major should Shawn consider? Why?

Scenario 2: Should I continue my education?

Maria is a married mother of two young boys ages five and seven and a part-time college student. Maria and her husband, Juan, are very proud of their Mexican heritage and value their marriage and family. They both think that it is important for Maria to spend time with the children. Maria learned to speak English as a second language and has made sure that her children speak both English and Spanish. While the children are in school, Maria has been attending college part-time with the goal of becoming a teacher's aide in a class for bilingual children. She has some experience as a teacher's aide and gets a great deal of satisfaction from helping the children.

Juan works in construction, and the family has sacrificed to come up with the money to pay for Maria to attend college. Maria has struggled to earn her associate's degree and is proud of her accomplishments. She values her education and wants her children to do well in school. Now Maria is considering continuing her education to earn the bachelor's degree so that she can become a teacher. She would enjoy having her own classroom, loves working with children, and would have a higher income as a teacher than she would as a teacher's aide. Maria's husband is concerned that she will spend too much time at college and will not be home for the children. He is also relieved that Maria has finished college and plans to work part-time to supplement the family income while the children are in school.

What are Maria's values? Should Maria continue her education?

Summing up Interests

Name _____   Date _____

Look back at your scores from the activity in this chapter titled "Learn about Your Interests." Rank the interest areas from 1 to 6 based on your scores, with 1 being the area you are most interested in.

_____ Realistic

_____ Investigative

_____ Artistic

_____ Social

_____ Enterprising

_____ Conventional

The areas that you ranked 1, 2, and 3 form a code that you can use to look up occupations that match your interests. For example, if A, R, and E are your first three choices, you can look up the code ARE in a career resource such as the *Occupations Finder** to find careers matching the artistic, realistic, and enterprising interests. Under this code, you would find occupations such as merchandise displayer, floral designer, pastry chef, and architect.

Write your interest code here:

The *Occupations Finder* is available in most college career centers. You can learn more about your interests and recommended occupations by taking the Strong Interest Inventory or other assessments, also available in most college career centers.

Using the *Occupations Finder*, or pages 258–262 in this chapter, the results of the Strong Interest Inventory or other assessments, list some careers that match your interest code above.

*John L. Holland, *The Occupations Finder* (Odessa, FL: Psychological Assessment Resources, 1996).

Name _____   Date _____

Look at the "Values Checklist" you completed on page 266 of this chapter. Choose the ten values most important to you and list them here.

_____   _____

_____   _____

_____   _____

_____   _____

_____   _____

Next, pick out the value that is most important and label it 1. Label your second most important value 2, and so on until you have picked out your top five values.

1. My most important value is_____. Why?

2. My second most important value is_____. Why?

3. My third most important value is _____. Why?

4. My fourth most important value is _____. Why?

5. My fifth most important value is _____. Why?

LEARNING OBJECTIVES

Read to answer these key questions:

- What are some employment trends for the future?

- What are work skills necessary for success in the 21st Century?

- How do I research a career?

- How do I plan my education?

- How can I make good decisions about my future?

- How can I obtain my ideal job?

- What is a dangerous opportunity?

© Stephen Coburn, 2008. Under license from Shutterstock, Inc.

Planning Your Career and Education

It is always easier to get where you are going if you have a road map or a plan. To start the journey, it is helpful to know about yourself, including your personality, interests, talents, and values. Once you have this picture, you will need to know about the world of work and job trends that will affect your future employment opportunities. Next, you will need to make decisions about which road to follow. Then, you will need to plan your education to reach your destination. Finally, you will need some job-seeking skills such as writing a resume and preparing for a successful interview.

Employment Trends

The world is changing quickly, and these changes will affect your future career. To assure your future career success, you will need to become aware of career trends and observe how they change over time so that you can adjust your career plans accordingly. For example, recently a school was established for training bank tellers. The school quickly went out of business and the students demanded their money back because they were not able to get jobs. A careful observer of career trends would have noticed that bank tellers are being replaced by automatic teller machines (ATM's) and would not have started a school for training bank tellers. Students observant of career trends would not have paid money for the training. It is probably a good idea for bank tellers to look ahead and plan a new career direction.

How can you find out about career trends that may affect you in the future? Become a careful observer by reading about current events. Good sources of information include:

- Your local newspaper, especially the business section
- News programs
- Current magazines
- Government statistics and publications
- The Internet

When thinking about future trends, use your critical thinking skills. Sometimes trends change quickly or interact in different ways. For example, since we are using e-mail to a great extent today, it might seem that mail carriers would not be as much in demand in the future. However, since people are buying more goods over the Internet, there has been an increased demand for mail carriers and other delivery services. Develop the habit of looking at what is happening to see if you can identify trends that may affect your future.

Usually trends get started as a way to meet the following needs:[1]

- To save money
- To reduce cost
- To do things faster
- To make things easier to use
- To improve safety and reliability
- To lessen the impact on the environment

The following are some trends to watch that may affect your future career. As you read about each trend, think about how it could affect you.

Baby Boomers, Generation X, and the Millennial Generation

About every twenty years, sociologists begin to describe a new generation with similar characteristics based on shared historical experiences. Each generation has different opportunities and challenges in the workplace.

The Baby Boomers were born following World War II between 1946 and 1964. Four out of every ten adults today is in this Baby Boom Generation.[2] Because there are so many aging Baby Boomers, the average age of Americans is increasing. Life expectancy is also increasing. By 2010 the projected life expectancy will be 78.5 years.[3] In the new millennium many more people will live to be 100 years old or more! Think about the implications of an older population. Older people need such things as health care, recreation, travel and financial planning. Occupations related to these needs are likely to be in demand now and in the future.

Those born between 1965 and 1977 are often referred to as Generation X. They are sometimes called the "baby bust" generation because fewer babies were born during this period than in the previous generations. There is much in the media about this generation having to pay higher taxes and social security payments to support the large number of aging Baby Boomers. Some say that this generation will not enjoy the prosperity of the Baby Boomers. Those who left college in the early nineties faced a recession and the worst job market since World War II.[4] Many left college in debt and returned home to live with their parents. Because of a lack of employment opportunities, many in this generation became entrepreneurs, starting new companies at a faster rate than previous generations.

Jane Bryant Quinn notes that in spite of economic challenges, Generation Xers have a lot going for them:[5]

- They have record-high levels of education, which correlate with higher income and lower unemployment. In 1993, 47 percent of 18- to 24-year-olds had at least some higher education. Also high school dropout rates were down.
- There is a demand for more skilled workers, so employers are more willing to train employees. Anthony Carnevale, chairman of the National Commission for Employment Policy, "sees a big demand for 'high-school plus'—a high school diploma plus technical school or junior college."
- Generation Xers are computer literate, and those who use computers on the job earn 10 to 15 percent more than those who don't.
- This group often has a good work ethic valued by employers. However, they value a balanced lifestyle with time for outside interests and family.
- As Baby Boomers retire, more job opportunities are created for this group.
- Unlike the Baby Boomers, this generation was born into a more integrated and more diverse society. They are better able than previous generations to adapt to diversity in society and the workplace.

Many of today's college students are part of the Millennial Generation born between 1977 and 1995. This generation is sometimes called Generation Y or the Echo Boomers since they are the children of the Baby Boomers.[6] This new generation of approximately 60 million is three times larger than Generation X and will eventually exceed the number of Baby Boomers. By 2010, they will become the largest teen population is U.S. history. As the Millennials reach college age, they will attend college in increasing numbers. In the next ten years, college enrollments will increase by approximately 300,000 students per year. Colleges will find it difficult to accommodate rapidly increasing numbers of students and as a result, the Millennial Generation will face increasingly competitive college admissions criteria.

Millennials are more ethnically diverse than previous generations with 34 percent ethnic minorities. One in four lives with a single parent. Three in four have working mothers. Most of them started using computers before they were five years old. Marketing researchers describe this new generation as "technologically adept, info-savvy, a cyber-generation, the clickeratti."[7] They are the connected generation, accustomed to cell phones, chatting on the Internet, and listening to downloaded music.

Young people in the Millennial Generation share a different historical perspective from the Baby Boom Generation. Baby Boomers remember the Viet Nam War and the assassinations of President John F. Kennedy and Martin Luther King. For Millennials school shootings such as Columbine and acts of terrorism such as the Oklahoma City bombing and the 9-11 attack on New York City stand out as important events. The Millennial Generation will see their main problems as dealing with violence, easy access to weapons, and the threat of terrorism.

Neil Howe and William Strauss paint a very positive picture of this new generation in their book *Millennials Rising: The Next Great Generation:*

- Millennials will rebel by tearing down old institutions that do not work and building new and better institutions. The authors share a quote from Shansel Nagia: "I like to think of my generation, the Class of 2000, as the Millennial Generation. We are the kids who are going to change things."
- Surveys show that this generation describes themselves as happy, confident, and positive.
- They are cooperative team players.
- They generally accept authority and respect their parents' values.
- They follow rules. The rates of homicides, violent crime, abortion, and teen pregnancy are decreasing rapidly.
- The use of alcohol, drugs, and tobacco is decreasing.
- Millennials have a fascination with and mastery of new technology.
- Their most important values are individuality and uniqueness.[8]

It is predicted that the world of work for the Millennials will be dramatically different. Previous generations anticipated having a lifetime career. By the year 2020, many jobs will probably be short-term contracts. This arrangement will provide cost savings and efficiency for employers and flexibility for employees to start or stop work to take vacations, train for new jobs, or meet family responsibilities. One in five people will be self-employed. Retirement will be postponed as people look forward to living longer and healthier lives.[9]

JOURNAL ENTRY #1

What generation are you in and how might this affect your future?

Moving from Goods to Services and Technology

Human society has moved through several stages. The first stage, about 20,000 years ago, was the hunting and gathering stage. During this time, society depended on the natural environment for food and other resources. When natural resources were depleted, the community moved to another area. The second stage, some 10,000 years ago, was the agricultural stage. Human beings learned to domesticate animals and cultivate crops. This allowed people to stay in one place and develop more permanent villages. About 200 years ago, industrial societies came into being by harnessing power sources to produce goods on a large scale.

Today in the United States we are evolving into a service, technology, and information society. Fewer people are working in agriculture and manufacturing. More people are working in service, technology, and information occupations. Futurists John Naisbitt, Patricia Aburdeen, and Walter Krechel note that we are moving toward a service economy based on high technology, rapid communications, biotechnology for use in agriculture and medicine, health care, and sales of merchandise.[10] Four out of five new jobs are in the service area.[11] Service occupations include health care, business, education, wholesale and retail trade, finance, insurance, real estate, transportation, communication, public utilities, and government.

The Department of Labor reported that most job growth since 1970 has been in the service area.[12] These are some service areas that are projected to increase in the coming decades:

- Health-care-related occupations will increase faster than any other service occupation. Two factors will contribute to this growth: an aging population has greater need for health services, and advances in technology and medication provide services and treatments that result in improved health care.
- Contracted-out business services will continue to increase. Businesses contract out services to operate more efficiently at a lower cost. These services include data processing, advertising, and security services.
- There will be a shift in work usually done in the home to outside service agencies. For example, people are increasingly eating out or eating prepared foods. As a consequence, jobs will increase in restaurants and related food industries.
- There will be increasing demand for child care, nursing homes, and home health-care services.
- The fastest growing occupations between 1998 and 2008 are expected to be computer related: computer engineers, computer support specialists, computer systems analysts, database administrators, and desktop publishers.[13]

The Effect of Automation

Automation is increasing in order to reduce the cost of goods and services. Jobs that involve simple repetitive tasks are being eliminated resulting in fewer unskilled jobs. Manufacturing jobs are being moved to Mexico, Taiwan, India and China. Another phase of automation is happening in the home. In the past, people bought dish washers and clothes washers to save time. New careers and products are evolving to save time in the home including preparing meals, cleaning the house, buying groceries and helping children with homework.

The Middle Class Is an Endangered Species

Author Joyce Lain Kennedy believes that the middle class is becoming an endangered species.[14] She states that many jobs traditionally held by the middle class have been "dumbed down," making them so simple that anyone can do them. These jobs pay very little and offer no benefits, no employment stability, and little opportunity for advancement. Young people often hold these jobs in their teens and twenties. Individuals who do not go on for education or training after high school often become stuck in these low-paying jobs.

One of the reasons for making these lower-level jobs simpler is that employers are concerned about the lack of skills of their employees. Kennedy states, "One third of today's workers will be unable to read well enough to qualify for entry-level jobs. Almost half of the firms in a recent survey say that between 15 percent and 35 percent of their current employees aren't capable of handling more complex tasks; about 10 percent say that up to half of their current workers do not have the skills needed for promotion."[15]

At the other end of the job continuum are jobs requiring a college education or training beyond high school. These high-end jobs often require technical or computer skills. These are the jobs that pay better and offer benefits. It seems that we are becoming a nation of haves and have-nots who are separated by their education and technical skills.

A Diverse Workforce

The workforce in the United States is becoming increasingly more diverse. Diversity includes many demographic variables such as race, religion, color, gender, national origin, disability, sexual orientation, age, education, geographic origin, and skill characteristics. Having an appreciation for diversity is important in maintaining a work environment that is open and allows for individual differences. Increasing diversity provides opportunities for many different kinds of individuals and makes it important to be able to have good working relationships with all kinds of people.

The U.S. Department of Labor[16] and the Bureau of Labor Statistics[17] have described some trends affecting the workplace:

- From 1998 to 2008, total employment is projected to increase from 140.5 million to 160.8 million. This is an increase of 14.4 percent.
- Because of the aging of the Baby Boomers, the average age of workers will rise.
- More women will be in the workforce. Women now comprise 47 to 50 percent of the workforce. Because women are still concentrated in traditionally women's jobs, they still earn only 76 cents for every dollar earned by a man.
- One third of new workers will be from minority populations. Hispanics and African Americans will continue to increase their representation in the workforce.
- There will be more immigrants than at any time since World War I.

Impact of the Internet

The Internet is having a profound effect on the way we communicate, work, and do business. Microsoft CEO Bill Gates has predicted that business will change more in the next ten years than in the last 50 years. In his book, *Business @ the Speed of Thought*[18], he summarizes the kinds of changes happening to businesses because of the Internet. These changes will affect the kinds of jobs that exist in the future.

- **E-mail.** The 2000s will be an age of speedy communication. Bill Gates predicts that within five years businesses will use the Internet more than the telephone. This rapid communication will help businesses to deliver goods and services faster.

- **E-commerce.** E-commerce is business conducted over the Internet. Department of Labor statistics show that e-commerce more than doubled between 1996 and 1997 from $15.5 billion to $38.8 billion. By 1998, sales exceeded $300 billion. By 2005, e-commerce is expected to reach $1 trillion.[19] Bill Gates describes Dell computers as an example of the most successful businesses using e-commerce:

  > Dell was one of the first major companies to move to e-commerce. A global computer supplier with more than $18 billion in revenue, Dell began selling its products online in mid-1996. The company's online business quickly rose from $1 million a week to $1 million a day. Soon it jumped to $3 million a day, then $5 million. It's now risen to $14 million.[20]

Businesses that do not use the Internet will be missing out on opportunities and may not be able to compete with businesses using e-commerce. Gates says that online sales will increase 45 percent per year, changing the nature of the way we do business. Online commerce will be increasingly used in finance, insurance, travel, online auctions, and computer sales. The increase in e-commerce may reduce the use of conventional stores, increase mail delivery services, and reduce inventory.

- **The paperless office.** In the future, businesses will increasingly use an intranet to take the place of numerous forms and papers. An intranet works much the same say as the Internet. It is a network used to share information within a company and is accessible only to those within the company. Using an intranet helps employees to access, organize, and file information in a fast and efficient way. There will be no more searching through piles of paper to find needed information.

- **Friction-free capitalism.** Bill Gates uses the term "friction-free capitalism" to describe a marketplace in which buyers and sellers can find each other easily. Consumers can use the Internet to find any product, and businesses can use it to find consumers interested in purchasing their products. Consumers can also gather information about products and find the best prices using the Internet.

Effects of the Internet on Business

- E-mail
- E-commerce
- Paperless office
- Friction-free capitalism
- Customer service
- Web lifestyle
- Web workstyle

- **Customer service.** The Internet will increasingly be used to provide customer service. For example, hotels can use the Internet to process reservations anywhere in the world. The consumer can access a digital photo of the hotel and room options. Many hotel rooms feature modem connections. Since the computer handles the details of the reservation, clerks will have more time for personal service.

- **The Web lifestyle.** Gates refers to the Web lifestyle as new hardware and software that will change the way we live. Because of rapid communication through the Internet, the people of the world will be drawn closer together. Personal computers and access to the Internet are becoming less expensive. More and more people will use the Web to get information, learn, and communicate.

One of the biggest changes is that consumers will shift to managing their finances online. Many will bank and pay bills electronically. When consumers pay bills online, the U.S. Commerce Department estimates that processing costs will drop more than $20 billion annually.[21] This will mean fewer people will be involved in the bill-paying process, and those who work in this area will be using a computer to do their jobs.

- **The Web workstyle.** Digital tools will change the roles and skills required of many workers in the future. Many workers will become freelancers, or free agents who work on a project basis. When a project is completed, they will move on to a different project, possibly in a different company. Because of the Web, workers can live in one place and work in another. Workers in the future will need to be more highly skilled.

The Web lifestyle will increasingly equalize opportunities for skilled people around the world. If you had to guess someone's approximate income today and were limited to a single polite question, a good one would be: "What country do you live in?" The reason is the huge disparity in average wages from country to country. In twenty years, if you want to guess somebody's income, the most telling question will be: "What's your education?"[22]

Gates thinks positively and says that these changes will empower people. People will be shifted from routine nonthinking work to more productive thinking work. He does not see people being replaced by computers. He states, "A good knowledge worker will add value to the computer." When workers are freed from the routine work, they can provide the human touch where it is important. "Workers are no longer a cog in a machine but rather are an intelligent part of the overall process."[23]

The Microprocessor

The microprocessor is a silicon chip containing transistors that determine the capability of a computer. In the past twenty years, the power of the microprocessor has increased more than one million times. In the next twenty years, the power will increase a million times again.[24] Because of the increased power of the microprocessor, it will be used in new ways and with new devices. Consider the "smart home" of the future:

At home, you'll be able to operate your PC by talking to it. It will automatically back up all your information, update its own software and synchronize itself with your TV, cell phone, handheld, and all the devices on your home network. The refrigerator in your kitchen will know how well stocked it is, suggest recipes based on what's available, and order more food from your online grocer. Your TV will double as an interactive shopping mall, letting you buy advertised products or clothes you saw in a sitcom. And if you don't want to watch TV, you'll be able to read an electronic book that knows your favorite authors and automatically downloads their latest novels. If you decide to read one of them, your bank account will be debited.[25]

The microprocessor is increasingly available to all and for less cost. The personal computer would have occupied an entire building 35 years ago. Today we have access to powerful computers that will play an ever greater role in our daily lives.

It's remarkable how we now take all that power for granted. Using a basic home PC costing less than $1,000, you can balance your household budget, do your taxes, write letters to friends and fax or e-mail them over the Internet, listen to CDs or the radio, watch the news, consult a doctor, play games, book a vacation, view a house, buy a book or a car. The list is endless.[26]

New Advances in Technology

Because we are living in the Information Age, information and technology workers are now the largest group of workers in the United States. Careers in Information Technology include the design, development, and support of computer software, hardware, and networks. Some newer jobs in this area include animators for video games, films, and videos as well as setting up Web sites and Internet security. There are also good opportunities for network programmers who can program a group of computers to work together. Because computer use has increased greatly, it is expected that computer-related jobs will expand by 40 percent or more in the next decade.[27]

In the future, computers will continue to become more powerful, mobile and connected. It is predicted that by 2018, microprocessors will be replaced by optical computers that function at the speed of light. Technology will be embedded in products used for entertainment as well as for home and business use. It is predicted that in the future, the desktop computer as we know it will cease to exist. Instead of a home computer, we will have computerized homes with sensors that monitor energy use and smart appliances with computer chips. Gestures, touch, and voice communication will rapidly replace computer keyboards. Nintendo Wii and the Iphone are current examples. Computers will move from homes and offices into human bodies. Microchips may be embedded in human bodies to monitor health conditions and to deliver medical care. Some futurists forecast a time when computer chips will be embedded in the brain and connected to the Internet. Of course computer security will become increasingly important with these new advances.[28]

Radiation and laser technologies will provide new technical careers in the future. It has been said that lasers will be as important to the 21st century as electricity was for the 20th century. New uses for lasers are being found in medicine, energy, industry, computers, communications, entertainment, and outer space. The use of lasers is creating new jobs and causing others to become obsolete. For example, many welders are being replaced by laser technicians who have significantly higher earnings. New jobs will open for people who purchase, install, and maintain lasers.

Careers in fiber optics and telecommunications are among the top new emerging fields in the 21st century. Fiber optics are thin glass fibers that transmit light. This new technology may soon make the copper wire obsolete. One of the most important uses of fiber optics is to speed up delivery of data over the Internet and to improve telecommunications. It is also widely used in medical instruments including laser surgery.

Another interesting development to watch is artificial intelligence software, which enables computers to recognize patterns, improve from experience, make inferences, and approximate human thought. Scientists at the MIT Artificial Intelligence Lab have developed a robot named Cog. Here is a description of Cog and its capabilities:

We have given it a multitude of sensors to "feel" and learn what it is like to be touched and spoken to. Cog's ability to make eye contact and reach out to moving objects is also meant to motivate people to interact with it. These features have taught Cog, among other things, to distinguish a human face from inanimate objects (this puts its development at about a 3-month-old's). It can also listen to music and keep rhythm by tapping on a drum (something a 5-year-old can do). One of the most startling moments in Cog's development came when it was learning to touch things. At one point, Cog began to touch and discover its own body. It looked so eerie and human, I was stunned.[29]

Beware of Outsourcing

To reduce costs and improve profits, many jobs in technology, manufacturing, and service are being outsourced to countries such as India, China, and Taiwan, where well-educated, English-speaking workers are being used to do these jobs. For example, programmers in India can produce software at only 10 percent of the cost of these services in the United States. Jobs that are currently being outsourced include accounting, payroll clerks, customer service, data entry, assembly line workers, industrial and production engineers, machine operators, computer-assisted design (CADD) technicians, purchasing managers, textile workers, software developers, and technical support. It is a good idea to consider this trend in choosing your future career and major. Jobs that are most likely to be outsourced are:[30]

- Repetitive jobs such as accounting
- Well-defined jobs such as customer service
- Small manageable projects such as software development
- Jobs in which proximity to the customer is not important, such as technical support

Jobs that are least likely to be outsourced include:

- Jobs with ambiguity such as top management jobs
- Unpredictable jobs such as troubleshooters
- Jobs that require understanding of the culture such as marketing
- Jobs that require close proximity to the customer such as auto repair
- Jobs requiring a high degree of innovation and creativity such as a product designer
- Jobs in entertainment, music, art, and design

To protect yourself from outsourcing:

- Strive to be the best in the field
- Be creative and innovative
- Avoid repetitive jobs that do not require proximity to the customer
- Choose a career where the demand is so high that it won't matter if some are outsourced
- Consider a job in the skilled trades. Carpenters, plumbers, electricians, hair stylists, construction workers, auto mechanics, and dental hygienists will always be in demand.

New Advances in Biology

Future historians may describe the 21st century as the biology century because of all the developments in this area. If you are interested in biology, it can lead to good careers in the future. One of the most important developments is the Human Genome Project that has identified the genes in human DNA, which is the carrier of genetic material. The research done on the human genome has been an impetus for development in some new careers in biotechnology and biomedical technology. Watch the news for future developments that will affect how we all live and work.

Biotechnology involves genetic engineering, gene splicing, and cloning to create and improve life forms. It will be used to create new manufacturing materials as well as solve problems in pollution and recycling. Biotechnology will also be used to develop new pharmaceuticals. About 90 percent of all drugs ever invented were developed since 1975, and about 6,000 new drugs are waiting for regulatory approval.[31] In the future, biotechnology may be used to find cures for diabetes, arthritis, Alzheimer's disease, and heart disease.

Biomedical technology is the field in which bionic implants are being developed for the human body. Scientists are working on the development of artificial limbs and organs including eyes, ears, hearts, and kidneys. A promising new development in this field is brain and computer interfaces. Scientists recently implanted a computer chip into the brain of a quadriplegic enabling him to control a computer and television with his mind.[32] Biotechnology also develops new diagnostic test equipment and surgical tools.

Increase in Entrepreneurship

An important trend for the new millennium is the increase in entrepreneurship, which means starting your own business. For the Baby Boom Generation, it was expected to have a job for life. Because of rapid changes in society and the world of work, New Millennials can expect to have as many as ten different jobs over a lifetime.[33] A growing number of entrepreneurs operate their small businesses from the home, taking advantage of telecommuting and the Internet to communicate with customers. While being an entrepreneur has some risks involved, there are many benefits, such as flexible scheduling, being your own boss, taking charge of your own destiny, and greater potential for future income if your company is successful. You won't have to worry about being outsourced either.

The Effect of Terrorism

Fear of terrorism has changed attitudes that will affect career trends for years to come. Terrorist attacks have created an atmosphere of uncertainty that has had a negative effect on the economy and has increased unemployment. For example, the airline industries are struggling financially as people hesitate to fly to their vacation destinations. People are choosing to stay in the safety of their homes, offices, cars, and gated communities. Since people are spending more time at home, they spend more money making their home comfortable. Faith Popcorn, who is famous for predicting future trends, has called this phenomenon "cocooning," which is "our desire to build ourselves strong and cozy nests where we can retreat from the world, enjoying ourselves in safety and comfort."[34] As a result, home remodeling and sales of entertainment systems are increasing.

Another result of terrorism is the shift toward occupations that provide value to society, and in which people can search for personal satisfaction.[35] More people volunteer their time to help others, and are considering careers in education, social work, and medical occupations. When people are forced to relocate because of unemployment they are considering moving to smaller towns that have a sense of community and a feeling of safety.

The Effect of Energy Shortages

The rising cost of oil and concerns about global warming will create new careers and products. Because of increased energy costs, manufacturing will become more expensive and recycling will become more cost effective. New energy efficient products such as lighting, appliances and cars will be in increasing demand. Scientists and engineers will continue to develop alternative sources of energy to decrease oil dependence.

The Need for Lifelong Education

In the past, the life pattern for many people was to graduate from school, go to work, and eventually retire. Because of the rapid changes in technology and society today, workers will need additional training and education over a lifetime. Education will take place in a variety of forms: community college courses, training on the job, private training sessions, and learning on your own. Those who do not keep up with the new technology will find that their skills quickly become obsolete. Those who do keep up will find their skills in demand.

While most of the fastest growing jobs will require at least an associate's degree, three out of four U.S. workers are in jobs that do not require a bachelor's degree. These workers will rely on short-term and on-the-job training. They will need good skills in reading, communication, and math to take advantage of these training opportunities.[36]

Nontraditional Workers

Unlike traditional workers, nontraditional workers do not have full-time, year-round jobs with health and retirement benefits. Employers are moving toward using nontraditional workers, including multiple jobholders, contingent and part-time workers, independent contractors, and temporary workers. Nearly four out of five employers use nontraditional workers to help them become more efficient, prevent layoffs, and access workers with special skills. There are advantages and disadvantages to this arrangement. Nontraditional workers have no benefits and risk unemployment. This arrangement can also provide workers with a flexible work schedule in which they work during some periods and pursue other interests or gain new skills when not working.

Companies Say No to Drugs and Alcohol

Problems related to drug and alcohol abuse in the workplace are widespread and costly. Drug and alcohol abuse result in decreased productivity, injuries, and fatalities in the workplace, higher unemployment, and lower income. Many employers screen applicants and employees for drug and alcohol abuse. In some cases, employees are directed to rehabilitation programs, which are costly to administer. Here are some interesting statistics related to drug and alcohol abuse in the workplace:

- Shortfalls in productivity and employment among individuals with alcohol or other drug-related problems cost the American economy $180.9 billion in 2002.[37]
- Although 70 percent of all current adult illegal drug users are employed,[38] use of most illicit drugs is substantially higher among the unemployed. The use of crack cocaine is ten times higher among unemployed persons than those with jobs.[39]
- Up to 40 percent of industrial fatalities and 47 percent of industrial injuries can be linked to alcohol consumption and alcoholism.[40]
- 60 percent of alcohol-related work performance problems can be attributed to employees who are not alcohol dependent but who occasionally drink too much on a work night or drink during a weekday lunch.[41]
- 21 percent of workers reported being injured or put in danger, having to redo work or to cover for a coworker, or needing to work harder due to others' drinking.[42]
- Workers who report having three or more jobs in the previous five years are about twice as likely to be current or past-year illicit drug users as those who have had two or fewer jobs.[43]

- Individuals with drinking problems or alcoholism at any time in their lives suffer income reductions ranging from 1.5 percent to 18.7 percent, depending on age and sex, compared with those with no such diagnosis.[44]

Top Jobs for the Future[45]

Based on current career trends, here are some jobs that should be in high demand for the next ten years.

Field of Employment	Job Titles
Business	Marketing Manager, Security and Financial Service, Internet Marketing Specialist, Advertising Executive, Buyer, Sales Person, Real Estate Agent, Business Development Manager, Marketing Researcher, Recruiter
Education	Teacher, Teacher's Aide, Adult Education Instructor, Math and Science Teacher
Entertainment	Dancer, Producer, Director, Actor, Content Creator, Musician, Artist, Commercial Artist, Writer, Technical Writer, Newspaper Reporter, News Anchor Person
Health	Emergency Medical Technician, Surgeon, Chiropractor, Dental Hygienist, Registered Nurse, Medical Assistant, Therapist, Respiratory Therapist, Home Health Aide, Primary Care Physician, Medical Lab Technician, Radiology Technician, Physical Therapist, Dental Assistant, Nurse's Aide
Information Technology	Computer Systems Analyst, Computer Engineer, Web Specialist, Network Support Technician, Java Programmer, Information Technology Manager, Web Developer, Data Base Administrator, Network Engineer
Law/Law Enforcement	Correction Officer, Law Officer, Anti-terrorist Specialist, Security Guard, Tax/Estate Attorney, Intellectual Property Attorney
Services	Veterinarian, Social Worker, Hair Stylist, Telephone Repair Technician, Aircraft Mechanic, Guidance Counselor, Occupational Therapist, Child Care Assistant, Baker, Landscape Architect, Pest Controller, Chef, Caterer, Food Server
Sports	Athlete, Coach, Umpire, Physical Trainer
Technology	Electrical Engineer, Biological Scientist, Electronic Technician, CAD Operator, Product Designer, Sales Engineer, Applications Engineer, Product Marketing Engineer, Technical Support Manager, Product Development Manager
Trades	Carpenter, Plumber, Electrician
Travel/Transportation	Package Delivery Person, Flight Attendant, Hotel/Restaurant Manager, Taxi Driver, Chauffeur, Driver

QUIZ
Career Trends of the Future

Test what you have learned by selecting the correct answer to the following questions:

1. Most students in college today are in this generation.
   a. The Baby Boom Generation
   b. Generation X
   c. The Millennial Generation

2. Use of the Internet will result in
   a. increased e-commerce.
   b. increased use of conventional stores.
   c. decreased mail delivery.

3. The largest group of workers in the United States are in
   a. manufacturing.
   b. information technology.
   c. agriculture.

4. Jobs unlikely to be outsourced include
   a. jobs that require close proximity to the customer.
   b. computer programming jobs.
   c. customer service jobs.

5. Future historians will describe the 21st century as the
   a. art and entertainment century.
   b. biology century.
   c. industrial development century.

How did you do on the quiz? Check your answers: 1. c, 2. a, 3. b, 4. a, 5. b

---

JOURNAL ENTRY #2

Do a quick review of the career trends listed above. How will these trends affect your future career?

Work Skills for the 21st Century

Because of rapid changes in technology, college students of today may be preparing for jobs that do not exist right now. After graduation, many college students find employment that is not even related to their college major. One researcher found that 48 percent of college graduates find employment in fields not related to their college major.[46] More important than college major, however, are the general skills learned in college that prepare students for the future.

To define skills needed in the future workplace, the U.S. Secretary of Labor created the Secretary's Commission on Achieving Necessary Skills (SCANS). Based on interviews with employers and educators, the members of the commission outlined foundation skills and workplace competencies needed to succeed in the workplace in the twenty-first century.[47] The following skills apply to all occupations in all fields and will help you to become a successful employee, regardless of your major. As you read through these skills, think about your competency in these areas.

Foundation Skills

Basic Skills

- Reading
- Writing
- Basic arithmetic
- Higher level mathematics
- Listening
- Speaking

Thinking Skills

- Creative thinking
- Decision making
- Problem solving
- Mental visualization
- Knowing how to learn
- Reasoning

Personal Qualities

- Responsibility
- Self-esteem
- Sociability
- Self-management
- Integrity/honesty

Workplace Competencies

Resources

- **Time.** Selects relevant goals, sets priorities, follows schedules
- **Money.** Uses budgets, keeps records, and makes adjustments
- **Materials and facilities.** Acquires, stores, and distributes materials, supplies, parts, equipment, space, or final products
- **Human resources.** Assesses knowledge and skills, distributes work, evaluates performance, and provides feedback

Interpersonal

- **Participates as a member of a team.** Works cooperatively with others and contributes to group efforts
- **Teaches others.** Helps others learn needed skills
- **Serves clients/customers.** Works and communicates with clients and customers to satisfy their expectations
- **Exercises leadership.** Communicates, encourages, persuades, and convinces others; responsibly challenges procedures, policies, or authority
- **Negotiates to arrive at a decision.** Works toward an agreement involving resources or diverging interests
- **Works with cultural diversity.** Works well with men and women and with people from a variety of ethnic, social, or educational backgrounds

Information

- **Acquires and evaluates information.** Identifies the need for information, obtains information, and evaluates it
- **Organizes and maintains information.** Organizes, processes, and maintains written or computerized records

- **Uses computers to process information.** Employs computers to acquire, organize, analyze, and communicate information

Systems

- **Understands systems.** Knows how social, organizational, and technological systems work and operates efficiently within them
- **Monitors and corrects performance.** Distinguishes trends, predicts impacts of actions on systems operations, takes action to correct performance
- **Improves and designs systems.** Develops new systems to improve products or services

Technology

- **Selects technology.** Judges which procedures, tools, or machines, including computers, will produce the desired results
- **Applies technology to tasks.** Understands the proper procedures for using machines and computers
- **Maintains and troubleshoots technology.** Prevents, identifies, or solves problems with machines, computers, and other technologies

Because the workplace is changing, these skills may be more important than the background acquired through a college major. Work to develop these skills and you will be prepared for whatever lies ahead.

How to Research Your Career

After you have assessed your personality, interests, values, and talents, the next step is to learn about the world of work. Try to find a match between your personal characteristics and the world of work. To learn about the world of work, you will need to research possible careers. This includes reading career descriptions, and investigating career outlooks, salaries, and educational requirements.

Career Descriptions

The career description tells you about the nature of the work, working conditions, employment, training, qualifications, advancement, job outlook, earnings, and related occupations. The two best sources of job descriptions are the *Occupational Outlook Handbook* and *Occupational Outlook Quarterly*. The *Handbook*, published by the Bureau of Labor Statistics, is like an encyclopedia of careers. You can search alphabetically by career or by career cluster.

The *Occupational Outlook Quarterly* is a periodical with up-to-date articles on new and emerging occupations, training opportunities, salary trends, and new studies from the Bureau of Labor Statistics. You can find these resources in a public or school library, college career center or at the College Success Website at http://www.college success1.com/Links9Career.htm.

Career Outlook

It is especially important to know about the career outlook of an occupation you are considering. Career outlook includes salary and availability of employment. How much does the occupation pay? Will the occupation exist in the future, and will there be employment opportunities? Of course you will want to prepare yourself for careers that pay well and have future employment opportunities.

You can find information about career outlooks in the sources listed above, current periodicals, and materials from the Bureau of Labor Statistics. The table on the next page, for example, lists the fastest growing occupations, occupations with the highest salaries, and occupations with the largest job growth. Information from the Bureau of Labor Statistics is also available online.

Employment Projections, 2002–2012

Ten Fastest-Growing Occupations

Medical assistants
Network systems and data
  communication analysts
Physician assistants
Social and human service assistants
Home health aides
Medical records and health information
  technicians
Physical therapist aides
Computer software engineers, applications
Computer software engineers, systems
  software
Physical therapist assistants

Ten Industries with the Fastest Wage and Salary Employment Growth

Software publishers
Management, scientific,
  and technical consulting
Community care for the elderly
Computer systems design
Employment services
Vocational rehabilitation services
Health-care services
Water and sewage systems
Internet and data processing services
Child day-care services

Ten Occupations with the Largest Job Growth

Registered nurse
Postsecondary teachers
Retail salespersons
Customer service representatives
Food workers
Cashiers
Janitors and cleaners
Operations managers
Waiters and waitresses
Nursing aides, orderlies, and
  attendants

Source: Bureau of Labor Statistics, 2004

Planning Your Education

Once you have assessed your personal characteristics and researched your career options, it is important to plan your education. If you have a plan, you will be able to finish your education more quickly and avoid taking unnecessary classes. You can begin work on your educational plan by following the steps below. After you have done some work on your plan, visit your college counselor or advisor to make sure that your plan is appropriate.

ACTIVITY
Steps in Planning Your Education

_____ 1. **Take your college entrance or assessment tests before you apply to colleges.** Most colleges require the Scholastic Aptitude Test (SAT) or their own local placement tests in order for you to be admitted. You can find information about these tests from your high school or college counseling center or online at http://www.ets.org/ or http://cbweb1.collegeboard.org/index.html. If you are attending a community college, check the college web site, Admissions Office or the Counseling Office to see what placement exams are required.

_____ 2. **Take English the first semester, and continue each semester until your English requirement is complete.** English courses provide the foundation for further college study. Your SAT or college placement test will determine what level of English you need to take. As a general rule, community colleges require one semester of college-level English. Four-year colleges and universities generally require two semesters or three quarters of college-level English. If your placement scores are low, you may be required to take review courses first.

_____ 3. **Start your math classes early, preferably in the first semester or quarter.** Many high paying careers require a long series of math classes, particularly in the sciences, engineering, and business. If you delay taking math courses until later, you may limit your career options and extend your time in college.

_____ 4. **Take the required general education courses.** Find out what your college requires for general education and put these classes on your plan. You will find this information in the college catalog. Be careful to select the correct general education plan. In community colleges, there are different plans for transfer and associate's degree students. At a university there may be different plans for different colleges within the university. Check with a college counselor or advisor to make sure you have the correct plan.

_____ 5. **Prepare for your major.** Consult your college catalog to see what courses are required for your major. If you are undecided on a major, take the general education courses and start working on a decision about your major. If you are interested in the sciences or engineering, start work on math in the first semester. Start on your major requirements as soon as possible so that you do not delay your graduation.

_____ 6. **Check prerequisites.** A prerequisite is a course that is required before taking a higher-level course. The college catalog lists courses offered and includes prerequisites. Most colleges will not let you register for a course for which you do not have the prerequisite. It is also difficult to succeed in an advanced course without taking the prerequisite first.

_____ 7. **Make an educational plan.** The educational plan includes all the courses you will need to graduate. Again, use the college catalog as your guide.

_____ 8. **Check your plan.** See your college counselor or advisor to check your plan. He or she can save you from taking classes that you do not need and help you to graduate in the minimum amount of time.

Making Good Decisions

Knowing how to make a good decision about your career and important life events is very important to your future, as this short poem sums up:

> *There is a choice you have to make, In everything you do.*
> *And you must always keep in mind, The choice you make,*
> *makes you.*[48]

Sometimes people end up in a career because they simply siezed an opportunity for employment. A good job becomes available and they happen to be in the right place at the right time. Sometimes people end up in a career because it is familiar to them because it is a job held by a member of the family or a friend in the community. Sometimes people end up in a career because of economic necessity. The job pays well and they need the money. These careers are the result of chance circumstances. Sometimes they turn out well, and sometimes they turn out miserably.

Whether you are male or female, married or single, you will spend a great deal of your life working. By doing some careful thinking and planning about your career, you can improve your chances of success and happiness. Use the following steps to do some careful decision making about your career. Although you are the person who needs to make the decision about a career, you can get help from your college career center or your college counselor or advisor.

Steps in Making a Career Decision

1. **Begin with self-assessment.**
    *   What is your personality type?
    *   What are your interests?
    *   What are your talents, gifts, and strengths?
    *   What is your learning style?
    *   What are your values?
    *   What lifestyle do you prefer?

2. **Explore your options.**
    *   What careers match your personal characteristics?

3. **Research your career options.**
    *   Read the job description.
    *   Investigate the career outlook.
    *   What is the salary?
    *   What training and education is required?
    *   Speak with an advisor, counselor, or person involved in the career that interests you.
    *   Choose a career or general career area that matches your personal characteristics.

4. **Plan your education to match your career goal.**
    *   Try out courses in your area of interest.
    *   Start your general education if you need more time to decide on a major.
    *   Try an internship or part-time job in your area of interest.

5. **Make a commitment to take action and follow through with your plan.**

6. **Evaluate.**
   - Do you like the courses you are taking?
   - Are you doing well in the courses?
   - Continue research if necessary.

7. **Refine your plan.**
   - Make your plan more specific to aim for a particular career.
   - Select the college major that is best for you.

8. **Change your plan if it is not working.**
   - Go back to the self-assessment step.

The Decision-Making Process

Types of Decisions

- Dependent
- Intuitive
- Planful

- **Dependent decisions.** Different kinds of decisions are appropriate in different situations. When you make a dependent decision, you depend on someone else to make the decision for you. The dependent decision was probably the first kind of decision that you ever made. When your parents told you what to do as a child, you were making a dependent decision. As an adult, you make a dependent decision when your doctor tells you what medication to take for an illness or when your stockbroker tells you what stock you should purchase. Dependent decisions are easy to make and require little thought. Making a dependent decision saves time and energy.

  The dependent decision, however, has some disadvantages. You may not like the outcome of the decision. The medication that your doctor prescribes may have unpleasant side effects. The stock that you purchased may go down in value. When students ask a counselor to recommend a major or a career, they are making a dependent decision. When the decision does not work, they blame the counselor. Even if the dependent decision does have good results, you may become dependent on others to continue making decisions for you. Dependent decisions do work in certain situations, but they do not give you as much control over your own life.

- **Intuitive decisions.** Intuitive decisions are based on intuition or a gut feeling about what is the best course of action. Intuitive decisions can be made quickly and are useful in dealing with emergencies. If I see a car heading on a collision path toward me, I have to swerve quickly to the right or left. I do not have time to ask someone else what to do or think much about the alternatives. Another example of an intuitive decision is in gambling. If I am trying to decide whether to bet a dollar on red or black, I rely on my gut feeling to make a choice. Intuitive decisions may work out or they may not. You could make a mistake and swerve the wrong way as the car approaches or you could lose your money in gambling.

- **Planful decisions.** For important decisions, it is advantageous to use what is called a planful decision. The planful decision is made after carefully weighing the consequences and the pros and cons of the different alternatives. The planful decision-making strategy is particularly useful for such decisions as:

- What will be my major?
- What career should I choose?
- Whom should I marry?

The steps in a planful decision-making process:

1.   State the problem.
When we become aware of a problem, the first step is to state the problem in the simplest way possible. Just stating the problem will help you to clarify the issues.

2.   Consider your values.
What is important to you? What are your hopes and dreams? By keeping your values in mind, you are more likely to make a decision that will make you happy.

3.   What are your talents?
What special skills do you have? How can you make a decision that utilizes these skills?

4.   Gather information.
What information can you find that would be helpful in solving the problem? Look for ideas. Ask other people. Do some research. Gathering information can give you insight into alternatives or possible solutions to the problem.

5.   Generate alternatives.
Based on the information you have gathered, identify some possible solutions to the problem.

6.   Evaluate the pros and cons of each alternative.
List the alternatives and think about the pros and cons of each one. In thinking about the pros and cons, consider your values and talents as well as your future goals.

7.   Select the best alternative.
Choose the alternative that is the best match for your values and helps you to achieve your goals.

8.   Take action.
You put your decision into practice when you take some action on it. Get started!

The Resume and Job Interview

After investing your time in achieving a college education, you will need some additional skills to get a job. Having a good resume and knowing how to successfully interview for a job will help you to obtain your dream job.

Your Resume

A resume is a snapshot of your education and experience. It is generally one page in length. You will need a resume to apply for scholarships, part-time jobs, or find a position after you graduate. Start with a file of information you can use to create your resume. Keep your resume on file in your computer or on your flash drive so that you can revise it as needed. A resume includes the following:

*   Contact information: your name, address, telephone number, and e-mail address
*   A brief statement of your career objective
*   A summary of your education:
    *   Names and locations of schools
    *   Dates of attendance
    *   Diplomas or degrees received
*   A summary of your work and/or volunteer experience

Tips for Writing a Resume

- Write clearly
- Be brief
- Be neat
- Be honest
- Have letters of reference
- Use good-quality paper
- Post resume online

- If you have little directly related work experience, a list of courses you have taken that would help the employer understand your skills for employment
- Special skills, honors, awards, or achievements
- References (people who can recommend you for a job or scholarship)

Your resume is important in establishing a good first impression. There is no one best way to write a resume. Whatever form you choose, write clearly and be brief, neat, and honest. If your resume is too lengthy or difficult to read, it may wind up in the trash can. Adjust your resume to match the job for which you are applying. This is easy to do if you have your resume stored on your computer. Update your resume regularly.

Ask for a letter of reference from your current supervisor at work or someone in a position to recommend you, such as a college professor or community member. Ask the person to address the letter "To Whom It May Concern" so that you can use the letter many times. The person recommending you should comment on your work habits, skills, and personal qualities. If you wait until you graduate to obtain letters of reference, potential recommenders may no longer be there or may not remember who you are. Always ask if you can use a person's name as a reference. When you are applying for a job and references are requested, phone the persons who have agreed to recommend you and let them know to expect a call.

Print your resume so that it looks professional. Use a good-quality white, tan, or gray paper.

You will probably need to post your resume online to apply for some scholarships and job opportunities. Having your resume on the computer will make this task easier.

The Cover Letter

When you respond to job announcements, you will send a cover letter with your resume attached. Address your letter to a specific person at the company or organization and spell the name correctly. You can call the personnel office to obtain this information. The purpose of the cover letter is to state your interest in the job, highlight your qualifications, and get the employer to read your resume and call you for an interview. The cover letter should be brief and to the point. Include the following items:

- State the job you are interested in and how you heard about the opening.
- Briefly state how your education and experience would be assets to the company.
- Ask for an interview and tell the employer how you can be contacted.
- Attach your resume.
- Your cover letter is the first contact you have with the employer. Make it neat and free from errors. Use spell check and grammar check and read it over again.

The Job Interview

Knowing how to be successful in an interview will help you to get the job that you want. Here are some ideas for being prepared and making a good impression.

- **Learn about the job.** Before the interview, it is important to research both the company and the job. This research will help you in two ways: you will know if the job is really the one you want, and you will have information that will help you to succeed at the interview. If you have taken the time to learn about the company before the interview, you will make a good impression and show that you are really interested in the job. Here are some ways that you can find this information:

- Your college or public library may have a profile describing the company and the products it produces. This profile may include the size of the company and the company mission or philosophy.
- Do you know someone who works for the company? Do any of your family, friends, or teachers know someone who works for the company? If so, you can find out valuable information about the company.
- The personnel office often has informational brochures that describe the employer.
- Visit the company website on the Internet.

- **Understand the criteria used in an interview.** The interviewer represents the company and is looking for the best person to fill the job. It is your job to show the interviewer that you will do a good job. Of course you are interested in salary and benefits, but in order to get hired you must first convince the interviewer that you have something to offer the company. Focus on what you can offer the company based on your education and experience and what you have learned about the company. You may be able to obtain information on salary and benefits from the personnel office before the interview.

    Interviewers look for candidates who show the enthusiasm and commitment necessary to do a good job. They are interested in hiring someone who can work as part of a team. Think about your education and experience and be prepared to describe your skills and give examples of how you have been successful on the job. Give a realistic and honest description of your work.

- **Make a good impression.** Here are some suggestions for making a good impression:

    - Dress appropriately for the interview. Look at how the employees of the company dress and then dress a little better. Of course your attire will vary with the type of job you are seeking. You will dress differently if you are interviewing for a position as manager of a surf shop or an entry-level job in an engineering firm. Wear a conservative, dark colored or neutral suit for most professional positions. Do not wear too much jewelry, and remove excess body piercings (unless you are working at a piercing shop). Cover any tattoos if they are not appropriate for the workplace.
    - Relax during the interview. You can relax by preparing in advance. Research the company, practice interview questions, and visualize yourself in the interview room feeling confident about the interview.
    - When you enter the interview room, smile, introduce yourself, and shake hands with the interviewer. If your hands are cold and clammy, go to the restroom before the interview and run warm water over your hands or rub them together.
    - Maintain eye contact with the interviewer and sit up straight. Poor posture or leaning back in your chair could be seen as a lack of confidence or interest in the job.

- **Anticipate the interview questions.** Listen carefully to the interview questions. Ask for clarification of any question you do not understand. Answer the questions concisely and honestly. It helps to anticipate the questions that are likely to be asked and think about your answers in advance. Generally, be prepared to talk about yourself, your goals, and your reasons for applying for the job. Here are some questions that are typically asked in interviews and some suggestions for answering them:

1. **What can you tell us about yourself?**
   Think about the job requirements, and remember that the interviewer is looking for someone who will do a good job for the company. Talk about your education and experience as it relates to the job. You can put in interesting facts about your

Tips for a Successful Job Interview

- Learn about job
- Understand criteria of interview
- Make a good impression
- Anticipate interview questions
- Send thank you note

Making a Good Impression

- Dress appropriately
- Relax
- Prepare in advance
- Smile
- Shake hands
- Introduce yourself
- Maintain eye contact
- Sit up straight

Tips for Answering Questions

- Listen carefully
- Ask for clarification
- Answer concisely and honestly

life and your hobbies, but keep your answers brief. This question is generally an ice breaker that helps the interviewer get a general picture of you and help you relax.

2. **Why do you want this job? Why should I hire you?**
Think about the research you did on this company and several ways that you could benefit the company. A good answer might be, "I have always been good at technical skills and engineering. I am interested in putting these technical skills into practice in your company." A not-so-good answer would be, "I'm interested in making a lot of money and need health insurance."

3. **Why are you leaving your present job?**
Instead of saying that the boss was horrible and the working conditions were intolerable (even if this was the case), think of some positive reasons for leaving such as:

   - I am looking for a job that provides challenge and an opportunity for growth.
   - I received my degree and am looking for a job where I can use my education.
   - I had a part-time job to help me through school. I have graduated and am looking for a career.
   - I moved (or the company downsized or went out of business).

   Be careful about discussing problems on your previous job. The interviewers might assume that you were the cause of the problems or that you could not get along with other people.

4. **What are your strengths and weaknesses?**
Think about your strengths in relation to the job requirements, and be prepared to talk about them during the interview. When asked about your weaknesses, smile and try to turn them into strengths. For example, if you are an introvert, you might say that you are quiet and like to concentrate on your work, but you make an effort to communicate with others on the job. If you are an extrovert, say that you enjoy talking and working with others, but you are good at time management and get the job done on time. If you are a perfectionist, say that you like to do an excellent job, but you know the importance of meeting deadlines, so you do the best you can in the time available.

5. **Tell us about a difficulty or problem that you solved on the job.**
Think about some problem that you successfully solved on the job and describe how you did it. Focus on what you accomplished. If the problem was one that dealt with other people, do not focus on blaming or complaining. Focus on your desire to work things out and work well with everyone.

6. **Tell us about one of your achievements on the job.**
Give examples of projects you have done on the job that have turned out well and projects that gave you a sense of pride and accomplishment.

7. **What do you like best about your work? What do you like least?**
Think about these questions in advance and use the question about what you like best to highlight your skills for the job. For the question about what you like the least, be honest but express your willingness to do the job that is required.

8. **Are there any questions that you would like to ask?**
Based on your research on the company, think of some specific questions that show your interest in the company. A good question might be, "Tell me about your company's plans for the future." A not-so-good question would be, "How much vacation do I get?"

Write a thank you note. After the interview, write a thank you note and express your interest in the job. It makes a good impression and causes the interviewer to think about you again.

 Keys to Success

Life Is a Dangerous Opportunity

Even though we may do our best in planning our career and education, life does not always turn out as planned. Unexpected events happen, putting our life in crisis. The crisis might be loss of employment, divorce, illness or death of a loved one. How we deal with the crisis events in our lives can have a great impact on our current well-being and the future.

The Chinese word for crisis has two characters: one character represents danger and the other represents opportunity. Every crisis has the danger of loss of something important and the resulting emotions of frustration, sorrow, and grief. But every crisis also has an opportunity. Sometimes it is difficult to see the opportunity because we are overwhelmed by the danger. A crisis, however, can provide an impetus for change and growth. A crisis forces us to look inside ourselves to find capabilities that have always been there but we just did not know it. If life goes too smoothly, there is no motivation to change. If we get too comfortable, we stop growing. There is no testing of our capabilities. We stay in the same patterns.

To find the opportunity in a crisis, focus on what is possible in the situation. Every adversity has the seed of a greater benefit or possibility. Expect things to work out well. Expect success. To deal with negative emotions, consider that feelings are not simply a result of what happens to us but of our interpretation of events. If we focus on the danger, we cannot see the possibilities.

As a practical application, consider the example of someone who has just lost a job. John had worked as a construction worker for nearly ten years when he injured his back. His doctor told him that he would no longer be able to do physical labor. John was 30 years old, had two children and large house and truck payments. He was having difficulty finding a job that paid as well as his construction job. He was suffering from many negative emotions resulting from his loss of employment.

John decided that he would have to use his brain rather than his back. As soon as he was up and moving, he started taking some general education courses at the local college. He assessed his skills and identified his strengths. He was a good father and communicated well with his children. He had wanted to go to college but got married early and started to work in construction instead. John decided that he would really enjoy being a marriage and family counselor. It would mean getting a bachelor's and a master's degree, which would take five or more years.

John began to search for a way to accomplish this new goal. He first tackled the financial problems. He investigated vocational rehabilitation, veteran's benefits, financial aid, and scholarships. He sold his house and his truck. His wife took a part-time job. He worked out a careful budget. He began to work toward his new goal with a high degree of motivation and self-satisfaction. He had found a new opportunity.

JOURNAL ENTRY #4

Describe a dangerous opportunity you have faced in your life.

JOURNAL ENTRIES

Planning Your Career and Education

Go to http://www.collegesuccess1.com/ for Word files of the Journal Entries

Success over the Internet

**Visit the *College Success Website* at
http://www.collegesuccess1.com/**

The *College Success Website* is continually updated with new topics and links to the material presented in this chapter. Topics include

- Future trends
- Planning your major
- Job descriptions
- Career outlooks
- Career information
- Salary
- Interests
- Self-assessment

- Exploring careers
- Hot jobs for the future
- Profiles of successful people
- Resume writing
- Interviewing
- The personal side of work
- Using the Internet for a job search
- Job openings
- Decision making
- How to write a resume and cover letter
- How to post your resume online

Contact your instructor if you have any problems in accessing the *College Success Website*.

Notes

1. Michael T. Robinson, "Top Jobs for the Future," from www.careerplanner.com, 2004.
2. Gail Sheehy, *New Passages* (New York: Random House, 1995), 34.
3. U.S. Census Bureau, 2008 Statistical Abstract, "Expectation of Life at Birth, 1970–2004," and Projections 2010 and 2015. Available at www.census.gov/compendia/statab/cats/
4. Jeff Giles, "Generalization X," *Newsweek*, June 6, 1994.
5. Jane Bryant Quinn, "The Luck of the Xers, Comeback Kids: Young People Will Live Better Than They Think," *Newsweek*, 6 June 1994, 66–67.
6. Ellen Neuborne, http://www.businessweek.com, 1999.
7. Claudia Smith Brison, http://www.thestate.com, 14 July 2002.
8. Neil Howe and William Strauss, *Millennials Rising: The Next Great Generation* (New York: Vintage Books, 2000).
9. Neuborne, www.businessweek.com, 1999.

10. John Naisbitt, Patricia Aburdeen, and Walter Kiechel III, "How We Will Work in the Year 2000," *Fortune,* 17 May 1993, 41–52.

11. Susan Sears and Virginia Gordon, *Building Your Career* (Englewood Cliffs, NJ: Prentice-Hall, 1998), 100.

12. "Futurework, Trends and Challenges for Work in the 21st Century," an adapted excerpt from a U.S. Department of Labor Report *Occupational Outlook Quarterly,* Summer 2000.

13. Ibid.

14. Joyce Lain Kennedy, *Joyce Lain Kennedy's Career Book* (Chicago, IL: VGM Career Horizons, 1993), 32.

15. Ibid.

16. U.S. Department of Labor, *Outlook 2000* (Washington, DC: U.S. Government Printing Office 1990).

17. Douglas Braddock, "Occupational Employment Projection to 2008," *Monthly Labor Review,* November 1999.

18. Bill Gates, *Business @ the Speed of Thought: Using a Digital Nervous System* (Warner, 1999). Excerpts available at www.speed-of-thought.com .

19. "Futurework, Trends and Challenges for Work in the 21st Century," an adapted excerpt from a U.S. Department of Labor Report, *Occupational Outlook Quarterly,* Summer 2000.

20. http://www.speed-of-thought.com.

21. Ibid.

22. Ibid.

23. Ibid.

24. Bill Gates, "Microprocessors Upgraded the Way We Live," *USA Today,* 22 June 1999.

25. Ibid.

26. Ibid.

27. "Tomorrow's Best Careers," from http://www.future-trends.com, 2004.

28. Dan Tynan, "The Next 25 Years in Tech," www.pcworld.com, January 30, 2008.

29. Anne Foerst, "A New Breed of 'Replicants' Is Redefining What It Means to Be Human," *Forbes ASAP,* 1999.

30. Michael T. Robinson, "Offshoring of America's Top Jobs," from http://www.careerplanner.com, 2004.

31. "Tomorrow's Best Careers," from http://www.future-trends.com, 2004.

32. Roxanne Khamsi, "Paralyzed Man Sends E-Mail by Thought," News @ Nature. Com, October 13, 2004.

33. Judith Kautz, "Entrepreneurship Beyond 2000," from www.smallbusinessnotes.com, 2004.

34. Faith Popcorn and Lys Marigold, *Clicking: 16 Trends to Future Fit Your Life, Your Work, and Your Business,* Harper Collins, New York, 1996.

35. James E. Challenger, "Career Pros: Terrorism's Legacy" from www.jobjournal.com, 2003.

36. "Futurework, Trends and Challenges for Work in the 21st Century," an adapted excerpt from a U.S. Department of Labor Report, Occupational Outlook Quarterly, Summer 2000.

37. American Management Association, *AMA Survey on Workplace Drug Testing and Drug Abuse Policies,* 1991, 1.

38. Office of National Drug Control Policy, "The Economic Costs of Drug Abuse in the United States, 1992-2002," from http://www.whitehousedrugpolicy.gov/publications, 2008.

39. NIDA, *National Household Survey on Drug Abuse: Race/Ethnicity, Socioeconomic Status, and Drug Abuse,* 1991, 19.

40. M. Bernstein and J.J. Mahoney, "Management Perspectives on Alcoholism: The Employer's Stake in Alcoholism Treatment," *Occupational Medicine,* 2, (1989): 223–32.

41. TW Mangione et al., *New Perspectives for Worksite Alcohol Strategies: Results from a Corporate Drinking Study*, JSI Research and Training Institute, 1998, 1.

42. Ibid., 2.

43. USDHHS, SAMHSA, *Drug Use among U.S. Workers: Prevalence and Trends by Occupation and Industry Categories*, 1996, 1.

44. Ibid.

45. Michael T. Robinson, "Top Jobs for the Future," CareerPlanner.com, 2008.

46. T. J. Grites, "Being 'Undecided' Could Be the Best Decision They Could Make," *School Counselor* 29 (1981): 41–46.

47. Secretary's Commission on Achieving Necessary Skills (SCANS), *Learning a Living: A Blueprint for High Performance* (Washington, DC: U.S. Department of Labor, 1991).

48. Quoted in Rob Gilbert, ed., *Bits and Pieces*, 7 October 1999.

Sample Cover Letter

Sara Student
222 College Avenue
San Diego, CA 92019
(619) 123-4567

June 20, 2009

Mr. John Smith
Director of Human Resources
Future Technology Company
111 Technology Way
La Jolla, CA 92111

Dear Mr. Smith:

At our college job fair last week, I enjoyed speaking with you about some new engineering jobs available at Future Technology Company. As you suggested, I am sending my resume. I am interested in your opening for an electrical engineer. Is there anything else I need to do to apply for this position?

While at UCSD, I gained experience in laboratory projects, writing scientific reports and preparing technical presentations. Some engineering projects that I completed relate to work done at your company:

- Constructed a programmable robot with motor and sensors
- Worked with a group of students on the design of a satellite communications system
- Completed lab projects on innovative fiber-optic fabrication techniques
- Proposed a design for a prosthetic device to help the visually impaired

For my senior design project, I used my knowledge of digital signal processing and systems integration to design and construct a voice modulator. This project involved applying theory to hardware and understanding information processing as well as the relation of a computer to its controlled devices.

I am excited about the possibility of continuing work in this field and would enjoy the opportunity to discuss my qualifications in more detail. I am available for an interview at your convenience. I look forward to hearing from you.

Sincerely,

Sara Student
Encl.: Resume

Sample Resume for a Recent College Graduate

Sara Student
222 College Avenue; San Diego, CA 92019
(619) 123-4567
saraengineer@aol.com

OBJECTIVE	Electrical Engineer
HIGHLIGHTS	Recent degree in Electrical Engineering Specialized coursework in electromagnetism, photonics and lasers, biomedical imaging devices, and experimental techniques
EDUCATION	B.S., Electrical Engineering, University of California, San Diego, CA, 2009 A.S. with Honors, Cuyamaca College, El Cajon, CA, 2007

KEY RELATED COURSES
- **Circuits and systems:** solving network equations, Laplace transforms, practical robotics development
- **Electromagnetism:** Maxwell's equations, wave guides and transmission, electromagnetic properties of circuits and materials
- **Experimental techniques:** built and programmed a voice processor; studied transducers, computer architecture, and interfacing; applied integrated construction techniques
- **Photonics and lasers:** laser stability and design, holography, optical information processing, pattern recognition, electro-optic modulation, fiber optics
- **Biomedical imaging devices:** microscopy, x-rays, and neural imaging; designed an optical prosthesis
- **Quantum physics:** uncertainty principle, wave equation and spin, particle models, scattering theory and radiation

SKILLS	**Computer Skills:** PSpice, Matlab, Java, DSP, Assembly Language, Unix, Windows, Microsoft Word, Excel, and PowerPoint **Technical Skills:** Microprocessors, circuits, optical components, oscilloscope, function generator, photovoltaics, signal processing, typing, SQUID testing **Personal Skills:** Leadership, good people skills, organized, responsible, creative, motivated, hard-working, good writing skills
EMPLOYMENT	Intern, Quantum Design, La Jolla, CA, Summer 2008 Computer Lab Assistant, UCSD, La Jolla, CA, 2007–2009 Teacher's Aide, Cuyamaca College, El Cajon, CA, 2004–2006 Volunteer, Habitat for Humanity, Tijuana, Mexico, 2000–2003
INTERESTS	Optics, computing, programming, physics, electronic music, sampling, marine biology, and scuba diving
ACHIEVEMENTS	Advanced Placement Scholar Dean's List, Phi Theta Kappa Honor Society Provost's Honors List

Name _____   Date _____

Use this worksheet to prepare a resume similar to the sample on page 310. Assume that you have graduated from college and are applying for your ideal career.

1. What is the specific job title of your ideal job?

2. What are two or three qualifications you possess that would especially qualify you for this job? These qualifications can be listed under Highlights on your resume.

3. List your degree or degrees, major, and dates of completion.

4. List five courses you will take to prepare for your ideal career. For each course, list some key components that would catch the interest of your potential employer. Use a college catalog to complete this section.

5. List the skills you would need in each of these areas.

   Computer skills:

   Technical or other job-related skills:

   Personal skills related to your job objective:

6. List employment that would prepare you for your ideal job. Consider internships or part-time employment.

7. What are your interests?

8. What special achievements or awards do you have?

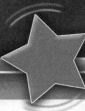

Interview Worksheet

Name _____   Date _____

Answer the following questions to prepare for the interview for your ideal job. If you do not know what your ideal job is, pretend that you are interviewing for any professional job. You may want to practice these questions with a classmate.

1. What can you tell us about yourself?

2. Why are you leaving your present job?

3. What are your strengths and weaknesses?

4. Tell us about a difficulty or problem that you solved on the job.

5. Tell us about one of your achievements on the job.

6. What do you like best about your work? What do you like least?

7. Are there any questions that you would like to ask?

Name _____   Date _____

Read each statement relating to skills needed for success in the workplace. Use the following scale to rate your competencies:

5 = Excellent   4 = Very good   3 = Average   2 = Needs improvement   1 = Need to develop

_____ 1. I have good reading skills. I can locate information I need to read and understand and interpret it. I can pick out the main idea and judge the accuracy of the information.

_____ 2. I have good writing skills. I can communicate thoughts, ideas, and information in writing. I know how to edit and revise my writing and use correct spelling, punctuation, and grammar.

_____ 3. I am good at arithmetic. I can perform basic computations using whole numbers and percentages. I can make reasonable estimates without a calculator and can read tables, graphs, and charts.

_____ 4. I am good at mathematics. I can use a variety of mathematical techniques including statistics to predict the occurrence of events.

_____ 5. I am good at speaking. I can organize my ideas and participate in discussions, and group presentations. I speak clearly and am a good listener. I ask questions to obtain feedback when needed.

_____ 6. I am a creative thinker. I can come up with new ideas and unusual connections. I can imagine new possibilities and combine ideas in new ways.

_____ 7. I make good decisions. I can specify goals and constraints, generate alternatives, consider risks, and evaluate alternatives.

_____ 8. I am good at solving problems. I can see when a problem exists, identify the reasons for the problem, and devise a plan of action for solving the problem.

_____ 9. I am good at mental visualization. I can see things in my mind's eye. Examples include building a project from a blueprint or imagining the taste of a recipe from reading it.

_____ 10. I know how to learn. I am aware of my learning style and can use learning strategies to obtain new knowledge.

_____ 11. I am good at reasoning. I can use logic to draw conclusions and apply rules and principles to new situations.

_____ 12. I am a responsible person. I work toward accomplishing goals, set high standards, and pay attention to details. I usually accomplish tasks on time.

_____ 13. I have high self-esteem. I believe in my self-worth and maintain a positive view of myself.

_____ 14. I am sociable, understanding, friendly, adaptable, polite, and relate well to others.

_____ 15. I am good at self-management. I know my background, skills, and abilities and set realistic goals for myself. I monitor my progress toward completing my goals and complete them.

_____ 16. I practice integrity and honesty. I recognize when I am faced with a decision that involves ethics and choose ethical behavior.

_____ 17. I am good at managing my time. I set goals, prioritize, and follow schedules to complete tasks on time.

_____ 18. I manage money well. I know how to use and prepare a budget and keep records, making adjustments when necessary.

_____ 19. I can manage material and resources. I can store and distribute materials, supplies, parts, equipment, space, or products.

_____ 20. I can participate as a member of a team. I can work cooperatively with others and contribute to group efforts.

_____ 21. I can teach others. I can help others to learn needed knowledge and skills.

_____ 22. I can exercise leadership. I know how to communicate, encourage, persuade, and motivate individuals.

_____ 23. I am a good negotiator. I can work toward an agreement and resolve divergent interests.

_____ 24. I can work with men and women from a variety of ethnic, social, or educational backgrounds.

_____ 25. I can acquire and evaluate information. I can identify a need for information and find the information I need.

_____ 26. I can organize and maintain information. I can find written or computerized information.

_____ 27. I can use computers to process information.

_____ 28. I have an understanding of social, organizational, and technological systems and can operate effectively in these systems.

_____ 29. I can improve the design of a system to improve the quality of products and services.

_____ 30. I can use machines and computers to accomplish the desired task.

_____ **Total**

Score your skills for success in the workplace

150–121   Excellent
120–91   Very good
90–61   Average
Below 60   Need improvement

Name _____   Date _____

If you need to improve or develop skills for success in the workplace, many are covered in this text. Use this text to learn about creative thinking, decision making, problem solving, mental visualization, learning style, reasoning, time management, money management, communications, and self-esteem. Other skills can be improved by taking courses in computer use and general education courses such as English, math, and speech.

From the previous list of workplace skills, make a list of five of your strong points. What do you do well?

From the list of workplace skills, make a list of five areas you need to improve or develop.

Think about how you can improve or develop the skills you listed above. Write your ideas here.

Checklist for a Satisfying Career

Name _____   Date _____

Read each statement and think about your current career choice or the options you are considering. Place a checkmark next to the items that are true about your career choice. Before you begin, you may want to review the self-assessment exercises that you have completed in this book and as part of this course.

My career choice (or tentative career choice) is:

_____ 1. My career matches the natural preferences of my personality type.

_____ 2. This career matches my interests. I would enjoy doing this type of work.

_____ 3. This career will allow me to live the lifestyle that I want.

_____ 4. This career matches my values (what I think is important).

_____ 5. This career matches my skills, aptitudes, talents, intelligences, and learning style.

_____ 6. I have the skills necessary to be successful in this career or I am willing to obtain these skills.

_____ 7. This career provides the kind of salary I need to live the way I want.

_____ 8. This career has a positive outlook for the future. The career will exist in the future and there will likely be job openings in this area.

_____ 9. I am willing to complete the education or training required to enter this career.

_____ 10. This career choice will help me to accomplish my lifetime goals.

Look at the items you have not checked above. Sometimes a career does not allow us to achieve everything we hope to do in our lives. Hobbies or recreational interests are important to satisfaction with life. Does your career choice give you the opportunity to pursue your hobbies and interests? Does it give you time for relaxation and recreation? Will you have time to spend with the people who are important in your life? Write your thoughts here.

Educational Planning Form (Semester System)

Name _____   Date _____

Student ID or SSN _____

Fall	Spring	Summer
Total units	Total units	Total units
Fall	Spring	Summer
Total units	Total units	Total units
Fall	Spring	Summer
Total units	Total units	Total units
Fall	Spring	Summer
Total units	Total units	Total units

Total units _____ Date of graduation _____

Counselor signature _____

The Planful Decision Strategy

Name _____   Date _____

Read the following scenario describing a college student in a problem situation. Then, answer the questions that follow to practice the planful decision strategy. You may want to do this as a group activity with other students in the class.

Rhonda is an 18-year-old student who is trying to decide on her major. She was a good student in high school, earning a 3.4 grade point average. Her best subjects were English and American history. She struggled with math and science but still earned good grades in these subjects. While in high school she enjoyed being on the debate team and organizing the African American Club. This club was active in writing letters to the editor and became involved in supporting a local candidate for city council.

Rhonda is considering majoring in political science and has dreams of eventually going to law school. Rhonda likes being politically involved and advocating for different social causes. The highlight of her life in high school was when she organized students to speak to the city council about installing a traffic light in front of the school after a student was killed trying to cross the street. The light was installed during her senior year.

Rhonda's family has always been supportive, and she values her family life and the close relationships in the family. She comes from a middle-income family that is struggling to pay for her college education. Getting a bachelor's degree in political science and going to law school would take seven years and be very expensive. There is no law school in town, so Rhonda would have to move away from home to attend school.

Rhonda's parents have suggested that she consider becoming a nurse and attending the local nursing college. Rhonda could finish a bachelor's degree in nursing in four years and could begin working part-time as a nurse's aide in a short time. A cousin in the family became a nurse and found a job easily and is now earning a good income. The cousin arranged for Rhonda to volunteer this summer at the hospital where she works. Rhonda enjoys helping people at the hospital. Rhonda is trying to decide on her major. What should she do?

1. State the problem.

2. Describe Rhonda's values, hopes, and dreams.

3. What special interests, talents, or aptitudes does she have?

4. What further information would be helpful to Rhonda in making her decision?

5. What are the alternatives and the pros and cons of each?

Alternative 1	
Pros:	Cons:
Alternative 2	
Pros:	Cons:
Alternative 3 (be creative!)	
Pros:	Cons:

6. Only Rhonda can choose what is best for her. If you were Rhonda, what would you do and why? Use a separate piece of paper, if necessary, to write your answer.

CHAPTER **10**

LEARNING OBJECTIVES

Read to answer these key questions:

- What is my personal communication style?

- What are some problems in communication?

- What are some techniques for being a good listener?

- What is the best way to communicate in a crisis situation?

- How does language affect behavior?

- What are some conflict management techniques?

- What are the qualities of a good friendship?

- How can I get along with my roommate?

- How can I improve my relationships?

- How is failure an opportunity for learning?

© Dmitriy Shironosov, 2008. Under license from Shutterstock, Inc.

Communication and Relationships

When you look back on your college experience, what you are most likely to remember and value are the personal relationships established while in college. These relationships can be a source of great pleasure or disappointment. What makes a good relationship? The answer to this question is complex and different for each individual. Good relationships begin with an understanding of personality differences and the components of effective communication. These skills can be useful in establishing satisfying friendships, happy marriages, effective parenting skills, and good relationships in the workplace.

Understanding Your Personal Communication Style

Becoming familiar with personality types can help you better understand yourself and others. Personality has a major impact on our style of communication. While we can make some generalizations about personality types, keep in mind that each individual is unique and may be a combination of the various types. For example, some people are a combination of introvert and extravert. The following descriptions will help you begin thinking about your own communication style and understanding others who are different. Remember that each personality type has positive and negative aspects. Knowledge of these differences can help individuals accentuate the positives and keep the negatives in perspective.

Introvert and Extravert Types

Communication Styles

- Introvert
- Extravert
- Sensing
- Intuitive
- Feeling
- Thinking
- Judging
- Perceptive

Extraverts are very social types who easily start conversations with friends as well as strangers. They know a lot of people and have many friends. They like going to parties and other social events and are energized by talking to people. They like to talk on the telephone and can read while watching TV, listening to music, or carrying on a conversation with someone else. They find talking easy and sometimes dominate the conversation. They find it more difficult to listen. They tend to talk first and think later, and sometimes regret that they have put their foot in their mouths.

In personal relationships, extraverts are fun to know and get along well with others. It is easy for them to make a date and do the talking. When extraverts are in conflict situations, they just talk louder and faster. They believe that the argument can be won if they can say just one more thing or provide more explanation. If there is a problem, extraverts want to talk about it right away. If they cannot talk about it, they become very frustrated.

The **introvert** is the opposite of the extravert. Introverts want to rehearse what they are going to say before they say it. They need quiet for concentration and enjoy peace and quiet. They have great powers of concentration and can focus their attention on projects for a long period of time. Because they tend to be quieter than extraverts, they are perceived as great listeners. Because they need time to think before talking, they often find it difficult to add their ideas to a conversation, especially when talking with extraverts. They often wish they could participate more in conversations. Because they are reserved and reflective, people often label the introvert as shy. In American society, introverts are the minority. There are three extraverts to every introvert. For this reason, the introvert is often pressured to act like an extravert. This can cause the introvert a great deal of anxiety.

The introvert often finds it difficult to start conversations or invite someone on a date. Introverts are often attracted to extraverts because they can relax and let the extravert do the talking. In conflict situations, the introverts are at a disadvantage. They will often withdraw from conflict because they need time to think about the situation and go over in their minds what to say. Introverts become stressed if they are faced with a conflict without advance notice.

Introverts and extraverts can improve their relationship by understanding each other and respecting their differences. The extravert can improve communication with the introvert by pausing to let the introvert have time to speak. He has to make a conscious effort to avoid monopolizing the conversation. Introverts can improve communication by making an effort to communicate. Introverts sometimes act like extraverts in social situations. Since this takes effort, they may need quiet time to relax and recharge after social events.

Imagine that two roommates are opposite types, extravert and introvert. The extravert enjoys talking and making noises. She will have guests, take telephone calls, and play music in the background while studying. These actions will cause the introvert to withdraw and leave the room to find a quiet place to study. These two roommates need to talk about their differences and do some compromising to get along with one another.

Sensing and Intuitive Types

Sensing types collect information through the senses. Their motto could be, "Seeing is believing." They are practical and realistic. They like communication to be exact and sequential. They want details and facts. They ask specific questions and want concrete answers. About 70 percent of the population of the United States is the sensing type.

In a dating situation, the sensing type focuses on actual experience. A sensor will describe the date in terms of what his or her companion looked like, how the food tasted, how the music sounded, and the feelings involved. In a dating situation, sensors talk about concrete events such as people they have known, experiences they have had, and places they have visited. Sensing types are generally on time for the date and get irritated if the other person is late. In conflict situations, sensing types argue the facts. They often don't see the big issues because they are concentrating on the accuracy of the facts.

Intuitive types gather information from the senses and immediately look for possibilities, meanings, and relationships between ideas. They are often ingenious and creative. Sensing types often describe intuitives as dreamers who have their heads in the clouds. They represent about 30 percent of the population.

In social situations such as dating, the intuitive person starts to fantasize and imagine what it is going to be like before it begins. The fantasies are often more exciting than the actual date. Conversations follow many different and creative trains of thought. Intuitive types are more likely to talk about dreams, visions, beliefs, and creative ideas, skipping from one topic to another. Sensing types sometimes have difficulty following the conversation. Intuitive types are less worried about being exactly on time. They believe that time is flexible and may not be on time for the date, much to the annoyance of sensing types. In conflict situations, intuitive types like to make broad generalizations. When sensing types remind them of the facts, they may accuse them of nit-picking.

Having both sensing and intuitive types in a relationship or business environment has many advantages, as long as these types can understand and appreciate one another. Sensing types need intuitive types to bring up new possibilities, deal with changes, and understand different perspectives. Intuitive types need sensing types to deal with facts and details.

Feeling and Thinking Types

Feeling types prefer to make decisions based on what they feel to be right or wrong based on their subjective values. They prefer harmony and are often described as tender-hearted. Other people's feelings are an important consideration in any decision they make. The majority of women (60 percent) are feeling types. In a conflict situation, feeling types take things personally. They prefer to avoid disagreements and will give in to reestablish a harmonious relationship.

Thinking types are logical, detached, analytical, and objective and make decisions based on these characteristics. They like justice and clarity. The majority of men (60 percent) are thinking types. In a conflict situation, thinking types use logical arguments. They often get frustrated with feeling types and think they are too emotional.

In a dating situation, the differences between feelers and thinkers can cause much misunderstanding and conflict. Thinking types strive to understand love and intimacy. Feeling types like to experience emotions. Thinking types process and analyze their feelings. For the thinker, love is to be analyzed. For the feeling types, love just happens.

Remember that while most women are feeling types and most men are thinking types, there are still 40 percent of women who are thinking types and 40 percent of men who are feeling types. Unfortunately because of gender stereotyping, feeling-type men are often seen as less masculine and thinking-type women are seen as less feminine.

There is much to gain from understanding and appreciating the differences between feeling and thinking types. Feeling types need thinking types to analyze, organize, follow policy, and weigh the evidence. Thinking types need feeling types to understand how others feel and establish harmony in relationships or in a business environment.

Judging and Perceptive Types

Judging types prefer their environment to be structured, scheduled, orderly, planned, and controlled. Judging types even plan and organize their recreation time. They need events to be planned and organized in order to relax. They are quick to make decisions and once the decisions are made, they find it difficult to change them. In the social scene, judging types schedule and plan the dates. When traveling, judging types carefully pack their suitcases using a list of essential items to make sure that nothing is forgotten. In conflict situations, judging types know that they are right. They tend to see issues in terms of right and wrong, good and bad, or black and white. It is difficult to negotiate with a judging type.

Perceptive types are very much the opposite of the judging types. They prefer the environment to be flexible and spontaneous. Perceptive types find it difficult to make a decision and stick to it because it limits their flexibility. Perceptive types like to collect information and keep the options open. After all, something better might come along and they do not want to be restricted by a plan or schedule. In a social situation, these types are playful and easygoing. They provide the fun and find it easy to relax. They often feel controlled by judging types. In a conflict situation, this type sees many options to resolve the situation. They have trouble resolving conflicts because they keep finding many possible solutions.

The preference for judging or perceiving has the most potential for conflict between individuals. Judging types can drive perceptive types crazy with their need for schedules, planning, and organization. Perceptive types drive the judging types crazy with their spontaneous and easygoing nature. In spite of these differences, judging and perceptive types are often attracted to one another. Judging types need perceptive types to encourage them to relax and have fun. Perceptive types need judging types to help them be more organized and productive. These two types need understanding and appreciation of each other to have a good relationship. They also need excellent communication skills.

It is often asked whether two people should consider personality type in establishing relationships or choosing a marriage partner. There are two theories on this. One theory is that opposites attract. If two people have opposite personality types, they will have the potential for using the strengths of both types. For example, if one marriage partner is a judging type, this person can manage the finances and keep the family organized. The perceptive type can provide the fun and help the other to relax and enjoy life. A disadvantage is that opposite types have great potential for conflict. The conflict can be resolved by understanding the other type and appreciating different strengths the opposite type brings to the relationship. The relationship cannot work if one person tries to change the other. Good communication is essential in maintaining the relationship.

Another theory is that like types attract. If you have a relationship with another person of the same type, your basic preferences are similar. However, even matching types will be different depending on the strength of each preference. Communication is easier when two people have similar views of the world. One disadvantage is that the relationship can become predictable and eventually uninteresting.

QUIZ
Communication Style

Test what you have learned by selecting the correct answer to the following questions.

1. Extraverts can help introverts improve communication by

    a. clearly explaining their point of view.
    b. pausing to give the introvert time to think and respond.
    c. talking louder and faster.

2. In a dating situation, sensing types are likely to talk about

    a. concrete events such as the weather or personal experiences.
    b. dreams and visions.
    c. creative ideas.

3. In a conflict situation, feeling types

    a. use logic to analyze the situation.
    b. engage in debate based on logical arguments.
    c. take things personally.

4. Perceptive types

    a. find it difficult to make a decision and stick to it.
    b. tend to decide quickly in order to finish the project.
    c. find it easy to be on time and meet deadlines.

5. In choosing a marriage partner it is best to

    a. choose a person with the same personality.
    b. choose a person with the opposite personality.
    c. be aware of each other's personality type to appreciate each other.

How did you do on the quiz? Check your answers: 1. b, 2. a, 3. c, 4. a, 5. c

---

JOURNAL ENTRY #1

Consider how the following terms affect your communication style: extravert, introvert, sensing, intuitive, feeling, thinking, judging, perceptive. What is your personal communication style?

Communication for Success

To be an effective communicator, it is important to be a good listener and speaker. Practice the techniques of good listening and use language that helps you enhance your success and establish good relationships.

Problems in Communication

Effective communication involves a loop in which a sender sends a message and a receiver receives the message. Communications are disrupted when:

- the receiver doesn't receive the message.
- the receiver hears the wrong message.
- the receiver doesn't care about the message.
- the receiver is more interested in talking than listening.
- the receiver only hears part of the message.
- the receiver only hears what she or he wants to hear.
- the receiver feels threatened by the sender.
- the sender didn't send the message correctly.
- the sender left out part of the message.
- the sender talks so much that nobody listens.
- the sender is not someone you want to hear.
- the sender is annoying.
- the sender was upset and did not mean to send the message.
- the sender assumes that you should know the message already.

There is a joke circulating on the Internet:

A man is driving up a steep, narrow mountain road. A woman is driving down the same road. As they pass each other, the woman leans out the window and yells, "Pig!" The man replies by calling the woman a name. They each continue on their way. As the man rounds the next corner, he crashes into a pig in the middle of the road. If only people would listen!

As you can see, there are many ways to disrupt communication. Just because a message was sent, does not mean that it was received. The first step in communication is to be a good listener. Many factors interfere with good listening. Do you recognize some of these reasons for not listening?

- **Message overload.** There is so much communication going on today that it is difficult to keep up with it all. There are stacks of paper, multiple e-mail messages, text messages, television, radio, and people who want to talk to you. Introverts may find this overwhelming, while extraverts may find it exciting. Both find it challenging to keep up with all these communications and to focus on the messages.

- **Worries and anxiety.** It is difficult to listen to other people when you are preoccupied with your own thoughts. You may be thinking about an upcoming test or paper that is due or worried about a personal relationship. While others are talking, you are thinking about something else of more immediate concern to yourself.

- **Rapid thought.** People think faster than they speak. We are capable of understanding speech at about 600 words per minute, but most people talk at 100 to 150 words per minute.[1] People use the spare time to become distracted. They daydream, think about what they will do next, or think about their reply.

Factors That Interfere with Good Listening

- Message overload
- Worries and anxiety
- Rapid thought
- Tired, overloaded or distracted
- Noise and hearing problems
- Faulty assumptions

- **Listening is hard work.** It takes effort to listen. It requires paying attention and striving to understand. People can't listen effectively if they are tired, overloaded, or distracted.

- **Noise and hearing problems.** Our world is becoming noisier. As people get older, many suffer from hearing loss. Younger persons are suffering hearing loss from listening to loud music. It is more difficult to get your message across when people can't hear everything you are saying.

- **Faulty assumptions.** People often make faulty assumptions. They may assume that other people also know the information, and therefore they do not communicate well. People listening may assume that they know the information already or that the information is easy, so it is not necessary for them to pay attention. Or they may assume the material is too difficult to understand and block it out.

- **Talking too much.** Since listening involves effort, people consider what they have to gain before they invest the effort in listening. They might think that there is more to gain in speaking than in listening. The speaker often feels that he or she has control. You might feel that in speaking you gain the attention or admiration of others. If you are speaking or telling a joke and everyone is listening, you feel important. Also, through speaking people release their frustration and think about their problems. They need to stop speaking in order to listen.

How to Be a Good Listener

Being a good listener takes practice and effort. Here are some tips on becoming a good listener:

- **Talk less.** It does no good to talk if no one is listening, if no one understands your message, or if your message is irrelevant to the situation. To have a better chance of communicating your message, it is important first to listen to gain an understanding of the other person and then to speak. In marriage counseling, a common technique is to have one person talk and express his or her point of view. Before the other person can talk, he or she has to accurately summarize what the previous person said. Too often people do not really listen; instead they are composing their own message in their head. It is a Native American custom that when members of the group assemble to talk about an important issue, a talking stick is used. Persons can only talk when they have the talking stick. When the person holding the talking stick is finished, it is passed to the next person who wants to talk. In this way only one person can talk at a time, and the others listen.

- **Minimize distractions.** For important conversations, turn off the TV or the music. Find quiet time to focus on the communication. Manage your internal distractions as well. Focus your attention on listening first and then speaking.

- **Don't judge too soon.** Try to understand first and then evaluate. If you judge too soon, you may not have the correct information and might make a mistake. People are especially vulnerable to this problem when their ideas do not agree with those of the speaker. They focus on defending their position without really listening to the other point of view.

- **Look for the main point.** You may become distracted or impatient with people who talk too much. Try to be patient and look for the main points. In a lecture, write these points down.

To Be a Good Listener
- Talk less
- Minimize distractions
- Don't judge too soon
- Look for main point
- Ask questions
- Feed back meaning
- Be careful with advice

- **Ask questions.** You will need to ask questions to make sure that you understand. Each person looks at the world in a different way. The picture in my mind will not match the picture in your mind. We will have a better idea of each other's pictures if we ask for more information.

- **Feed back meaning.** This communication technique involves restating the speaker's ideas in your own words to check the meaning. This is important because speakers often

  - say one thing and mean something else.
  - say something but don't mean it, especially if emotions are involved.
  - speak in a way that causes confusion.

Feeding back meaning has two important benefits. It helps speakers to clarify their thoughts. It helps listeners make sure that they have received the correct message. Here are several ways to feed back meaning:

1. **Restate what has been said.** Sometimes this is called parroting. It is useful for clarifying information, but sometimes it annoys people if you use it too much.

   Statement: Turn right at the light.
   Feedback: Okay. So you want me to turn right at the light?

2. **Ask for clarification.**

   Statement: Take the next exit on the freeway.
   Feedback: Do you mean this exit coming up now or the next one?

   Statement: Pig! (referring to the joke about the man and woman on the mountain road)
   Feedback: What do you mean by "pig"?
   Statement: Be careful. There is a pig in the road ahead.

3. **Reword the message to check your understanding.** First, restate what you have heard and then ask for clarification. This is called active listening.

   Statement: Turn in the draft of your paper next week.
   Feedback: You want the draft next week. Does that include the outline, the draft of the entire paper, and the bibliography? Should it be typed, or is handwritten okay?

   Statement: Don't worry about your grade on this quiz.
   Feedback: You said not to worry about my grade on this quiz. Does that mean that the grade won't count or that I can make up the quiz?

   Statement: I need this project completed by Friday.
   Feedback: So this project needs to be done by Friday. What parts do you want included and how would you like me to do it?

4. **Listen for feelings.** Feelings get in the way of clear thinking. A person may say one thing and mean something else.

   Statement: Just forget about it!
   Feedback: I'm confused. You ask me to forget about it, but you sound angry.

5. **Use your own words to restate what the speaker has said.** In this way, you help the speaker to clarify his or her thoughts and hopefully to come up with some solutions.

   Statement: I wish I didn't have to work so much. I'm getting behind in school, but I have bills to pay. I have to work.

Feedback: You seem to be caught in a bind between school and work.
Statement: That's right. I just can't keep working so much. Maybe I
              should go check out financial aid and scholarships.

- **Be careful about giving advice.** Whenever possible, listen closely and be an active listener. In this way, the person speaking to you has a way to clarify his or her thoughts and think about alternatives. When you listen, it is tempting to offer advice because you may have had similar experiences. You can share your experiences and offer suggestions, but beware of giving advice for these reasons:
    - If you give advice and it turns out badly, you may be blamed.
    - If you give advice and it turns out right, the person may become dependent on you.
    - People are unique individuals with unique life situations. Something that works for one person may not work for another person at all.

Helpful Communication in a Crisis Situation

Most people have been in a situation where their friends or family are in distress and need immediate help. If you become aware of a dangerous or critical situation, seek professional help. Go to your college counseling center, a community service organization, your doctor, or a religious leader for help. Here are some general ideas for being a helpful listener:

- Let the person talk. Talking helps to clarify thinking.
- Paraphrase or feed back meaning.
- Avoid being critical. Comments such as "You asked for it" or "I told you so" do not help. They just make the person angry.
- Help the person analyze the situation and come up with alternatives for solving the problem.
- Share your experiences but resist giving advice.
- Ask questions to clarify the situation.
- Offer to be supportive. Say, "I'm here if you need me" or "I care about you."
- Let people express their feelings. It is not helpful to say, "Don't feel sad," for example. A person may need to feel sad and deal with the situation. The emotion can be a motivation for change.
- Don't minimize the situation. Saying, "It's only a grade (job, promotion)," minimizes the situation. It might not be important to the listener, but it is causing pain for the speaker. Give him or her time to gain perspective on the problem.
- Replace pity with understanding. It is not helpful to say, "You poor thing."

The following anonymous poem summarizes some ideas on how to be a helpful listener.

When I ask you to listen to me
   and you give me advice
   you have not done what I asked.

When I ask you to listen to me
   and you begin to tell me why I shouldn't feel that way,
   you are trampling on my feelings.

When I ask you to listen to me
   and you feel you have to do something to solve my problem,
   you have failed me, strange as that may seem.

Listen! All I asked was that you listen.
Not talk or do—just hear me.
Advice is cheap: 50 cents will get you both Dear Abby and
Billy Graham in the same newspaper.
And I can do for myself; I'm not helpless.
Maybe discouraged and faltering, but not helpless.

When you do something for me that I can and need to do
for myself, you contribute to my fear and weakness.

But, when you accept as a simple fact that I do feel what I feel,
no matter how irrational, then I can quit trying to convince
you and can get about the business of understanding what's
behind this irrational feeling.
And when that's clear, the answers are obvious and I
don't need advice.

Irrational feelings make sense when we understand what's
behind them.

Perhaps that's why prayer works, sometimes, for some people
because God is sometimes mute and doesn't give advice or
try to fix things. He often listens and lets you
work it out for yourself.

So please listen and hear me. And, if you want to
talk, wait a minute for your turn; and I'll listen to you.[2]

QUIZ
Communication for Success, Part I

Test what you have learned by selecting the correct answer to the following questions.

1. One of the biggest problems with communication is that the message sent is not always the message that is

    a. appreciated.
    b. intended.
    c. received.

2. To be a good listener, it is important to remember that

    a. it is important to listen first, so that you can understand before speaking.
    b. it is important to talk first to make sure the other has heard your point of view.
    c. it is important to assume that the other knows what you are talking about.

3. Feeding back meaning is

    a. responding to questions.
    b. restating what has been said to check understanding.
    c. unnecessary because some people find it irritating.

4. Giving advice is

    a. generally not a good idea.
    b. only a good idea if you know what is best.
    c. a good idea if the other person does not know what to do.

5. In a crisis situation, it is best to

    a. tell the person not to feel sad.
    b. show your pity for the person.
    c. let the person talk in order to clarify thinking.

How did you do on the quiz? Check your answers: 1. c, 2. a, 3. b, 4. a, 5. c

The Language of Responsibility

The way we use language reflects our willingness to take responsibility for ourselves and affects our relationships with others. Knowing about "I" and "you" messages, as well as how we choose certain words, can help us to improve communications. We can become aware of how our thoughts influence our behavior and communication. We can choose to use cooperation in dealing with conflicts.

"I" and "You" Statements

When communicating, watch how you use the pronouns "I" and "you." For example, if you walk in and find your apartment a mess, you might say to your roommate, "Just look at this mess! You are a slob!" Your roommate will probably be angry and reply by calling you an equally offensive name. You have accomplished nothing except becoming angry and irritating your roommate. Using the pronoun "you" and calling a person a name implies that you are qualified to make a judgment about another person. Even if this is true, you will not make any friends or communicate effectively.

"You" statements label and blame. They demand a rebuttal. They cause negative emotions and escalate the situation. How would you react to these statements?

> You must be crazy.
> You are really a jerk!

You would probably get angry and think of a nasty reply in return. When you use an "I" message, you accept responsibility for yourself. You might say something like this:

> I don't understand.
> I feel angry.

There are many ways to make "I" statements. Instead of calling your roommate a slob, you could:

1. Make an observation. Describe the behavior:

   Your things are all over the floor.

2. State your feelings. Tell how you feel about the behavior:

   I get angry when I have to step over your things on the floor.

3. Share your thoughts. Say what you think about the situation, but beware of disguised "you" messages such as, "I think you are a slob."

   I think it is time to clean up.

4. State what you want:

   Please pick up your things.

5. State your intentions. Say what you are going to do:

   If you do not pick up your things, I will put them in your room.

Here are some examples of "I" statements that can be used to express various feelings:

To express anger	To express sadness
I don't like	I feel disappointed
I feel frustrated	I am sad that
I am angry that	I feel hurt
I feel annoyed	I wanted
I want	I want

To express fear	To say you are sorry
I feel worried	I feel embarrassed
I am afraid	I am sorry
I feel scared	I feel ashamed
I do not want	I didn't want
I need, I want	I want

A complete "I" message describes the other person's behavior, states your feelings, and describes the effect of the other's behavior on you. For example, when your things are all over the floor (behavior), I feel angry (feeling) because I have to pick up after you (how it affects me). A variation on the "I" message is the "we" message. The "we" statement assumes that both persons need to work on the problem. For example, "We need to work on this problem so that we don't have to argue."

Words Are Powerful

The words that we choose have a powerful influence on behavior. One of the least powerful words is the word "should." This word is heard frequently on college campuses:

I should do my homework.
I should go to class.
I should get started on my term paper.

The problem with "should" is that it usually does not lead to action and may cause people to feel guilty. If you say, "I should get started on my term paper," the chances are that you will not start on it.

If you say, "I might get started on my term paper," at least you are starting to think about possibilities. You might actually get started on your term paper. If you say, "I want to get started on my term paper," the chances are getting better that you will get started. You are making a choice. If you say, "I intend to start on my term paper," you have at least expressed good intentions. The best way to get started is to make a promise to yourself that you will start. The words "should," "might," "want," "intend," and "promise" represent a ladder of powerful communication. As you move up the ladder, you are more likely to accomplish what you say you will do. This ladder moves from obligation to promise, or a personal choice to act:

The Ladder of Powerful Speaking

"I promise" or "I will"

"I intend to"

"I want to"

"I might"

"I should"

Next time you hear yourself saying that you "should" do something, move one more step up the ladder. Move from obligation to making a personal decision to do what is important to you. For example, if a friend wants to borrow money from you, which response is the most powerful?

* I really should pay the money back.
* Well, I might pay the money back.
* I really want to pay the money back.
* I intend to pay the money back.
* I promise to pay the money back.

Negative Self-Talk

Self-talk is what you say to yourself. It is the stream of consciousness or the little voice in your head. This self-talk affects how you communicate with others. If your self-talk is negative, you will have lower self-esteem and find it more difficult to communicate with others. There are some common irrational beliefs that lead to negative self-talk. Becoming aware of these beliefs can help you to avoid them.

* **I have to be perfect.**
  If you believe this, you will think that you have to be a perfect communicator and deliver flawless speeches. Since this goal is unattainable, it causes stress and anxiety. If you believe in this idea, you may try to pretend or act as if you were perfect. This takes up a lot of energy and keeps others from liking you. Everyone makes mistakes. When people stop trying to be perfect and accept themselves as they are, they can begin to relax and work on the areas needing improvement. They can write papers and make speeches knowing that they will probably make mistakes, just like the rest of the human population.

* **I need the approval of everyone.**
  A person who believes this finds it necessary to have the approval of almost everyone. Much energy is spent in gaining approval from others. If approval is not obtained, the person may feel nervous, embarrassed, or apologetic. It is not possible to win the approval of everyone because each individual is unique. Those who constantly seek approval will sacrifice their own values and what they think is right just to please others.

* **That's always the way it is.**
  People who believe this statement are making a generalization. They take a few events and use them to predict the future or exaggerate their shortcomings. Here are some examples:

  * I'm not a technical person. I can't install my computer.
  * I'm not good at numbers. I'll never to able to pass algebra.
  * Some husband (wife) I am! I forgot our anniversary.
  * You never listen to me.

Beliefs that Lead to Negative Self-Talk

* I have to be perfect.
* I need everyone's approval.
* That's always the way it is.
* You made me feel that way.
* I'm helpless.
* If something bad can happen, it will.

Notice the absolute nature of these statements. Absolute statements are almost always false and lead to anger and negative thinking. Remember that with a positive attitude, things can change in the future. Just because it was one way in the past does not mean it has to be the same in the future. Beware of "always" and "never" statements.

- **You made me feel that way.**
  Your own self-talk, rather than the actions of others, is what causes emotions. No one can make you feel sad or happy. You feel sad or happy based what you say to yourself about an event. If someone makes a negative comment about you, you can say to yourself that it is only the other person's opinion and choose how you react. Your reactions and emotions depend on how much importance you decide to attach to the event. People tend to react strongly to a comment if it is from someone they care about.

  People also do not cause the emotions of others. Some people do not communicate honestly because they are afraid of causing negative emotions in the other person. They may hesitate to tell someone how they really feel. This lack of honesty leads to increasing hostility over time and difficulties in communication.

- **I'm helpless.**
  If you believe that what happens to you is beyond your control, you will be unlikely to do something to make the situation better. Here are some examples of helpless self-talk:

  - I'm a shy person. It is hard for me to talk to people.
  - I won't consider that career. Women are always discriminated against in that field.
  - It's difficult for me to meet people.

  Believing such statements, shy people don't attempt to talk to others, women limit their career options, and people give up trying to make friends. Believe that there is a way to change, and you can make your life better.

- **If something bad can happen, it will happen.**
  If you expect the worst, you may take actions that make it happen. If you expect that your speech will be a disaster, you may not prepare or you may forget your notes or props. If you believe that you will not pass the interview and will never get hired, you may not even apply for the job or attempt the interview. If you believe that your personal relationships will not get better, you will not invest the effort to make things better. There will be times when you make a poor speech, get turned down for a job, or have a relationship fail. Learn from these mistakes and do better the next time.

Barriers to Effective Communication

We all want to communicate effectively and get along with people whom we care about. We want to get along with our families, be a good parent, have friends at school, and get along with the boss and our coworkers on the job. Life is just more enjoyable when we have good communication with others. Watch for these barriers to effective communication:

- **Criticizing.**
  Making negative evaluations of others by saying, "It's your fault" or "I told you so," causes anger, which gets in the way of communication.

- **Name-calling and labeling.**
  If you call someone a name or put a label on them, they will attack you rather than communicate with you in any meaningful way.

- **Giving advice.**
  Giving advice may be viewed as talking down to a person. The person may resent your advice and you as well.

- **Ordering or commanding.**
  If you order someone to do something, they are likely to sabotage your request.

- **Threatening.**
  Trying to control someone by making threats causes resentment.

- **Moralizing.**
  Preaching about what a person should or should not do doesn't work because it causes resentment.

- **Diverting.**
  Changing the subject to talk about your own problems tells the person that you do not care about them.

- **Logical arguing.**
  Trying to use facts to convince without taking feelings into account is a barrier to communication. Present your facts and state your point of view, but respect the other person's feelings and different point of view.[3]

QUIZ
Communication for Success, Part II

Test what you have learned by selecting the correct answer to the following questions.

1. The following is a good example of an "I" statement.
   a. I think you need to explain.
   b. I do not understand.
   c. I think you are crazy.

2. "You" statements
   a. put the blame where it needs to be.
   b. results in anger and rebuttal.
   c. are effective communication tools.

3. Which statement is the most powerful?
   a. I should get started on my paper.
   b. I want to get started on my paper.
   c. I will get started on my paper.

4. The following statement is an irrational belief.
   a. I have to be perfect.
   b. I don't need the approval of everyone.
   c. I make mistakes sometimes.

5. This technique is used in effective communication:
   a. moralizing.
   b. logical arguing.
   c. listen and then respond.

How did you do on the quiz? Check your answers: 1. b, 2. b, 3. c, 4. a, 5. c

Dealing with Conflict

There are several ways to approach a conflict. In every conflict there is the potential to be a winner or a loser.

Approaches to Conflict

- Win-Lose
- Lose-Lose
- Compromise
- Win-Win

- **Win-Lose.**
  With this approach to conflict management, one person wins and the other loses, just as in a game or sport. Competition is part of the win-lose approach. In competition, power is important. In sports, the best and most powerful team wins.

  There are many kinds of power, however. Power may be based on authority. Examples might include your boss at work, your teacher, or even your parents. Another kind of power is based on mental ability or cleverness. Sometimes battles are not won by the strongest, but by the cleverest person. Another kind of power is majority rule. In many settings in a democratic society, the person with the most votes wins.

  In many situations, we cannot avoid the win-lose approach. Only one team can win, only one person can get the job, and only one person can marry another. In some circumstances the person you are communicating with does not want to cooperate but to compete.

  The problem with this approach is that there is only one winner. What happens to the loser? The loser can feel bad, resent the winner, give up, or try again for victory. These are not always the best alternatives.

- **Lose-Lose.**
  Lose-lose is another option for resolving conflicts. Both parties lose. Both parties strive to be winners, but the struggle causes damage to both sides. Wars are often lose-lose situations. In World War II dropping an atomic bomb caused the surrender of Japan, but it contaminated the environment with radioactive material and set a dangerous precedent for nuclear war. Recently Russia was able to stop a civil war by destroying Grozny, the capital of Chechnya. The city became nearly uninhabitable. Everyone lost. On an interpersonal level, divorce can be a lose-lose situation if the struggle becomes destructive to both parties.

- **Compromise.**
  Another approach to solving conflict is compromise, where both parties to the conflict have some of their needs met. Both make some sacrifice in order to resolve the situation. For example, the buyer and seller of a used car may agree on a price somewhere between what the seller wants to get and the buyer wants to pay. As long as both parties are satisfied with the outcome, the results are satisfactory. Difficulties arise when people are asked to compromise their values. If they must compromise on something that is truly important, they may be dissatisfied with the outcome.

- **Win-Win.**
  In a win-win approach, both parties work together to find a solution that meets everyone's needs. There is no loser. To reach a win-win solution, set aside competition and replace it with cooperation. This is often difficult to do because emotions are involved. Put aside emotions to discuss the issue. This may mean waiting until both parties have had the opportunity to calm down. This approach can be impossible, however, when one person wants to cooperate and the other person wants to win.

These are the steps in a win-win approach:

1. **Identify the problem.** Identify the problem as your own. If your roommate is having a party and you cannot study, it is your problem. You need to find a quiet place to study.
2. **Set a good time to discuss the issue.** When you are feeling angry is usually not a good time to discuss issues. Set a time when both parties can focus on the problem. A good rule is to wait twenty-four hours to let the emotions cool down and gain some perspective.

3. **Describe your problem and needs.** Use "I" messages. Resist the temptation to label and call names. Goodwill is important.

4. **Look at the other point of view.** Understand the other person's needs, and make sure the other person understands your needs.

5. **Look for alternatives that work for both parties.**

6. **Decide on the best alternative.**

7. **Take action to implement the solution.**

The win-win approach is a good tool for effective communication and maintaining good relationships.

JOURNAL ENTRY #2

Think of a conflict that you have had recently. How could you have applied the steps of a win-win approach to resolving that conflict?

Friendships

College provides the opportunity to make new friends. These friends can broaden your perspective and make your life richer and more enjoyable. What do you value in a friendship? How can you establish and maintain good friendships?

ACTIVITY

Friendship is a relationship that involves trust and support. Beyond this basic definition, we all have different ideas about what is important in a friendship. Here is a list of common qualities of friends. Place a checkmark next to those qualities that are important to you in establishing your personal friendships.

A friend is a person who:

_____ can keep information confidential.   _____ spends time with me.

_____ is loyal.   _____ has a sense of humor.

_____ can be trusted.   _____ is independent.

_____ is warm and affectionate.   _____ has good communication skills.

_____ is supportive of who I am.   _____ is an educated person.

_____ is honest.   _____ is an intelligent person.

_____ is a creative person.   _____ knows how to have fun.

_____ encourages me to do my best.   _____ cares about me.

What are the top three qualities you would look for in a friend? List them below.

1. _____

2. _____

3. _____

The friends that you choose can have a big influence on your life, so it is important to choose them wisely. In college and in the workplace, you will have the opportunity to make new friends who can add a new dimension and perspective to your life. For example, if your friends have goals for the future and believe that completing college is important, you will be more likely to finish your own education. If your friends distract you with too many activities outside of school, your college performance may suffer.

Some students naturally make friends easily, others find making new friends more difficult. Here are some ideas for making new friends:

- **Be a good listener.** Spend equal time listening and talking. If you are doing all the talking, the other person is likely to feel left out of the conversation. Show interest in the other person's interests and ideas.
- **Talk about yourself.** Let others get to know you by sharing your interests, where you come from, and what is important to you. In this way, you can find mutual interests to enjoy.

- **Be supportive and caring.** We all have good days and bad ones. Help your friends to celebrate the good days and be supportive through life's challenges. Showing that you care is the basis of developing trust and friendship.
- **Be a friend.** Treat your friends the way you would like to be treated.
- **Spend time with your friends.** It is difficult to maintain relationships if you do not spend time sharing activities. Make spending time with friends a high priority.
- **Accept your friends for who they are.** Everyone has good and bad qualities. Accept the idea that you are not going to be able to change people to match your expectations.
- **Show appreciation.** Say thank you and make honest compliments. Think of something positive to say.
- **Be assertive.** This means that you ask for what you want and that you don't give in to doing something that you don't want to do. Being assertive means that you have the right to your feelings and opinions. There is a fine line, though, between being assertive and being aggressive. Aggressive behavior is domineering, rude, and intimidating. Aggressive individuals act without consideration of other people's rights and feelings.
- **Be selective.** Not everyone makes a good friend. Make friends with people you respect and admire. Stay away from people who are critical or make you feel unhappy. Avoid those who cause you to do things that you do not want to do. Choose friends that make you happy and encourage you to do your best.

JOURNAL ENTRY #3
What are the qualities you look for in a good friend?

Roommates

Getting along with a roommate can be a challenge. It can be your best or worst college experience or somewhere in between. The key to getting along with a roommate is to understand differences and to work on compromise or win-win solutions. Making a wise choice of a roommate can make the situation much easier. Below are some areas of possible disagreement for roommates:

- **Neatness.** Some students like to keep their rooms neat and others can tolerate messiness.
- **Smoking.** Some students like to smoke and others are offended by smoking.
- **Noise.** Some students need quiet for study while others like to study with music and friends.
- **Guests.** Some students like to have guests in the room, others do not want guests.
- **Temperature.** Some like it warm and some like it cold.
- **Studying.** Is the room a place to study or to have fun?
- **Borrowing.** Some think that borrowing is okay and some do not.
- **Sleeping.** Some go to bed early and some go to bed late. Some need quiet for sleeping.

If you have a choice of roommates, it is a good idea to discuss the above issues in advance. Even best friends can part company over some of these issues. If you are assigned a roommate, discuss the above issues to avoid conflict later on. Aim for win-win solution or at least a compromise. If there is some conflict, following these guidelines may help.

1. Discuss problems as they arise. If you do not discuss problems, it is likely that anger and resentment will increase, causing a more serious problem at a later date.
2. Ask for what you want. Subtle hints often do not work.
3. Be nice to your roommate and treat him or her as you would want to be treated.
4. Be reasonable and overlook small problems. No one is perfect.

Relationships

A relationship starts as a friendship and then moves a step further. A relationship involves emotional attachment and interdependence. We often get our ideas about good relationships through practice and trial and error. When we make errors, the results are often painful. Although we all have different ideas about what constitutes a good relationship, at a minimum it includes these components:

- Love and caring
- Honesty
- Trust
- Loyalty
- Mutual support
- Acceptance of differences

Relationships between Men and Women

According to John Gray, popular author of *Men Are from Mars, Women Are from Venus,* men and women have such different values and needs in a relationship, it is as if they came from different planets.[4] He states that men generally value power, competency, efficiency, and achievement. He says, "A man's sense of self is defined through his ability to achieve results." While women are fantasizing about romance, a man is fantasizing about "powerful cars, faster computers, gadgets, gizmos, and new and more powerful technology."[5] The worst thing that women can do to men, according to Gray, is to offer unsolicited advice or to try to change them. These actions conflict with men's needs for power and competence and imply that they don't know what to do or can't do it on their own. We can communicate our honest feelings about our partner's behavior and ask for what we want and need. However, we should not use our feelings and requests to manipulate another person to change. Gray identifies the most important needs for men as trust, acceptance, appreciation, admiration, approval, and encouragement.

Gray says that women generally value love, communication, beauty, and relationships. Their sense of self-worth is defined through their feelings and the quality of their relationships. The worst thing that men can do to women is to offer solutions too quickly when women are talking about their feelings, rather than listening and understanding those feelings. When this happens, women get frustrated and feel a lack of intimacy. It is possible to listen carefully and understand these feelings without necessarily agreeing with them. The most important needs for women are caring, understanding, respect, devotion, validation, and reassurance.

Gray's ideas about men and women parallel the thinking and feeling dimensions of personality presented earlier. Men are 60 percent thinking types and women are 60 percent feeling types. His ideas are interesting for discussion and apply in many relationships, but it is important to be aware of gender stereotypes. Remember that 40 percent of women are thinking types and 40 percent of men are feeling types, so not all individuals will fit into the same categories that Gray describes.

Although Gray proposes that men and women generally differ in what they consider most important, he lists the following twelve components of love.[6] Men and women can improve their relationships when they demonstrate the following:

1. **Caring.** Show that you are interested and concerned about each other.

2. **Trust.** Have a positive belief in the intentions and abilities of each other.

3. **Understanding.** Listen without judgment and without presuming that you understand the feelings of the other person. In this way both men and women can feel free to discuss what is important to them.

4. **Acceptance.** It is probably not a good idea to marry a person if you think you can change him or her into the ideal person you have in mind. Love your partner without trying to change him or her. No one is perfect; we are each a work in progress. The key is to trust the people we love to make their own improvements.

5. **Respect.** Have consideration for the thoughts and feelings of each other.

6. **Appreciation.** Acknowledge the behavior and efforts of your partner. Appreciation can be in the form of a simple thank you or sending cards or flowers.

7. **Devotion.** Give priority to the relationship so that the other person feels important.

8. **Admiration.** Show approval for the unique gifts and talents of your partner.

9. **Validation.** Do not argue with feelings. Each person has a right to his or her own feelings. We can acknowledge, try to understand, and respect the feelings of another without necessarily agreeing with them.

10. **Approval.** Show approval by acknowledging the goodness and satisfaction you have with each other.

11. **Reassurance.** Show reassurance by repeatedly showing that you care, understand, and respect each other.

12. **Encouragement.** Notice the good characteristics of each other and provide encouragement and support.

How to Survive the Loss of a Relationship

Relationships require work and good communication to keep them going strong. Relationships also change over time as people grow and change. As we search for our soul mates, we may need to end some relationships and start new ones. This process can be very painful.

Following the break up of a relationship, people generally go through three predictable stages:

1. Shock or denial
2. Anger or depression
3. Understanding or acceptance[7]

Dealing with pain is a necessary part of life. Whether the pain is a result of a loss of a relationship or the death of someone important to you, there are some positive steps you can take along the road to acceptance and understanding.

- Recognize that a loss has taken place and give yourself time to adjust to this situation. The greater the loss, the more time it will take to feel better. In the meantime, try to keep up with daily routines. It is possible to feel sad and to go to work and to school. Daily routines may even take your mind off your troubles for a while.
- It is healthy to feel sad and cry. You will need to experience the pain to get over it. It is not helpful to deny pain, cover it up, or run away from it because it will take longer to feel better.
- Talk to a friend or a counselor. Talking about how you feel will help you to understand and accept the loss.
- Don't punish yourself with thoughts that begin "If only I had . . ."
- Realize that there is a beginning and an end to pain.
- Get plenty of rest and eat well.
- Accept understanding and support from friends and family.
- Ask for help if you need it.
- Don't try to get the old relationship going again. It will just prolong the pain.
- Anticipate a positive outcome. You will feel better in the future.
- Beware of the rebound. It is not a good idea to jump into a new relationship right away.
- Beware of addictive activities such as alcohol, drugs, smoking, or overeating.
- Take time to relax and be kind to yourself.
- Use exercise as a way to deal with stress and feel better.
- Keep a journal to help deal with your emotions and learn from the situation.[8]

JOURNAL ENTRY #4

What are the qualities you look for in a good relationship?

Keys to Success

Failure Is an Opportunity for Learning

Everyone makes mistakes and experiences failure. This is the human condition. There is also a saying that falling down is not failure but not getting up is. If you can view failure as an opportunity for learning, you can put it into perspective and continue making progress toward your goals. It has been said that the famous inventor Thomas Edison tried 9,999 times to invent the light bulb. When asked if he was going to fail 10,000 times, he answered, "I didn't fail. I just discovered another way not to invent the light bulb." Failure allows you to collect feedback about how you are doing.

Imagine that your life is like a ship heading toward a destination. Sometimes the sailing is smooth, and sometimes the water is choppy and dangerous and knocks you off course. Failure acts like the rudder of the ship. It helps you to make adjustments so that you stay on course. Too often we do not learn from failure because shame and blame get in the way. Gerard Nierenberg, author of *Do It Right the First Time*, advocates the "no shame, no blame" approach to dealing with errors, mistakes, or failure.[9] The first step is to identify the mistake that has been made. What went wrong? Then you look at how much damage has been done. The next step is to take an honest look at what caused the problem. The last step is to figure out a way to fix the problem and see that it does not happen again. There is no shame or blame in the process. Following this approach results in fewer errors and failures.

Harold Kushner has another view about failure:

> Life is not a spelling bee, where no matter how many words you have gotten right, if you make one mistake you are disqualified. Life is more like a baseball season, where even the best team loses one-third of its games and even the worst team has its days of brilliance. Our goal is not to go all year without ever losing a game. Our goal is to win more than we lose, and if we can do that consistently enough, then when the end comes, we will have won it all.[10]

Like a baseball player, if you lose a game, analyze what went wrong and keep on practicing. Remember that you will eventually be a winner. Everyone remembers that Babe Ruth was a great baseball player and that he had 714 home runs. People do not remember that he also struck out 1,330 times. If you can look honestly at your mistakes and learn from them, you can have many winning seasons.

JOURNAL ENTRY #5

Describe a situation in which you have been disappointed with the results. Was there an opportunity to learn from the situation?

JOURNAL ENTRIES

Communication and Relationships

Go to http://www.collegesuccess1.com/ for Word files of the Journal Entries

Success over the Internet

Visit the *College Success Website* at
http://www.collegesuccess1.com/

The *College Success Website* is continually
updated with new topics and links to the material
presented in this chapter. Topics include

- Expectations in relationships
- Common mistakes in relationships

- Beginning, enhancing, and ending relationships
- Dealing with anger
- Personality and relationships

Contact your instructor if you have any problems in accessing the *College Success Website*.

Notes

1. A. Wolvin and C. G. Coakley, *Listening*, 3rd ed. (Dubuque, IA: W. C. Brown, 1988), 208.
2. *Care of the Mentally Ill* (F.A. Davis, 1977).
3. T. Gordon, *Parent Effectiveness Training* (New York: McGraw-Hill, 1970).
4. John Gray, *Men Are from Mars, Women Are from Venus* (New York: HarperCollins, 1992).
5. Ibid., 16.
6. Ibid., 133–37.
7. Melba Colgrove, Harold Bloomfield, and Peter McWilliams, *How to Survive the Loss of a Love* (New York: Bantam Books, 1988).
8. Adapted from Colgrove, Bloomfield, and McWilliams, *How to Survive the Loss of a Love.*
9. Gerard Nierenberg, *Doing It Right the First Time* (New York: John Wiley and Sons, 1996).
10. Harold Kushner, *Becoming Aware* (Dubuque, IA: Kendall/Hunt).

Communication Scenarios

Name _____   Date _____

In the following scenarios, think about how personality type influences communication style. Knowing about your personality type and understanding opposite types can help to improve your communication. Your instructor may want to do this as a group activity in the classroom.

1. An introvert and an extravert are having an argument.

    How is the introvert likely to act?

    How is the extravert likely to act?

    How can the extravert improve communication?

    How can the introvert improve communication?

2. A sensing and an intuitive type are on a date.

    What is the sensing person likely to talk about?

    What is the intuitive type likely to talk about?

3. A thinking type and a feeling type are dating.

    When there are problems in the relationship, how is the thinking type likely to approach the problem?

    How will the feeling type approach the problem?

    How can the thinking type improve communication?

    How can the feeling type improve communication?

4. A judging type and a perceptive type are married. The judging type likes to keep the house neat and orderly. The perceptive type likes creative disorder. How can they resolve this conflict?

Your Personal Communication Style

Name _____   Date _____

1. How does being an **introvert** or an **extravert** (or combination) affect your communication style?

2. How does being a **sensing** or **intuitive** type (or combination) affect your communication style?

3. How does being a **thinking** or **feeling** type (or combination) affect your communication style?

4. How does being a **judging** or **perceptive** type (or combination) affect your communication style?

"I" and "You" Messages

Name _____   Date _____

Part 1

"You" messages label, judge, and blame; they demand counterattack.

"I" messages describe yourself and help improve understanding.

Examples:

You are rude.	I feel upset.
You make me mad.	I feel angry.
You must be crazy.	I don't understand.

Change the following statements from a "you" message to an "I" or "we" message.

1. Your class is boring.

2. That was a stupid joke.

3. You gave me an F.

4. You don't understand.

Part 2

For each situation below, state the behavior, the consequences, and your feelings in any order.

Example: When you play your stereo this loud after midnight (behavior), I can't sleep (consequence) and I get really irritable (feelings).

1. Your date, who is supposed to arrive at 6:00, arrives at 7:00. The dinner you have fixed is ruined and you won't have time to catch that late movie after dinner. What do you say?

   _____

   _____

2. A student who sits next to you in class constantly asks you questions and tries to talk to you during the lecture. You find it difficult to concentrate and take notes. What do you say?

   _____

   _____

   _____

Rewrite the Script

Name _____   Date _____

Rewrite the script in the following scenario using "I" messages to try to improve the situation and come up with a win-win solution.

Eric and Jason are roommates who have known each other since childhood. Because they are good friends, they decide to be roommates in college. They rent an apartment together and sign a one-year lease.

Eric: Look at this place. It's trashed! You're really a pig! There are pieces of leftover pizza and empty beer bottles everywhere from that party you had. Your stupid friends spilled soda on the floor and broke the lamp. Are you going to pay for that?

Jason: Why do you always have to be so hostile? We were just having some fun. I was going to clean it up in the morning but I accidentally slept in. Then I had to go to class. Do you want me to miss class and fail? I'm still going to clean it up. Chill out!

Eric: Maybe I wouldn't be so irritated if you guys didn't keep me up all night. I had a test this morning at 8:00. You don't think of anyone but yourself. How can you be so irresponsible?

Jason: Whatever, dude.

Name _____   Date _____

Find at least three people over the age of 40. Ask them these three questions and write your notes below. Your instructor may ask you to share your answers with the class.

1. If you were 18 years old again, what would you do differently?

2. What is the best decision that you made between the ages of 18 and 22?

3. What advice would you give to a person who is 18 years old?

Name _____ Date _____

What is your definition of friendship?

What are the five most important qualities of a good friend?

1.

2.

3.

4.

5.

Join with some other students in the class to share your ideas.

Relationships

Name _____ Date _____

For five minutes, brainstorm your ideas about what constitutes an ideal relationship. Remember that a relationship involves caring and interdependence.

What are the five most important qualities of an ideal relationship?

1.

2.

3.

4.

5.

A good relationship requires the cooperation and caring of two people. What steps can you take to improve your present relationships?

Communication Exercise

Name _____   Date _____

List 10 ideas from this chapter that will help you to improve communication with others who are important to you.

1.

2.

3.

4.

5.

6.

7.

8.

9.

10.

© Yuri Arcurs, 2008. Under license from Shutterstock, Inc.

Thinking Critically and Creatively

Your college experience will help you to develop critical and creative thinking skills. Critical thinking involves analyzing data, generating alternatives, and solving problems. Creative thinking helps you to find new ideas to solve problems in your personal and professional life.

Critical Thinking

Critical thinking involves questioning established ideas, creating new ideas, and using information to solve problems. In critical thinking reasoning is used in the pursuit of truth. Part of obtaining a college education is learning to think critically. Understanding the concepts of critical thinking will help you to be successful in college courses in which critical thinking is used.

Beyond college, critical thinking is helpful in being a good citizen and a productive member of society. Throughout history, critical thinkers have helped to advance civilization. Thoughts that were once widely accepted were questioned, and newer and more useful ideas were introduced. For example, it was once assumed that blood-sucking leeches were helpful in curing diseases. Some critical thinkers questioned this practice, and the science of medicine was advanced. It was not so long ago that women were not allowed to vote. Critical thinkers questioned this practice so that women could participate in a democratic society.

A lack of critical thinking can lead to great tragedy. In his memoirs, Adolf Eichmann, who played a central role in the Nazis' killing of six million Jews during World War II, wrote:

> From my childhood, obedience was something I could not get out of my system. When I entered the armed services at the age of 27, I found being obedient not a bit more difficult than it had been during my life at that point. It was unthinkable that I would not follow orders. Now that I look back, I realize that a life predicated on being obedient and taking orders is a very comfortable life indeed. Living in such a way reduces to a minimum one's own need to think.[1]

Critical and creative thinking are closely related. If you can think critically, you have the freedom to be creative and generate new ideas. The great American jurist and philosopher Oliver Wendell Holmes noted:

> There are one-story intellects, two-story intellects, and three-story intellects with skylights. All fact-collectors who have no aim beyond their facts are one-story men. Two-story men compare, reason, generalize, using the labor of the fact-collectors as their own. Three-story men idealize, imagine, predict—their best illumination comes from above through skylights.

Use the information in this chapter to become a three-story intellect with skylights. And by the way, even though Oliver Wendell Holmes talks about men, women can be three-story intellects too.

Fallacies in Reasoning

To think critically, you need to be able to recognize fallacies in reasoning.[2] Fallacies are patterns of incorrect reasoning. Recognizing these fallacies can help you to avoid them in your thinking and writing. You can also become aware of when others are using these fallacies to persuade you. They may use these fallacies for their own purpose, such as power or financial gain.

The function of education is to teach one to think intensively and to think critically. Intelligence plus character—that is the goal of true education.

Martin Luther King, Jr.

If it was so, it might be; and if it were so, it would be; but as it isn't, it ain't. That's logic.

Lewis Carroll

- **Appeal to authority.** It is best to make decisions by reviewing the information and arguments and reaching our own conclusions. Sometimes we are encouraged to rely on experts for a recommendation because they have specialized information. Obviously, we need to have trust in the experts to accept their conclusions. However, when we cite some person as an authority in a certain area when they are not, we make an appeal to a questionable authority. For example, when a company uses famous sports figures to endorse a product, a particular brand of athletic shoes or breakfast cereal, they are appealing to a questionable authority. Just because the athletes are famous, does not mean they are experts on the product they are endorsing. They are endorsing the product to earn money. Many commercials you see on TV use appeals to a questionable authority.

- **Jumping to conclusions.** When we jump to conclusions, we make hasty generalizations. For example, if a college student borrows money from a bank and does not pay it back, the manager of the bank might conclude that all college students are poor risks and refuse to give loans to other college students.

- **Making generalizations.** We make generalizations when we say that all members of a group are the same, as in

  All lawyers are greedy.
  All blondes are airheads.

  Of course, your occupation does not determine whether or not you are greedy, and the color of your hair does not determine your intelligence. Such thinking leads to harmful stereotypes and fallacies in reasoning. Instead of generalizing, think of people as unique individuals.

- **Attacking the person rather than discussing the issues.** To distract attention from the issues, we often attack the person. Political candidates today are routinely asked about personal issues such as extramarital affairs and drug use. Of course personal integrity in politicians is important, but attacking the person can serve as a smokescreen to direct attention away from important political issues. Critical thinkers avoid reacting emotionally to personalities and use logical thinking to analyze the issues.

- **Appeal to common belief.** Just because something is a common belief does not mean that it is true. At one time people believed that the world was flat and that when you got to the edge of the earth, you would fall off. If you were to survey the people who lived in that period in history, the majority would have agreed that the earth was flat. A survey just tells us what people believe. The survey does not tell us what is true and accurate.

- **Appeal to common practice.** Appealing to common practice is the "everyone else is doing it" argument. Just because everyone else does it doesn't mean that it is right. Here are some common examples of this fallacy:

  It is okay to cheat in school. Everyone else does it.
  It is okay to speed on the freeway. Everyone else does it.
  It is okay to cheat on your taxes. Everyone else does it.

- **Appeal to tradition.** Appeal to tradition is a variation of the "everyone else is doing it" argument. The appeal to tradition is "we've always done it that way." Just because that is the way it has always been done doesn't mean it is the best way to do it. With this attitude, it is very difficult to make changes and improve our ways of doing things. While tradition is very important, it is open to question. For example, construction and automotive technology have traditionally been career choices for men but not for women. When women tried to enter or work in these

Fallacies in Reasoning

- Appeal to authority
- Jumping to conclusions
- Making generalizations
- Attacking the person
- Appeal to common belief
- Appeal to common practice
- Appeal to tradition
- Two wrongs
- Domino theory
- Wishful thinking
- Scare tactics
- Appeal to pity
- Appeal to loyalty
- Appeal to prejudice
- Appeal to vanity
- False causes
- Straw man/woman
- Cult behavior

© Zits Partnership. Reprinted with Special Permission of King Features Syndicate.

careers, there was resistance from those who did not want to change traditions. This resistance limited options for women.

- **Two wrongs.** In this fallacy, it is assumed that it is acceptable to do something because other people are doing something just as bad. For example, if someone cuts you off on the freeway, you may assume that it is acceptable to zoom ahead and cut in front of his or her car. The "two wrongs" fallacy has an element of retribution, or getting back at the other person. The old saying, "Two wrongs do not make a right," applies in this situation.

- **The slippery slope or domino theory.** The slippery slope or domino theory is best explained with an example. A student might think: If I fail the test, I will fail this class. If I fail this class, I will drop out of college. My parents will disown me and I will lose the respect of my friends. I will not be able to get a good job. I will start drinking and end up homeless. In this fallacy, the negative consequences of our actions are only remotely possible, but are assumed to be certain. These dire consequences influence people's decisions and change behavior. In this situation, it is important to evaluate these consequences. One does not necessarily lead to the other. If you fail the test, you could study and pass the next test. As a child you were probably cautioned about many slippery slopes in life:

  Brush your teeth or your teeth will fall out.
  Do your homework or you will never get into college and get a good job.

ACTIVITY
Practice Matching Fallacies in Reasoning, Part I

The column on the left contains examples of fallacies in reasoning. Match these examples with the name of the fallacy on the right.

Example:

_____ 1. Women should not be automotive mechanics.

_____ 2. The best sports shoes are those endorsed by famous athletes.

_____ 3. It is OK for athletes to take drugs to enhance their performance. They all do it.

_____ 4. All women with red hair get angry easily.

_____ 5. If you fail the test, you are a failure for life.

_____ 6. To defeat a politician, research his personal background and let the public know of any past mistakes.

_____ 7. Since some children steal, children should not be allowed into the store without their parents.

_____ 8. All sharks are dangerous and should be killed.

_____ 9. If someone insults you, you should insult them back.

Fallacy:

A. Appeal to authority

B. Appeal to tradition

C. Common practice

D. Two wrongs

E. Attack the person

F. Making generalizations

G. Appeal to a common belief

H. Slippery slope

I. Jumping to conclusions

Answers: 1. B, 2. A, 3. C, 4. F, 5. H, 6. E, 7. I, 8. G, 9. D

• **Wishful thinking.** In wishful thinking an extremely positive outcome, however remote, is proposed as a distraction from logical thinking. For example, a new sports stadium may be proposed. Extremely positive outcomes may be presented, such as downtown redevelopment, the attraction of professional sports teams, increased revenue, and the creation of jobs. Opponents, on the other hand, might foresee increased taxes, lack of parking, and neglect of other important social priorities such as education and shelter for the homeless. Neither position is correct if we assume that the outcomes are certain and automatic. Outcomes need to be evaluated realistically.

Wishful thinking is often used in commercials to sell products. Here are a few examples:

Eat what you want and lose weight.
Use this cream and look younger.
Use this cologne and women will be attracted to you.
Invest your money and get rich quick.

• **Appeal to fear or scare tactics.** Sometimes people appeal to fear as a way of blocking rational thinking. I once saw a political commercial that showed wolves chasing a person through the forest. It was clearly designed to evoke fear. The message was to vote against a proposition to limit lawyers' fees. The idea was that if lawyers' fees were limited, the poor client would be a victim of limited legal services.

This commercial used scare tactics to interfere with rational thinking about the issue.

- **Appeal to pity.** In an appeal to pity, emotion is used to replace logic. It is what is known as a "sob story." Appeals to pity may be legitimate when used to foster charity and empathy. However, the sob story uses emotion in place of reason to persuade and is often exaggerated. College faculties often hear sob stories from students having academic difficulties:

    Please don't disqualify me from college. I failed all my classes because I was emotionally upset when my grandmother died.

    Please don't fail me in this class. If you fail me, my parents will kick me out of the house and I will not be able to get health insurance.
    If you fail me in this class, I won't be eligible to play football and my future as a professional will be ruined.

- **Appeal to loyalty.** Human beings are social creatures who enjoy being attached to a group. We feel loyalty to our friends, family, school, communities, teams, and favorite musicians. Appeals to loyalty ask you to act according to the group's best interests without considering whether the actions are right or wrong. Critical thinkers, however, do not support an idea just to show support for a group with which they identify.

    Peer pressure is related to the loyalty fallacy. With peer pressure, members of a group may feel obliged to act in a certain way because they think members of the group act that way. Another variation of the loyalty fallacy is called the bandwagon argument. It involves supporting a certain idea just to be part of the group. This tendency is powerful when the group is perceived to be powerful or "cool." In elections, people often vote for the candidate that is perceived to be the most popular. If everyone else is voting for the candidate, they assume the candidate must be the best. This is not necessarily true.

- **Appeal to prejudice.** A prejudice is judging a group of people or things positively or negatively, even if the facts do not agree with the judgment. A prejudice is based on a stereotype in which all members of a group are judged to be the same. Speakers sometimes appeal to prejudice to gain support for their causes. Listen for the appeal to prejudice in hate speeches or literature directed against different ethnicities, genders, or sexual orientations.

- **Appeal to vanity.** The appeal to vanity is also known as "apple polishing." The goal of this strategy is to get agreement by paying compliments. Students who pay compliments to teachers and then ask for special treatment are engaging in apple polishing.

- **Post hoc reasoning, or false causes.** Post hoc reasoning has to do with cause and effect. It explains many superstitions. If I play a good game of golf whenever I wear a certain hat, I might conclude that the hat causes me to play a good golf game. The hat, however, is a false cause of playing a good game of golf. I may feel more comfortable wearing my lucky hat, but it is a secondary reason for playing well. I play well because I practice my golf skills and develop my self-confidence. In scientific research, care is taken to test for false causes. Just because an event regularly follows another event does not mean that the first event caused the second event. For example, when the barometer falls, it rains. The falling barometer does not cause the rain; a drop in atmospheric pressure causes the rain. If falling barometers caused the rain, we could all be rainmakers by adjusting our barometers.

- **Straw man or woman.** Watch for this fallacy during election time. Using this strategy, a politician creates a misleading image of someone else's statements, ideas, or beliefs to make them easy to attack. For example, politicians might accuse their opponents of raising taxes. That may only be part of the story, however. Maybe their opponents also voted for many tax-saving measures. When politicians or anyone else uses the straw man fallacy, they are falsifying or oversimplifying. Use your critical thinking to identify the straw man or woman (political opponent) in the next election. Of course you don't have to be a politician to use this strategy. People use this strategy when they spread gossip or rumors about someone they want to discredit.

- **Cult behavior.** Cults and doomsday forecasters spread unorthodox and sometimes harmful beliefs with great fervor. These thoughts are perpetuated through mind-control techniques. With mind control, members of a group are taught to suppress natural emotions and accept the ideas of the group in exchange for a sense of belonging. These groups do not allow members to think critically or question the belief system. Mind control is the opposite of critical thinking. It is important to use critical thinking when you encounter beliefs for which there is no hard evidence. An example is the Heavensgate cult:

> It all seems perfectly ludicrous: 39 people don their new sneakers, pack their flight bags and poison themselves in the solemn belief that a passing UFO will whisk them off to Wonderland.[4]

ACTIVITY
Practice Matching Fallacies in Reasoning, Part II

The column on the left contains examples of fallacies in reasoning. Match these examples with the name of the fallacy on the right.

Example:

Fallacy:

_____1. You look really nice today. Can I ask you a favor?   A. Wishful thinking

_____2. I'll vote for a woman because I am a woman.   B. Scare tactics

_____3. Earn $10,000 a month by working part time at home.   C. Appeal to pity

_____4. If you fail me on this test, the coach will not let me play next week.   D. Appeal to loyalty

_____5. I'm more likely to win if I wear my lucky socks.   E. Appeal to prejudice

_____6. If you vote for this politician, she will raise taxes.   F. Appeal to vanity

_____7. If you don't buy this car, you are putting your family at risk.   G. Post hoc reasoning

_____8. All large dogs are dangerous.   H. Straw man or woman

_____9. The leader knows what is best for me.   I. Cult behavior

Answers: 1. F, 2. D, 3. A, 4. C, 5. G, 6. H, 7. B, 8. E, 9. I

JOURNAL ENTRY #1

Fallacies in reasoning are frequently used in advertisements and politics. From your personal experience, describe two examples of fallacies in reasoning.

How to Become a Critical Thinker

The Critical Thinking Process

When thinking about a complex problem, use these steps in the critical thinking process:

1. **State the problem in a clear and simple way.** Sometimes the message is unclear or obscured by appeals to emotion. Stating the problem clearly brings it into focus so that you can identify the issue and begin to work on it.

2. **Identify the alternative views.** In looking at different views, you open your mind to a wider range of options. The diagram entitled "Alternative Views" below gives a perspective on point of view. For every issue, there are many points of view. The larger circle represents these many points of view. The individual point of view is represented by a dot on the larger circle. Experience, values, beliefs, culture, and knowledge influence an individual's point of view.

3. **Watch for fallacies** in reasoning when looking at alternative views.

4. **Find at least three different answers.** In searching for these different answers, you force yourself to look at all the possibilities before you decide on the best answer.

5. **Construct your own reasonable view.** After looking at the alternatives and considering different answers to the problem, construct your own reasonable view. Practice this process using the critical thinking exercises at the end of this chapter.

Alternative Views[3]

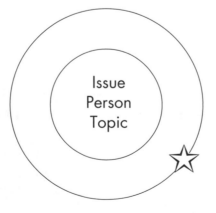

Issue Person Topic

⭐ Individual Point of View Based on:
- Experience
- Values
- Beliefs
- Culture
- Knowledge

Tips for Critical Thinking

1. **Be aware of your mindset.** A mindset is a pattern of thought that you use out of habit. You develop patterns of thinking based on your personal experiences, culture, and environment. When the situation changes, your old mindset may need to change as well.

2. **Be willing to say, "I don't know."** With this attitude you are open to exploring new ideas. In today's rapidly changing world, it is not possible to know everything. Rather than trying to know everything, it is more important to be able to find the information you need.

3. **Practice tolerance for other people's ideas.** We all have a different view of the world based on our own experiences and can benefit from an open exchange of information.

4. **Try to look for several answers and understand many points of view.** The world is not either-or or black-and-white. Looking at all the possibilities is the first step in finding a creative solution.

5. **Understand before criticizing.** Life is not about justifying your point of view. It is important to understand and then offer your suggestions.

6. **Realize that your emotions can get in the way of clear thinking.** We all have beliefs that are important to us. It is difficult to listen to a different point of view when someone questions your personal beliefs. Open your mind to see all the alternatives. Then construct your reasonable view.

7. **Notice the source of the information you are analyzing.** Political announcements are required to include information about the person or organization paying for the ad. Knowing who paid for an advertisement can help you understand and evaluate the point of view that is being promoted.

8. **Ask the question, "What makes the author think so?"** In this way you can discover what premises the author is using to justify his or her position.

9. **Ask the question, "So what?"** Ask this question to determine what is important and how the author reached the conclusion.

> If there is any secret of success, it lies in the ability to get the other person's point of view and see things from his angle as well as from your own.
>
> Henry Ford

Universal Intellectual Standards to Assure Quality Thinking[4]

Clarity	Can you provide the details or an example?
Accuracy	Is it really true and how can we check it?
Precision	What are the specific details?
Relevance	How does it relate to the problem or how does it help us with the issue?
Depth	What are some of the complexities of the problem?
Breadth	Do we need to consider another point of view?
Logic	Does it make sense?
Fairness	Are we considering all relevant viewpoints?

Critical Thinking Tips

- Be aware of your mindset.
- Say "I don't know."
- Be tolerant.
- Look for several answers.
- Understand.
- Recognize emotions.
- Examine the source.
- Ask, "Why?"
- Ask, "So what?"

Critical Thinking over the Internet

The Internet is revolutionizing the way we access and retrieve information today. Through the use of search engines, websites, electronic periodicals, and online reference materials, it is possible to find just about any information you need. The Internet is also full of scams, rumors, gossip, hoaxes, exaggerations, and illegal activity. Anyone can put anything on the Internet. You will need to apply critical thinking to the information that you find on the Internet. Author Reid Goldsborough offers these suggestions for thinking critically about material on the Internet:

- **Don't be fooled by appearances.** It is easy to create a flashy and professional-looking website. Some products and services are legitimate, but some are scams.

- **Find out about the person or organization providing the information.** There should be links to a home page that lists the author's background and credentials. You need to be skeptical if the author is not identified. If you cannot identify the person who authored the website, find out what organization sponsored the site. Most of the Internet resources cited in this text are provided by educational or government sources. It is the goal of these organizations to provide the public with information.

- **Look for the reason the information was posted.** What is the agenda? Keep this in mind when evaluating the information. Many websites exist to sell a product or influence public opinion.

- **Look for the date that the information was created or revised.** A good website posts the date of creation or revision.

- **Try to verify the information elsewhere,** especially if the information is at odds with common sense or what you believe to be true. Verify the information through other websites or your local library.[5]

How to Recognize a Scam

Use your critical thinking skills to recognize a scam or hoax. How can you recognize a scam? Here are some signs to watch for:

- **Be aware of big promises.** If something sounds too good to be true, it probably is a hoax. If you are promised $5,000 a month for working part time out of your home, be careful. If you are offered a new TV in a box for $50, the box may contain stolen goods or even rocks!

- **The word "free" is often used to catch your attention to make a sale.** Few things in life are free.

- **A similar tactic is to offer money or a prize.** The scam goes like this: "Congratulations! You have just won a . . ." Be especially careful if you have to pay money to claim your prize.

- **Beware of high-pressure tactics.** A common scam is to ask you to pay money now or the price will go up. Take your time to think carefully about your expenditures. If the deal is legitimate, it will be there tomorrow.

- **To avoid identity theft, be careful about disclosing personal information** such as social security numbers and credit card numbers. Disclose this information only to people and organizations you know and trust.

- **If you suspect a scam, research the offer on the Internet.** Use a search engine such as yahoo.com or google.com and type in the word "scam." You can find descriptions of many different types of scams. You can also find information on the latest scams or file a complaint at the Federal Trade Commission website at www.ftc.gov

> ## QUIZ
> # Critical Thinking
>
> Test what you have learned by selecting the correct answer to the following questions.
>
> 1. Critical thinking involves
>   a. being critical of other's opinions.
>   b. identifying alternative views.
>   c. finding only one correct answer.
>
> 2. To be a critical thinker it is important to
>   a. understand before criticizing.
>   b. justify your point of view.
>   c. tell yourself that you know the answer.
>
> 3. Construct your reasonable view by
>   a. advocating for your point of view.
>   b. always defending your mindset.
>   c. first considering different answers.
>
> 4. An Internet site is legitimate if it
>   a. looks professional.
>   b. has useful information.
>   c. has an identifiable and reputable source.
>
> 5. If you are offered something that is too good to be true,
>   a. be thankful for your good fortune.
>   b. suspect that it could be a scam.
>   c. it could be a good investment.
>
> How did you do on the quiz? Check your answers: 1. b, 2. a, 3. c, 4. c, 5. b

> **JOURNAL ENTRY #2**
>
> How would you use the critical thinking process to determine what political candidate to elect?

Creative Thinking

What Is Creativity?

To see creativity in action all we need to do is to look at young children. Movie producer Steven Spielberg describes their creativity:

> The greatest quality that we can possess is curiosity, a genuine interest in the world around us. The most used word—and I have five kids, so I know what I'm talking about—the most used word in a child's vocabulary is "why." A child doesn't blindly accept things as they are, doesn't blindly believe in limits, doesn't blindly believe in the words spoken by some authority figure like me.[6]

The creative individual asks why and uses divergent thinking. **Divergent thinking** is the ability to discover many alternatives. J. P. Guilford, a researcher on creativity, said that "the person who is capable of producing a large number of ideas per unit of time, other things being equal, has a greater chance of having significant ideas."[8] Divergent thinking is useful in careers requiring creativity, such as the arts, science, and business. Creativity helps in the enjoyment of outside activities such as hobbies that help us to lead satisfying lives. Creativity and divergent thinking are important in generating alternatives necessary for effective problem solving and coming up with creative solutions to the challenges we all face in life. Guilford defines creative behavior as follows:

> The individual who behaves creatively is oriented toward selecting and solving meaningful problems, using an inner drive to recombine his or her storehouse of experiences in new ways. In attacking problems, he or she does not act as a conformist; instead, he or she pioneers often, is not afraid to fail frequently, but is productive in the long run.[7]

The Three S's of Creativity: Sensitivity, Synergy, and Serendipity

Questions are the creative acts of intelligence.

Frank Kingdon

The creative process involves sensitivity, synergy, and serendipity. Creative persons use their **sensitivity** to discover the world and spot problems, deficiencies, and incongruities. A person who is sensitive asks, "Why does this happen?" Sensitive persons are also inventive and ask the question, "How can I do this?" They are problem finders as well as problem solvers.

Synergy occurs when two or more elements are associated in a new way and the result is greater than the sum of the parts. For example, imagine a machine that combines the telephone, the computer, the television, and a music player. The combining of these familiar devices into one machine is changing the way we live. Another example of synergy is the old saying, "Two heads are better than one." When two or more people work together and share ideas, the result is often greater than what one person could produce alone. This is the essence of creativity.

The word **serendipity** is attributed to Horace Walpole, who wrote a story about the Persian princes of Serendip. The princes made unexpected discoveries while they were looking for something else. Serendipity is finding something by a lucky accident. You can only take advantage of a lucky accident if you look around and find new meaning and opportunity in the event. An example of serendipity comes from a story about the famous musician Duke Ellington. He was playing at an outdoor concert when a noisy plane flew over the stage. He changed the tempo of the music to go with the sounds of the airplane and directed the plane along with the orchestra. Another example of serendipity is Alexander Fleming's discovery of penicillin. He was growing bacteria in his lab when a spore of *penicillium notatum* blew in the window, landed on the bacteria, and killed it. Instead of throwing away a ruined experiment, he discovered the antibiotic penicillin, one of the most important medical discoveries ever made.

Creative Thinking Techniques

- **Brainstorming.** One of the most important components of creativity is the ability to use divergent thinking to generate many ideas or alternatives. Brainstorming is one of the most frequently used techniques to develop divergent thinking. The key to brainstorming is to delay critical judgment to allow for the spontaneous flow of ideas. Critical judgment about the merit of ideas can hinder the creative process if it is applied too early. Here are the rules of brainstorming:

- Generate a large quantity of ideas without regard to quality. This increases the likelihood that some of the ideas will be good or useful.
- Set a time limit to encourage quick thinking. The time limit is generally short, from three to five minutes.
- Set a goal or quota for the number of ideas you want to generate. The goal serves as a motivator.
- The wilder and more unusual the ideas, the better. It is easier to tame down crazy ideas than to think up new ideas.
- Use synergy by brainstorming with a group of people. Build on other people's ideas. Sometimes two ideas combined can make one better idea.
- Select the best ideas from the list.

- **Relaxed attention.** Can you imagine being relaxed and paying attention at the same time? Robert McKim describes this as the paradox of the Ho-hum and the Aha![8] To be creative it is first necessary to relax. The brain works better when it is relaxed. By relaxing, the individual releases full energy and attention to the task at hand. Athletes and entertainers must master the art of relaxation before they can excel in athletics or entertainment. If the muscles are too tense, blood flow is restricted and energy is wasted. However, totally relaxed individuals cannot think at all. They might even be asleep!

  Some tension, but not too much, is needed to think and be creative; hence the term "relaxed attention." In the creative process, the person first thinks about a task, problem, or creation and then relaxes to let the ideas incubate. During this incubation period, the person often gets a flash of insight or feeling of "Aha!" Famous artist Pablo Picasso described this process:

  > For me creation first starts with contemplation, and I need long, idle hours of meditation. It is then that I work most. I look at flies, at flowers, at leaves and trees around me. I let my mind drift at ease, just like a boat in the current. Sooner or later, it is caught by something. It gets precise. It takes shape . . . my next painting motif is decided.[9]

  As a student you can apply the principle of relaxed attention to improve your creativity. If you are thinking about a problem and get stuck, relax and come back to it later. Take a break, do something else, or even sleep on it. You are likely to come up with creative inspiration while you are relaxing. Then get back to solving the problem and pay attention to it.

- **Use idea files.** Keep files of ideas that you find interesting. People in advertising call these "swipe files." No one creates in a vacuum. Some of the best creative ideas involve recombining or building on the ideas of others or looking at them from a different perspective. This is different from copying other people's ideas; it is using them as the fertilizer for creative thinking.

  As a college student, you might keep files of the following:

  - Interesting ideas and their sources for use in writing term papers
  - Information about careers
  - Information for your resume
  - Information that you can use to apply for scholarships
  - Ideas related to your hobbies
  - Ideas for having fun
  - Ideas for saving money

- **Practice using visualization and imagination.** Visualizing and imagining are important in the creative process. Young children are naturally good at these two

Creative Thinking Techniques

- Brainstorming
- Relaxed attention
- Idea files
- Visualization and imagination
- Read
- Keep a journal
- Think critically

skills. What happens as we grow older? As we grow older, we learn to follow the rules and color between the lines. We need rules to have an orderly society, yet we need visualization and imagination to move forward and create new ideas. Don't forget to use and practice visualization and imagination.

Visualization and imagination can be fun and interesting activities to help you relax. We have often been told not to daydream, but daydreams can be a tool for relaxation as well as creativity. It is important to come back to reality once we are finished daydreaming. The last step in the creative process is doing something with the best of our creative ideas.

- **Read.** One of the best ways to trigger your creativity is to read a wide variety of materials, including newspapers, magazines, novels, nonfiction books, and articles on the Internet. The ideas that you discover will provide background information, helping you gain perspective on the world, and give you ideas for making your own contributions. When you read, you expose your mind to the greatest people who have ever lived. Make reading a habit.

- **Keep a journal.** Keep a journal of your creative ideas, thoughts, and problems. Writing often will help you think clearly. When you write about your problems, it is almost like having your own private therapist. In college your journal can be a source of creative ideas for writing term papers and completing assignments.

- **Think critically.** Approach learning with a sense of awe, excitement, and skepticism. Here is another paradox! Creative and critical thinkers have much in common. Both ask questions, look at the world from different perspectives, and generate new alternatives.

QUIZ
Creative Thinking

Test what you have learned by selecting the correct answer to the following questions.

1. Divergent thinking is a creative thinking technique that involves:

   a. defending the correct answer.
   b. selecting the one best alternative.
   c. the ability to discover many different alternatives.

2. The following saying is a good definition for synergy:

   a. Seeing is believing.
   b. Two heads are better than one.
   c. Practice makes perfect.

3. Serendipity is:

   a. finding something by a lucky accident.
   b. finding something humorous in the situation.
   c. improvising while playing music.

4. When using relaxed attention as a creative process,

   a. the creative person is totally relaxed.
   b. the creative person is focusing attention.
   c. the creative person first thinks about the problem and then relaxes.

5. For brainstorming, it is important to:

   a. select the best ideas as a last step.
   b. consider only the good ideas.
   c. consider only the workable ideas.

How did you do on the quiz? Check your answers: 1. c, 2. b, 3. a, 4. c, 5. a

JOURNAL ENTRY #3
Describe at least two creativity techniques that you use or are willing to try.

Keys to Success

Learn to Laugh at Life

Have a laugh at life and look around you for happiness instead of sadness. Laughter has always brought me out of unhappy situations. Even in your darkest moment, you usually can find something to laugh about if you try hard enough.

—Red Skelton

All of us face difficult times in life; but if we can learn the gift of laughter, it is easier to deal with the difficulties.

Just putting a smile on your face can help. German psychologist Fritz Strack had his subjects watch a cartoon with a pencil in their mouths. Half of his subjects held the pencil between their teeth, which made them laugh. The other half of his subjects held the pencil between their lips, which made them frown. The smiling group thought that the cartoon was funnier. It seems that there is a connection between our physical responses and our internal feelings. The physical act of smiling actually makes you feel happier.[10]

If you do not feel happy, smile and pretend to feel happy. Neurophysicist Richard Hamilton says that if you pretend to be happy, you actually feel better because positive thoughts and behavior impact the biochemistry of the brain. Positive thinking helps the brain produce seratonin, a neurotransmitter linked with feelings of happiness.[11] The path to achieving your goals is much smoother if you choose to be happy. So smile and be happy. Then work on making positive changes in your life.

JOURNAL ENTRIES

Thinking Critically and Creatively

Go to http://www.collegesuccess1.com/ for Word files of the Journal Entries

Success over the Internet

Visit the *College Success Website* at http://www.collegesuccess1.com/

The *College Success Website* is continually updated with new topics and links to the material presented in this chapter. Topics include

- Critical thinking in college-level courses
- Techniques for thinking excellently

- The core concepts of critical thinking
- Avoiding scams

Contact your instructor if you have any problems in accessing the *College Success Website.*

Notes

1. Roger Cohen, "Nazi Leader's Notes Cite 'Obedience' as Reason for His Genocidal Actions," *San Diego Union Tribune,* 13 August 1999.
2. Information in this section is adapted from the Institute for Teaching and Learning website Mission Critical at http://www.sjsu.edu/depts/itl/index.html.
3. Idea contributed by Vangie Meneses, Dean of Counseling, Cuyamaca College, El Cajon, CA.
4. Richard Paul and Linda Elder. "The Miniature Guide to Critical Thinking," The Foundation for Critical Thinking, www.criticalthinking.org, 2008.
5. Reid Goldsborough, "Teaching Healthy Skepticism about Information on the Internet," *Technology and Learning,* January 1998.
6. Steven Spielberg, commencement address at the University of Southern California, 1994.
7. Sidney Parnes, Ruth Noller, and Angelo Biondi, *Guide to Creative Action* (New York: Charles Scribner's Sons, 1977), 52.
8. Ibid., 9.
9. Robert McKim, *Experiences in Visual Thinking* (Monterey, CA: Brooks/Cole, 1972).
10. Joan Smith, "Nineteen Habits of Happy Women," *Redbook Magazine,* August 1999, 68.
11. Ibid.

Crime and Punishment

Name _____   Date _____

In 1974, at the age of 19, Doris Drugdealer was arrested for selling $200 worth of heroin to an undercover police officer in Michigan. She received a 10–20 year prison sentence for this crime. After serving about 8 months of her sentence, she decided that she could not tolerate prison and with the help of her grandfather, plotted an escape. She used a work pass to walk away from prison. In May, 2008, after 34 years, Doris was captured again by detectives who matched fingerprints from her driver's license to her prison records.

Doris said that in 1974 she was a "stupid little . . . hippie-ish girl . . . a pothead." During the 34 years that Doris evaded prison, she worried every day that she would be caught. While looking at a sunset, she would marvel at her freedom and wonder if the past would catch up with her. She was very careful to lead the life of a model citizen and even volunteered for Common Cause, an organization that promotes government ethics and accountability. She married an executive and had three children and lived a comfortable life in an upper middle class neighborhood in California. She never told her family about her past. Her husband of 23 years stated that he loved his wife as much as the day they were married and that she was a "person of the highest integrity and compassion" and had dedicated her life to raising her children. She taught her children to be responsible citizens and to avoid drugs. Her husband said that the arrest "was the next worst thing to having a death in the family." Doris worried about the effect of her arrest on her son who had just graduated from high school and her older daughters. A neighbor commented that it would not be useful to society to send Doris back to prison.

Undercover drug officers believed that Doris had connections to "higher ups" in the drug world and was a teenage leader in a 1970's drug ring. They found $600 in her apartment, paraphernalia for cutting heroin and pictures of her with other drug dealers. Doris described herself as a recent high school graduate who was strapped for cash, working at a minimum wage job and driving a $400 car. She said that every day of her life she regretted getting herself into this situation. She was extradited back to Michigan to serve her original prison term. Her family and friends submitted a plea for clemency to the governor of Michigan. Should the governor grant her clemency?

Use your critical thinking to analyze this situation. Your professor may use this exercise as a group discussion. Use the Critical Thinking Worksheet that follows for your analysis.

This exercise is based on excerpts from "Former Fugitive Drawing Sympathy" and "Captured Fugitive Now Waiting for Extradition, and to Learn Fate" from the San Diego Union Tribune, May 1 and 2, 2008. From CollegeScope/College and Career Success by Dr. Marsha Fralick

Critical Thinking Worksheet: Crime and Punishment

Name _____   Date _____

Use the summary of the news article on crime and punishment to answer the questions below. Discuss the issues with a group of students in your class and then write your reasonable point of view.

1. State the problem as simply and clearly as you can.

2. Describe the values and point of view of Doris Drugdealer.

3. Describe the values and point of view of her husband.

4. Describe the values and point of view of her children.

5. Describe the values and point of view of her neighbors.

6. Describe the legal and societal issues.

7. After discussing the issues and looking at different points of view, what is your reasonable point of view? Why? Include a brief description of your values. Use the back of this sheet of paper to explain your point of view.

From CollegeScope/College and Career Success by Dr. Marsha Fralick

Name _____ Date _____

Brainstorming Rules

• Quantity is more important than quality.
• Do not censure your ideas or the ideas of others.
• See if you can generate ten ideas in five minutes.
• Feel free to be wild and crazy.
• When brainstorming in a group, you may build on other people's ideas and combine them in new ways.
• Select your best ideas when you are finished.

A. How is this peanut like you (the college student)?

1.

2.

3.

4.

5.

6.

7.

8.

9.

10.

Put an asterisk (*) next to your best ideas. If all of your ideas are best, give yourself the freedom to put down some of your not-so-good ideas on the next try. Share them with the class.

B.   How is this peanut like going to college?

1.

2.

3.

4.

5.

6.

7.

8.

9.

10.

Put an asterisk (*) next to your best ideas. Share your best ideas with the class.

LEARNING OBJECTIVES

Read to answer these key questions:

- How long can I expect to live in the new millennium?

- What are the best ideas on nutrition for maintaining optimum health?

- What are the dangers of smoking, alcohol abuse and other drugs?

- How can I protect others and myself from HIV/AIDS and other sexually transmitted diseases?

- Why is it important to get enough sleep?

- What is stress and how can I deal with it?

- What are some relaxation techniques?

- How can I make positive changes in my life?

© JupiterImages Corporation.

Maintaining a Healthy Lifestyle

Getting a college education is an investment in the quality of your life in the future. Enjoying this increased quality of life depends on maintaining your good health. What you do every day affects your future health. The ordinary choices you make such as what you eat and how much you exercise, avoiding harmful substances, protecting the body, relaxing, getting enough sleep, and thinking positively will have a big effect on how long you will enjoy good health and reap the benefits of your education.

Life Expectancy

How long can you expect to live in the new millennium? Since life expectancy is increasing, it is possible that you might live to be 100 years or older. Life expectancy depends on heredity, environment and lifestyle. Heredity cannot be changed, but environment and lifestyle depend on personal choice. The choices made at a young age can have a major impact on health in later life.

U.S. Life Expectancy		
Year	Male	Female
1900	48.2	51.1
1940	60.8	65.2
1950	65.6	71.1
1960	66.6	73.3
1970	67.1	74.7
1980	70.0	77.4
1990	71.8	78.8
2000	74.1	79.5
2004	75.2	80.4

Source: National Center for Health Statistics[1]

Scientists have been studying centenarians around the world to identify the secrets of longevity.[2] It has been found that 90 percent of centenarians remain functionally independent until age 92. From studies of identical twins that were separated at birth and reared apart, it has been determined that 20 to 30 percent of longevity is genetically determined. The most important factor in longevity is lifestyle. One group that has been studied is the Seventh Day Adventists in Utah. They avoid alcohol, caffeine, and tobacco and live an average of eight years longer than the average American.

Another group that has been studied is centenarians who live in Okinawa, Japan. These centenarians get plenty of physical and mental exercise. Their diet is rich in fruits and vegetables containing fiber and antioxidants that protect against cancer, heart disease, and stroke. Their diets are low in fat and salt, and they eat more soy than any other population on earth. Soy contains flavonoids that protect against cancer. They practice a dietary philosophy called hara hachi bu, which means eating until 80 percent full. Seiryu Toguchi of Okinawa was a centenarian who lived to be 105 years old. Here is a description of a typical day for him:[3]

　. . . He wakes at 6 A.M., in the house in which he was born, and opens the shutters. "It's a sign to my neighbors," he says, "that I am still alive." He does stretching exercises along with a radio broadcast, then eats breakfast: whole-grain rice and miso soup with vegetables. He puts in two hours of picking weeds in his 1,000 sq. ft.

field. . . . A fellow has to make a living, so Toguchi buys rice and meat with the profits from his produce. At 12:30 Toguchi eats lunch: goya stir fry with egg and tofu. He naps for an hour or so, then spends two more hours in his field. After dinner he plays traditional songs—a favorite is Spring When I Was 19—on the three-stringed sanchin and makes an entry in his diary as he has done every night for the past decade. "This way," he says, "I won't forget my Chinese characters. It's fun. It keeps my mind sharp."

The best advice for living a long and healthy life is to eat sensibly, exercise, and find activities that keep you mentally alert.

Balance Nutrition and Exercise for Good Health

Balancing good nutrition with exercise contributes to a long and healthy life. A good diet helps you to enjoy life and feel your best. It helps children to grow and develop and to do well in school. Being informed about the basic principles of nutrition can help you to make healthful choices. The federal government has proposed dietary guidelines that take into account age, gender, and level of exercise.[4]

Aim for a healthy weight. Maintaining a healthy weight is one of the keys to a long and healthy life. Being overweight increases the risk of high blood pressure, high blood cholesterol, heart disease, stroke, diabetes, cancer, arthritis, and breathing problems. Researchers believe that 55 percent of Americans are overweight and about 25 percent are obese.[5] The problem of overweight children and adults is a major health concern today. The best way to lose weight is by establishing patterns of healthy eating and exercise.

Americans are struggling with how to maintain a healthy weight. Some are turning to crash diets that severely restrict calories and food choices. Crash diets are not recommended because the weight loss is temporary and the body can be deprived of important nutrients. Another serious problem is eating disorders such as anorexia that can lead to serious health problems, and even death in severe cases. Symptoms of an eating disorder include a preoccupation with food or body weight, dramatic weight loss, excessive exercise, self-induced vomiting, and abuse of laxatives. Anyone with these symptoms should consult a health care provider.

We don't stop playing because we grow old, we grow old because we stop playing.

George Bernard Shaw

ACTIVITY

The Body Mass Index (BMI) is a commonly used method of evaluating a person's weight.
It is based on the ratio of weight to height. To calculate your BMI, first answer these two questions:

1.   What is your height in inches? _____

2.   What is your weight in pounds? _____

Calculate your BMI using the following formula:

$$BMI = (705 \times body\ weight) \div (height \times height)$$

Example: A person who is 66 inches tall and weighs 155 pounds:

$$BMI = (705 \times 155) \div (66 \times 66) = 25$$

Calculate your BMI here. To evaluate your weight, locate your BMI in the chart below.

Body Mass Index Categories[6]

BMI	Weight
Less than 18.5	Underweight
18.5–24.9	Normal weight
25–29.9	Overweight
30 and above	Obese

There are some exceptions to consider when using BMI to evaluate weight:

•   Body builders and other athletes may have a higher BMI because muscle weighs more than fat.
•   For the elderly, a BMI between 25 and 27 may be healthier and protect against osteoporosis.
•   The BMI is not designed to be used with children.

Another way to evaluate your weight is to simply measure around your waist. A measurement of over 35
inches for women or 40 inches for men places a person at greater risk of health problems. If your BMI is over
25 or your waist measurement increases, reduce calories and increase activity.

JOURNAL ENTRY #1
Based on your BMI, do you need to lose or gain weight?

Here are some suggestions for managing your weight:

- Be physically active.
- Choose healthy foods.
- Choose foods low in fat and sugars.
- Eat sensible portions.
- Lose weight slowly.

Be physically active each day. There are many benefits to regular physical activity:

- Increases your fitness, endurance, and strength
- Maintains healthy bones, muscles, and joints
- Helps in managing weight
- Lowers risk of cardiovascular disease, colon cancer, and Type 2 diabetes
- Promotes psychological well-being
- Reduces depression and anxiety

Two kinds of physical activity are recommended. Aerobic activity speeds up your heart rate and breathing and increases cardiovascular fitness. Strength and flexibility exercises such as lifting weights and stretching help to maintain strong bones. Choose activities that you enjoy and include them in your daily routine. It is important to remain active throughout your life.

New federal guidelines suggest the need for 30 to 60 minutes of moderately intense physical activity each day. These activities could include an hour of walking, slow swimming, leisurely bicycle riding, or golfing without a cart. More intense exercise such a jogging can provide needed exercise in a shorter time.[7]

Use the government suggested dietary guidelines to guide your food choices. In 2005, The U.S. Department of Agriculture (USDA) revised dietary guidelines to balance what we eat with level of activity. The USDA created a suggested individualized nutrition plan based on age, gender and level of physical activity. This plan is called MyPyramid Plan and is available online at:

http://www.mypyramid.gov/

This plan helps to guide food choices for optimum good health. The dietary guidelines are represented by a pyramid with a figure climbing stairs to remind us to balance what we eat with physical activity. In the pyramid, the food bands run from

Cathy by Cathy Guisewite. Dist. by Universal Press Syndicate. Reprinted by permission. All rights reserved.

top of the pyramid to the base. The different sizes of the bands show the proportion of foods we should eat from each food group. The bands are wider at the base to remind us to eat most of our foods without solid fat and added sugars. The MyPyramid Plan divides foods into these categories from left to right: grains, vegetables, fruits, oils, milk, and meat/beans.

Source: U.S. Department of Agriculture, http://www.mypyramid.gov/, 2005

The grains category includes whole grain bread, cereal, rice or pasta. It includes any foods made from wheat, rice, oats, cornmeal, barley, or other cereal grains. For example, foods in the grain category include bread, pasta, oatmeal, breakfast cereals, tortillas and grits. It is important the word "whole" is on the list of product ingredients. Grains provide fiber, essential nutrients and aids in weight management. It is recommended that we consume at least three or more ounces of grains daily depending on age, gender and level of physical activity. What counts as an ounce of grains?

- One slice of bread
- One 6 inch tortilla
- One-half of a "mini" bagel
- One cup of cereal
- One-half cup of cooked cereal
- One-half cup of cooked rice
- One pancake
- Three cups popcorn
- One-half cup cooked spaghetti

The vegetables category includes a variety of vegetables including dark green or orange vegetables, dry beans and peas, starchy vegetables such as corn and potatoes and other vegetables. The amount of vegetable required ranges from one to two and a half cups depending on age, gender and level of physical activity. What counts as a cup of vegetables?

- One cup of any raw or cooked vegetable
- One cup of vegetable juice
- Two cups of leafy green vegetables
- One large ear of corn
- One medium potato

The fruits category includes a variety of fresh, frozen, canned or dried fruits or fruit juices. It is suggested to go easy on fruit juices because of their higher caloric content. Fruits and vegetables provide necessary fiber and protect the body from diseases such as cancer. The daily recommended amount of fruits is one to two cups depending on age, gender and activity level. What counts as a cup of fruit?

- One small apple
- One large banana
- One large orange
- Eight strawberries
- One cup of grapes
- One cup of 100 percent fruit juice

The oils category is the smallest section of the pyramid since they contain about 120 calories per tablespoon. The amount of oil consumed needs to be limited to fit in the total daily caloric allowance. Oils are defined as fats that are liquid at room temperature including olive oil, corn oil, canola oil, or sunflower oil. It is suggested that most fat should come from fish, nuts and vegetable oils and to limit solid fats such as butter, margarine, or lard. Some foods are naturally high in oils including nuts, avocados, olives and some fish. Oils contain essential fatty acids and are the major source of vitamin E in the diet. The recommended amount of oils ranges from three to seven teaspoons depending on age, gender and activity level. Most Americans get all the oils they need from:

- Nuts
- Fish
- Cooking oil
- Salad dressings

The milk category includes foods made from milk, such as cheeses and yogurt. If the food maintains its calcium content when processed, it remains part of the food group. Foods such as cream cheese, cream and butter are not included in the group. Milk food choices should be non-fat or low fat. The daily recommended amount of milk products is two to three cups depending on age, gender and level of activity. The milk group provides calcium for bone health over a lifetime. What counts as one cup of milk?

- One and a half ounces of hard cheese (cheddar, mozzarella, Swiss)
- One-third of a cup shredded cheese
- Two ounces processed American cheese
- Two cups cottage cheese
- One 8 ounce container of yogurt

The meat and beans category includes low-fat or lean meat and poultry. Other examples include eggs, dry beans and peas, nuts and seeds and fish. This group of foods provides proteins that serve as the basic building blocks of the human body. The daily recommendation is two to six ounces depending on age, gender and activity level. What is equivalent to an ounce of meat?

- One-quarter cup of dry beans
- One egg
- One tablespoon peanut butter
- One-half ounce of nuts

Under the USDA guidelines, each person has a budget for some discretionary calories. These calories should not be used to replace the essential nutrients, but can provide extra energy for the body. Discretionary calories include added sugars and fats and range from 100–300 calories for most people, depending on activity level. Discretionary calories can be used for eating more of the essential foods or eating some foods with higher fat or sugar content. This category includes items such as butter, gravy, sauces, candy, soda, desserts, beer or wine. Most people exceed their number of discretionary calories, so limit this category especially if you need to lose weight.

Here are some examples of recommended food consumption based on age, gender, and activity levels. In these examples, 30 to 60 minutes of physical activity are assumed:

	Female Age 6	Female Age 18	Male Age 18	Male Age 50
Grains	5 oz.	6 oz	10 oz.	8 oz.
Vegetables	1.5 cups	2.5 cups	3.5 cups	3 cups
Fruits	1.5 cups	2 cups	2.5 cups	2 cups
Oils	4 teas.	6 teas.	8 teas.	7 teas.
Milk	2 cups	3 cups	3 cups	3 cups
Meat/Beans	4 oz.	5.5 oz.	7 oz.	6.5 oz.
Extra Calories from Fat and Sugar	170	265	425	360
Total Calories	1400	2000	2800	2400

Here are some suggestions for making healthy food choices:

• In establishing a pattern of healthy eating, it is recommended that plant foods form the foundation of a good diet. Two-thirds of the dinner plate should be covered with fruits, vegetables, whole grains, and beans. Use meats and dairy products in moderation and use fats and sweets sparingly. This type of diet is helpful in controlling weight as well as reducing your risk of cancer.[9]

• Eat a variety of grains daily, especially whole grains. Whole grains include brown rice, cracked wheat, graham flour, whole-grain corn, oatmeal, popcorn, barley, whole rye, and whole wheat. Whole grains provide vitamins, minerals, and fiber that helps you to feel full with fewer calories.

• Eat a variety of fruits and vegetables daily. Eating many kinds and colors of fruits and vegetables provides important vitamins and minerals. Enjoy five servings of fruits and vegetables each day with at least two servings of fruit and three servings of vegetables.

• Limit the use of solid fats such as butter, lard, margarines, and partially hydrogenated shortenings. Solid fats raise blood cholesterol and increase your chances of coronary heart disease. Use vegetable oils instead. Aim for a fat intake of no more that 30 percent of your calories.

• Moderate your intake of sugar. Foods containing added sugars have added calories and little nutritional value. The number one source of added sugar is soft drinks. Drink water instead of or in addition to soft drinks. Sweets, candies, pies, cakes, cookies, and fruit drinks are also major sources of added sugars. Eating too many foods with added sugar contributes to weight gain or eating less of the nutritious foods. Added sugar also contributes to tooth decay.

- Choose and prepare foods with less salt. Eating too much salt can increase your chances of having high blood pressure. High salt intake causes the body to secrete calcium, which is necessary for healthy bones. Only small amounts of salt occur naturally in foods. Most salt is added during food processing. Eat fresh fruits and vegetables to avoid eating too much salt.

QUIZ
Nutrition

Test what you have learned by selecting the correct answer to the following questions.

1. If you are not an athlete and your BMI is over 25, it is probably a good idea to:

   a. Severely limit caloric intake.
   b. Go on a diet that limits food choices.
   c. Reduce calories and increase activities.

2. The MyPyramid Plan suggests that we need to balance:

   a. Our eating habits and our lifestyle.
   b. Our desserts and vegetables.
   c. What we eat with our physical activity.

3. In the MyPyramid Plan, an ounce of grain is equivalent to:

   a. Two cups of cooked spaghetti
   b. One cup of cooked rice
   c. One half cup of cooked cereal

4. In the MyPyramid Plan, the recommended amount of oils consumed in a day is:

   a. 3–7 tablespoons
   b. 3–7 teaspoons
   c. One-half cup

5. In the MyPyramid Plan, the daily recommended amount of foods in the meat and beans category is:

   a. 2–6 ounces
   b. 8–12 ounces
   c. 15–20 ounces

6. For most people, daily discretionary calories range from:

   a. 100–300 calories
   b. 100–600 calories
   c. 500–1000 calories

7. It is suggested that two-thirds of the dinner plate be covered with:

   a. Potatoes
   b. Plant foods such as fruits, vegetables, whole grains and beans
   c. Meats, fish or poultry

How did you do on the quiz? Check your answers: 1. c, 2. c, 3. c, 4. b, 5. a, 6. a, 7. b

JOURNAL ENTRY #2

Make some intention statements about improving your nutrition.
I intend to . . .

Avoiding Addictions to Smoking, Alcohol, and Other Drugs

Smoking, abusing alcohol, or using illegal drugs can interfere with your success in college, on the job and in life. These addictions can cause illness and a shortened life expectancy. Knowledge in these areas will help you make the best choices to maintain your quality of life.

Smoking Tobacco: A Leading Cause of Preventable Illness and Death

Smoking is widespread in our society. One in every four adults in the United States smokes and one in every three teenagers smokes. Tobacco use is the leading cause of preventable illness and death in the United States.[10] One out of every five deaths in the United States is related to smoking. Each year over 430,000 Americans die too young as a result of smoking related illnesses.[11] Imagine that three jumbo jets carrying 400 people each crashes every day of the year. This is similar to the number of people who die each year from smoking-related illnesses.

Smoking is related to a variety of illnesses:

- Smoking damages and irritates the respiratory system. Smoking a package of cigarettes a day is like smearing a cup of tar over the respiratory tract. Smoking causes lung cancer, emphysema, and chronic bronchitis.
- Smoking affects the heart and circulatory system. Smoking causes premature coronary heart disease and several types of blood-vessel diseases.
- Smoking increases the probability of having strokes, which damage the brain and often leaves a person with permanent disabilities.
- Smoking affects the eyes and vision. It is speculated that smoking causes vision loss by restricting blood flow to the eyes. Recent studies have connected smoking with macular degeneration, an irreversible form of blindness. Cataracts, or clouding of the lenses of the eyes, is also associated with smoking.
- Smoking irritates the eyes, nose, throat, and gums and can lead to cancer of the mouth, throat, or esophagus.
- Smoking is associated with osteoporosis, the thinning of bones due to mineral loss.
- During pregnancy, smoking damages the developing fetus causing miscarriages, low birth weight, developmental problems, and impaired lung function at birth.
- Smoking causes premature facial wrinkling due to vasoconstriction of the capillaries of the face.[12]

Why is smoking such a major health problem? It is because smoking is an addiction that is difficult to overcome. Only 20 percent of smokers who decide to quit smoking are successful on a long-term basis.[13] For those who are successful in quitting, tobacco-related health risks are improved over time. Although smoking cessation is difficult, it is worth the investment in improved healthy living. Refraining from smoking, along with a healthy diet and exercise, can increase your life span by as much as ten years.[14] For help with smoking cessation, visit your physician or college health office. The resources on the College Success website provide helpful hints for giving up smoking.

Alcohol

Each year many college students die as a result of excessive drinking. Some students drink and drive and die in car accidents. Others die from alcohol poisoning or alcohol-related accidents. Excessive drinking is a factor in poor college performance and high dropout rates. Studies have shown that heavy drinking causes brain damage and interferes with memory.[15] Having some knowledge about alcohol use can help you to make choices to ensure your future quality of life.

ACTIVITY
Alcohol Abuse Quiz

Read each statement and decide if it is true or false. Place a checkmark in the appropriate column.

True	False	
		Alcohol abuse is the third leading health problem in the United States behind heart disease and cancer.
		Thirteen percent of people in the United States have a problem with alcohol dependency.
		Alcohol is the most abused drug worldwide.
		Alcohol use or dependency reduces one's lifespan by ten years.
		Alcohol is involved in 50 percent of all traffic fatalities and homicides.
		Alcohol is involved in two thirds of college student suicides.
		Alcohol is a major factor in HIV infection.
		Alcohol is involved in 90 percent of college rapes.
		Women are at higher risk than men of serious medical conditions related to alcohol use.
		The age span 18 to 21 is the period of heaviest alcohol consumption for most drinkers in the United States.
		Each year college students spend about $5.5 billion on alcohol, mostly beer.
		College students drink enough beer each year to fill an Olympic size swimming pool on every campus in the United States.
		Students spend more money on beer than they do on books, soda, coffee, juice, and milk combined.
		Excessive alcohol use leads to memory loss and neurological problems.
		More students drink than use cocaine, marijuana, or cigarettes combined.

How did you do on the quiz? All of the above statements are true. The fact that all of the above statements are true points to the serious nature of alcohol abuse on college campuses and in society in general.[16]

Binge Drinking

Heavy drinking causes students to miss class and fall behind in schoolwork. College students who are considered binge drinkers are at risk of many alcohol-related problems. Binge drinking is simply drinking too much alcohol at one time. In men, binge drinking is defined by researchers as drinking five or more drinks in a row. In women it is drinking four or more drinks in a row.[17] It takes about one hour to metabolize one drink, so it would take five hours to metabolize five drinks. Researchers estimate that two out of five college students (44 percent) are binge drinkers.[18] Students who are binge drinkers are 21 times more likely to:

- Be hurt or injured
- Drive a car after drinking
- Get in trouble with campus or local police
- Engage in unprotected sex
- Engage in unplanned sexual activity
- Damage property
- Fall behind in schoolwork
- Miss class[19]

It is particularly significant that there is a connection between binge drinking and driving. Among frequent binge drinkers, 62 percent of men and 49 percent of women said that they had driven a car after drinking. About half of the students in this study reported being a passenger in a car in which the driver was high or drunk.[20] A drink is defined as:

- A 12-ounce beer
- A four-ounce glass of wine
- A shot of liquor (1.5 ounces of 80-proof distilled spirits) straight or in a mixed drink

National studies on alcohol consumption in colleges find that students are less likely to participate in binge drinking when they put a high priority on studying, have special interests or hobbies, and participate in volunteer activities. The majority of college students (56 percent nationally) either abstains from drinking or drinks in moderation. Students least likely to be binge drinkers are African American, Asian, 24 years or older, or married. Students at highest risk for binge drinking include intercollegiate athletes and members of fraternities and sororities. Students most likely to be binge drinkers are white, male, and under 24 years of age.[21]

Blood Alcohol Content (BAC)

The amount of alcohol in your blood is referred to as blood alcohol content (BAC). It is recorded in milligrams of alcohol per 100 milliliters of blood. For example, a BAC of .10 means that 1/10 of 1 percent or 1/1,000 of your total blood is alcohol. BAC depends on the amount of blood in your body, which varies with your weight, and the amount of alcohol consumed over time. The liver can only process one drink per hour. The rest builds up in the bloodstream. Below are listed the effects of increasing BAC:

.02   Mellow feeling, slight body warmth, less inhibited
.05   Noticeable relaxation, less alert, less self-focused, coordination impairment begins, most people reach this level with one or two drinks
.08   Drunk driving limit, definite impairment in coordination and judgment

.10   Noisy, possible embarrassing behavior, mood swings, reduction in reaction times
.15   Impaired balance and movement, clearly drunk
.30   Many lose consciousness
.40   Most lose consciousness, some die
.50   Breathing stops, many die[22]

The above figures point out some important facts for college students. It does not take many drinks to reach the drunk driving limit. Most people reach the drunk driving limit if they have one to three drinks depending on weight and time since the last drink. BAC increases if you are lighter weight or if you have just had a drink. As the BAC increases, more serious effects occur. Tragically, each year college students die from alcohol poisoning, which occurs when large quantities of alcohol are consumed in a short period of time. This sometimes occurs during the hazing periods in college fraternities and sororities. Colleges are taking steps to stop hazing on college campuses nationwide.

Increased Risks for Women

Because women absorb and metabolize alcohol differently than men do, they are at greater risk of alcohol-related problems. Women have less body water than men and achieve a higher concentration of alcohol in the blood after drinking the same amount as men. Women are more likely to develop liver damage, brain damage, and heart damage. Some research has suggested that women who are moderate to heavy drinkers are at higher risk for breast cancer.[23]

Besides considering health effects, women need to be concerned about personal safety when alcohol is being used. When alcohol is being consumed, women are at higher risk of becoming the victims of violent crime. Among frequent binge drinkers, women report higher rates of rape and nonconsensual sex.[24]

What Is Moderate Drinking?

If adults choose to drink alcohol, it is recommended that they drink in moderation.[25] Moderation is defined as no more than one drink per day for women or two drinks per day for men. Drinking more than this can increase the risks for car accidents, high blood pressure, stroke, violence, suicide, and certain types of cancer. Women who drink during pregnancy increase the risk of birth defects. Too much alcohol causes social and psychological problems, cirrhosis of the liver, inflammation of the pancreas, and damage to the brain and heart. Heavy drinkers are also at risk for malnutrition since alcohol contains calories that may be substituted for more nutritional foods.

It has been found that drinking in moderation may lower the risk of coronary heart disease in men over the age of 45 and women over the age of 55. However, there are other factors contributing to a healthy heart including a healthy diet, exercise, avoidance of smoking, and maintaining a healthy weight.

There are certain people who should not drink:

- Children and adolescents
- Individuals of any age who cannot restrict their drinking to moderate levels
- Women who are pregnant or who are likely to become pregnant
- Individuals who drive or operate machinery that requires skill, attention, or coordination
- Individuals taking over-the-counter or prescription drugs that interact with alcohol

Warning Signs of Alcoholism

Alcoholics Anonymous has published twelve questions to determine if alcohol is a problem in your life. Answer these questions honestly:

1. Have you ever decided to stop drinking for a week or so but could only stop for a couple of days?
2. Do you wish people would mind their own business about your drinking and stop telling you what to do?
3. Have you ever switched from one kind of drink to another in the hope that this would keep you from getting drunk?
4. Have you ever had to have a drink upon awakening during the past year? Do you need a drink to get started or to stop shaking?
5. Do you envy people who can drink without getting into trouble?
6. Have you had problems connected with drinking during the past year?
7. Has your drinking caused problems at home?
8. Do you ever try to get extra drinks at a party because you do not get enough?
9. Do you tell yourself you can stop drinking any time you want to, even though you keep getting drunk when you don't mean to?
10. Have you missed days of work or school because of drinking?
11. Do you ever have blackouts from drinking, when you cannot remember what happened?
12. Have you ever felt that your life would be better if you did not drink?

If you answered yes to four of the above questions, it is likely that you have a problem with alcohol.

Other Drugs

While alcohol is the most commonly used drug, street drugs such as marijuana, cocaine, LSD, methamphetamines, rohypnol (the "date rape drug"), ecstasy, ketamine (a PCP-like anesthetic), and heroin interfere with the accomplishment of life goals. Clark Carr, President of Narconon, describes the following impact of illegal drug usage:

> One of the worst impacts of street drugs is their impact on ambition. Drugs have insidious yet devastating effects upon children and their ability to envision hopes and dreams. Ambition enables a person to learn to enjoy life and to pursue happiness without drugs, but it can be destroyed through drug use. When a person is intoxicated by drugs, important functions are adversely affected, including concentration, recording, and recalling. These tools are essential to learning, and without them education is impaired. Addiction becomes the all-consuming focus of activities aimed at procuring more drugs. Education, careers, relationships, and life itself take a back seat.[26]

People take drugs in order to feel better. However the high from taking drugs is followed by a low which is relieved by taking more drugs, leading to addiction. With increased drug use, the lows get lower and it becomes more difficult to reach a high. Drugs have varying levels of toxicity, but they all stress the body's nervous, digestive, respiratory, circulatory and reproductive systems. The problem is that drugs can become life destroying. Anyone contemplating taking drugs should ask these four questions:

1. Are the benefits going to outweigh the liabilities?
2. Will I experience more pleasure than pain, or more pain than pleasure?

3. Will the pleasure be temporary? How will I feel tomorrow?
4. Will the drug do more harm than good?

Answering these questions honestly can help you to make the right choices. Having an addiction to smoking, alcohol, or illegal drugs can be difficult to control. If you need help with problems caused by drug or alcohol addiction, see your physician or contact your college health office. The *College Success Website* contains useful links to help you to cope with addictive behavior and make some positive changes in your life.

QUIZ
Avoiding Addictions

Test what you have learned by selecting the correct answer to the following questions.

1. The leading cause of preventable death in the United States is

   a. car accidents.
   b. smoking-related illnesses.
   c. obesity.

2. The most abused drug worldwide is

   a. marijuana.
   b. cocaine.
   c. alcohol.

3. Binge drinking for men is defined as

   a. five drinks in a row.
   b. seven drinks in a row.
   c. ten drinks in a row.

4. Depending on weight and time of last drink, a person generally reaches the drunk driving limit of .08 with

   a. one to three drinks.
   b. three to five drinks.
   c. five to nine drinks.

5. Moderate drinking for women is defined as

   a. one drink per day.
   b. two drinks per day.
   c. three drinks per day.

How did you do on the quiz? Check your answers: 1. b, 2. c, 3. a, 4. a, 5. a

Protecting Yourself from HIV/AIDS and Other Sexually Transmitted Diseases

HIV/AIDS has been described as the worst plague in modern history. AIDS is the fourth leading cause of death in the world. It is estimated that by 2020, the number of people dying from AIDS will be approximately equal to all people killed in wars in the twentieth century.[27] New drugs have been developed that inhibit the growth of the virus that leads to AIDS, but there is still no cure for AIDS. These new medications are extending the healthy life of infected patients.[28] Since AIDS continues to be a leading cause of death among Americans ages 25 to 44, knowing how to protect yourself from

HIV/AIDS and other sexually transmitted diseases is an important survival skill.[29] The U.S. Centers for Disease Control and Prevention provides some helpful information to minimize your risk of infection.[30]

What is HIV? HIV is the human immunodeficiency virus that causes AIDS. The virus kills the "CD4" cells that help your body fight off infection.

What is AIDS? AIDS is the acquired immunodeficiency syndrome. It is the disease you get when HIV destroys the body's immune system. Normally your immune system helps to fight off illness. When the immune system is destroyed, you can become very sick and die.

How is HIV acquired? HIV is acquired in the following ways:

- It is acquired by having unprotected sex (sex without a condom) with someone who has HIV. The virus can be in an infected person's blood, semen, or vaginal secretions. It can enter the body through tiny cuts or sores on the skin, or the lining of the vagina, penis, rectum, or mouth.
- It is acquired by sharing a needle and syringe to inject drugs or by sharing equipment used to prepare drugs for injection with someone who has HIV.
- HIV can be acquired from a blood transfusion received before 1985. Since 1985, blood is tested for HIV.
- Babies born to women who are HIV positive can become infected during pregnancy, birth, or breast-feeding.

You cannot get HIV from the following:

- Working with or being around someone who has HIV
- Sweat, tears, spit, clothes, drinking fountains, phones or toilet seats
- Insect bites or stings
- Donating blood
- A closed-mouth kiss

What are the best ways to protect yourself? Here are some guidelines:

- Don't share needles or syringes for injecting drugs, steroids, vitamins or for tattooing or body piercing. Germs from an infected person can stay in the needle and then be injected into the next person using the needle.
- Don't have sex. This is truly "safe sex."
- If you choose to have sex, have sex with only one partner that you know doesn't have HIV and is only having sex with you.
- Use a latex condom every time you have sex. This is referred to as "safer sex."
- Don't share razors or toothbrushes because of the possibility of contact with blood.
- If you are pregnant, get tested for HIV. Drug treatments are available to reduce the chances of your baby being infected with HIV.

How do I know if I have HIV or AIDS? A person can have HIV or AIDS and feel perfectly healthy. The only way to know is to get tested. Most college health offices and your local health department offer confidential testing.

What other diseases are spread through sexual activity? There are more than 25 different diseases spread through sexual activity. There are 19 million new cases of sexually transmitted diseases (STDs) each year, half of them in young people ages 15–24.[31] According to the Centers for Disease Control and Prevention, these diseases can "result in severe health consequences, cancer, impaired fertility, premature birth, infant death and disability."[32] The increase in STD's has paralleled the AIDS epidemic. The guidelines for protecting against HIV apply to other STDs as well.

The most common STDs in the United States include chlamydia, gonorrhea, syphilis, genital herpes, human papillomavirus, hepatitis B, trichomoniasis, and bacterial vaginosis. Bacterial diseases such as gonorrhea, syphilis, and chlamydia can be cured with antibiotics. Viral diseases such as herpes, hepatitis, and genital warts can be treated but not cured. A vaccine has been developed to prevent hepatitis B, and it is recommended that teenagers and college students obtain this vaccination to avoid the serious liver damage that can result from this disease.

Women suffer the most from STDs because they have more frequent and serious complications from them than men do. Many STDs can be passed to the fetus, newborn, or infant before, during, or after birth. Chlamydia and gonorrhea can lead to pelvic inflammatory disease (PID), which can cause chronic pelvic pain, infertility, or potentially fatal ectopic pregnancies. The human papilloma virus (HPV) can increase the risk of cervical cancer in women. A new vaccine for HPV has just become available and is recommended for girls and women ages 11 to 26. It is most effective for girls and women who have not been exposed to HPV and is effective in preventing 70 percent of the cancers caused by HPV.

JOURNAL ENTRY #3

What steps can college students take to protect themselves from HIV/AIDS and other sexually transmitted diseases?

Getting Enough Sleep

College students often miss out on sleep while cramming for exams, enjoying an active social life, and trying to balance work and school. However, getting enough sleep is important for learning. Without enough sleep, long-term memory is impaired and concentration is difficult.[33] If you are sleep-deprived, it is more difficult to read and study and store information in long-term memory.

Getting enough sleep is important for optimal brain function. Nobel Laureate Thomas Crick, who studies the brain at the Salk Institute in California, has proposed that the purpose of sleep is to allow the brain to "take out the trash."[34] Sleep gives the brain time to process the day's events, store what is needed, and delete irrelevant material. Sleep is necessary to properly store the experiences of each day in the brain. It is believed that sleeping helps the brain to replenish its energy supplies.[35]

Not getting enough sleep results in a decline in mental performance. Colonel Gregory Belenky of the Walter Reed Army Institute of Research studied the effects of sleeplessness on military personnel.[36] He found that mental performance declined by 25 percent in every 24-hour sleepless period. Another researcher found that being awake for 24 hours causes the same mental impairment as being drunk.[37] After 24 hours of continuous simulated combat, artillery teams lost track of where they were and what they were firing at. During the Persian Gulf War, sleep-deprived soldiers lost a sense of where they were and began firing on their own tanks, destroying two of them. Lack of sleep impairs higher cognitive functions such as critical thinking. It becomes more difficult to make decisions, pay attention to detail, and react to new information. College students who stay up all night studying for exams suffer from the same declines in mental performance.

Depriving yourself of sleep also has negative impacts on your health.[38] Lack of sleep can make you less energetic, increase your irritability, cause depression, and make you accident-prone. It is estimated that sleepy drivers cause about 100,000 car accidents each year. Lack of sleep can harm brain cells, weaken the immune system, and decrease muscle-building growth hormones. Blood levels of the stress hormone cortisol are increased. Sleep deprivation can cause increased stress, memory impairment, risk of illness, and the growth of fat instead of muscle. Researchers are now finding evidence that lack of sleep hastens the aging process.[39]

So, how much sleep do you need? Everyone has different needs for sleep. One way to determine your personal need for sleep is to think about how much sleep you get at the end of a long vacation when you do not have to get up at a certain time. At first you may sleep longer to make up for any sleep deficits. Toward the end of the vacation, you will probably be getting the amount of sleep your body needs for optimum performance. Gregory Belenky recommends, "If you simply want to put one foot in front of the other, five hours will do. But if you want to be doing things where you're required to think, plan, or anticipate, then you probably need eight or eight and a half hours of sleep."[40] It is interesting to note the current research shows that it is not healthy to sleep more than eight hours because too much sleep can alter sleep patterns and lead to sluggishness, fatigue and other health problems.[41]

> ### JOURNAL ENTRY #4
> Are you getting enough sleep for optimum performance in school and to maintain good health? If not, what is your plan to get more sleep?

Stress and Relaxation

One of the major challenges in life is dealing with stress and being able to relax. For college students, it is important to realize that too much stress interferes with memory, concentration, and learning. After graduation, it is important to be able to deal with stress on the job.

What Is Stress?

Imagine that you are a cave man or woman. You come out of your cave and notice that the sun is up and the birds are chirping. You are feeling good and your heart rate is normal. All of a sudden you hear a twig snap. You look to your right and notice a large saber-toothed tiger. You have two choices. You can either fight the tiger or take flight. This is called the "fight or flight" reaction to stress.

The body produces some powerful hormones to help give you the strength to fight or to run away. These hormones increase your heart rate and metabolism to give you quick energy. During the fighting or fleeing, the stress hormones are used up and the body returns to normal. The problem today is that the stresses we face are not saber-toothed tigers and we do little physical fighting or running away. The stress hormones still accumulate and we no longer use them up.

Is all stress bad? Imagine a world where there is absolutely no stress. While the thought is intriguing, it would probably be very boring. Some stress is positive and essential for well-being. For example, when we run a race, play a game of football, or act in a play, we experience stress, but it provides excitement and motivation. When a teacher announces a test, a little stress can cause the student to study for the test. Hans Selye, a famous researcher on stress, called this positive type of stress "eustress." He even went so far as to suggest, "Without stress, there could be no life."[42]

Hans Selye described negative stress as "distress." Distress has several physical symptoms that are uncomfortable and detract from good health. These symptoms can range from headaches, stomachaches, and sleeplessness to serious health problems such as high blood pressure, heart disease, and stroke. It is helpful to know some relaxation techniques to deal with the distress.

Get Aerobic Exercise

Aerobic exercise is simply exercise that raises your heart rate and exercises your heart. It includes activities such as walking, running, swimming, dancing, and playing sports. It is recommended that people do some type of aerobic exercise three to five times a week. In addition to strengthening the heart, aerobic exercise burns up stress hormones and allows us to relax.

One of the best relaxation techniques is to find some physical activities that you enjoy and participate in them often. It often requires some planning to fit these activities in our busy schedules. It is important to see these activities as a priority and to take time to enjoy them.

Practice Stress-Reducing Thoughts

Much of the stress we experience is a result of the thoughts we have in our heads, specifically, negative self-talk. We experience a situation, we say negative things to ourselves about it, and the result is an emotional reaction that causes stress. This sequence of events is referred to as the ABCs of emotions:

Situation (A) ⟶ Self-statement (B) ⟶ Emotion (C)

For example, Nicole is caught in rush hour traffic. She wonders why traffic is not moving. She watches the light, hoping that she can make it through the intersection before the light changes to red. She gets angry when the car in front of her stops just as the light changes to yellow. She has to wait for another light. She glances at her watch and watches the time go by as she sits in traffic. She thinks about all the things she needs to do at home. She realizes that she needs to stop at the grocery store to get something for dinner. She thinks about getting fast food on the way home but remembers that she has spent too much money this month. Besides, she realizes that the fast food is not good for her diet. Finally she arrives home at 6:04 p.m. She has a headache and feels stressed out.

Here is an analysis of this situation using the ABCs of emotion:

Situation (A)   ⟶ Self-statement (B)   ⟶ Emotion (C)

Traffic jam (A) ⟶ Negative self-statement (B) ⟶ Angry, stressed (C)

Negative self-statements run through Nicole's head as she deals with the traffic jam:

- Why does this always happen to me?
- Why are the cars ahead so slow?
- Stupid drivers! Can't they move any faster?
- I'm always broke.
- I'll never lose weight.

As a result of these statements, Nicole feels angry and stressed out and even has a headache. Let's look at a different way of handling this situation. Diane is also caught in rush hour traffic. She thinks to herself, "Rush hour traffic. Oh, well. Can't do anything about that." She decides to relax. She turns on her favorite radio station and enjoys the music. She notices the trees and plants along the side of the road and notices that spring is coming. She notices a new restaurant along the way and decides to try it out next Saturday night. She starts to think about spring break and how she will spend her vacation time. She anticipates the warm greetings of her family when she arrives home. She arrives home at 6:04 p.m. with a smile on her face. Let's analyze this situation:

Situation (A) $\longrightarrow$ Self-statement (B) $\longrightarrow$ Emotion (C)

Traffic jam (A) $\longrightarrow$ Positive self-statements (B) $\longrightarrow$ Happy (C)

When you are trying to deal with a stressful situation, listen to your self-statements. What are you saying to yourself? If these statements are negative, you will have negative emotions and will be stressed out. Think of some positive, stress-reducing thoughts that you can use in stressful situations. Here are some examples, but you will be better off to think up some of your own:

- That's the way it goes. No use getting upset.
- It's not the end of the world.
- Keep cool.
- It's no big deal.
- Relax.
- Life's too short to let this bother me.
- It's their problem.
- Life's like that.
- Be happy.
- I'll just do the best I can.
- No need to worry.

Take Action to Resolve Your Problems

If you have problems that are causing stress, take action to resolve them. Here are some steps you can take to solve problems and reduce stress:

- Concentrate your efforts on doing something about the problem.
- Seek information on how to solve the problem. This step may involve doing research or speaking to others.
- Make a plan of action.
- Make it a priority to solve the problem.
- Do what needs to be done to solve the problem, one step at a time.

Psychological Hardiness

Psychologists have studied people who are psychologically hardy.[43] These individuals are able to deal with stress in a positive way and avoid the negative consequences of stress. How do they stay healthy in spite of high-powered jobs and constant challenges? People who are stress resistant have a positive attitude toward life and the challenges it presents. Psychologically hardy individuals have the following qualities:

- They are open to change. They view change as a challenge rather than a threat.

- They have a feeling of involvement in whatever they are doing. They are committed to their occupations and endeavors.
- They have a sense of control over events rather than a feeling of powerlessness. Having a sense of control is essential to good mental health.

Some of the hardiest individuals were those who survived the concentration camps during World War II. In spite of enduring extreme hardships, some found the strength to survive their ordeal and to live well-adapted lives. Scientists studying these survivors discovered that they used several resources for survival. Knowledge and intelligence was one resource. With knowledge and intelligence, these people could see many ways of dealing with the situation and were able to choose the best alternative. These survivors also had a strong sense of identity. They were confident and powerful individuals. Another important resource was a strong social network that gave people the collective strength to survive.

Other Relaxation Techniques

Another way to deal with stress is to practice some physical and mental relaxation techniques. Here are a few suggestions:

- Listen to soothing music. Choose music that has a beat that is slower than your heart rate. Classical or new age music can be very relaxing.
- Take a few deep breaths.
- Focus on your breathing. If you are thinking about breathing, it is difficult to think about your worries.
- Lie down in a comfortable place and tense and relax your muscles. Start with the muscles in your head and work your way down to your toes. Tense each muscle for five to ten seconds and then release the tension completely.
- Imagine yourself in a pleasant place. When you are actually in a beautiful place, take the time to make a mental photograph. Memorize each detail and then close your eyes to see if you can still recall the scene. Return to this place in your mind when you feel stressed. Some people visualize the mountains, the beach, the ocean, a mountain stream, waterfalls, a tropical garden, or a desert scene. Choose a scene that works for you.
- Use positive thinking. Look for the good things in life and take the time to appreciate them.
- Maintain a healthy diet and get enough exercise.
- Practice yoga or Tai Chi.
- Keep things in perspective. Ask yourself, "Will it be important in ten years?" If so, do something about it. If not, just relax.
- Focus on the positives. What have you learned from dealing with this problem? Has the problem provided an opportunity for personal growth?
- Discuss your feelings with a friend who is a good listener or get professional counseling.
- Keep your sense of humor. Laughter actually reduces the stress hormones.
- Maintain a support network of friends and loved ones.
- Practice meditation. It is a way of calming the mind.
- Get a massage or give one to someone else.

JOURNAL ENTRY #5
What stress management techniques work best for you?

Making Positive Changes in Your Life

You are probably aware of the importance of implementing many of the ideas in this chapter. However, actually making some positive changes is difficult. Dr. James Prochaska has studied the process of change and identifies the six stages:[44]

1.   Precontemplation.

In this stage, a person denies that there is a problem and is not ready to change. If the habit causes difficulties, the person may blame the problems on others, especially those who are pressuring for change. There are two ways to move out of this stage. One way is through an increasing awareness or knowledge of the problem. Another way is through emotional arousal. For example, a person may see another dying of lung cancer and decide that it is time to quit smoking.

2.   Contemplation.

In this stage a person begins to be aware of a problem and thinks seriously about taking some action. He or she weighs the pros and cons, the benefits and sacrifices, and thinks about the difficulty of change. People can only move to the next stage when they develop the self-confidence to believe that they can make a change. In the example of smoking cessation, at this stage a person would begin to look at the negative consequences of smoking but would consider change difficult.

3.   Preparation.

During this stage, people develops a strategy for change. They realize that change is necessary and desire to make the change. They discuss the change with friends and find the needed resources to make the change. They set an actual date to take action. In our smoking example, a person would start talking with friends and family members about quitting smoking and would set a time to stop smoking.

4.   Action.

This is the "just do it" stage. Without action, the goal cannot be accomplished. This stage requires some commitment. A person trying to quit smoking might just stop smoking "cold turkey" or cut down on their daily smoking by a specific amount.

5.   Maintenance.

Once you have reached your goal, maintenance is the next step. This stage is the most difficult one as people struggle with the impulse to return to old patterns. Once a person has stopped smoking, the real test is maintaining the behavior.

6.   Termination.

This is permanent change. It is a time when temptations stop. Many people find it difficult to reach this stage.

Six Stages of Change

1.   Precontemplation
2.   Contemplation
3.   Preparation
4.   Action
5.   Maintenance
6.   Termination

What is important to realize about Prochaska's model is that change is a process and that there will be slip-ups along the way. His research shows that successful changers experience some failures along the way. However, he suggests that action that fails is better than no action at all. His research shows that those who tried to act and failed were more likely to succeed in the future. In one study of 200 people who made New Year's resolutions and were still keeping them two years later, the subjects had an average of fourteen lapses before they were successful in keeping their resolutions.

Setbacks in the process of change are natural and it is important not to give up. The process of change is difficult, but rewarding when you can follow through. When you are successful, you enjoy better health and gain confidence in your ability to make positive changes.

Live to Be 100

It is possible that you could live to be 100 years old. Of course, if you live to be 100, you will want to be healthy and capable of enjoying your life. Many people are doing this already.

John Glenn, the world's oldest astronaut at age 77, returned from space in 1998. Dr. John Charles joked "he did pretty good for a 40-year old guy."[45] He suffered no more bone or muscle loss than the younger astronauts on the mission, and his heart rate was slightly better than the younger astronauts. Doctors were so impressed with John Glenn's physical condition that they decided to take better care of their own health. How does John Glenn stay fit? He has taken care of himself over his lifetime. He walks several miles a day, does some light weight training, and eats a balanced diet. He challenges the notion that seniors are frail individuals. Glenn enjoyed the ride and is encouraging NASA to send more senior citizens into orbit.

Sarah "Sadie" Delaney wrote a best-selling novel with her sister Bessie at age 104. It contained their reminiscences of a century of achievement of African American women. They shared memories of slavery, segregation, and racism that they had experienced during their lives. Sadie lived to be 109 years old and Bessie died at age 104. They were from a family of ten children, all of whom went to college. Their mother was a teacher and taught the children self-discipline, compassion, and confidence. When Bessie and Sadie were asked how they had lived so long, Bessie said, "Honey, we never married; we never had husbands to worry us to death." Sadie added, "Don't get married just because he looks pretty. He's got to have good genes and have some sense."[46]

Mae Laborde became an actress at age 93. She has played the role of Vanna White (40 years in the future), appeared on MadTV and faced down the Grim Reaper in a commercial about the elderly without health insurance. She is always smiling, has a positive attitude and is ready to take on the world. She says it is never too late to follow your dreams.

Jerry Bloch at age 81 became the oldest man to climb El Capitan Mountain in Yosemite National Park. He chose the toughest and most challenging route up the mountain because he felt it might be his last mountain-climbing adventure because he was getting older.

Jeanne Calment passed away in 1997 at the age of 122. She was the oldest living person at that time. She was quite active into her old age. She took up fencing at age 85, rode a bicycle at age 100, and produced a rap CD at age 121. During her younger life she engaged in activities such as playing the piano, tennis, roller-skating, bicycling, swimming, hunting, and going to the opera. She was never bored and remained spirited and mentally sharp until the end. She became known for her wit and humor. One of her sayings was, "I've never had but one wrinkle, and I'm sitting on it."

Since you may live to be 100, take some advice from the experts: exercise to stay physically fit, be careful about whom you marry, stay active, have a positive attitude and maintain your sense of humor.

JOURNAL ENTRY #6

Write at least five intention statements about improving your health. I intend to . . .

JOURNAL ENTRIES

Maintaining a Healthy Lifestyle

Go to http://www.collegesuccess1.com/ for Word files of the Journal Entries

Success over the Internet

Visit the *College Success Website* at http://www.collegesuccess1.com/

The *College Success Website* is continually updated with new topics and links to the material presented in this chapter. Topics include:

- Health Topics A–Z
- Wellness
- Men and women's health topics
- Resources for smoking cessation
- Pregnancy
- Sexually transmitted diseases
- HIV/AIDS
- Planned parenthood
- Nutrition
- Fitness

- Addictive behavior (drugs, alcohol, smoking)
- Resources for dealing with addiction to drugs, alcohol, or smoking
- Treatment centers for alcohol and drug problems
- Internet addictions
- Sleep problems
- Stress
- Panic attacks
- Anxiety
- Mental health

Contact your instructor if you have any problems in accessing the *College Success Website*.

Notes

1. U.S. Department of Health and Human Services, Centers for Disease Control and Prevention, National Center for Health Statistics, 2003. Available at http:www.cdc.gov/nchs/fastats/lifexpec.htm
2. Richard Corliss and Michael Lemonick, "How to Live to be 100," *Time,* August 30, 2004.
3. Ibid.
4. U.S. Department of Agriculture http://www.mypyramid.gov, 2005.
5. Associated Press, "Americans' Obesity Spurs Plan by Government to Trim the Fat," *San Diego Union Tribune,* 31 May 2000.
6. U.S. Department of Agriculture, *Body Mass Index and Health*, March 2000.
7. U.S. Department of Agriculture http://www.mypyramid.gov, 2005.

8. U.S. Department of Agriculture http://www.mypyramid.gov, 2005.

9. Associated Press, "Proper Diet Urged to Fight Cancer, Not Supplements," *San Diego Union Tribune,* 5 September 2000.

10. U.S. Department of Health and Human Services, Centers for Disease Control and Prevention, http://www.cdc.gov/tobacco, 2002.

11. Andrew Bridges, "Doctors May Push Smoking Age of 21," *San Diego Union Tribune,* 21 February 2002.

12. Paul H. Brodish, *The Irreversible Health Effects of Cigarette Smoking*, prepared for the American Council on Science and Health, June 1998.

13. Ibid.

14. Gary Fraser and David Shavlik, "Ten Years of Life," *Archives of Internal Medicine,* 161, no. 13 (9 July 2001).

15. "Binge Drinking Affects Brain, Memory," from http://www.alcoholism.about.com.

16. Samuel Autman, "CSU Panel Urges Offensive against Alcohol Abuse," *San Diego Union Tribune,* 8 May, 2001. Lewis Eigan, *Alcohol Practices, Policies and Potentials of American Colleges and Universities*, U.S. Department of Health and Human Services, 1991. National Institute on Alcohol Abuse and Alcoholism, U.S. Department of Health and Human Services, *Are Women More Vulnerable to Alcohol's Effects?* 1999. Pacific Institute for Research and Evaluation, *Cost of Underage Drinking*, U.S. Department of Justice, 1999. Also from http://www.alcoholism.about.com and http://www.stopcollegebinging.com.

17. Henry Wechsler and Toben Nelson, "Binge Drinking and the American College Student: What's Five Drinks?" *Psychology of Addictive Behaviors,* 15, no. 4, (2001): 287–91.

18. Henry Wechsler, *Binge Drinking on America's College Campuses: Findings from the Harvard School of Public Health College Alcohol Study*, 2000.

19. Henry Wechsler, "College Binge Drinking in the 1990s: A Continuing Problem," *Journal of American College Health,* 48 (2000): 199–210.

20. Ibid.

21. Henry Wechsler, *Findings from the Harvard School of Public Health College Alcohol Study*, 2000, http://www.hsph.harvard.edu/cas.

22. From http://www.habitsmart.com/bal.html.

23. National Institute on Alcohol Abuse and Alcoholism, U.S. Department of Health and Human Services, Alcohol Alert, No. 46, *Are Women More Vulnerable to Alcohol's Effects?* 1999.

24. Henry Wechsler, Kuo Lee, and H. Lee, Harvard School of Public Health, 1999.

25. U.S. Department of Agriculture, *Dietary Guidelines for Americans, 2000.*

26. Clark Carr, "There is No Free Ride," *Freedom* (1998).

27. Lawrence Altman, "Peak of AIDS Epidemic Still to Come, U.N. Says," *San Diego Union Tribune,* 3 July 2002.

28. E. J. Mundell, "Hope for AIDS Cure Remains Alive," WashingtonPost.com, January 5, 2007.

29. U.S. Centers for Disease Control and Prevention, *Comprehensive HIV Prevention Messages for Young People*, 2002.

30. U.S. Centers for Disease Control and Prevention, National Center for HIV, STD, and TB Prevention, Divisions of HIV/AIDS Prevention, *HIV and AIDS: Are You at Risk?* 2000.

31. U.S. Centers for Disease Control and Prevention, "Surveillance 2006: Trends in Sexually Transmitted Diseases in the United States 2006," http://cdc.gov/STD/trends2006.htm.

32. Cheryl Clark, "Sex Cops Help Find Those Who Spread Diseases," *San Diego Union Tribune,* 11 March 2002.

33. Darryl E. Owens, "Sleep's Impact on Learning A to Zzzzz," *San Diego Union Tribune,* 2 October 2000.

34. Scott LaFee, "A Chronic Lack of Sleep Can Lead to the Big Sleep," *San Diego Union Tribune,* 8 October 1997.
35. Ronald Kotulak, "Skimping on Sleep May Make You Fat, Clumsy and Haggard," *San Diego Union Tribune,* 14 June 1998.
36. Gregory Belenky, Walter Reed Army Institute of Research, *Sleep, Sleep Deprivation, and Human Performance in Continuous Operations,* 1997.
37. Lindsey Tanner, "AMA Backs 80-hour Workweek Limit for Doctors-in-Training," *San Diego Union Tribune,* 21 June 2002.
38. Ronald Kotulak, "Skimping on Sleep."
39. Nicole Ziegler Dizon, "Aging Men's Flab Tied to a Lack of Deep Sleep," *San Diego Union Tribune,* 16 August 2000.
40. From http://www.thirdage.com/cgi-bin/NewsPrint.cgi, 2002.
41. Francesco Cappuccio, Warwick Medical School, "Researchers Say Lack of Sleep Doubles Risk of Death . . . But So Can Too Much Sleep," http://www2warwick,ac.uk, 2008.
42. From http://www.stress.org, 2002.
43. Maya Pines, "Psychological Hardiness: The Role of Challenge in Health," *Psychology Today,* December 1980.
44. James Prochaska, "What It Takes to Change," *Health Net News,* Fall 1997.
45. Katherine Rizzo, "John Glenn, 77, Handled Space Like a Young Man," *San Diego Union Tribune,* 29 January 2000.
46. Chelsea Carter, "Sarah 'Sadie' Delany, 109, Wrote Best Seller with her Sister at 104," *San Diego Union Tribune,* 1999.

Ollie American's Diet

Name _____   Date _____

Read the following description of Ollie American's diet and analyze it by answering the following questions about food groups, servings, and daily activity.

Ollie American gets up in the morning and heads for school. On the way to school, he stops at a convenience store and grabs a 32-ounce soda and a bag of chips. He sips the soda and eats the chips on the way to school. He feels energized and ready to face the day. Around mid-morning he starts to feel a little tired and goes to the vending machine during a break in class. He buys a can of soda and a candy bar to last him through the morning. At lunch, Ollie American is starving, so he and his friends head for a local fast-food place. Ollie orders a large hamburger with everything on it, a large order of fries, and a soda.

After class, Ollie heads for home. For relaxation, he spends a couple of hours playing a video game. Since this is Monday evening football night, Ollie is having some friends over to watch the game. The group puts their money together to order several large pepperoni pizzas. They decide to stop at the store on the way home to purchase some beer and chips to go with the pizza. During the game, Ollie has about half of a large pizza, a half bag of chips, and has four cans of beer.

Ollie has noticed that he is starting to gain weight. He is six feet tall and weighs 230 pounds.

1. What is Ollie's body mass index (BMI)?

    BMI = (705 × body weight) ÷ by (height × height)

2. According to Ollie's BMI, is he considered obese?

3. Ollie is eating many foods that belong in the discretionary calories category (high in sugar or fat). What foods are contributing to Ollie's weight gain?

4. Use the government suggested dietary guidelines to analyze Ollie's diet. This exercise assumes that Ollie is a male, 21 years old, and does not exercise regularly.

Food Groups	Recommended	List Actual Food Choices
Grains	8 ounce equivalents (1 ounce equivalent is about 1 slice of bread, 1 cup dry cereal, or ½ cup rice or pasta)	How many ounces?
Vegetables	3 cups (Includes dark green, orange, starchy, dry beans and peas and other veggies)	How many cups?
Fruits	2 cups	How many cups?
Oils	7 teaspoons	How many teaspoons?
Milk	3 cups (1½ ounces of cheese = 1 cup milk, a large pizza contains 16 ounces of cheese)	How many cups?
Meat and Beans	6.5 ounces (1 ounce equivalent is 1 ounce of meat, poultry or fish, 1 T. peanut butter, ½ oz. nuts, ¼ oz. dry beans or peas)	How many ounces?
Discretionary Calories	360 calories	List foods high in fat or sugar.

5. What suggestions would you make to help Ollie choose a more healthy diet and lose weight?

How Healthy Is Your Diet?

Name _____   Date _____

Use the following worksheet to analyze your diet. This plan is based on 2000 calories. Go to www.mypyramid.gov to find your individualized recommendations.

Food Groups	Recommended	List Actual Food Choices
Grains	6 ounce equivalents (1 ounce equivalent is about 1 slice of bread, 1 cup dry cereal, or ½ cup rice or pasta)	How many ounces?
Vegetables	2½ cups (Includes dark green, orange, starchy, dry beans and peas and other veggies)	How many cups?
Fruits	2 cups	How many cups?
Oils	6 teaspoons	How many teaspoons?
Milk	3 cups (1½ ounces of cheese = 1 cup milk, a large pizza contains 16 ounces of cheese)	How many cups?
Meat and Beans	5.5 ounces (1 ounce equivalent is 1 ounce of meat, poultry or fish, 1 T. peanut butter, ½ oz. nuts, ¼ oz. dry beans or peas)	How many ounces?
Discretionary Calories	100–300 calories	List foods high in fat or sugar.

1. How much do you exercise daily outside of your daily routine?

2. Compare your results to the recommended dietary guidelines. What did you discover?

3. What changes will you make in your exercise routine and diet in the future?

Critical Thinking about Alcohol Abuse

Name _____   Date _____

College officials nationwide are searching for ways to deal with alcohol abuse on college campuses. Consider these yearly statistics:*

- 1700 college students die from alcohol-related injuries including motor vehicle crashes.
- 696,000 students are assaulted by other students who have been drinking.
- 97,000 are victims of alcohol related sexual assault or date rape.
- 2.1 million students drive under the influence.
- 25 percent of students report academic consequences as the result of drinking (missing classes or doing poorly on exams or papers).
- Each year about 300 college students die of alcohol poisoning as a result of drinking contests or hazing rituals that result in blood alcohol levels of higher than .3. One fraternity student drank the equivalent of 22 beers in a two hour period. He went to sleep and never woke up.

You may want to discuss these questions with groups of students in your classroom.

1. What should students know about alcohol abuse? (binge drinking, alcohol poisoning, driving under the influence)

2. What actions can be taken to change the college culture of binge drinking?

*"A Snapshot of Annual High-Risk College Drinking Consequences," http://collegedrinkingprevention.gov/StatsSummaries/snapshot. aspx, 2008.

Health Assessment

Name _____   Date _____

Go to www.livingto100.com and use the Living to 100 Life Expectancy Calculator to assess your health habits.

What are your good health habits?

What are some areas you need to improve?

Based on the above list, write three intention statements for maintaining good health in the future.

1.

2.

3.

Substance Abuse

Name _____   Date _____

The following is a group activity to raise your awareness of substance abuse issues.

1.   For five minutes, brainstorm with the class the problems that result from substance abuse.

2.   For ten minutes, brainstorm some solutions to the problem of substance abuse.

3.   Share your best ideas with the class.

Stress-Reducing Thoughts

Name _____   Date _____

The following story is based on a news article about road rage. As you read the article, think about Mr. Road Rage and the negative thoughts he was thinking. What stress-reducing thoughts could have been used to avoid these tragic results? Then answer the questions below. You may want to do this as a group exercise with some of your classmates.

Mr. Road Rage, who shot a man as a result of a traffic-related altercation, was sentenced to nineteen years in prison today. He was a quiet man with no previous criminal record. People at his place of work where he was employed as a computer programmer were surprised to learn what had happened. Mr. Road Rage was not a violent man. He had even tried to get out of the Navy as a conscientious objector because he hated violence.

What happened? Mr. Rage was on the way home from work when some teenagers on bicycles cut right in front of him. Mr. Rage almost hit them. He was so angry that he stopped to talk with the teenagers. They began to call each other names and exchange obscene gestures. One of the teenagers became so angry with Mr. Rage that he threw his bicycle at Mr. Rage's car, making a small dent. The teenagers quickly left the scene. Mr. Rage continued to his apartment complex where he saw one of the teenagers involved in the altercation. He went to his apartment and got an old gun and decided that he would make a citizen's arrest of the teenager. The teenager resisted; and during the scuffle that ensued, the gun went off and the teenager was killed.

During Mr. Rage's murder trial, one of his colleagues at work said that Mr. Rage's behavior was completely out of character. He never imagined that such an incident could occur.

1. List the negative thoughts that might have been going through Mr. Rage's head during this incident.

2. What stress-reducing thoughts could Mr. Rage have used to avoid this situation?

3. Make a list of stress-reducing thoughts that you can use in stressful situations.

What Is Your Stress Index?*

Name _____   Date _____

Do you frequently: Yes   No

1. Neglect your diet?   _____   _____

2. Try to do everything yourself?   _____   _____

3. Blow up easily?   _____   _____

4. Seek unrealistic goals?   _____   _____

5. Fail to see the humor in situations others find funny?   _____   _____

6. Act rude?   _____   _____

7. Make a big deal out of everything?   _____   _____

8. Look to other people to make things happen?   _____   _____

9. Have difficulty making decisions?   _____   _____

10. Complain you are disorganized?   _____   _____

11. Avoid people whose ideas are different from your own?   _____   _____

12. Keep everything inside?   _____   _____

13. Neglect exercise?   _____   _____

14. Have only a few supportive relationships?   _____   _____

15. Use psychoactive drugs, such as sleeping pills and tranquilizers, without
    physician approval?   _____   _____

16. Get too little rest?   _____   _____

17. Get angry when you are kept waiting?   _____   _____

18. Ignore stress symptoms?   _____   _____

19. Procrastinate?   _____   _____

20. Think there is only one right way to do something?   _____   _____

21. Fail to build in relaxation time?   _____   _____

22. Gossip?   _____   _____

23. Race through the day?   _____   _____

24. Spend a lot of time lamenting the past?   _____   _____

25. Fail to get a break from noise and crowds?   _____   _____

*From Andrew Slaby, *Sixty Ways to Make Stress Work for You.*

Score 1 for each yes answer and 0 for each no. Total score: _____

1–6   There are a few hassles in your life. Make sure, though, that you aren't trying so hard to avoid problems that you shy away from challenges.

7–13   You've got your life in pretty good control. Work on the choices and habits that could still be causing some unnecessary stress in your life.

14–20   You're approaching the danger zone. You may well be suffering stress-related symptoms and your relationships could be strained. Think carefully about choices you've made and take relaxation breaks each day.

Above 20   Emergency! You must stop now, rethink how you are living, change your attitudes, and pay scrupulous attention to your diet, exercise, and relaxation programs.

CHAPTER **13**

© Mandy Godbehear, 2008. Under license from Shutterstock, Inc.

Appreciating Diversity

Our schools, our workplaces, and our nation are becoming more diverse. Gaining an understanding and appreciation of this diversity will enhance your future success. Understanding yourself and having pride in your unique characteristics is the first step in the process. Self-knowledge includes information about your personality, interests, talents, and values. Earlier in this text you had the opportunity to begin this exploration. This chapter challenges you to examine some additional characteristics that make you a unique individual and to take pride in yourself while respecting differences of others.

Diversity Is Increasing

Another word for diversity is differences. These differences do not make one group inferior or superior. Differences are not deficits; they are just differences. Look around your classroom, your place of employment, or where you do business. You will notice people of a variety of races, ethnic groups, cultures, genders, ages, socioeconomic levels, and sexual orientations. Other differences that add to our uniqueness include religious preference, political affiliation, personality, interests, and values. It is common to take pride in who we are and to look around and find people who share our view of the world. The challenge is to be able to look at the world from the point of view of those who are different from us. These differences provide an opportunity for learning.

Our schools and communities are becoming increasingly diverse. In the United States, one in every five students has a parent born in a foreign country. Nationwide, non-Latino whites make up only 63 percent of the population. The current population includes 16 percent African Americans, 15 percent Latinos, and 5 percent Asians. California, one of the most populous states, is leading the nation in diversity. There is no single group in the majority: 43 percent are Latinos, 36 percent are non-Latino whites, 9 percent are African Americans, and 8 percent are Asian.[1] In New Mexico, Hawaii, and the District of Columbia, non-Latino whites are also in the minority.[2]

In our schools, places of work, and communities, we increasingly study, work, and socialize with people from different ethnic groups. This morning I talked with a student from Mexico and another from France. My classes have students from Mexico, Japan, Argentina, and Iraq. A colleague called on the phone and we spoke in Spanish. He invited me to a Greek café and deli where we ate Greek salad and purchased feta cheese and baklava. This diversity provides a different perspective and products from other countries enrich our lives. It requires an open mindedness and respect for differences for it all to work.

We also live in a **global economy**. Increased trade among the nations of the world requires an understanding and appreciation of cultural differences. The United States is in the center of the largest free-trade area in the world. In 1994, the North American Free Trade Agreement (NAFTA) created a free-trade area that includes Canada, the United States, and Mexico. This act resulted in a freer flow of goods among these countries and an increase in international business. The success of this international business depends on increased cooperation and problem solving among these nations. Free-trade agreements will probably be expanded to other countries in Latin America in the near future.

Another major step toward the global economy was the creation of a single currency in Europe, the euro, which was successfully launched on January 1, 2002. The purpose of this largest money changeover in history is to establish a system in which people, goods, services, and capital can move freely across national borders. The European countries using the euro have made their economies more competitive by facilitating trade, travel, and investment.

International trade accounts for a quarter of all economic activity in the United States.[3] All we have to do is look around us to see that many of the foods and products we use in our daily lives come from other countries.

Last night Jessica invited friends over for dinner and made stir fried vegetables with chicken. She used ingredients from Viet Nam, Thailand, Italy, Japan and Mexico. These foods were all purchased at her local grocery store. The guests ate dinner on plates made in Malaysia and drank wine from Australia. The next morning she got up and dressed in a shirt made in the Dominican Republic and pants made in Mexico. She then put on her walking shoes which were made in Thailand and listened to Jamaican music on her iPod that was made in China. For breakfast she ate a banana grown in Honduras and drank coffee from Colombia. She drove to school in a car that was made in Japan.

Global trade brings us many new and inexpensive products and is having a major impact on the economy and careers of the future.

Changes in technology have made an awareness and appreciation of diversity more important. The world is becoming an **electronic village** connected by an array of communication and information technologies: computers, the Internet, communications satellites, cell phones, fax machines, and the myriad of electronic devices that are an integral part of our lives today. These devices make rapid communication possible all over the world and are essential for international business and trade. The Internet is like a vast information superhighway and each computer is an on ramp to the highway. Those who do not have a computer or lack computer skills will be left off the highway and have limited access to information and opportunities.

The increased use of the Internet offers both great opportunities and challenges. The Internet can help to break down barriers between people. When communicating with someone over the Internet, differences such as race, age, religion, or economic status are not obvious. The flow of information and ideas is unrestricted, and people with similar interests can communicate easily with one another. There is great potential for use as well as misuse of the Internet as well. Chat groups may share information about medical conditions or treatments, or hate groups can use the Internet to promote their political agendas.

The Internet presents new challenges for communicating since nonverbal cues are often missing. Looking at a person's face or listening to the tone of voice adds a great deal to communication. A new type of "netiquette" has evolved as a result. For example, using all caps is a form of YELLING! Increasingly words are shortened and changed for ease of communication resulting in a type of Internet grammar. Understanding Web pages in a different language is another new challenge.

JOURNAL ENTRY #1
How will the global economy and the electronic village affect your future?

Benefits of Diversity

- Gain critical thinking skills
- Pride in self and culture
- Learn from others
- Improve inter-personal skills
- Learn flexibility
- Develop cultural awareness

Why Is Diversity Important?

Having an understanding and appreciation of diversity can help you to be successful at school and work. Here are some benefits:

- **Gain skills in critical thinking.** Critical thinking requires identifying different viewpoints, finding possible answers, and then constructing your own reasonable view. Critical thinking skills are one of the expected outcomes of higher education. Many of your college assignments are designed to teach these skills. Whether you are writing an essay in an English class, participating in a discussion in a history class, or completing a laboratory experiment, critical thinking skills will help you to complete the task successfully.

Critical thinking skills are also helpful in finding good solutions to problems or challenges you might find at work. For example, for a business manager, an important task is helping employees to work together as a team. The critical thinking process results in greater understanding of others and better problem-solving skills. To stay competitive, businesses need to find creative solutions for building better products and providing good customer service. Critical thinking skills help people work together to come up with good ideas to make a business a success.

- **Have pride in yourself and your culture.** Having pride in yourself is the foundation of good mental health and success in life. Sonia Nieto did research on a group of successful students. These students had good grades, enjoyed school, had plans for the future, and described themselves as successful. Nieto found that "one of the most consistent, and least expected, outcomes to emerge from these case studies has been a resoluteness with which young people maintain pride and satisfaction in their culture and the strength they derive from it."[4] Having pride in yourself and your culture is an important part of high self-esteem and can help you to become a better student and worker. Having good self-esteem provides the confidence to accept and care for others. The best schools and workplaces provide an environment where people can value their own culture as well as others. With respect between different cultures, ideas can be freely exchanged and the door is opened to creativity and innovation.

  The world is constantly changing and we must be ready to adapt to new situations. Sometimes it is difficult to balance "fitting in" and maintaining our own cultural identity. Researchers have described a process called **transculturation,** in which a person adapts to a different culture without sacrificing individual cultural identity. One study of Native Americans showed that retention of traditional cultural heritage was an important predictor of success. A Native American student described the process this way: "When we go to school, we live a non-Indian way but we still keep our values. . . . I could put my values aside just long enough to learn what it is I want to learn but that doesn't mean I'm going to forget them. I think that is how strong they are with me."[5] Cultural identity provides strength and empowerment to be successful.

- **Gain an ability to network and learn from others.** In college you will have the opportunity to learn from your professors and other students who are different from yourself. You may have professors with very different personality styles and teaching styles. Your success will depend on being aware of the differences and finding a way to adapt to the situation. Each student in your classes will also come from a different perspective and have valuable ideas to add to the class.

  It is through networking with other people that most people find a job. You are likely to find a job through someone you know such as a college professor, a student in one of your classes, a community member, or a referral from a previous employer. Once you have the job, you will gain proficiency by learning from others. The best managers are open to learning from others and help different people to work together as a team. No matter how educated or experienced you become, you can always learn from others. Bill Cosby once told a graduating class at Washington University, "Don't ever think you know more than the person mopping the floor."[6] Every person has a different view of the world and has important ideas to share.

- **Improve interpersonal skills.** A popular Native American proverb is that you cannot understand another person until you have walked a few miles in their moccasins. Being able to understand different perspectives on life will help you to improve your personal relationships. Good interpersonal skills bring joy to our personal relationships and are very valuable in the workplace. The Secretary of

Labor's Commission on Achieving Necessary Skills (SCANS) identifies having good interpersonal skills as one of the five critical competencies needed in the workplace. Workers need to work effectively in teams, teach others, serve customers, exercise leadership, negotiate to arrive at a decision, and work well with cultural diversity.[7] Efficiency and profits in any industry depend on good interpersonal skills and how well workers can provide customer service.

- **Learn to be flexible and adapt to the situation.**   These two qualities are necessary for dealing with the rapid change that is taking place in our society today. We learn these qualities by successfully facing personal challenges. If you are a single parent, you have learned to be flexible in managing time and resources. If you served in the military overseas, you have learned to adapt to a different culture. If you are a new college student, you are probably learning how to be independent and manage your own life. Flexibility is a valuable skill in the workplace. Today's employers want workers who can adapt, be flexible and solve problems.

- **Develop cultural awareness.**   Cultural awareness is valuable in your personal life and in the workplace. In your personal life, you can have a wider variety of satisfying personal relationships. You can enjoy people from different cultural backgrounds and travel to different countries.

In a global economy, cultural awareness is increasingly important. Tuning into cultural differences can open up business opportunities. For example, many companies are discovering that the buying power of minorities is significant. They are developing ad campaigns to sell products to Asians, Latinos, African Americans, and other groups.

Companies now understand that cultural awareness is important in international trade. American car manufacturers could not understand why the Chevy Nova was not selling well in Latin America. In Spanish, "No va" means "It doesn't go" or "It doesn't run." Kentucky Fried Chicken found out that "Finger-lickin' good" translates as "Eat your fingers off" in Chinese! Being familiar with the culture and language of different countries is necessary for successful international business.

JOURNAL ENTRY #2

Why is an understanding and appreciation of diversity important to your future?

Vocabulary for Understanding Diversity

Knowing some basic terms will aid in your understanding of diversity.

Race. Race refers to a group of people who are perceived to be physically different because of traits such as facial features, color of skin, and hair.

Ethnicity. Ethnicity refers to a sense of belonging to a particular culture and sharing the group's beliefs, attitudes, skills, ceremonies, and traditions. An ethnic group usually descends from a common group of ancestors usually from a particular country or geographic area.

Ethnocentrism. Ethnocentrism is the belief that one's own ethnic, religious, or political group is superior to all others.

Culture. Culture is the behavior, beliefs, and values shared by a group of people. It includes language, morals, and even food preferences. Culture includes everything that we learn from the people around us in our community.

Gender, sex. Gender refers to cultural differences that distinguish males from females. Different cultures raise men and women to act in specified ways. Sex refers to anatomical differences.

Sexism. Sexism is a negative attitude or perception based on sex.

Stereotype. A stereotype is a generalization that expresses conventional or biased ideas about people in a certain group. Stereotypes can lead to discrimination based on these ideas. They cause us to view others in a limited way and reduce our ability to see people as individuals.

Prejudice. A prejudice is a prejudgment of someone or something. Prejudices are often based on stereotypes and reflect a disrespect for others. Sometimes people who are prejudiced are insecure about their own identities.

Discrimination. Discrimination happens when people are denied opportunities because of their differences. Prejudice and stereotype are often involved.

Racism. Racism occurs when one race or ethnic group holds a negative attitude or perception of another group. It is prejudice based on race. Anthropologists generally accept that the human species can be categorized into races based on physical and genetic makeup. These scientists accept the fact that there is no credible evidence that one race is superior to another. People who believe that their own race is superior to another are called racists.

Cultural pluralism. Each group celebrates the customs and traditions of their culture while participating in mainstream society.

Genocide. Genocide is the deliberate and systematic destruction of a racial, political, or cultural group. It can include the destruction of the language, religion, or cultural practices of a group of people.

Understanding Diversity

There are 6.6 billion people in the world today. Statistics provided by the Population Reference Bureau and the United Nations can give us a better understanding of diversity in the world today. By geographic area, the world's population can be broken down into these percentages:[8]

61	Asians
14	Africans
11	Europeans
9	Central and South Americans
5	North Americans (Canada and the United States)

If visitors from outer space were to visit the earth and report back about the most common human being found, they would probably describe someone of Asian descent. Statistics also show that approximately 50 percent of the world population suffers from malnutrition and 80 percent live in substandard housing. Moreover, 6 percent of the population living in the United States, Japan, and Germany, own half of the wealth of the world. In addition, continuous wars and fighting among the people of the earth have contributed to human suffering and the flight of many refugees.

As children, we accept the values, assumptions, and stereotypes of our culture. We use our own culture as a filter to understand the world. Because of this limited perception, people often consider their culture to be superior and other cultures to be inferior.[9] The belief that one's own culture, religious, or political group is superior to others is called **ethnocentrism.** Native Americans have argued that the celebration of Columbus Day, commemorating the discovery of the new world by Christopher Columbus, is an example of ethnocentrism. In reality the Native Americans lived here long before Christopher Columbus arrived in 1492.

Ethnocentrism can lead to discrimination, interpersonal conflict, and even wars between different groups of people. In extreme cases, it can even lead to **genocide**, the deliberate and systematic destruction of a racial, political, or cultural group. History is full of examples of genocide. In the United States, Native Americans were massacred and their land was confiscated in violation of treaties. In Mexico and South America, the Spanish conquerors systematically destroyed native populations. During World War II, six million Jews were killed. Pol Pot and the Khmer Rouge killed millions of Cambodians. Unfortunately genocide continues today in various conflicts around the world.

An understanding of the harmful effects of stereotypes is necessary to improve our understanding and appreciation of diversity. A **stereotype** is an assumption that all members of a group are alike. For example, a tall African American woman in one of my classes was constantly dealing with the assumption that she must be attending college to play basketball. Actually she was very academically oriented and not athletic at all.

All of us use stereotypes to understand people different from ourselves. Why does this happen? There are many different reasons:

- It is a fast way to make sense of the world. It requires little thought.
- We tend to look for patterns to help us understand the world.
- We are often unable or unwilling to obtain all the information we need to make fair judgments about other people.
- Stereotypes can result from fear of people who are different. We often learn these fears as children.
- The media promotes stereotypes. Movies, magazines, and advertisements often present stereotypes. These stereotypes are often used as the basis of humor. For example, the media often uses people who are overweight in comedy routines.

The problem with stereotypes is that we do not get to know people as individuals. All members of a culture, ethnic group, or gender are not alike. If we make assumptions about a group, we treat everyone in the group the same. Stereotypes can lead to prejudice and discrimination. For example, a person who is overweight may find it more difficult to find a job because of stereotyping.

Psychologists and sociologists today present the idea of **cultural relativity** in which different cultures, ethnic groups, genders, and sexual orientations are viewed as different but equally valuable and worthy of respect.[10] These differences between cultures can help us learn new ideas that can enrich our view of the world. It can also promote greater understanding and better relationships among individuals and nations.

QUIZ
Understanding Diversity, Part I

Test what you have learned by selecting the correct answer to the following questions.

1. The belief that one's own ethnic, religious, or political group is superior to all others is called

    a. cultural pluralism.
    b. cultural relativity.
    c. ethnocentrism.

2. The assumption that all members of a group are alike is

    a. discrimination.
    b. stereotype.
    c. prejudice.

3. The deliberate destruction of a racial, cultural, or political group of people is called

    a. genocide.
    b. racism.
    c. ethnocentrism.

4. Most people on the earth are

    a. North Americans.
    b. Europeans.
    c. Asians.

5. Cultural relativity is defined as

    a. the belief that one's own ethnic group is superior.
    b. groups that are viewed as different, but equally valuable.
    c. an ethnic group that descends from a common group of ancestors.

How did you do on the quiz? Check your answers: 1. c, 2. b, 3. a, 4. c, 5. b

A New Look at Diversity:
The Human Genome Project

Although the people of the world represent many racial, ethnic, and cultural groups, biologists are taking a new look at diversity by learning about human genes. Genes are composed of segments of DNA that determine the transmission of hereditary traits by controlling the operation of cells. Cells are the basic building blocks of the human body.

The Human Genome Project, a multibillion-dollar and multinational government-sponsored research project to map all human genes, was completed in 2003. This map is a catalog of all the genetic information contained in human cells. They have identified the genes and determined the sequence of the 3 billion chemical base pairs in human DNA. Although the project is completed, analysis of the data will continue for many years.[11] The human genome is considered a biological treasure chest that will allow scientists to discover how a body grows, ages, stays healthy, or becomes ill. This knowledge is invaluable in discovering new medications and improving health.

Results of the human genome project show that we are all genetically similar while having unique individual differences. One of the interesting findings is that "as scientists have long suspected, though the world's people may look very different on the outside, genetically speaking humans are all 99.9 percent identical."[12] While we are genetically very similar, each individual can be identified by his or her genetic code. With the exception of identical twins, each individual human being is slightly different because of the unique combination of DNA letters inherited from one's parents.

Dr. Craig Venter, head of Celera Genomics Corporation, has stated that "race is a social concept, not a scientific one."[13] While it may be easy to look at people and describe them as Caucasian, African, or Asian, there is little genetic material to distinguish one race from another. Venter says, "We all evolved in the last 100,000 years from the same small number of tribes that migrated out of Africa and colonized the world."[14] Very few genes control traits that distinguish one race from another, such as skin color, eye color, and width of nose. These outward characteristics have been able to change quickly in response to environmental pressures. People who lived near the equator evolved dark skin to protect them from ultraviolet radiation. People who lived farther from the equator evolved pale skins to produce vitamin D from little sunlight. The genes responsible for these outward appearances are in the range of .01 percent of the total. Researchers on the human genome project agree that **there is only one race, the human race**.

The human genome project will be important for understanding the human body and will help us to find ways to prevent or cure illnesses. It may also provide new information for critical thinking about the idea of ethnocentrism and discover some basic ways in which all human beings are similar.

Communicating across Cultures

Human beings communicate through the use of symbols. A symbol is a word that stands for something else. Problems in communication arise when we assume that a symbol has only one meaning and that everyone understands the symbol in the same way. For example, we use the word "dog" to stand for a four-legged animal that barks. However, if I say the word "dog," the picture in my mind probably doesn't match the picture in your mind because there are many varieties of dogs. I might be picturing a Chihuahua while you are picturing a German Shepherd. Language becomes even more complex when we have multiple meanings for one symbol. Consider the ways we use the word "dog":

- She is a dog. (She is unattractive.)
- He is a dog. (He is promiscuous.)
- He is a lucky dog. (He is fortunate.)
- It's a dog. (It is worthless.)
- Just dog it. (Just do enough to get by.)
- He went to the dogs. (He was not doing well.)
- He was in the doghouse. (He was in trouble.)
- Let sleeping dogs lie. (Leave the situation alone.)
- My dogs hurt. (My feet hurt.)
- He put on the dog. (He assumed an attitude of wealth or importance.)
- These are the dog days of summer. (These are hot days when people feel lazy.)
- The book is dog-eared. (The corners of the pages are bent.)
- He led a dog's life. (He was not happy.)
- May I have a doggy bag? (May I have a bag for my leftovers?)
- Doggone it! (I am frustrated!)
- I am dog-tired. (I am very tired.)

Imagine how a computer would translate the above sentences. The translations would be incomprehensible since there are so many variations in meaning depending on the context.

The problem of communication becomes even more difficult for those who are learning English. People who speak a different language might not understand the word "dog" at all because they use a different symbol for the object. Even after studying the language, it is easy to misinterpret the meaning of the word "dog." A recent immigrant was horrified when he was offered a hot dog at a ball game. He thought that this was a civilized country and was surprised that we ate dogs!

The symbols we use to stand for objects are arbitrary, complex, and dependent on our culture, language, and frame of reference. As a result, misunderstandings are common. When my son was very young, he was very frightened by noises on the roof of our house. He was afraid that aliens had landed. He said that he was certain there were aliens on the roof and that Dad said he had seen them too. I later found out that his father said that he had seen illegal aliens, or undocumented workers, in our neighborhood. It is strange that in the English language we use the word "alien" to refer to someone from outer space and someone from a different country. The "aliens" in my son's case turned out to be raccoons playing on the roof. The words that we use have a powerful influence on our lives and can make clear communication difficult.

Both verbal and nonverbal symbols have different meaning in different cultures. George Henderson in his book *Cultural Diversity in the Workplace*,[15] gives the example of the common thumbs-up gesture, which we commonly interpret as "okay." In Japan the same gesture means money. In Ghana and Iran it is a vulgar gesture similar to raising your middle finger in the United States. Another example is silence. In the United States, if a teacher asks a question and no one responds right away, the situation is uncomfortable. In Native American cultures, the person who remains silent is admired. Many Asian students listen more than they speak. According to a Zen proverb, "He who knows does not speak and he who speaks does not know." Think about how different our communications, especially business and sales techniques, would have to be in order to be effective in different cultures.

Here are some ideas to help improve your communications with people who are culturally different from you or speak a different language:

- Be sensitive to the fact that communication is difficult and that errors in understanding are likely.
- Remember that the message sent is not necessarily the message received.
- Give people time to think and respond. You do not have to fill in the silence right away.
- Check your understanding of the message. Rephrase or repeat the information to make sure it is correct. Ask questions.
- If you feel insulted by the message, remember that it is quite possible that you could be misinterpreting it. (Remember all the meanings for "dog" listed above.)
- If you are having problems communicating with someone who speaks a different language, speak slowly and clearly or use different words. Talking louder will not help.
- Remain calm and treat others with respect. Be patient.
- Find a translator if possible.
- Study a different language. This will help in understanding other cultures and the different ways that other cultures use symbols.
- Before traveling to a different country, read about the culture and learn some basic phrases in the language used. This will help you to enjoy your travel and learn about other cultures. Attempting to speak the language will show others that you care about and respect the culture.
- Sometimes nonverbal communication can help. If you are adventurous or desperate, smile and act out the message. Be aware that nonverbal communication can be misunderstood also.
- Don't forget your sense of humor.

Understanding Sexual Orientation

One of the causes of stereotyping and the resulting prejudice and discrimination is fear and lack of knowledge of those who are different. Prejudice and discrimination against gays and other minorities has sometimes led to hate crimes. For example, in 1998, Mathew Shepard, a gay student at the University of Wyoming, was lured from a bar, beaten, and tied to a log fence where he was left during cold weather. He died five days later. His murderers received life sentences in prison. At Mathew's funeral, protesters held up signs saying, "God hates fags."[16] (The term "faggot," which comes from the Latin word for a bundle of sticks, may refer to the time of the Inquisition when gays were burned at the stake along with witches.)[17]

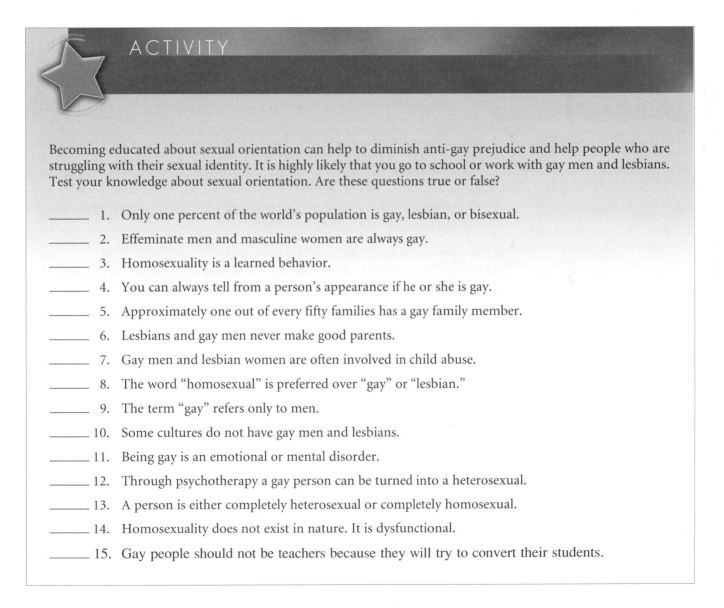

ACTIVITY

Becoming educated about sexual orientation can help to diminish anti-gay prejudice and help people who are struggling with their sexual identity. It is highly likely that you go to school or work with gay men and lesbians. Test your knowledge about sexual orientation. Are these questions true or false?

_____ 1. Only one percent of the world's population is gay, lesbian, or bisexual.

_____ 2. Effeminate men and masculine women are always gay.

_____ 3. Homosexuality is a learned behavior.

_____ 4. You can always tell from a person's appearance if he or she is gay.

_____ 5. Approximately one out of every fifty families has a gay family member.

_____ 6. Lesbians and gay men never make good parents.

_____ 7. Gay men and lesbian women are often involved in child abuse.

_____ 8. The word "homosexual" is preferred over "gay" or "lesbian."

_____ 9. The term "gay" refers only to men.

_____ 10. Some cultures do not have gay men and lesbians.

_____ 11. Being gay is an emotional or mental disorder.

_____ 12. Through psychotherapy a gay person can be turned into a heterosexual.

_____ 13. A person is either completely heterosexual or completely homosexual.

_____ 14. Homosexuality does not exist in nature. It is dysfunctional.

_____ 15. Gay people should not be teachers because they will try to convert their students.

All of the above statements are false and represent myths about gay men and lesbians. The corrected information below is provided by PFLAG, which stands for Parents, Families and Friends of Lesbians and Gays. This organization provides information on its website at: www.pflagla.org. An organization called Rainbow Bridge also provides educational materials on gays and lesbians.

1. It is estimated that about ten percent of the world's population is gay, lesbian, or bisexual.
2. Effeminate men and masculine women can be heterosexual. Some gay persons fit this stereotype, but most look and act like individuals from the heterosexual majority.
3. No one knows how sexual orientation is determined. Homosexuality is not something that one chooses to be or learns to be. As children, gay men and lesbians are not taught or influenced by others to be homosexual. Various theories about sexual orientation have been proposed, including ones citing genetic or inborn hormonal factors.[18]
4. Most gay men and lesbians look and act like individuals from the heterosexual majority.
5. Approximately one out of four families has a gay member.
6. Gay men and lesbians can make good parents. Children of gay and lesbian parents are no different in any aspects of psychological, social or sexual development from children in heterosexual families. These children tend to be more tolerant of differences.
7. Gay men and lesbians are rarely involved in child abuse. In the United States, heterosexual men commit 90 percent of all sexual child abuse. The molesters are most often fathers, stepfathers, grandfathers, uncles, or boyfriends of the mothers.
8. The term "gay man" or "lesbian" is preferred over the term "homosexual."
9. The term "gay" refers to both men and women.
10. All cultures have gay men and lesbians.
11. Being gay is not an emotional or mental disorder.
12. Psychotherapy has not been successful in changing a person's sexual orientation.
13. Based on Dr. Alfred Kinsey's research, few people are predominantly heterosexual or homosexual. Most people fall on a continuum between the two extremes. A person on the middle of the continuum between heterosexual and homosexual would be a bisexual. Bisexuals are attracted to both sexes.[19]
14. Research suggests that homosexuality is "natural." It exists among all animals and is frequent among highly developed species.[20]
15. Homosexual seduction is no more common than heterosexual seduction. Most gay teachers fear they will be fired if it is found out that they are gay.[21]

How to Appreciate Diversity

Having an appreciation for diversity enriches all of us. Poet Maya Angelou has described the world as a rich tapestry and stressed that understanding this concept can enrich and improve the world:

> It is time for us to teach young people early on that in diversity there is beauty and strength. We all should know that diversity makes for a rich tapestry, and we must understand that the threads of the tapestry are equal in value, no matter their color; equal in importance, no matter their texture.[22]

Here are some ways to appreciate diversity:

- Educate yourself about other cultures and people who are different from you. Read about or take courses on the literature or history of another culture or learn another language.
- Explore your own heritage. Learn about the cultures that are part of your family history.
- Value diversity and accept the differences of others.
- View differences as an opportunity for learning.
- Realize that you will make mistakes when dealing with people from other cultural backgrounds. Learn from the mistakes and move on to better understanding.
- Work to understand differences of opinion. You do not have to agree, but respect different points of view.
- Travel to other countries to discover new ideas and cultures.
- Think critically to avoid stereotypes and misconceptions. Treat each person as an individual.
- Avoid judgments based on physical characteristics such as color of skin, age, gender, or weight.
- Put yourself in the other person's place. How would you feel? What barriers would you face?
- Make friends with people from different countries, races, and ethnic groups.
- Find some common ground. We all have basic needs for good health, safety, economic security, and education. We all face personal challenges and interests. We all think, feel, love, and have hope for the future.
- Be responsible for your own behavior. Do not participate in or encourage discrimination.
- Do good deeds. You will be repaid with good feelings.
- Learn from history so that you do not repeat it. Value your own freedom.
- Challenge racial or homophobic remarks or jokes.
- Teach children and young people to value diversity and respect others. It is through them that we can change the world.

Stages of Ethical Development

After much study, Harvard University professor William Perry developed the theory that students move through stages of ethical development.[23] Students move through these patterns of thought and eventually achieve effective intercultural communication.

Stage 1: Dualism

In this stage we view the world in terms of black or white, good or bad, "we" versus "they." Role models and authorities determine what is right. The right answers exist for every problem. If we work hard, we can find the correct answers and all will be well. Decisions are often based on common stereotypes.

Stage 2: Multiplicity

At this stage we become aware that there are multiple possibilities and answers. We know that authorities can disagree on what is right and wrong. We defend our position, but acknowledge that on any given issue everyone has a right to his or her own opinion.

Stage 3: Relativism

As we learn more about our environment and ourselves, we discover that what is right is based on our own values and culture. We weigh the evidence and try to support our opinions based on data and evidence.

Stage 4: Commitment in Relativism

At this stage we look at our environment and ourselves and make choices. In an uncertain world, we make decisions about careers, politics, and personal relationships based on our individual values. We make certain commitments based on the way we wish to live our lives. We defend our own values but respect the values of others. There is openness to learning new information and changing one's personal point of view. This position allows for the peaceful coexistence of different points of views and perspectives. It is at this point that we become capable of communicating across cultures and appreciating diversity.

QUIZ
Understanding Diversity, Part II

Test what you have learned by selecting the correct answer to the following questions.

1. Results of the human genome project show that humans are

    a.   80 percent identical.
    b.   50 percent identical.
    c.   99.9 percent identical.

2. Problems in communication occur when we assume that

    a.   a symbol has only one meaning.
    b.   words have many meanings.
    c.   it is easy to match the picture in one person's mind to a picture in another person's mind.

3. The thumbs up gesture

    a.   means "okay" in Japan.
    b.   is a vulgar gesture in Iran.
    c.   is understood in the same way in all cultures.

4. The following statement about sexual orientation is generally accepted as true:

    a.   sexual orientation is not something one chooses or can change.
    b.   some cultures do not have gay men and lesbians.
    c.   homosexuality is a learned behavior.

5. In the last stage of ethical development, commitment in relativism, we

    a.   view the world in terms of "good" and "bad."
    b.   become aware of multiple possibilities.
    c.   defend our own values but respect the values of others.

How did you do on the quiz? Check your answers: 1. c, 2. a, 3. b, 4. a, 5. c

Student Perspectives on Diversity

The following are some student comments on the subject of diversity. Many students have faced incidents of discrimination and hope for a better future.

I am always faced with problems because I'm black or my hair is long or because I am a large man. I wish people could be more sensitive and love me as a person and not judge me based on what I look like.

I am frequently discriminated against because of my religion. I feel really bad when it happens and it hurts a lot.

I have always faced discrimination because of my sexual orientation and will probably continue to experience discrimination in the future. If you are part of a minority, discrimination is inevitable. The key is to not let it drag you down so that you become a second-class citizen. That can be accomplished by taking pride in who you are and then working to fight against discrimination.

I come from Japan. I noticed that people here think their culture is better than any other. I think it's not bad to love your culture, but it is important to be open to other cultures.

There is a story I tell my children about words being nails. When we speak, we pound our nails into the other person's spirit. We can go back and apologize for hurtful words and maybe that removes the nail, but it still leaves a hole in the spirit.

If you constantly hear people say that you are not as good as another, you eventually start to believe it.

I've been discriminated against because I am female and a blonde. When I hear blonde jokes, I've learned to laugh with people most of the time, but it still hurts my feelings.

Discrimination is passed on to the next generation because a child believes what a parent tells them. We need to teach our children tolerance for differences.

Discrimination hurts people's feelings and doesn't allow them to become successful in life because they lose confidence and self-esteem.

Because I am black, salespeople tend to follow me around in the store thinking I am going to steal something. People of different races call me "nigger."

When I was younger, I used to wear thick glasses. People would call me names such as "four eyes," "nerd," "dork," and "geek." I can look back and laugh at this now, but it made me feel inferior. Discrimination is based on ignorance and hate.

Black kids used to mistreat me because I was not as black as them.

Once when I was ten years old, I was playing in the park. I noticed this Caucasian kid playing on the slide and he was about to fall off the slide. I went over to catch him and the mother ran over to me and told me to take my hands off of him and that she would rather have him fall than to have some "nigger" put her hands on him. I will never forget this incident!

When I was younger, my father frequently made negative comments about women. Because of his prejudice, I felt less worthy of getting equal treatment for equal education and work. Now my father is trying to overcome this mindset, and I plan to graduate from college to earn equal pay with men.

It is sad that humans can be so cruel to one another. I hope someday this will all end and we can live in peace with one another.

By celebrating diversity, all the people of the world could come together and have peace.

Keys to Success

Diversity Is Valuable and People Are Important

In 1963 Dr. Martin Luther King, Jr., made a famous speech in which he said, "I have a dream that my four little children will one day live in a nation where they will not be judged by the color of their skin, but by the content of their character." Because of his message of brotherhood and understanding, his birthday is celebrated as a national holiday. Tragically, King was assassinated because of his strong stand against racism. We are still working toward his ideal of brotherly love.

When I ask students to describe what success means to them, they often talk about having a good career, financial stability, owning a home, and having a nice car. Some students mention family and friends and people who are important to them. Understanding diversity and appreciating other people can add to your personal success and enjoyment of life.

To gain perspective on what is important to your success, it is interesting to think about what

people will say about you after you die. What will you think is important at the end of your life? If you can ponder this idea, you can gain some insight into how to live your life now. Go to the following web site:

http://www.lindaellisonline.com/
The_Dash_Poem_Copyright_Linda_Ellis.htm

Read "The Dash"
By Linda Ellis

Learn to understand, respect, and appreciate the different people in your life. Take time to love those who are important to you. Focus on cooperation and teamwork on the job. Don't forget about the people you meet on your road to success; they are important too. Having an understanding and appreciation of diversity will make the world a better place to live in too.

JOURNAL ENTRY #4
What is the most important thing you would want to be said in your eulogy?

JOURNAL ENTRIES

Appreciating Diversity

Go to http://www.collegesuccess1.com/ for Word files of the Journal Entries

Success over the Internet

Visit the *College Success Website* at
http:www.collegesuccess1.com/

The *College Success Website* is continually updated with new topics and links to the material presented in this chapter. Topics include

- Tolerance
- Ways to fight hate

- Diversity and multicultural resources
- Asian-Pacific students
- Latinos
- Women
- Minorities

Contact your instructor if you have any problems in accessing the *College Success Website.*

Notes

1. Robert Rosenblatt and Robert Duke, "A New Boom in U.S. Student Population, Census Finds; Count: Enrollment of 49 Million Equals 1970 Record. But Immigration Is a Concern, Especially in California," *Los Angeles Times,* 23 March 2001.
2. Brian Melly, "One in Three Californians is Hispanic; Whites Minority, Census Shows," *Associated Press,* 29 March 2001.
3. David Broder, "Congress Wants to Shape Trade Debate," *San Diego Union Tribune,* 7 November 2001.
4. Sonia Nieto, *Affirming Diversity: The Sociopolitical Context of Multicultural Education* (New York: Longman, 1996), 283.
5. Terry Huffman, "The Transculturation of Native American College Students," in *American Mosaic: Selected Readings on America's Multicultural Heritage,* ed. Young Song and Eugene Kim (Englewood Cliffs, NJ: Prentice-Hall, 1993), 211–19.
6. Richard Bucher, *Diversity Consciousness* (Englewood Cliffs, NJ: Prentice-Hall, 2000), 119.

7. Secretary's Commission of Achieving Necessary Skills (SCANS), U.S. Department of Labor, *Learning a Living: A Blueprint for High Performance*, 1991.

8. World population statistics from the Population Reference Bureau website: http://www.prb.org/pdf07/07WPDS_Eng.pdf, 2008, and the United Nations website: www.un.org/esa/population, 2008.

9. H. Triandis, "Training for Diversity," paper presented at the annual meeting of the American Psychological Association, San Francisco, 1991.

10. Benjamin Lahey, Psychology: An Introduction (Dubuque, IA: Brown and Benchmark, 1995), 20. "Human Genome Project Information", U.S. Department of Energy Office of Science, http://www.ornl.gov/sci/techresources/Human_Genome/home.shtml, 2008.

11. "Human Genome Project Information," U.S. Department of Energy, Office of Science, http://www.ornl.gov/sci/techresources/Human_Genome/home.shtml, 2008.

12. Sue Goetinck Ambrose, "First Look at Genome Data Leaves Scientists in 'Awe'," *San Diego Union Tribune*, 11 February 2001.

13. Natalie Angier, "Do Races Differ? Not Really, Genes Show," *New York Times*, 22 August 2000.

14. Ibid.

15. George Henderson, *Cultural Diversity in the Workplace: Issues and Strategies* (Westport, CT: Praeger, 1994.

16. "Mourners Gather to Honor Gay Murdered in Wyoming," *Bellingham Herald*, 17 October 1998, A8.

17. California Rainbow Bridge pamphlet, 2000.

18. American Psychological Association, from http://www.apa.org.pubinfo.html, 2001.

19. Ibid.

20. Ibid.

21. Ibid.

22. Maya Angelou, *Wouldn't Take Nothing for My Journey Now* (New York: Random House, 1993).

23. William G. Perry, "Cognitive and Ethical Growth: The Making of Meaning," in *The Modern American College* by Arthur Chickering and Associates (Jossey-Bass, 1981), 76–116.

Exploring Stereotypes

Name _____   Date _____

Part 1. We are all familiar with **common stereotypes** of certain groups. Think about how these groups are often portrayed in the media. Quickly complete each statement.

1. All athletes are _____

2. All lawyers are _____

3. All male hairdressers are _____

4. All construction workers are _____

5. All redheads are _____

6. All people with AIDS are _____

7. All people on welfare are _____

8. All young people are _____

9. All old people are _____

10. All men are _____

11. All women are _____

12. All A students are _____

Part 2. Your instructor will ask you to share the above stereotypes with the class. Then discuss these questions.

1. What prejudices result from such stereotypes?

2. What is the source of these prejudices?

3. What harm can come from these prejudices?

Exploring My Culture

Name _____   Date _____

Everyone has a unique cultural background based on many different factors. Answer these questions to explore your unique culture.

1. Describe where you grew up and the school you attended.

2. What beliefs did you learn from your family?

3. What beliefs did you learn from your teachers? How would your teachers describe you as a student?

4. How has your religious training or lack of religious training affected your beliefs?

5. If you are in a relationship, describe how your partner has affected your beliefs.

6. If you have children, how have your values and beliefs changed?

7. Are the beliefs you grew up with right for you today? Why or why not?

LEARNING OBJECTIVES

Read to answer these key questions:

- What is my life stage?

- How does positive thinking affect my future success?

- What are some beliefs of successful people?

- What are some secrets to achieving happiness?

© Lucas Allen White, 2008. Under license from Shutterstock, Inc.

Looking Toward the Future

Psychologists have identified life stages that we all go through. Knowing about life stages can help you to understand where you are now and where you might be in the future. Positive thinking is also a powerful tool for achieving life goals. Learn to use your attitudes and beliefs to enhance your future success. Many of you have happiness as one of your lifetime goals. This chapter ends with some useful ideas about how to achieve happiness in your life.

Life Stages

A number of researchers believe that adults progress through a series of orderly and predictable stages in which success or failure at each stage has an influence on later stages. Understanding these stages can help you to understand where you are now and where you are headed in the future. Life stage theorists include Erik Erikson and Daniel Levinson. Gail Sheehy, author of *Passages* and *New Passages*, is a journalist who has summarized and popularized current research on life stages.[1]

Erik Erikson

Erik Erikson proposes that human beings progress through eight stages of psychosocial development in a fixed order.[2] These stages are turning points, or crises, and the outcome of each turning point will determine future personality development. Each crisis has two possible outcomes; one is negative and the other positive. For example, the first turning point happens during the first year of life. He titles this stage trust vs. mistrust. If the infant's parents and caregivers provide consistent, caring, and adequate treatment, the infant learns to trust the world as a safe place. If the infant is abused or not cared for adequately, he or she will learn that the world is an unsafe place. The sense of trust or mistrust is carried with the individual throughout life. Erickson identifies seven stages, which range from ages zero to age 65 and beyond.

1. **Basic trust vs. mistrust (age 0–1).**
Based on the parents' care, the infant learns to trust others and feel comfortable in the world or learns to distrust a world that is perceived to be unsafe.

2. **Autonomy vs. shame and doubt (age 1–3).**
Between the ages of one and three children learn to feel competent by feeding themselves, learning to use the toilet, and playing alone. If they do not accomplish these tasks successfully, children learn to doubt their own abilities.

3. **Initiative vs. guilt (age 3–5).**
During this stage, children learn to plan their own activities within the parents' guidelines. If the children do not learn these tasks, they develop guilt over their misbehavior.

4. **Industry vs. inferiority (age 5–11).**
In this stage children learn to meet the demands of parents, teachers, and peers. They learn to clean their rooms, do their homework, and ride a bike, for example. If they accomplish these tasks successfully, they learn that their effort (industry) leads to success. If they do not learn these tasks, Erikson believes that they develop a lifelong feeling of inferiority.

5. **Identity vs. role confusion (age 11–18).**
During this stage the child develops his or her identity. It is also during this stage that the child starts to prepare for work by gaining insights into personality, interests, and values as well as learning about the world of work. If these tasks are not successfully accomplished, the result is confusion over his or her role in life.

Philosophy is perfectly right in saying that life must be understood backward. But one forgets the other clause—that it must be lived forward.

Soren Kierkegaard

6. **Intimacy vs. isolation (age 18–40).**
This is an adult stage of development in which relationships are formed with a partner. The task is to develop loving and committed relationships with others that partially replace the bonds with parents. If this task is not completed, the adult remains isolated from others and has difficulty establishing meaningful relationships. He or she is less capable of full emotional development.

7. **Generativity vs. stagnation (age 40–65).**
During this adult stage, the person contributes to future generations through raising children, helping others, developing products, or coming up with creative new ideas. At this time, the person continues to grow and produce, but puts unfulfilled dreams aside and finds meaning in work and family. If this task is not accomplished, growth is stopped and the person becomes stagnant and self-centered.

8. **Integrity vs. despair (age 65 plus).**
At this stage, people reap the benefits of all that they have done during their life and accept the fact that life is temporary. If this task is not accomplished, the individual is in despair and struggles to find meaning in life.

JOURNAL ENTRY #1
What is your life stage according to Erik Erikson?

Daniel Levinson

The research and writing by Daniel Levinson has been very useful in understanding adult development and career development.[3] Levinson proposes four stages in adult development:

1. Pre-adulthood
2. Early adulthood (age 17–45)
3. Middle adulthood (age 40–60)
4. Late adulthood (age 60–65)

Each of these stages of adulthood alternates between stable and transitional periods. Stable periods last six to seven years, during which people pursue their goals and create a desired structure in their lives. Transitional periods last four to five years, during which people question and reappraise the structure and consider making changes. These transitional periods provide the opportunity for growth and reflection.

These stable and transitional periods are related to age. Levinson's research showed that people do vary a little on the onset or termination of each stage, but generally by not more than two years. He also believes that people go through these stages in a fixed sequence during which certain developmental tasks present themselves in a fixed order. How a person deals with these developmental tasks has a big impact on later life. Transitional and stable periods, including developmental tasks, are summarized below. As you read each description, think about your life stage and where you may be headed in the future.

- **Age 17–22 Transitional Period.**
  The task here is to move from adolescence to young adulthood and to separate from parents.

- **Age 22–28 Stable Period.**
  This is a period of settling down and creating life structure, while still keeping the options open to explore jobs and relationships.

- **Age 28–33 Transitional Period.**
  During this period, adults reappraise their current life structure. There is the feeling that if a change is to be made, it must be made before it is too late.

- **Age 33–40 Stable Period.**
  During this time, adults build clear work, family, and leisure roles. The need to attain one's dream is powerful and intense. Levinson says that this stage ends with a BOOP (Becoming One's Own Person). Women often have the challenge of balancing work and family roles at this time.

- **Age 40–45 Transitional Period.**
  This is a time of turmoil. Up to 80 percent of men and 85 percent of women experience a moderate to severe crisis at this time.[4] At this point there is an awareness of human mortality and the feeling that half of life is now over. There is often a generational shift at this point; adults may have teenage children, and their parents are getting old or have passed away. At this point adults assess their progress toward accomplishing their dream. If the dream has not been accomplished, there is a sense of failure. If the dream has been accomplished, the person considers whether it was worth the effort and wonders, "Is this all there is?" Women are often juggling three roles: career, marriage, and motherhood. Only 4 percent of women manage to have it all: marriage, motherhood, and a full-time career.[5] Efforts to combine these roles often do not provide the satisfaction that women expect.

- **Age 45–50 Stable Period.**
  During this period, adults work on stable life structures for the middle years. They often have more autonomy and flexibility in choosing roles.

- **Age 50–55 Transitional Period.**
  Adults continue to work on questions raised during the midlife crisis.

- **Age 55–60 Stable Period.**
  Adults work on stable life structures.

- **Age 60–65 Transitional Period.**
  Adults deal with retirement transitions.

JOURNAL ENTRY #2

What is your life stage according to Daniel Levinson?

Gail Sheehy

Gail Sheehy is a journalist who became famous in 1976 for her book *Passages*. She continued to survey current research on life stages in her 1995 book, *New Passages*. In her later book she looks at the research as well as historical events to describe some new trends in adult life stages. She notes that because of increasing life spans, earlier theories of life stages need to be updated. Previous theories of life development covered a life span to age 65. Sheehy notes that women today who reach 50 (without developing cancer or heart disease) can expect to live to be 92 years old. Men who are healthy and live to age 65 can expect to live until the age of 81.[6] She quotes the president of a nursing home: "Twenty years ago I'd see 40-year-olds bringing in their 60-year-old parents. Now I'm seeing seventy-year-olds bringing in their ninety-year-old parents."[7]

The good news is that we will all be living longer and healthier lives in the years to come. In terms of life stages, Sheehy states that "the territory of the mid-forties, fifties and sixties and beyond is changing so fundamentally it now opens up whole new passages and stages of life." She asks us to "stop and recalculate. Imagine the day you turn 45 as the infancy of another life . . . a second adulthood in middle life."[8] She divides adult life stages into the stages:

- Provisional adulthood (18–30)
- First adulthood (30–45)
- Second adulthood (45–85)

Provisional Adulthood and the Try-Out 20s (age 18–30)

This stage is traditionally characterized by two opposing goals: (1) a desire for exploration and (2) a desire for stability. Historically this was a time to finish one's education move away from the parents' home to start a career and family. Young people are now living at home longer, and the period of adolescence has been extended. The author notes that of unmarried American men between 25 and 34, more than one third are still living at home.[9] She describes a dramatic shift that occurs around the age of 30. "Before the shift men and women feel unable to make clear choices or cope with life's vicissitudes without expecting some help from parents. After the shift they feel confident enough in their own values to make their own choices and competent enough in life skills to set a course."[10]

Some challenges for the Try-Out 20s include coping with a rapidly changing world:

- Views on marriage are changing. Young women have seen their mothers struggling to balance career, marriage, and children. Many young people are delaying marriage into the 20s or 30s or are deciding not to get married at all.
- Sheehy notes that in previous generations the enemies were external: wars, communism, and the nuclear bomb. Today for many young people, the enemies are internal: drugs, guns, and violence.
- The world has become more unpredictable and violent. Many teenagers do not feel safe in their schools or communities.
- There is a growing gap between the rich and poor.
- There is increased competition for jobs.
- Young people have to reassess their morals, as they become full of fear and anxiety about sex outside of marriage.
- Many worry that they are being educated for jobs that no longer exist.

Some positives include the following:

- This group is becoming more educated: by age 20 to 24, 58 percent of women and 53 percent of men have some college education or have graduated from college.
- Because of increased education, this group will be better able to adapt to change and to do freelance or free-agent work.
- This generation is becoming more ethnically diverse and is more receptive to multiculturalism.
- They will participate in great advances in technology and biotechnology.
- This group will use the Internet to conduct business in a more efficient way than ever before.
- Since young people are waiting longer to marry, they may have fewer divorces.[11]

First Adulthood: The Turbulent 30s and the Flourishing 40s

Thirty-year-olds step into first adulthood with questions about who they are and what life is all about. They pay the rent or mortgage, make the car payment, and take care of the children. Maybe they used to say that someone over 30 could not be trusted. Now they are 30 themselves and become conscious that they are getting older. At age 35, they take inventory and ask, "Is half of my life over? Is this what it is all about?" These questions are the beginning of a mid-life crisis. Since people are living longer, half of their life is not over at age 35. The mid-life crisis used to happen around age 38–43. Gail Sheehy suggests that the mid-life crisis is now often delayed until the mid-40s.

A **mid-life crisis** is a major transition in life in which we question what we did during the first half of our life. The central issue in mid-life is dealing with growing older and our own mortality. During this time adults make major changes in their lives. They may start a new hobby, change careers, go back to school, start a new business, get a divorce, or buy a new sports car. During this transition adults often go through what Gail Sheehy calls middlescence, which she defines as adolescence the second time around. She gives this example:

> "At forty-eight I lost forty pounds, looked younger than I did at forty and took up a long-repressed passion—music," says a typical homemaker. Jeannie enrolled in music school to study electric bass and drums. She now plays in a garage rock band with 18-year-old boys. She already has planned her antidote to "hardening of the attitudes." After 65 she plans to launch a heavy metal band called Guns and Geezers.[12]

Men and women are often at a crossroads going in different directions during this mid-life transition. If women married and had children, their children are often grown, and there is a void in their lives. This is called the "empty nest" syndrome. At this stage in life, women may look to a career and work as a source of fulfillment and motivation. At the same point many men think about future retirement and spending more time in leisure activities. They often become more interested in family. They realize that no one ever wished on his deathbed that he had put in more time at the office. Because men and women are struggling with their identity and often have different goals in life during this period, divorce is often the outcome.

While the mid-life crisis can be dangerous, it can have some positive outcomes. Adults look at their lives and make changes that lead to continued growth and enjoy-

Reprinted with Special Permission of King Features Syndicate.

ment of life. The mid-life crisis is a gateway to a new beginning or second adulthood. Half of life is not over; half of life lies ahead, and adults can take advantage of their experiences in the first half of life to find exciting new opportunities in the second half.

Second Adulthood: The Ages of Mastery and Integrity

The second adulthood begins with the resolution of the mid-life crisis at around age 45 and goes to age 85 or longer. We expect that people will be living into their eighties and nineties and leading healthy and productive lives. Sheehy divides the second adulthood into two stages: the Age of Mastery (45–65) and the Age of Integrity (65–85 or beyond).[13]

The Age of Mastery (45–65) marks the apex of life in which people have a stable psychological sense of mastery. People face the second half of life with fifty years of experience in living. Sheehy states that "45 represents the old age of youth, while 50 initiates the youth of Second Adulthood." She compares life to watching a play:

> It's as though when we are young, we have seen only the first act of the play. By our forties we have reached the climactic second-act curtain. Only as we approach fifty does the shape and meaning of the whole play become clear.[14]

People in their fifties are more serene about their mortality. At age 35, our mortality becomes a realization and at age 40, it becomes a terrifying idea. We try to turn back the clock. At age 50, we are better able to accept the aging process. We have had experience with life and have successfully dealt with many challenges. At this age, many may even feel physically fit and devote time to exercise and better health. The question is, "How long do I want to live and how can I invest my time in my mental and physical health?"

Successful aging does not happen automatically. To age successfully, people need to look at their priorities and determine what is most important in life. Successful aging means taking an active part in life rather than being sedentary and inactive. The central question of this age is a search for the meaning of life. People find meaning by searching for their passion. They need to find what they really enjoy and do it.

Many Baby Boomers (born between 1946 and 1965) are now approaching this age. Sheehy notes that one-third of all women in the United States today have passed their fiftieth birthday. At this age, women are independent, enjoy learning new skills, start new careers, and begin new adventures. They enjoy greater well-being than at any other time in life. Sheehy found that education is a key factor to well-being and happiness at this age. Of the women she surveyed, those who measured near the top on the scale of well-being had completed college or earned a graduate degree.[15] She also reports that women who are age 50 say that this age feels like "an optimistic, can-do stage of life."[16]

Men face more difficult times in their fifties. Men frequently base their identity on their career; and many men in their fifties are unemployed, underemployed or hate their jobs. They are often the victims of an economy that is downsizing.[17] Sheehy believes that men at this age need to move from competing in the workplace to connecting with people who are important to them. Men may try to connect with children and family, but the children may have already left home. She also notes that men from age 45 to 64 who live with their wives live ten years longer than their unmarried counterparts.[18] One of the male participants in Sheehy's surveys states that he had to come to realize that "a lot of good friendships is better than a lot of money."[19]

The Age of Integrity (65–85 and beyond) is a new life stage resulting from the extended average life span. In the "serene sixties," only ten percent of Americans 65 and older have a chronic health problem that restricts them from carrying on a major activity. Those who do have chronic health problems are often suffering as a result of neglecting their health at earlier ages.[20] In the sixties, most people are healthy and looking forward to using their experience with life to make contributions to their families and community. An example of a woman in the "serene sixties" is Deborah Szekely, a pioneer in creating fitness spas. She says that life can be divided into three parts:

> The first third of life is devoted to being a child, learning in school and at home. The next third is spent working as hard as you're able and being rewarded for it. The final third is perhaps the most important: taking a role in making the world better for the next generation.[21]

People who have lived to the Age of Integrity have learned to deal with life. They have passed through many stages and dealt with many crises. They have learned how to put life into perspective. Gail Sheehy cites a study of Harvard men done over a period of years in which it was found that "even the most painful and traumatic events in childhood had virtually no effect on the well-being of these men in their mid-sixties."[22] It takes about sixty-five years for human beings to finally figure it all out and to be happy with their lives!

Retirement is one of the most difficult transitions in the Age of Integrity. It used to be that people worked for about thirty years and then retired. However, if a person retires at age 65, there are still twenty to thirty years of life to live. A new idea is serial retirement. A person retires from one career and enters a new career and retires again. This happens because of the need to stay active and involved as well as the need to extend financial resources over a longer life span. It is difficult to predict how much money will be needed to retire twenty or thirty years into the future. To successfully move through the retirement transition, people need to continue to grow and learn how to play after a life of work.

Gail Sheehy summarizes some of the research on factors contributing to health and well-being in the sixties and beyond.[23]

- Having mature love (a wife, husband, partner) is more important than money or power.
- Continued growth experiences and feeling an excitement about life help people to feel happy.
- It is important to find your passion and pursue it.
- Exercise is the most important factor in retarding the aging process. It was found that men and women who walk a half-hour a day cut their mortality rates in half.[24]

Many people are living to the age of 90 to 100. Gail Sheehy describes the **characteristics of successful centenarians:**

> Characteristics of healthy centenarians, garnered from a number of studies, are these: most have high native intelligence, a keen interest in current events, a good memory, and few illnesses. They tend to be early risers, sleeping on average between six and seven hours. Most drink coffee, follow no special diets, but generally prefer diets high in protein, low in fat. There is no uniformity in their drinking habits, but they use less medication in their lifetimes than many old people use in a week. They prefer living in the present, with changes, and are usually religious in the broad sense. All have a degree of optimism and a marked sense of humor. Life seems to have been a great adventure.[25]

Sheehy defines successful aging as "sageing." Sageing is defined as "the process by which men and women accumulate wisdom and grow into the culture's sages."[26] The stages of our lives are like a spiral pattern. We move through successive stages gaining understanding and experience. Erik Erikson and his wife, Joan, wrote a book in their eighties titled *Vital Involvement in Old Age*, in which they described the patterns of the life cycle and how we learn from experience:

> The life cycle does more than extend itself into the next generation. It curves back on the life of the individual, allowing . . . a reexamination of earlier stages in a new form.[27]

Writer F. Scott Fitzgerald said that we need to learn "to accept life not as a series of random events but as path of awakening."[28] We learn and grow and develop over a lifetime. Knowing about the stages of our lives helps us to realize that as long as we continue to grow and develop, we can awaken to each new day with the prospect of continued satisfaction and enjoyment of life.

JOURNAL ENTRY #3

What is your life stage according to Gail Sheehy?

QUIZ
Understanding Life Stages

Test what you have learned by selecting the correct answer to the following questions.

1. Erik Erikson believes that all human beings pass through eight stages of development

   a. that last ten years for each stage.
   b. in a random pattern.
   c. in a fixed order.

2. According to Erikson, the main task of the identity vs. role confusion stage (age 11–18) is

   a. learning to follow the rules of society.
   b. discovering personality and interests in preparation for work.
   c. forming intimate relationships.

3. Daniel Levinson says that stages of adult development alternate between

   a. stable and transitional periods.
   b. calm and stressful periods.
   c. integrity and despair.

4. The midlife crisis is defined as

   a. a brief period of insanity.
   b. a major transition in which we question what we did in the first half of life.
   c. the realization that half of life is over.

5. Factors contributing to successful aging include

   a. increasing time for relaxation.
   b. continuing exercise throughout life.
   c. reflecting on past accomplishments.

How did you do on the quiz? Check your answers: 1. c, 2. b, 3. a, 4. b, 5. b

Thinking Positively about Your Life

Thinking positively about yourself and your life is one of the most important skills you can learn for your future success. Following are some ways to practice positive thinking.

Believe in Yourself

Anthony Robbins defines belief as "any guiding principle, dictum, faith, or passion that can provide meaning and direction in life . . . Beliefs are the compass and maps that guide us toward our goals and give us the surety to know we'll get there."[29] The beliefs that we have about ourselves determine how much of our potential we will use and how successful we will be in the future. If we have positive beliefs about ourselves, we will feel confident and accomplish our goals in life. Negative beliefs get in the way of our success. Robbins reminds us that we can change our beliefs and choose new ones if necessary.

> The birth of excellence begins with our awareness that our beliefs are a choice. We usually do not think of it that way, but belief can be a conscious choice. You can choose beliefs that limit you, or you can choose beliefs that support you. The trick is to choose the beliefs that are conducive to success and the results you want and to discard the ones that hold you back.[30]

The Self-Fulfilling Prophecy

The first step in thinking positively is to examine your beliefs about yourself, your life, and the world around you. Personal beliefs are influenced by our environment, significant events that have happened in life, what we have learned in the past, and our picture of the future. Beliefs cause us to have certain expectations about the world and ourselves. These expectations are such a powerful influence on behavior that psychologists use the term "self-fulfilling prophecy" to describe what happens when our expectations come true.

For example, if I believe that I am not good in math (my expectation), I may not try to do the assignment or may avoid taking a math class (my behavior). As a result, I am not good in math. My expectations have been fulfilled. Expectations can also have a positive effect. If I believe that I am a good student, I will take steps to enroll in college and complete my assignments. I will then become a good student. The prophecy will again come true.

Psychologist Robert Rosenthal has done some interesting research on the self-fulfilling prophecy. He describes the following experiment:

> Twelve experimenters were each given five rats that were taught to run a maze with the aid of visual cues. Six of the experimenters were told that their rats had been specially bred for maze-brightness; the other six were told that their rats had been bred for maze-dullness. Actually, there was no difference between the rats. At the end of the experiment, researchers with "maze-bright" rats found superior learning in their rats compared to the researchers with "maze-dull" rats.[31]

Rosenthal also did experiments with human subjects. Students in an elementary school were given an IQ test. Researchers told the teachers that this was a test that

> If I believe I cannot do something, it makes me incapable of doing it. But when I believe I can, then I acquire the ability to do it, even if I did not have the ability in the beginning.
>
> Mahatma Gandhi

would determine "intellectual blooming." An experimental group of these students was chosen at random and teachers were told to expect remarkable gains in intellectual achievement in these children during the next eight months. At the end of this time, researchers gave the IQ test again. Students in the experimental group in which the teachers expected "intellectual blooming" actually gained higher IQ points than the control group. In addition, teachers described these students as more "interesting, curious and happy" than the control group. The teachers' expectations resulted in a self-fulfilling prophecy.

To think positively, it is necessary to recognize your negative beliefs and turn them into positive beliefs. Some negative beliefs commonly heard from college students include the following:

> I don't have the money for college.
> English was never my best subject.
> I was never any good at math.

When you hear yourself saying these negative thoughts, remember that these thoughts can become self-fulfilling prophecies. First of all, notice the thought. Then see if you can change the statement into a positive statement such as:

> I can find the money for college.
> English has been a challenge for me in the past, but I will do better this time.
> I can learn to be good at math.

If you believe that you can find money for college, you can go to the financial aid office and the scholarship office to begin your search for money to attend school. You can look for a better job or improve your money management. If you believe that you will do better in English, you will keep up with your assignments and ask the teacher for help. If you believe that you can learn to be good at math, you will attend every math class and seek tutoring when you do not understand. Your positive thoughts will help you to be successful.

Positive Self-Talk and Affirmations

Self-talk refers to the silent inner voice in our heads. This voice is often negative, especially when we are frustrated or trying to learn something new. Have you ever had thoughts about yourself that are similar to these:

> How could you be so stupid!
> That was dumb!
> You idiot!

> Human beings can alter their lives by altering their attitude of mind.
>
> William James

ACTIVITY

What do you say to yourself when you are angry or frustrated? Write several examples of your negative self-talk.

We are what we think.
All that we are arises
With our thoughts.
With our thoughts
we make the world.

Buddha

Negative thoughts can actually be toxic to your body. They can cause biochemical changes that can lead to depression and negatively affect the immune system.[32] Negative self-talk causes anxiety and poor performance and is damaging to self-esteem. It can also lead to a negative self-fulfilling prophecy. Positive thoughts can help us build self-esteem, become confident in our abilities, and achieve our goals. These positive thoughts are called affirmations.

If we make the world with our thoughts, it is important to become aware of the thoughts about ourselves that are continuously running through our heads. Are your thoughts positive or negative? Negative thoughts lead to failure. What we hear over and over again shapes our beliefs. If you say over and over to yourself such things as, "I am stupid," "I am ugly," or "I am fat," you will start to believe these things and act in a way that supports your beliefs. Positive thoughts help to build success. If you say to yourself, "I'm a good person," "I'm doing my best," or "I'm doing fine," you will begin to believe these things about yourself and act in a way that supports these beliefs. Here are some guidelines for increasing your positive self-talk and making affirmations:

1. Monitor your thoughts about yourself and become aware of them. Are they positive or negative?
2. When you notice a negative thought about yourself, imagine rewinding a tape and recording a new positive message.
3. Start the positive message with "I" and use the present tense. Using an "I" statement shows you are in charge. Using the present tense shows you are ready for action now.
4. Focus on the positive. Think about what you want to achieve and what you can do rather than what you do not want to do. For example, instead of saying, "I will not eat junk food," say, "I will eat a healthy diet."
5. Make your affirmation stronger by adding an emotion to it.

6. Form a mental picture of what it is that you want to achieve. See yourself doing it successfully.

7. You may need to say the positive thoughts over and over again until you believe them and they become a habit. You can also write them down and put them in a place where you will see them often.

Here are some examples of negative self-talk and a contrasting positive affirmations:

Negative: I'm always broke.

Affirmation: I feel really good when I manage my finances. See yourself taking steps to manage finances. For example, a budget or savings plan.

Negative: I'm too fat. It just runs in the family.

Affirmation: I feel good about myself when I exercise and eat a healthy diet. See yourself exercising and eating a healthy diet.

Negative: I can't do this. I must be stupid.

Affirmation: I can do this. I am capable. I feel a sense of accomplishment when I accomplish something challenging. See yourself making your best attempt and taking the first step to accomplish the project.

ACTIVITY

Select one example of negative self-talk that you wrote earlier. Use the examples above to turn your negative message into a positive one and write it here.

Visualize Your Success

Visualization is a powerful tool for using your brain to improve memory, deal with stress, and think positively. Coaches and athletes study sports psychology to learn how to use visualization along with physical practice to improve athletic performance. College students can use the same techniques to enhance college success.

If you are familiar with sports or are an athlete, you can probably think of times when your coach asked you to use visualization to improve your performance. In baseball, the coach reminds players to keep their eye on the ball and visualize hitting it. In swimming, the coach asks swimmers to visualize reaching their arms out to touch the edge of the pool at the end of the race. Pole-vaulters visualize clearing the pole and sometimes even go through the motions before making the jump. Using imagery lets you practice for future events and pre-experience achieving your goals. Athletes imagine winning the race or completing the perfect jump in figure skating. In this way they prepare mentally and physically and develop confidence in their abilities.

Just as the athlete visualizes and then performs, the college student can do the same. It is said we create all things twice. First we make a mental picture, and then we create the physical reality by taking action. For example if we are building a house, we first get the idea; then we begin to design the house we want. We start with a blueprint and then build the house. The blueprint determines what kind of house we construct. The same thing happens in any project we undertake. First we have a mental picture and then we complete the project. Visualize what you would like to accomplish in your life as if you were creating a blueprint. Then take the steps to accomplish what you want.

As a college student, you might visualize yourself in your graduation robe walking across the stage to receive your diploma. You might visualize yourself in the exam room confidently taking the exam. You might see yourself on the job enjoying your future career. You can make a mental picture of what you would like your life to be and then work toward accomplishing your goal.

Hope for the Best

Believing that you will accomplish your goals and build a good future for yourself can help you to be successful. One research study showed that for entering college freshmen, level of hope was a better predictor of college grades than standardized tests or high school grade point average.[33] Students with a high level of hope set higher goals and worked to attain those goals. Hopeful people use positive self-talk and believe that the future will be good. They change goals and plans when necessary. People who are not hopeful about the future use negative self-talk and become victims of the negative self-fulfilling prophecy.

Successful Beliefs

Steven Covey's book, *The 7 Habits of Highly Successful People* has been described as one of the most influential books of the 20th century.[34] In 2004 he released a new book called *The 8th Habit: From Effectiveness to Greatness.*[35] These habits are based on beliefs that lead to success.

1. **Be proactive.**
   Being proactive means accepting responsibility for your life. Covey uses the word "response-ability" for the ability to choose responses. The quality of your life is based on the decisions and responses that you make. Proactive people make things happen through responsibility and initiative. They do not blame circumstances or conditions for their behavior.

> The future first exists in imagination, then planning, then reality.
>
> R.A. Wilson

2. **Begin with the end in mind.**
   Know what is important and what you wish to accomplish in your life. To be able to do this, you will need to know your values and goals in life. You will need a clear vision of what you want your life to be and where you are headed.

3. **Put first things first.**
   Once you have established your goals and vision for the future, you will need to manage yourself to do what is important first. Set priorities so that you can accomplish the tasks that are important to you.

4. **Think win-win.**
   In human interactions, seek solutions that benefit everyone. Focus on cooperation rather than competition. If everyone feels good about the decision, there is cooperation and harmony. If one person wins and the other loses, the loser becomes angry and resentful.

5. **First seek to understand, then to be understood.**
   Too often in our personal communications, we try to talk first and listen later. Often we don't really listen; we use this time to think of our reply. It is best to listen and understand before speaking. Effective communication is one of the most important skills in life.

6. **Synergize.**
   A simple definition of synergy is that the whole is greater than the sum of its parts. If people can cooperate and have good communication, they can work together as a team to accomplish more than each individual could do separately. Synergy is also part of the creative process.

7. **Sharpen the saw.**
   Covey shares the story of a man who was trying to cut down a tree with a dull saw. As he struggled to cut the tree, someone suggested that he stop and sharpen the saw. The man said that he did not have time to sharpen the saw, so he continued to struggle. Covey suggests that we need to take time to stop and sharpen the saw. We need to stop working and invest some time in ourselves by staying healthy physically, mentally, spiritually, and socially. We need to take time for self-renewal.

8. **Find your voice, and inspire others to find theirs.**
   Believe that you can make a positive difference in the world and inspire others to do the same. Covey says that leaders "deal with people in a way that will communicate to them their worth and potential so clearly that they will come to see it in themselves." Accomplishing this ideal begins with developing one's own voice or "unique personal significance."[36]

Successful Beliefs

- Be proactive
- Begin with the end in mind
- Put first things first
- Think win-win
- First seek to understand, then to be understood
- Synergize
- Sharpen the saw
- Find your voice, and inspire others to find theirs

QUIZ
Positive Thinking

Test what you have learned by selecting the correct answer to the following questions.

1. When teachers were told to expect "intellectual blooming" in their students,

    a. students gained IQ points at the end of the year.
    b. students had the same IQ at the end of the year.
    c. students became frustrated because of high teacher expectations.

2. Positive self-talk results in

    a. lower self-esteem.
    b. over confidence.
    c. higher self-esteem.

3. The statement, "We create all things twice," refers to

    a. doing the task twice to make sure it is done right.

    b. creating and refining.
    c. first making a mental picture and then taking action.

4. A win-win solution means

    a. winning at any cost.
    b. seeking a solution that benefits everyone.
    c. focusing on competition.

5. The statement by Steven Covey, "Sharpen the saw," refers to

    a. proper tool maintenance.
    b. studying hard to sharpen thinking skills.
    c. investing time to maintain physical and mental health.

How did you do on the quiz? Check your answers: 1. a, 2. c, 3. c, 4. b, 5. c

Secrets to Happiness

> The three grand essentials of happiness are: something to do, someone to love, and something to hope for.
>
> Thomas Chalmers

Many of you probably have happiness on your list of lifetime goals. It sounds easy, right? But what is happiness, anyway?

Psychologist Martin Seligman says that real happiness comes from identifying, cultivating, and using your personal strengths in work, love, play, and parenting."[37] You have identified these strengths by learning about your personality type, learning style, interests, and values.

Seligman contrasts authentic happiness with hedonism. He states that a hedonist "wants as many good moments and as few bad moments as possible in life."[38] Hedonism is a shortcut to happiness that leaves us feeling empty. For example, we often assume that more material possessions will make us happy. However, the more material possessions we have, the greater the expectations, and we no longer appreciate what we have.

> Suppose you could be hooked up to a hypothetical "experience machine" that, for the rest of your life, would stimulate your brain and give you any positive feelings you desire. Most people to whom I offer this imaginary choice refuse the machine. It is not just positive feelings we want, we want to be entitled to our positive feelings. Yet we have invented myriad shortcuts to feeling good: drugs, chocolate, loveless sex, shopping, masturbation, and television are all examples. (I am not, however, suggesting that you should drop these shortcuts altogether.) The belief that we can rely on shortcuts to happiness, joy, rapture,

comfort, and ecstasy, rather than be entitled to these feelings by the exercise of personal strengths and virtues, leads to the legions of people who in the middle of great wealth are starving spiritually. Positive emotion alienated from the exercise of character leads to emptiness, to inauthenticity, to depression, and as we age, to the gnawing realization that we are fidgeting until we die.[39]

Most people assume that happiness is increased by having more money to buy that new car or HDTV. However, a process called hedonistic adaptation occurs which makes this type of happiness short lived. Once you have purchased the new car or TV, you get used to it quickly. Soon you will start to think about a better car and a bigger TV to continue to feel happy. Seligman provides a formula for happiness:[40]

$$\text{Happiness} = S + C + V$$

In the formula S stands for set range. Psychologists believe that 50 percent of happiness is determined by heredity. In other words, half of your level of happiness is determined by the genes inherited from your ancestors. In good times or bad times, people generally return to their set range of happiness. Six months after receiving a piece of good fortune such as a raise, promotion, or winning the lottery, unhappy people are still unhappy. Six months after a tragedy, naturally happy people return to being happy.

The letter C in the equation stands for circumstances such as money, marriage, social life, health, education, climate, race, gender, and religion. These circumstances account for 8 to 15 percent of happiness. Here is what psychologists know about how these circumstances affect happiness:

- Once basic needs are met, greater wealth does not increase happiness.
- Having a good marriage is related to increased happiness.
- Happy people are more social.
- Moderate ill health does not bring unhappiness, but severe illness does.
- Educated people are slightly happier.
- Climate, race, and gender do not affect level of happiness.
- Religious people are somewhat happier than nonreligious people.

The letter V in the equation stands for factors under your voluntary control. These factors account for approximately 40 percent of happiness. Factors under voluntary control include positive emotions and optimism about the future. Positive emotions include hope, faith, trust, joy, ecstasy, calm, zest, ebullience, pleasure, flow, satisfaction, contentment, fulfillment, pride, and serenity. Seligman suggests the following ideas to increase your positive emotions:

- Realize that the past does not determine your future. The future is open to new possibilities.
- Be grateful for the good events of the past and place less emphasis on the bad events.
- Build positive emotions through forgiving and forgetting.
- Work on increasing optimism and hope for the future.
- Find out what activities make you happy and engage in them. Spread these activities out over time so that you will not get tired of them.
- Take the time to savor the happy times. Make mental photographs of happy times so that you can think of them later.
- Take time to enjoy the present moment.
- Build more flow into your life. Flow is the state of gratification we feel when totally absorbed in an activity that matches our strengths.

Are you interested in taking steps to increase your happiness? Here are some activities proposed by Sonya Lyubomirsky, a leading researcher on happiness and author of *The How of Happiness*.[41] Choose the ones that seem like a natural fit for you and vary them so that they do not become routine or boring. After putting in some effort to practice these activities, they can become a habit.

1.   Express gratitude.

Expressing gratitude is a way of thinking positively and appreciating good circumstances rather than focusing on the bad ones. It is about appreciating and thanking the people who have made a positive contribution to your life. It is feeling grateful for the good things you have in life. Create a gratitude journal and at the end of each day write down things for which you are grateful or thankful. Regularly tell those around you how grateful you are to have them in your life. You can do this in person, by phone, in a letter or by email. Being grateful helps us to savor positive life experiences.

2.   Cultivate optimism.

Make it a habit of looking at the bright side of life. If you think positively about the future, you are more likely to take the effort to reach your goals in life. Spend some time thinking or writing about your best possible future. Make a mental picture of your future goals as a first step toward achieving them. Thinking positively boosts your mood and promotes high morale. Most importantly, thinking positively can become a self-fulfilling prophecy. If you see your positive goals as attainable, you are more likely to work toward accomplishing them and invest the energy needed to deal with obstacles and setbacks along the way.

3.   Avoid overthinking and social comparison.

Overthinking is focusing on yourself and your problems endlessly, needlessly and excessively. Examples of overthinking include, "Why am I so unhappy?," "Why is life so unfair?," or "Why did he/she say that?." Overthinking increases sadness, fosters biased thinking, decreases motivation and makes it difficult to solve problems and take action to make life better.

Social comparison is a type of overthinking. In our daily lives, we encounter people who are more intelligent, beautiful, richer, healthier or happier. The media fosters images of people with impossibly perfect lives. Making social comparisons can lead to feelings of inferiority and loss of self-esteem.

Notice when your are overthinking or making comparisons with others and stop doing it. Use the yell "Stop" technique to refocus your attention. This technique involves yelling "Stop" to yourself or out loud to change your thinking. Another way to stop overthinking is to distract yourself with more positive thoughts or activities. Watch a funny movie, listen to music or arrange a social activity with a friend. If these activities are not effective, try writing down your worries in a journal. Writing helps to organize thoughts and to make sense of them. Begin to take some small steps to resolve your worries and problems.

4.   Practice acts of kindness.

Doing something kind for others increases your own personal happiness and satisfies our basic need for human connection. Opportunities for helping others surround us each day. How about being courteous on the freeway, helping a child with homework, or helping your elderly neighbor with yard work? A simple act of kindness makes you feel good and often sets off a chain of events in which the person who receives the kindness does something kind for someone else.

5.   Increase flow activities.

Flow is defined as intense involvement in an activity so that you do not notice the passage of time. Musicians are in the flow when they are totally involved in their music. Athletes are in the flow when they are totally focused on their sport. Writers are in the

Finish each day and be done with it. You have done what you could; some blunders and absurdities have crept in; forget them as soon as you can. Tomorrow is a new day; you shall begin it serenely and with too high a spirit to be encumbered with your old nonsense.

Ralph Waldo Emerson

flow then they are totally absorbed in writing down their ideas. The key to achieving flow is balancing skills and challenges. If your skills are not sufficient for the activity, you will become frustrated. If your skills are greater than what is demanded for the activity, you will become bored. Work often provides an opportunity to experience flow if you are in a situation in which your work activities are matched to your skills and talents.

As our skills increase, it becomes more difficult to maintain flow. We must be continually testing ourselves in ever more challenging activities to maintain flow. You can take some action to increase the flow in your life by learning to fully focus your attention on the activity you are doing. It is important to be open to new and different experiences. To maintain the flow in your life, make a commitment to lifelong learning.

6.   Savor life's joys.

Savoring is the repetitive replaying of the positive experiences in life and is one of the most important ingredients of happiness. Savoring happens in the past, present and future. Think often about the good things that have happened in the past. Savor the present by relishing the present moment. Savor the future by anticipating and visualizing positive events or outcomes in the future.

There are many ways to savor life's joys. Replay in your mind happy days or events from the past. Create a photo album of your favorite people, places and events and look at it often. This prolongs the happiness. Take a few minutes each day to appreciate ordinary activities such as taking a shower or walking to work. Engage the senses to notice your environment. Is it a sunny day? Take some time to look at the sky, the trees and plants. Landscape architects incorporate art work, trees and flowers along the freeways to help drivers to relax on the road. Notice art and objects of beauty. Be attentive to the present moment and be aware of your surroundings. Picture in your mind positive events you anticipate in the future. All of these activities will increase your "psychological bank account" of happy times and will help deal with times that are not so happy.

7.   Commit to accomplishing your goals.

Working toward a meaningful life goal is one of the most important things that you can do to have a happy life. Goals provide structure and meaning to our lives and improves self-esteem. Working on goals provides something to look forward to in the future.

The types of goals that you pursue have an impact on your happiness. The goals that have the most potential for long term happiness involve changing your activities rather than changing your circumstances. Examples of goals that change your circumstances are moving to the beach or buying a new stereo. These goals make you happy for a short time. Then you get used to your new circumstances and no longer feel as happy as when you made the initial change. Examples of goals that change your activities are returning to school or taking up a new sport or hobby. These activities allow you to take on new challenges which keep life interesting for a longer period of time. Choose intrinsic goals that help you to develop your competence and autonomy. These goals should match your most important values and interests.

8.   Take care of your body.

Engaging in physical activity provides many opportunities for increasing happiness. Physical activity helps to:

- Increase longevity and improve the quality of life.
- Improve sleep and protect the body from disease.
- Keep brains healthy and avoid cognitive impairments.
- Increase self-esteem.
- Increase the opportunity to engage in flow.
- Provide a distraction from worries and overthinking.

> Happiness consists more in small conveniences or pleasures that occur every day, than in great pieces of good fortune that happen but seldom.
>
> Benjamin Franklin

> An aim in life is the only fortune worth finding.
>
> Robert Louis Stevenson

David Myers, a professor of psychology at Hope College in Michigan, is a leading researcher on happiness. He says that 90 percent of us are naturally happy. He adds that if most of us "were characteristically unhappy, the emotional pain would lose its ability to alert us to an unusual and possibly harmful condition."[42]

Just as you have made a decision to get a college degree, make a decision to be happy. Make a decision to be happy by altering your internal outlook and choosing to change your behavior. Here are some suggestions for consciously choosing happiness.

1. Find small things that make you happy and sprinkle your life with them. A glorious sunset, a pat on the back, a well-manicured yard, an unexpected gift, a round of tennis, a favorite sandwich, a fishing line cast on a quiet lake, the wagging tail of the family dog, or your child finally taking some responsibility—these are things that will help to create a continual climate of happiness.[43]

2. Smile and stand up straight. Michael Mercer and Maryann Troiani, authors of *Spontaneous Optimism: Proven Strategies for Health, Prosperity and Happiness,* say that "unhappy people tend to slouch, happy people don't. . . . Happy people even take bigger steps when they walk."[44]

3. Learn to think like an optimist. "Pessimists tend to complain; optimists focus on solving their problems."[45] Never use the word "try"; this word is for pessimists. Assume you will succeed.

4. Replace negative thoughts with positive ones.

5. Fill your life with things you like to do.

6. Get enough rest. If you do not get enough sleep, you will feel tired and gloomy. Sleep deprivation can lead to depression.

7. Learn from your elders. Psychologist Daniel Mroczek says that "people in their sixties and seventies who are in good health are among the happiest people in our society. . . . They may be better able to regulate their emotions, they've developed perspective, they don't get so worried about little things, and they've often achieved their goals and aren't trying to prove themselves."[46]

8. Reduce stress.

9. Take charge of your time by doing first things first.

10. Close relationships are important. Myers and Mroczek report higher levels of happiness among married men and women.[47]

11. Keep things in perspective. Will it matter in six months to a year?

12. Laugh more. Laughter produces a relaxation response.

Keys to Success

Keys to Success: You Are What You Think

Sometimes students enter college with the fear of failure. This belief leads to anxiety and behavior that leads to failure. If you have doubts about your ability to succeed in college, you might not go to class or attempt the challenging work required in college. It is difficult to make the effort if you cannot see positive results ahead. Unfortunately, failure in college can lead to a loss of confidence and lack of success in other areas of life as well.

Henry Ford said that "what we believe is true, comes true. What we believe is possible, becomes possible." If you believe that you will succeed, you will be more likely to take actions that lead to your success. Once you have experienced some small part of success, you will have confidence in your abilities and will continue on the road to success. Success leads to more success. It becomes a habit. You will be motivated to make the effort necessary to accomplish your goals. You might even become excited and energized along the way. You will use your gifts and talents to reach your potential and achieve happiness. It all begins with the thoughts you choose.

Watch your thoughts; they become words.
Watch your words; they become actions.
Watch your actions; they become habits.
Watch your habits; they become character.
Watch your character; it becomes your destiny.[48]

—Frank Outlaw

To help you choose positive beliefs, picture in your mind how you want your life to be. Imagine it is here now. See all the details and experience the feelings associated with this picture. Pretend it is true until you believe it. Then take action to make your dreams come true.

JOURNAL ENTRY #4

Write five intention statements about increasing your future happiness. I intend to . . .

 JOURNAL ENTRIES

Looking Toward the Future

Go to http://www.collegesuccess1.com/ for Word files of the Journal Entries

Success over the Internet

**Visit the *College Success Website* at
http://www.collegesuccess1.com/**

The *College Success Website* is continually
updated with new topics and links to the material
presented in this chapter. Topics include

- Adult development
- Happiness

- Self-improvement
- Self-esteem
- Sports psychology
- How to be successful

Contact your instructor if you have any problems in accessing the *College Success Website*.

Notes

1. Gail Sheehy, *Passages* (New York: E.P. Dutton, 1976) and *New Passages* (New York: Random House, 1995).
2. Erik H. Erikson, *Childhood and Society* (New York: W.W. Norton, 1963).
3. D. J. Levinson and J. D. Levinson, *Seasons of a Woman's Life* (New York: Knopf, 1996). D. J. Levinson, C. N. Darrow, E. B. Klein, M. H. Levinson, and B. McKee, *Seasons of a Man's Life* (New York: Knopf, 1978).
4. D. J. Levinson, "A Conception of Adult Development," *American Psychologist* 41 (1986): 107.
5. Levinson and Levinson, *Seasons of a Woman's Life*, 372.
6. Sheehy, *New Passages*, 5–6.
7. Ibid., 7.
8. Ibid., 6.
9. Ibid., 49.
10. Ibid., 52.
11. Ibid., 43–53.
12. Ibid., 140.
13. Ibid., 145.
14. Ibid., 150.
15. Ibid., 189.
16. Ibid., 191.
17. Ibid., 264.
18. Ibid., 335.
19. Ibid., 277.
20. Ibid., 351.
21. Ibid., 395.
22. Ibid., 356.
23. Ibid., 384.
24. Ibid., 426.
25. Ibid., 427.
26. Ibid., 420.
27. Erik Erikson, *Vital Involvement in Old Age* (New York: Brunner/Mazel, 1974), 112.
28. Sheehy, *New Passages*, 429.
29. Anthony Robbins, *Unlimited Power* (New York: Fawcett Columbine, 1986), 54–55.

30. Ibid., 57.
31. Robert Rosenthal, "Self-Fulfilling Prophecy," *Psychology Today,* September 1968.
32. Joan Smith, "Nineteen Habits of Happy Women," *Redbook Magazine,* August 1999, 68.
33. Daniel Goleman, "Hope Emerges a Key to Success in Life," *New York Times,* 24 December 1991.
34. Stephen R. Covey, *The Seven Habits of Highly Effective People* (New York: Simon and Schuster, 1989).
35. Stephen R. Covey. *The 8th Habit, from Effectiveness to Greatness* (New York: Free Press, 2004).
36. Ibid
37. Martin Seligman, *Authentic Happiness, Using the New Positive Psychology to Realize Your Potential for Lasting Fulfillment.* New York: Free Press, p. xiii.
38. Ibid, p. 6.
39. Ibid, p. 8.
40. Ibid, p. 45.
41. Sonya Lyubomirsky, *The How of Happiness* (New York: The Penguin Press, 2008).
42. Quoted in Joan Smith, "Nineteen Habits of Happy Women," *Redbook Magazine,* August 1999, 66.
43. Boal, "Happy Daze."
44. Quoted in Smith, "Nineteen Habits of Happy Women."
45. Ibid.
46. Ibid.
47. Ibid.
48. Rob Gilbert, ed., *Bits and Pieces* (Fairfield, NJ: The Economics Press), Vol. R, No. 40, p. 7, copyright 1998.

Measure Your Success

Name _____ Date _____

Now that you have finished the text, complete the following assessment to measure your improvement. Compare your results to the assessment taken at the beginning of class.

Directions: Read the following statements and rate how true they are for you at the present time.

5 Definitely true
4 Mostly true
3 Somewhat true
2 Seldom true
1 Never true

_____ I am motivated to be successful in college.

_____ I know the value of a college education.

_____ I know how to establish successful patterns of behavior.

_____ I can concentrate on an important task until it is completed.

_____ I am attending college to accomplish my own personal goals.

_____ I believe to a great extent that my actions determine my future.

_____ I am persistent in achieving my goals.

_____ **Total points for Motivation**

_____ I can describe my personality type.

_____ I can list careers that match my personality type.

_____ I can describe my personal strengths and talents based on my personality type.

_____ I understand how my personality type affects how I manage my time and money.

_____ I know what college majors are most in demand.

_____ I am confident that I have chosen the best major for myself.

_____ Courses related to my major are interesting and exciting to me.

_____ **Total points for Personality and Major**

_____ I can describe my learning style.

_____ I can list study techniques that match my learning style.

_____ I understand how my personality affects my learning style.

_____ I understand the connection between learning and teaching style.

_____ I understand the concept of multiple intelligences.

_____ I can list my multiple intelligences.

_____ I create my own success.

_____ **Total points for Learning Style and Intelligence**

_____ I have a list or mental picture of my lifetime goals.

_____ I know what I would like to accomplish in the next four years.

_____ I spend my time on activities that help me accomplish my lifetime goals.

_____ I effectively use priorities in managing my time.

_____ I can balance study, work, and recreation time.

_____ I generally avoid procrastination on important tasks.

_____ I am good at managing my money.

_____ **Total points for Managing Time and Money**

_____ I know memory techniques and can apply them to my college studies.

_____ I can read a college textbook and remember the important points.

_____ I know how to effectively mark a college textbook.

_____ I can quickly survey a college text and select the main ideas.

_____ I generally have good reading comprehension.

_____ I can concentrate on the material I am reading.

_____ I am confident in my ability to read and remember college level material.

_____ **Total points for Memory and Reading**

_____ I know how to listen for the main points in a college lecture.

_____ I am familiar with note-taking systems for college lectures.

_____ I know how to review my lecture notes.

_____ I feel comfortable with writing.

_____ I know the steps in writing a college term paper.

_____ I know how to prepare a speech.

_____ I am comfortable with public speaking.

_____ **Total points for Taking Notes, Writing, and Speaking**

_____ I know how to adequately prepare for a test.

_____ I can predict the questions that are likely to be on the test.

_____ I know how to deal with test anxiety.

_____ I am successful on math exams.

_____ I know how to make a reasonable guess if I am uncertain about the answer.

_____ I am confident of my ability to take objective tests.

_____ I can write a good essay answer.

_____ **Total points for Test Taking**

———— I can describe my vocational interests.

———— I can list careers that match my vocational interests.

———— I can list my top five values.

———— I generally consider my most important values when making decisions.

———— My actions are generally guided by my personal values.

———— My personal values motivate me to be successful.

———— I can balance work, study and leisure activities.

———— **Total points for Interests and Values**

———— I understand how current employment trends will affect my future.

———— I know what work skills will be most important for the 21st century.

———— I have an educational plan that matches my academic and career goals.

———— I know the steps in making a good career decision.

———— I have a good resume.

———— I know how to interview for a job.

———— I know how to choose a satisfying career.

———— **Total points for Career and Education**

———— I understand how my personality affects my communication style.

———— I know how to be a good listener.

———— I can use some basic techniques for good communication.

———— I can identify some barriers to effective communication.

———— I know how to deal with conflict.

———— I feel confident about making new friends in college and on the job.

———— I am generally a good communicator.

———— **Total points for Communication and Relationships**

———— I have the skills to analyze data, generate alternatives, and solve problems.

———— I can identify fallacies in reasoning.

———— I can apply the steps of critical thinking to analyze a complex issue.

———— I am willing to consider different points of view.

———— I can use brainstorming to generate a variety of ideas.

———— I am good at visualization and creative imagination.

———— I am generally curious about the world and can spot problems and opportunities.

———— **Total points for Critical and Creative Thinking**

_____ I understand the basics of good nutrition.

_____ I understand how to maintain my ideal body weight.

_____ I exercise regularly.

_____ I avoid addictions to smoking, alcohol, and drugs.

_____ I protect myself from sexually transmitted diseases.

_____ I generally get enough sleep.

_____ I am good at managing stress.

_____ **Total points for Health**

_____ I understand the concept of diversity and know why it is important.

_____ I understand the basics of communicating with a person from a different culture.

_____ I understand how the global economy will affect my future career.

_____ I understand how the concept of the electronic village will affect my future.

_____ I am familiar with the basic vocabulary of diversity.

_____ I try to avoid stereotypes when dealing with others who are different than me.

_____ I try to understand and appreciate those who are different from me.

_____ **Total points for Diversity**

_____ I understand the theories of life stages.

_____ I can describe my present developmental stage in life.

_____ I have self-confidence.

_____ I use positive self-talk and affirmations.

_____ I have a visual picture of my future success.

_____ I have a clear idea of what happiness means to me.

_____ I usually practice positive thinking.

_____ **Total points for Future**

_____ I am confident of my ability to succeed in college.

_____ I am confident of my ability to succeed in my career.

_____ **Total additional points**

Total your points:

_____ Motivation

_____ Personality and Major

_____ Learning Style and Intelligence

_____ Time and Money

_____ Memory and Reading

_____ Test Taking

_____ Taking Notes, Writing, and Speaking

_____ Interests and Values

_____ Career and Education

_____ Communication and Relationships

_____ Critical and Creative Thinking

_____ Health

_____ Diversity

_____ Future

_____ Additional Points

_____ **Grand Total Points**

If you scored

450–500   You are very confident of your skills for success in college. Maybe you do not need this class?

400–449   You have good skills for success in college. You can always improve.

350–399   You have average skills for success in college. You will definitely benefit from taking this course.

Below 350   You need some help to survive in college. You are in the right place to begin.

(Use these scores to complete the exercise "Chart Your Success," as in Chapter 1. Note that the additional points are not used in the chart.)

Success Wheel

Name _____ Date _____

Use your scores from "Measure Your Success" to complete the following success wheel. Use different colored markers to shade in each section of the wheel.

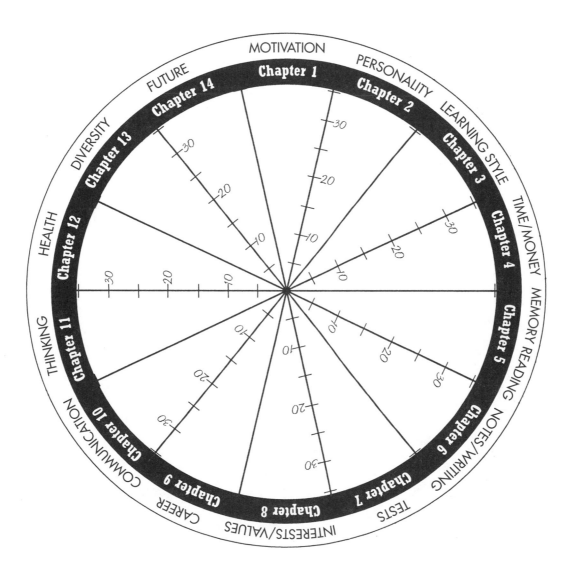

Compare your results to those on this same assessment in Chapter 1. How much did you improve?

Thinking about Your Life Stage

Name _____ Date _____

1. According to Erikson's seven life stages, what is your life stage? _____

    _____

    _____

2. What is your next life stage? _____

    _____

    _____

3. According to Levinson, are you in a stable or transitional period? _____

4. How do Gail Sheehy's ideas about life stages differ from those of Erik Erikson and Daniel Levinson?

    _____

    _____

5. According to Gail Sheehy, what is your life stage?

    _____

    _____

6. What is a mid-life crisis? Can you avoid one?

    _____

    _____

7. What are some ideas for successful aging?

_____

_____

Positive Thinking

Name _____   Date _____

Below are some negative thoughts. Transform each negative statement into a positive statement that could help a student to be successful. You may want to do this exercise as part of a group in your classroom.

Example: Negative thought: I have never been any good in math.
             Positive thought: I have had difficulty with math in the past, but I can do better this time.

1. I can't find a job.

    _____

2. I can never manage to save any money.

    _____

3. I hate physical education. Why do I have to take that class anyway?

    _____

4. I'm not very good at job interviews.

    _____

5. I'll never pass that test.

    _____

6. I'll never finish my college degree.

    _____

7. I was never good in school. I just want to play sports.

    _____

8. I'm not smart enough to do that.

    _____

9. Some people have all the luck.

    _____

Visualize Your Success

Name _____   Date _____

To be successful, you will need a clear mental picture of what success means to you. Take a few minutes to create a mental picture of what success means to you. Include your education, career, family life, lifestyle, finances, and anything else that is important to you. Make your picture as specific and detailed as possible. Write about this picture or draw it in the space below. You may wish to use a mind map, list, outline, or sentences to describe your picture of success.

Happiness Is . . .

Name _____   Date _____

Think of small things and big things that make you happy. List or draw them in the space below.

Intentions for the Future

Name _____   Date _____

Look over the table of contents of this book and think about what you have learned and how you will put it into practice. Write ten intention statements about how you will use the material you have learned in this class to be successful in the future.

1.

2.

3.

4.

5.

6.

7.

8.

9.

10.

Course Evaluation

Name _____   Date _____

1. What did you think of this course?
   _____ A.   This was one of the best courses I ever had.
   _____ B.   This course was excellent.
   _____ C.   This course was very good.
   _____ D.   This course was satisfactory.
   _____ E.   This course was not satisfactory.

2. How helpful was this course in choosing a major or career or confirming you choice of a major or career?
   _____ A.   Extremely helpful
   _____ B.   Very helpful
   _____ C.   Helpful
   _____ D.   Not helpful
   _____ E.   Unknown

3. How helpful was this course in improving your chances for success in college?
   _____ A.   Extremely helpful
   _____ B.   Very helpful
   _____ C.   Helpful
   _____ D.   Not helpful
   _____ E.   Unknown

4. How helpful was this course in improving your chances for success in your future career?
   _____ A.   Extremely helpful
   _____ B.   Very helpful
   _____ C.   Helpful
   _____ D.   Not helpful
   _____ E.   Unknown

5. How helpful was this course in building your self-confidence?
   _____ A.   Extremely helpful
   _____ B.   Very helpful
   _____ C.   Helpful
   _____ D.   Not helpful
   _____ E.   Unknown

6. Please rate the textbook used for this class.
   _____ A.   Outstanding
   _____ B.   Excellent
   _____ C.   Satisfactory
   _____ D.   Needs Improvement

7. Please rate the instructor in this class.
   _____ A.　　Outstanding
   _____ B.　　Excellent
   _____ C.　　Satisfactory
   _____ D.　　Needs Improvement

8. Would you recommend this course to a friend?
   _____ A.　　Yes
   _____ B.　　No

9. Do you plan to continue your college studies next semester?
   _____ A.　　Yes
   _____ B.　　No

10. Please tell what you liked about this class and how it was useful to you.

11. Do you have any suggestions for improving the class or text?

Index